Citizenship, Democracies, and Media Engagement among Emerging Economies and Marginalized Communities

Emmanuel K. Ngwainmbi
Editor

Citizenship, Democracies, and Media Engagement among Emerging Economies and Marginalized Communities

palgrave
macmillan

Editor
Emmanuel K. Ngwainmbi
Independent Scholar
Elizabeth City, NC
USA

ISBN 978-3-319-56214-8 ISBN 978-3-319-56215-5 (eBook)
DOI 10.1007/978-3-319-56215-5

Library of Congress Control Number: 2017937292

Cover illustration: Cover by Sam Johnson

Printed on acid-free paper

This Palgrave Macmillan imprint is published by Springer Nature
The registered company is Springer International Publishing AG
The registered company address is: Gewerbestrasse 11, 6330 Cham, Switzerland

Preface

The world has witnessed the rapid emergence of regional organizations, the rise of individualism, increasing social media use playing a pivotal role in stopping dictatorial regimes and the election of new governments, and extreme advances in technology facilitating the strengthening of local economies, especially within the first 10 years of the twenty-first century. The widespread uses of the internet have granted citizens around the world unprecedented electronic access to alternative media and communication resources and have given rise to regionalization, particularly in the global South where bureaucratic and dictatorial regimes had restricted access to normal ways of living.

The information and communication technology (ICT) breakthrough has sowed the seeds for future control of political and economic systems inside the new nation states. As the World Wide Web and other forms of social media developed and expanded through the 1990s, no one foresaw their impact on national security, human rights abuses and protection, and other social foibles, and on communities and cities in wealthy, politically stable, as well as fragile and economically emerging states today. The resulting globalization has transformed human identity and redefined local and national space and international law, raising new questions about citizenship and nationality. With forced integration at the political, diplomatic, economic, social, and environmental levels, a redefinition of what constitutes civic space and a more intense examination of how new social movements affect lives occur almost daily.

The open internet, clearly the most powerful form of communication and information dissemination, has allowed young people access to information about previous actions and policies that put their countries on the wrong side of political and economic growth. In many developing countries, more young people are using Facebook, blogs, WhatsApp, and other internet platforms to forge political and social change. In Tunisia, Egypt, Libya, and other parts of North Africa, and in the Middle East, they have used those applications to share information denouncing regimes, organize rallies, stay motivated, and even to protect their colleagues from being attacked by government authorities. We have noticed a similar trend in Cameroon, where people of Southern Cameroonian heritage, through social media broadcasts and text messaging, mobilized themselves and influenced international opinion to establish themselves as citizens of an independent state. In North Africa, social media activists have shifted their focus from denouncing oppression on the streets to turning their Facebook pages and blogs into spaces of resistance and sustainable activism.

Elsewhere, citizenship is up for sale. Wealthy persons can purchase citizenship for as little as $100,000 without physically being in another country. According to a report on *60 Minutes* (a CBS news magazine) on January 1, 2017, any individual can obtain a passport in Malta or the Dominican Republic, Barbuda, or St. Kitts after answering questions online and going through a background check. These countries reportedly look for wealthy people, the "crème de la crème," says Prime Minister of Antigua and Barbuda Gaston Browne, who confirmed that for $250,000 people are screened by the US intelligence service and meet with local authorities for five days. Vast sums of money flow into those countries, but national and global security is guaranteed to be at stake, since persons with criminal backgrounds in one country can easily become citizens in those cash-strapped countries and use their new passports to travel to other nations.

As rapid changes occur in our world, scholars and students need information packages to help them understand these changes, their causes, and their impacts, especially in Africa and Asia. This book is an edited collection of essays in which the authors provide some explanations of these complex problems. The title, *Citizenship, Democracies, and Media Engagement among Emerging Economies and Marginalized Communities*, comes from the idea that putting together new developments in cyber media use and citizens' reactions to governments' decisions can help national and international policymakers to plan better futures.

This book examines diplomatic relationships between local authorities and populations in fast-growing economies like China, India, and Brazil, and the large economies (UK, France, Germany, and the USA), revealing unique qualities and existing challenges among under-served groups in countries striving to emerge from poverty. The book offers a context in which some emerging economies in Africa, the Caribbean, South America, the Middle East, and Asia could chart their socioeconomic futures through regular democratic practice. The volume addresses human rights policies, diplomatic practices, and citizen journalism as paradigms for sustainable growth in those countries.

Using hundreds of references and data from existing physical and electronic texts, scholars and practitioners with research backgrounds on Africa, the Middle East, South America, North America, and India offer a broad range of perspectives on the changing face of democracy and markets in those countries, and on human rights, political communication, citizen journalism, international law and diplomacy, and political science. Through practical experience in the selected countries and field research, scholars are able to show how personal and national freedoms, as well as business deals, have been negotiated in a bid to create a new socioeconomic culture within these nations.

We prefer the term "tribe," rather than "ethnic" or "linguistic group" that is used by most scholars, as the former denotes historicity and a social group existing before the infiltration or arrival of external forces. Functionally, we see the tribe as a group of people who are dependent on their immediate surroundings—fauna and flora—for their livelihood: men, women, and children who are mostly self-sufficient, and are not integrated into the national society. We feel that to ask appropriate questions around the definition or redefinition of "citizenship" and the challenges that states seeking a middle ground face between developing their economies and embracing media-induced external cultural patterns, one should appreciate the space and ways of the indigenous group—the tribe.

About 1000 ethnic groups in Africa, Asia, and the Middle East, each with a common and distinctive culture, religion, and language, are among emerging markets in the world today. These markets are slightly different from communities, where ethnic groups use a single language and practice a religion. For clarity, we see the town and the city within the defined borders of the nation state as part of the "indigenous" or emerging community. By looking at those indigenous groups in the context of the new communities wired with global information technology, we may force the debate on how emerging economies and marginalized communities are handling issues of social media, broadcast media, and other forms of ICT.

We acknowledge that the internet and its social media tools have been instrumental in facilitating political uprisings, and we argue that while ICT has facilitated the exchange of information among people and organizations, governments and policymakers continue to ignore its capacity to disintegrate the nation and, in some cases, create economic chaos. We cite the militia and special interest groups in Libya, Chad, Mexico, Tunisia, Yemen, Eritrea, and the Democratic Republic of Congo, which have used social media to share information and galvanize the public against political authorities. Then there are the terrorist cells in Iraq, Afghanistan, Syria, and Nigeria that destroy infrastructure and lives, rendering those countries politically unstable and causing foreign investors to suspend plans to set up their businesses in such territories. The ultimate result is that unemployment rates increase in those politically fragile nations, and the probability of civil unrest remains high. Similarly, the chances of foreign nationals migrating to such countries and seeking citizenship become limited.

We hope that through this volume, readers may have a clear understanding of how the socioeconomic gap between the so-called developed and emerging countries can be bridged. Some of the major issues discussed include:

- Political science and communication theories on democratization in developing countries.
- How public policy, international relations, and cyber communications (the internet, social media) have contributed to national democratic movements, including challenges and best practices.
- How the media, democracy, and electoral processes have influenced emerging democracies.
- How various organizations use and misuse poll data in measuring national democratic activities.
- How the ruling party influences the electoral process, including via corruption.
- Whether election observer missions add any value to the democratic process.

- Whether regular municipal, legislative, parliamentary, and presidential elections are necessary or even authentic.
- The role of the geopolitical landscape and neighboring countries in mitigating democracy.
- Whether experts can provide local media coverage to measure democracy.

The book includes several case studies on diplomacy toward emerging economies, focusing on how economic inequality is slowing the practice of healthy democracy in some developing countries and how thriving local democracies serve as a marketplace for foreign investments. Another study on public policies and social practices highlights the power of media advocacy and strategic networking in transforming norms and changing policies. It draws out implications for the study and practice of persuasion communication, arguing that without strategic advocacy and coalition building, it will be nearly impossible to achieve any significant change.

The book brings out two key problems caused by globalization: the scramble for and retrieval of local space by foreign entities; and the challenge for indigenous groups of protecting local resources against foreign "hawks." A chapter reviews the communication actions needed to ensure peaceful coexistence between the native population and the government sector in Guyana over land titling. The book offers suggestions for socioeconomic changes to build democracy and equality, specifically how countries can reform their democracies to grow their social and economic institutions by using existing best practices, expatriates, and citizens in the Diaspora, as well as ways of building sustainable progressive democratic practices.

We feel that this book will be useful to political science, international communication, and international relations and diplomacy students, as well as researchers, scholars, diplomats, transnational business executives, and practitioners. Political scientists, policy scholars, development communication scholars, political communication scholars, researchers, international law and human rights experts, and legal scholars will find the content insightful and useful. Institutes for the study of human rights, minority studies, and international and cross-cultural studies programs may also find the material useful. After reading this book, readers will have the opportunity to explore media and citizenship, popular media, democracy and development in Africa, media studies, diversity teaching, and education in a multicultural society, and topics related to how the media engages with small and large communities. Simply put, the book presents the media as a community watchdog, messenger, and organizer.

We also hope that those interested in citizen media, democracy and development, modern sociocultural anthropology, human rights, or cross-cultural studies will draw essential knowledge from this book. We note, however, that the book is not a lens through which we can see citizenship, democratic movements, and the media's role in emerging economies and marginalized communities around the world. Rather, we suggest that readers see this book as a hint to discussion on how globalization and mass media engagement affect the wellbeing of some communities, states, regions, citizens, and political actors in social and economic terms. Here, we see the media as the nucleus or foundation on which a state can grow its economy, improve its sociopolitical condition, or measure the safety and security of its borders. In tandem, the book presents the media as an arbiter of public interests, a peacemaking tool, a mechanism for promoting the agendas of politicians and governments, and an agent for constructing a new national identity.

Elizabeth City, USA, January 2017 Emmanuel K. Ngwainmbi

Acknowledgements

The editor of this volume wishes to thank the managers of the following publications for granting permission for the following titles:

Journal of Development and Communication Studies, *Journal of Mass Communication & Journalism*, and *African Journal of Political Science and International Relations* previously published:

Kalulu, Mavuto. "Media Exposure of Corruption and Re-election Chances of Incumbent Parties in Africa" *Journal of Development & Communication Studies 3* (2014): 511–526.

Fayoyin, A., and Ngwainmbi, K. E. "Use and Misuse of Data in Advocacy, Media and Opinion Polls in Africa: Realities, Challenges, and Opportunities" *Journal of Development & Communication Studies 3* (2014a): 527–543.

Ngwainmbi, K. Emmanuel "The Mediatization of Violence: A Model for Utilizing Public Discourse and Networking to Counter Global Terrorism." *Journal of Mass Communication & Journalism 6* (2016): 1–8.

LaMonica, Christopher. "Moving Beyond "Illiberal Democracy" in Sub-Saharan Africa: Recalling the Significance of Local Governance." *African Journal of Political Science and International Relations* on July 9, *7* (2015): 268–283.

Contents

Editor and Contributors

About the Editor

Emmanuel K. Ngwainmbi the volume editor, has served as a tenured, full professor at several universities, and lectures in Asia, Europe, the USA, and Africa about globalization and the socioeconomic impact of information technology on indigenous cultures. These include George Washington University and Howard University (DC), St. Thomas University (FL), Jackson State University (MS), and Morgan State University (MD). He is also a senior communication adviser for United Nations agencies and other intergovernmental bodies, and has directed some communications programs in the USA and abroad. He has published 14 books and numerous articles in journals and magazines, and serves on the boards of professional national, regional, and international organizations in communication and other social science fields. He is an independent communication consultant, adjunct Professor at the University of North Carolina, Charlotte, Department of Communication, and Editor-in-Chief of *the Journal of Mass Communication and Journalism.*

Contributors

Adebayo Fayoyin (Ph.D.) is an expert in advocacy, external relations and social and behavioral change communications with over 20 years field experience in various development agencies, including USAID,

UNICEF, and UNFPA. He currently serves as the regional communication adviser for UNFPA East and Southern Africa, providing strategic oversight and technical assistance for 23 countries in the region. He has held various full-time and honorary faculty positions in communication institutions in Nigeria, Kenya, and South Africa. His current areas of research are advocacy and social development, strategic communication, and impact of new media on oral media. He has published articles in the *Asian Pacific Journal of Research, Journal of Social Studies, Journal of Communication*, and *Journal of Development and Communication Studies.*

Nagamallika Gudipaty (Ph.D.) is Associate Professor in the Department of Communication at the English and Foreign Languages University, Hyderabad, India. Her current research interests are political communication and journalism studies. She has published in *Media Asia*, *International Journal of Development Communication*, and *Journal of Media and Development.* She has also developed course material for open universities in India. Her recent contributions include a chapter each in Health and the Media: Essays on the Effects of Mass Communication (2016) (McFarland Books) and Educational Policy Reforms: National Perspectives (2017) (Bloomsbury).

Mavuto Kalulu (Ph.D.) holds a degree in economics from the University of Mississippi, where he taught economics for six years. He is currently working as a policy analyst with the Arkansas Center for Research in Economics at the University of Central Arkansas. His research interests include public choice and political economics, especially corruption and its effect on the electoral process in developing countries.

Jean-Claude Kwitonda teaches communication at Ohio University and is a Ph.D. candidate in the Department of Communication Studies. He obtained his MA in international affairs (with a concentration in communication and development studies) at the Ohio University Center for International Studies. He has presented papers on global neoliberalism at various conferences. His research interests include (the many) meanings of global neoliberalism and its discursive reinvention. His research that synthesizes the different meanings of global neoliberalism has appeared in the *Journal of Critical Discourse Studies.*

Christopher LaMonica (Ph.D.) is Associate Professor of Government and Lead Academic Advisor at the US Coast Guard Academy in Connecticut. A graduate of Harvard University's Kennedy School of Government and Boston University, he has served as a Visiting Scholar at the New Zealand Defense Force and some European universities. Before entering academia, he worked with leading international development organizations including USAID and the International Energy Agency of the OECD. Notable books include Horror in Paradise: Frameworks for Understanding the Crises of the Niger Delta of Nigeria (Carolina Academic Press, Africa Series) and Local Government Matters: The Case of Zambia (VDM Verlag/Lambert Academic Press). He teaches comparative politics, African politics, international relations, international political economy, the politics of North Africa and the Middle East, and the politics of race and ethnicity.

Johannes Muntschick (Ph.D.) is research fellow and lecturer in the Department of International Relations at the Johannes Gutenberg University Mainz (Germany). He has obtained degrees in political science and the teaching profession from the Otto-Friedrich-University, Bamberg, Germany. His major research interests include regionalism inside and outside Europe, international institutions, as well as statehood, conflicts, and war economies in Africa. In his dissertation, "Regionalism and External Influence: The Southern African Development Community (SADC) and the Ambivalent Impact of the EU on Regional Integration," Muntschick analyzes the formation, dynamics, and performance of regionalism in the SADC. His recent publications in edited volumes, including Mapping Agency: Comparing Regionalisms in Africa (2013), and in journals such as Politische Vierteljahresschrift (2013) and Journal of Common Market Studies (2014), focus on the impact of extra-regional actors on regional integration in southern Africa.

Srinivas Pathunkala (Ph.D.) is Assistant Professor in the Department of Communication at the English and Foreign Languages University, Hyderabad (Telangana), India, and School of Interdisciplinary Studies at EFL University, Hyderabad. He has 14 years' experience in the field of Television Journalism and Journalism Studies. He has served as a Communication Manager for DDS, a grassroots non-governmental organization, and as Coordinator of Community Radio and Video Projects based in Pastapur, Zaheerabad, Medak, Andhra Pradesh (India).

He has worked as TV Reporter for Maa TV during 2003–07 and 24 hours news channel HMTV for the establishment of Research and Reference wing.

Ashlie Perry (Ph.D.) is an Assistant Professor of Security Studies at Endicott College in Beverly, MA. She holds a Ph.D. in global affairs/ security studies from Rutgers University (NJ) and an MA in clinical psychology from Valdosta State University (GA). Her research interests include identity politics, terrorism, collective action, and gendered crimes. She teaches courses ranging from political psychology to terrorism studies. Her recent work includes "Terrorism as Genocide: Killing with 'Intent'" in *Journal of Global Analysis.*

Jose Luis Velasco (Ph.D.) is a full-time researcher at the Institute for Social Research of Mexico's National Autonomous University (UNAM). He holds a Ph.D. in political science from Boston University (MA). He usually teaches courses on political theory and comparative politics, at graduate level. His publications include Insurgency, Authoritarianism and Drug Trafficking in Mexico's "Democratic" Transition (Routledge, 2005).

List of Figures

List of Tables

PART I

Paradigmatic Approaches of Media Engagement and Social Mobilization

CHAPTER 1

An External Examination of Emerging Democratic Institutions and the Problem of Social and Economic Security

Emmanuel K. Ngwainmbi

The two world wars that took place in the twentieth century destroyed the infrastructures and landscapes of most countries and caused a great deal of poverty and distrust among nations. The countries in the global north, especially those with advanced technology, good democratic institutions, strong security and political influence were able to rebuild their

Emmanuel K. Ngwainmbi has researched the socioeconomic impact of information technology on indigenous cultures. He is currently an independent high-level communication specialist and Editor-in-Chief of the Journal of Mass Communication and Journalism. At the moment, his research focuses on the socioeconomic impact of information technology on indigenous cultures. In this chapter, he focuses on how the widespread use of ICT (information and communication technology) threatens the security of countries just beginning to adopt democracy, discusses the obstacles to the development of democracy, and offers suggestions for progressive democracy and socioeconomic development in African countries.

E.K. Ngwainmbi (✉)
Matthews, NC , USA

E.K. Ngwainmbi (ed.), *Citizenship, Democracies, and Media Engagement among Emerging Economies and Marginalized Communities*,
DOI 10.1007/978-3-319-56215-5_1

institutions much sooner than countries with a fragile government. But that seemed to change in the latter part of the century when the world governing body, the United Nations Organization (UNO/UN), introduced governing policies aimed at improving diplomatic relations among nation states. By creating and managing such inter-governmental bodies as the United Nations Human Rights Council responsible for enhancing and protecting human rights around the world, and the United Nations Development Program which advocates for change and connects countries to knowledge, experience and resources to help people build a better life and provides expert advice, training, and grants support to developing countries, with increasing emphasis on assistance to the least developed countries the world governing body has often reasserted its role as key advocate for global peace and socio-economic change.

The work of the UN has, to a great extent, been enhanced by advancements in information and communication technology. The launching of the World Wide Web in the early 1990s and later the introduction of social communication gadgets like the I-phone, WhatsApp, IMO, and Viber, have allowed businesses to find new markets for their goods and services, and governments to redefine or protect their national interests, among other noteworthy activities. However, with the ongoing terrorist acts within countries and beyond national borders, facilitated by the widespread use of cyber media resources, it seems that no government, business, or military group foresaw ICT's negative impact on national security.

The UN Peace Keeping forces and observer missions charged with ensuring the prevalence of peace and the promotion of democratic modus operandi in all nations of the world have experienced measurable success when groups resolved their conflicts and in some cases considered national interest over personal ambition.

In short, the resulting process of globalization has not only redefined our identity, it has raised new debates about what constitutes local and national space, citizenship and nationality. With the advent of information and communication technology, nations have been integrating at the regional, political, diplomatic, economic, social, and environmental levels at an alarmingly fast pace. To that end, the question of what constitutes local space and how new social movements and business negotiations affect lives must be examined and answers sought if nations intend to maintain their own identity. Otherwise, the nation-state, nationality, or heritage will soon become a thing of the past.

The Cultural Context of Understanding an Emerging Democratic Institution or Community

The term "globalization" is understood as the opening up of countries to free trade and the growing interdependence of world markets, and coming under the responsibility of organisms of the United Nations, multilateral pacts, and agreements (e.g., Court 2001). In practical terms, however, globalization has taken on new meanings: acculturation and socioeconomic marginalization. For Court (2001), a senior member of the Pontifical Academy of Social Sciences, the cultural dimension (also described elsewhere as the "cultural industry") includes those institutions protected by law, such as schools, universities, and the media (p. 189). Court sees globalization within the context of individual freedom. The phenomenon contains a psychosocial element in which the person's right to express the self intermingles with social reality. Court (2001) writes:

> [Globalization] presupposes that the human person rationally understands that despite his or her different ethnic and historical-cultural origins he or she is a free subject and also conscious of the causation of his or her acts, something which includes, as a consequence, his or her responsibility. (p. 190)

This implies freedom of expression and the right to be treated with dignity and equality. From a sociological standpoint, respecting individual cultures is as important as the interdependence of countries' economic resources or having free access to world markets. Thus, ideally, activities involving open access to global markets are expected to include sensitivity to, or at least respect for, individual freedoms and cultural heritage.

Socioeconomic marginalization refers to the deliberate exclusion or relegation of communities with rich economic and social potential to the fringes of global society. Marginalization also relates to undermining the potential of a community in such disciplines as education, sociology, psychology, politics, or economics. Activists for development and some scholars in the area of national development are convinced that people in rural communities, minorities, subgroups, and those in densely populated urban centers with low income levels and high unemployment rates are considered less important, and are hence overlooked when it comes to distributing knowledge and financial resources. Consequently, their opinions are not seen as important.

Marginalized Communities

We explain the term marginalization through the prism of social, economic, political, and educational platforms. It gets the most attention in social psychology and political science. Both schools claim that the most dominant paradigm is "social marginalization," where groups are excluded from the mainstream and treated with no respect, based on their ethnic origin, race, gender, religion, sexual preference, low economic status, or all of these. A group or individual is marginalized or powerless when it has been excluded from having economic, social, and political opportunities that others enjoy, and deprived of the ability for self-determination. Further, a community is marginalized when knowledge of its cultural, political, or economic assets is limited and responsible parties fail to invest in it. Education, job allocation, fair treatment of the poor and voiceless, and full and unbiased application of the rule of law are among the major determinants of an unmarginalized community. Phobias, lack of access to information, limited knowledge, misinformation, political fragility, weak diplomatic and business negotiation skills, and negative media coverage of a community make that community less desirable and less respected by other communities. With the increase in information technology, particularly the internet, cell phones, and other mass media tools, some communities are more marginalized than others. Thus, community psychology should avoid two complementary mistakes: the individualization of social problems and the neglect of the subjective experience of social actors (Burton and Kagan 2003).

The World Wide Web and the Plight of Emerging Democratic Institutions

Researchers have described the period from January 1, 1990 to December 31, 1999 as the Gregorian calendar, because the content of the internet not only granted countries around the world instant access to alternative media and communication resources, it also exposed everyone to multiple cultures, creative thinking, and creative action. That period also created a wave of regionalism, particularly in the global South, where bureaucratic and autocratic regimes had restricted access to former ways of living (Hettne and Söderbaum 1998; Harrell 1995). The internet opened doors for powerful nations to collect intelligence in new nation states emerging from political colonization, reach their elected or self-appointed leaders, or negotiate diplomatic relations. Industrialized countries welcomed the ICT revolution, because they had the resources to create, control, and distribute ICT content. Conversely, the new nation states, with their fragile governments, weak currencies, low educational standards, widespread poverty, limited access to electricity, and tightly controlled press, could not compete for equality in cyber-mediated information technology.

The unfair advantage in information and communication practice for once rendered the debate over the New World Information and Communication Order (NWICO) useless. We may recall that NWICO, the subject of what is known as the MacBride Commission, had advocated but failed to address the unbalanced free flow of information from the developed countries to developing ones, which left the latter psychologically, economically, socially, and spiritually dependent. Those who introduced the World Wide Web and forms of social media to the rest of the world may not have foreseen the damage such media would inflict on national security, nor their impact on human rights abuses in rich countries as well as in politically fragile states. Thus, the Internet can be considered the most dubious agent in the "cultural industry" in the sense that it facilitates the exchange of information and data that promotes good and bad practices around the world.

Media as a Global Terrorism Public Relations Agent

Television networks in both politically powerful and fragile states have been covering terrorism with such frequency that terrorism itself seems to be an interesting stunt. Media ratings skyrocket whenever there is a breaking story about bombings and killings led by terrorists. The media continue to exploit attacks in public places around the world, largely for the benefit of their operational efficiency, information gathering, recruitment, fundraising, and propaganda schemes (Nacos 2002). International relations scholars contend that technologies have improved the capability of groups and cells in the areas of proselytizing coordination, security, mobility, and lethality (Ngwainmbi 2016). In the case of the group known as ISIS, it has become clear that information technology has enhanced the ability of terrorist cells around the world to coordinate terrorist activities, and has strengthened their engagement with the media to share their message with the global community (Ngwainmbi 2016).

Those who expect television, clearly the most influential channel for mass audience reach, to be the watchdog for citizen protection could be dumbfounded when they realize that television networks put more emphasis on telling than educating. CNN International, Al Jazeera, BBC, France 24, and other global information networks spend more time covering news and sharing expert views on terrorist plans and programs. By prioritizing terrorism on their agenda instead of focusing on socioeconomic issues that integrate regions, television networks are giving terrorists free publicity and validating terrorism. The fact that shortly after each bombing in virtually every city or community ISIS has released a statement to the media stating that it is responsible for the act clearly suggests that the terrorist network recognizes its importance as a news maker and needs to make itself continually relevant to the media and to world citizens.

ICT Products as a Conduit for Meaningful Change

Despite the negative social impact of the internet as described above, strategic use of its products may have a positive influence on both politically and economically fragile nations and powerful leaders. With the help of ICT, diplomatic relations between powerful nations and new nation states have improved to the extent that there are fewer dictatorial and monarchical regimes in the world today than in the early 1990s. Through televised United Nations (UN) conferences and missions involving ambassadors, senior government officials, and heads of state, citizens have been able to assess and select their leaders, propose policies, and mobilize themselves accordingly. Meetings of heads of state have led to the formation of continental political bodies and executive/administrative branches to promote peaceful international coexistence and friendship. Mediated communication systems have certainly enhanced the image, networking, and productivity of high-level, world-class groups such as the Group of Twenty (G20), European Union (EU), African Union, and North American Trade Organization (NATO).

The world governing body for football (FIFA), and regional bodies such as the Confederation of North, Central American and Caribbean Association Football (CONCACAF), the Confederation of African Football (CAF), and the European Champions League (ECL), have successfully exploited electronic media to promote peace and friendship among nations. The emergence of regional communities also helps to advance regional economic, security, and infrastructure cooperation. The UN has put in place regional commissions around the world to foster intra-regional integration, international cooperation for growth, and the economic and social development of member states. The Economic Commission for Africa (ECA) reported that multiple transitions dominated Africa's development in the first half of the 1990s. In some countries the transition has run concurrently from war to peace, from one-party rule to multi-party governance, from apartheid to non-racial democracy, from command economies dominated by governments and sheltered from imports to free markets, private enterprise, and more liberal trade (UNECA 1996).

In the global South, particularly southern and southeastern Africa, integration and parallel institution building can be proper measures to strengthen democratic governance, since a transnational policy agreement for institutional "lock-in" implies that member countries are committed to maintaining specified local norms and practices of democracy. The South African Development Community (SADC) is a case in point. Furthermore, the EU provides sound evidence for the success of this mechanism, given the transformation of the formerly authoritarian and communist European countries to stable democracies in the course of their EU membership.

Conversely, fragile states contribute to global instability and violence and "illiberal democracy," especially when their representatives are not involved in the design of safety laws. The central governments in West, Central, and East Africa appear to undermine the abilities of traditional leaders in facilitating the implementation of national policies in local communities. Coups and coup attempts seem to be a never-ending phenomenon in Africa, with Nigeria, Chad, Niger, Congo, and Cameroon among countries that experienced them in the distant past, and Burkina Faso, Libya, Tunisia, Egypt, and Burundi undergoing them in the last five years alone. Pakistan and Syria, Chile and Cuba, and other countries undergoing regime transitions and economic crises also face variable degrees of urbanization. In cities where the population is over a million, one is bound to find political divisions, crime, and considerably high poverty rates. There are 500 cities around the world hosting more than a million inhabitants with varying cultural backgrounds, of which 80% are in emerging economies in Africa, South America, and Asia. As Robert Muggah (2015) has stated in his article "Preventing Fragile Cities from Becoming Failed Cities," fast-growing medium-sized cities will decide the security, stability, and sustainable development of the world in the twenty-first century. That presupposes challenges in governance, employment, and economic disparity to be placed in the laps of national governments as human mobility and domestic political crises take people to different national borders.

Globalization has affected the economic and political foundations of every country, as well as the cultural industry. Already in the USA, UK, and several European countries touted as the having the most advanced democracies in the world, citizenship or *jus sanguinis* is not only determined by one's place of birth, but also by one or both parents who are already citizens of that country. Children born in the USA are citizens by virtue of the Fourteenth Amendment's Citizenship Clause. Civil rights, constitutional, and immigration law and policy expert Kristin A. Collins (2014) reminds us that the statutes governing parent–child citizenship transmission are race neutral in the USA. The derivative nature of citizenship determination in the USA today presupposes the same determination of citizenship in countries at the infant stage of democratic governance, because the USA has a strong political influence in those countries.

There are also legitimate concerns that powerful foreign governments and rich international companies have compromised and devalued local space, original values, and group dynamics (Ngwainmbi 2004, 2007). The process of globalizing communities has the potential to erode the national sovereignty of the weakest and poorest states, while widening the technological divide among states; on the other hand, it tends to provide an enabling environment for greater respect for human rights and gender equality (Amuwo 2002, p. 67). More crucially, the fast pace with which changes are taking place in transnational social and economic activities raises more questions about whether democracy and democratization are the right trends in modern society. The ease with which both the educated and uneducated are utilizing new and old information products without proper vetting from IT experts, social scientists, and local governments is causing users to create and disseminate new languages and media content to vulnerable users. The ongoing activity in the free global information superhighway—the internet and forms of social media—has undermined and in some cases damaged worldviews of Islam, Christianity, Buddhism, and other belief systems that have shaped specific philosophies of life for their respective groups, as well as having an impact on feminism and gender politics. In a nutshell, globalization has transformed the human identity and redefined local and national spaces and international law, raising new questions about citizenship and nationality.

The Fallacy of Globalization and Trade Negotiation

Globalization has deepened economic inequality between poor small countries and advanced ones. Part of the reason for the imbalance in global economic growth is that developing countries are rarely represented in negotiations that concern them directly, as London School of Economics and Political Science professor Robert Hunter Wade (2004) has observed. The former World Bank economist has argued that developing countries cannot afford the cost of hotels, offices, and salaries in places like Washington, DC and Geneva, which must be paid not in dollars but hard currency bought at market exchange rates. They resort to hiring expensive external consultants to negotiate for them. To this extent, Wade's argument makes sense. Over the years, a given developing country could spend much money hiring external negotiators who understand the negotiation dynamics and could close relatively better deals on its behalf than could nationally selected negotiators.

When it comes to multilateral trade, negotiations can either make or break a country's economy, strengthen its leverage among its neighbors, or deplete its resources. Trade negotiation certainly plays a predominant role for any state, but for developing countries it has become the central tool to leapfrog stages of economic development.

Multilateral trade talks have existed since the foundation of the General Agreement on Tariffs and Trade (GATT) in 1947, but talks have become more complex and important for developing countries. This is why such countries have increased their resources to strengthen their participation in negotiations, as opposed to the 1950s and 1960s when they were still setting up their systems of governance and felt they had little to gain from exporting products and little to lose from excluding imports. The Fourth Ministerial Conference in Doha, Qatar in November 2001 provided a platform for ministers from developing countries to address negotiations and implementation of the modalities of the World Trade Organization (WTO) agreements, among other subjects. The developing countries were an important part of the alliance that helped anti-subsidy negotiations in agriculture to take place. Page (2003) rightly considers the Doha meeting as evidence of the ability of developing countries to influence outcomes, writing: "A clearer victory, in agriculture and other areas, was that the meeting accepted that special and differential treatment (allowing different policies by developing countries and requiring different policies towards them) would be 'an integral part' of any final settlement. The Doha meeting also extended the times for Least Developed to comply with subsidy and intellectual property rules" (pp. 4, 5).

Globalization and Demographic Change

Inevitably, global economic development and demographic shifts are interrelated in the ways in which governments and parastatals implement social policies, and in how access to healthcare services and finances helps determine the birth and death rates of persons in a given community. Shifts in demographics or demographic transitions (from high birth and death rates to low birth and death rates or vice versa) cannot occur without significant changes in economic performance. Thus, conditions that promote the sustenance of emerging markets can also create an environment for the long-term care of an aging population, as well as for high birth rates. To this end, lawmakers and business executives can spark demographic transitions in their respective countries by creating jobs, drastically reducing the number of highly skilled workers leaving the country, improving their healthcare facilities, and implementing programs for the adult population.

A major policy research report co-published by the World Bank and Oxford University Press claims that the number of people living in poverty decreased by 200 million in the 18 years from 1980 to 1998 (World Bank 2002). Wade (2004) has disputed the World Bank's poverty numbers, claiming that they were subject to a large margin of error, probably biased downward, and probably made the trend look rosier than it was (p. 581). The 2015–2016 *Global Monitoring Report*, jointly produced by the World Bank and the International Monetary Fund (IMF), details the decline of those living in global poverty, reclassified as living on $1.90 or less a day. The report forecast that this would be 9.6% of the world's population in 2015, a projected 200 million fewer people living in extreme poverty than in 2012 (World Bank 2015/2016). It revises global economic growth projections for 2015 down to 3.3% because of lower growth prospects in emerging markets. Current World Bank Group President Jim Yong Kim's optimism in the following statement should not surprise anyone: "With the right set of policies, this era of demographic change can be turned into one of sustained development progress." As argued above, however, any sustained positive demographic shift requires planning and coordination between government agencies and the executives of private businesses.

Globalization might undermine cultural diversity as multinational corporations practice a certain kind of consumerist culture, in which products and commodities promoted through global marketing campaigns exploit basic material desires, forcing consumers to resort to clandestine methods to obtain those products. The more people from different ethnic and cultural backgrounds intermingle in a community where indigenous people have long practiced their customs and followed local and national laws, the more indigenous and citizenship status will be compromised. A combination of the family, race, and social principles, or the financial standing of the immigrant family, and not birth, determines citizenship status. In many Western countries, marriage between an immigrant and a national can qualify the former as a citizen, while children born to that couple are automatic citizens. However, this *laissez-faire* attitude also exists in the USA, where democracy was established by the founding fathers. For example, Collins (2014) identifies a complex set of statuses in the law on children born to American parents outside the USA, demonstrating that a gender-based law established in 1855 by the US Congress decreeing that a foreign woman married to an American man would be automatically an American citizen "was shaped by the logic of racial hierarchy and exclusion that informed American nationality law."[1]

It has been argued that some developing countries are more globalized than others, where change is based on the ratio of trade to gross domestic product (GDP). The World Bank's publication *Globalization, Growth, and Poverty* (2002) distinguishes "newly globalizing" countries, also known as "more globalized" countries, from "non-globalized" countries or "less globalized" countries. By declaring that the former have had faster economic growth, no increase in inequality, and a faster reduction of poverty than the latter, the World Bank concludes that globalization plays a role in poverty alleviation. A country can be "less globalized" if its climatic, health, and political conditions are not convenient for external business entities.

Perhaps the most succinct and controversial arguments have been made by a group of sociologists at Emory University (GA), who state:

- Multinational corporations promote a certain kind of consumerist culture, in which standard commodities, promoted by global marketing campaigns exploiting basic material desires, create similar lifestyles—"Coca-Colonization."[2]
- Backed by the power of certain states, Western ideals are falsely established as universal, overriding local traditions—"cultural imperialism."
- New institutions have an inherently rationalizing thrust, making all human practices more efficient, controllable, and predictable, as exemplified by the spread of fast food—"McDonaldization."[3]
- The USA exerts hegemonic influence in promoting its values and habits through popular culture and the news media—"Americanization."[4]

These sociologists also think that globalization will foster diversity in the following ways:

- Interaction across boundaries leads to the mixing of cultures in particular places and practices—pluralization.
- Cultural flows occur differently in different spheres and may originate in many places—differentiation.
- Integration and the spread of ideas and images provoke reactions and resistance—contestation.
- Global norms or practices are interpreted differently according to local tradition; the universal must take particular forms—globalization.
- Diversity has itself become a global value, promoted through international organizations and movements, not to mention nation states—institutionalization.[5]

In a democratic society is no longer an issue or something to be settled by argument or evidence; it is now a reality in global cultural politics. Locals invariably and easily embrace the food, clothes, or music of other groups, as such elements do not compromise their principles or threaten their safety. However, the rudiments of local languages that define a group's heritage and its way of life are being diluted by immigrants from various countries who continue to use their own languages. The situation is compounded by the widespread use of the internet, cell phones, and other forms of social media. The internet can be accessed only in the major languages, which forces non-speakers of those languages to learn the techniques of communicating in them, risking the frequency with which they express themselves in the medium with which they are most comfortable—their mother tongue. Thus, globalization is a leading factor in the erosion of minority languages. With 40% of the world's 7000 languages at risk of disappearing, a unique vision of the world could be lost.[6] The mission of the Alliance for Linguistic Diversity to accelerate, strengthen, and increase efforts to document and revitalize endangered languages deserves support from respective governments in fragile states and the international community, especially educational institutions and funding agencies.[7]

Globalization as a Promoter of Cultural Discord

While nation-centric thinkers continue to point to globalization as the killer of small groups' languages in particular, and national identity in general, religious fanatics believe that the main objective of Western media is to spread Judeo-Christian values around the world. This notion has been expounded by Jan Nederveen Pieterse (2009). Prefacing the third edition of his groundbreaking work *Globalization and Culture: Global Mélange*, Pieterse (2009, p. ix) has clearly noted that keynotes of globalization literature have been critiques of neoliberalism and American hegemony. As he further states, for 200 years (since 1800) globalization was shaped and determined by North–South relations, with a clear, overwhelming dominance of the North in economic, political, and cultural spheres.

He disputes the view held by nation-centric scholars that the world is a melting pot of civilizations and that globalization does not lead to cultural hegemony. Rather, globalization in cultural terms tends toward a global mélange, a form of hybridization. Whether or not hybridization does in fact lead to differentialism and convergence, as Pieterse contends, no one can deny that information technology is rapidly changing the world. It is flooding individuals with unfiltered information and knowledge, and making users in developing countries vulnerable to media content, selectively creating more emerging economies and marginalizing communities, and widening the gap between politically stable and fragile nations. Social media, the internet, and cable television networks have granted unfettered public access to happenings around the world, leaving users in politically fragile states with no ability to control the information they receive.

Unfortunately, the KARMA syndrome might also be affecting powerful nations with the proliferation of global terrorism, if we choose to believe media reports that the recent terrorist happenings are in retaliation against the infiltration of such nations into the religious and political affairs of Islamic nations.

Although arguably their primary intention for creating the Internet and other mass media systems was to spread Western democracy and Judea-Christian ideologies around the world in order to gain control of other landscapes and minds, the plan of the US and its Western allies seems to have backfired. Persons and sects disgruntled with the political and economic practices in these countries are not only communicating and collaborating with the militia in non-Christian nations destroy symbols of Western civilization in their own country. They are joining terrorist networks in Islamic countries for the same purpose. Hence, the KARMA syndrome of territorial control has become symptomatic; it is in a way, a psychological disease that is collectively affecting and has now promoted a religious warfare between historically rich Judea-Christian nations in the West and traditionally Islamic nations in the Middle East.

The Plight of Fragile States

Powerful nations and international corporations lobby their governments to open new routes to markets and services in states with weak political authority. The leaders of the aid-receiving states are often forced to come to the negotiating table with diplomats and diplomatic missions backed by special interest groups, and international organizations like the UN, World Bank, and other regional groups.

To fully understand the plight of fragile states, particularly those in the least developed region—Africa—we have to look at the governing approach utilized by their leaders, before examining environmental factors. Political scientists and development scholars have successfully argued that Africa's continuing reliance on foreign aid has increased the opportunities for bilateral and multilateral aid agencies to influence policymaking in the region.[8] This was particularly so in the early 1990s, when donors began to show interest in promoting political change in addition to economic reforms. Democratic political reforms were emphasized as key factors in the determination of future economic assistance for Africa.[9] That led to donor countries dictating terms of governance and imposing their own political reforms. The problem with the introduction of these reforms is that a uniform set of democratic ideals was applied in all countries that requested aid, undermining the varied fundamental principles, cultural values, and pre-exisiting governance techniques among the aid-receiving states. So one is persuaded to ask whether economic development is a necessary precondition for achieving democracy, or whether other non-economic factors can help democracy. These are particularly important issues with practical implications for foreign assistance and self-governance.

Even for those developing countries that have managed to refuse assistance from foreign governments and intergovernmental organizations, changes in the environment could be having a negative impact on the national political climate and causing more economic hardship for local institutions and populations. For example, indigenous groups in Guyana, and those in areas of gold and diamond mining in South Africa, Tanzania, Ghana, Mali, Zimbabwe, and Cameroon, were displaced from their homes due to timber exploitation and other forms of massive deforestation led by foreign companies. Mining companies are attracted to developing countries because there are lower environmental and safety standards.[10] In order to establish mines, vegetation is cleared and native people are often forced out of their homes, which creates a loss of biodiversity in fauna and flora and has numerous physiological and psychological impacts on humans.[11] Another environmental impact caused by mining is tailings dumping and leakage. The leftover material from mining, known as tailings, is often dumped in rivers, which contaminates water with metals.[12] Such conditions only promote poverty and mistrust in public officials, since they do not provide adequate compensation for displaced indigenous people whose ancestral space (ritual sites, worship grounds) and family real estate have been destroyed.

Further, global warming and upheavals in politically fragile states have led to massive displacement and migration of people, further complicating the ability of leaders in both fragile and politically stable states to manage national borders while maintaining the political status quo. In more detail, changes in the climate have had adverse effects on human communities and ecosystems, including increasing food insecurity, exposure to disease, loss of livelihood, and worsening poverty and dependency for poorer countries and emerging economies. Nicole Detraz and Leah Windsor (2014, pp. 127–146) rightly remind us that climate debates are now focusing attention on climate migrants, people who are displaced by the environmental stresses caused by climate change, with the emphasis on state security issues while leaving the gender implications largely unexplored. In their examination of population movement and the securitization of climate migration, these authors find that gender helps focus attention on the human security implications of climate migration and offers a useful discourse for climate policymaking. Beyond the role of gender in shaping policy around malleable futures for global communities is the way in which higher education can foster civic education and public engagement beyond national borders. With the introduction of learning compacts in the USA since 1985, students are trained to participate in the life of the community in order to improve conditions for others and help shape the community's future. The engagement in democratic deliberation and advocacy and other forms of political action does not only negotiate the parameters of the rights and duties of national citizenship, it has the potential to educate and civilize local communities and urban areas alike.

The situation is more complex for young states that have only been holding elections for the last 50 years, which observer delegations describe as peaceful, free, and fair. During the second decade of the twenty-first century, most of these countries have witnessed little or no significant improvement in their social, economic, or infrastructure development. Even with the decades-old interventions of the UN, a global governing body that was sett up to promote peace among nations, human rights abuses are still rampant worldwide, including in advanced democratic systems like the USA, where police brutality and unfair incarceration of minorities are rife.

Thus internal challenges are not merely germane to fragile states. Freedom has also been attacked in emerging economies as well. Take the case of emerging economies like Mexico, where drug cartels assassinate journalists for covering drug trafficking and drug-related violence, or Guyana, whose government, according to media reports, failed to protect the rights of indigenous people to secure land, creating a hostile environment for national unity. In India, public figures use social media for political mobilization. There, the use of Web 2.0 technologies has made it easy for political parties, social activists, and young people to share knowledge and views and take action in real time. Meti et al. (2005) have reported that politicians use social media to communicate with their audience and to call them either to protest or to vote. In inner cities in the USA, police brutality against black and Hispanic people is rife, exposing inequities in civil rights. In India, Bhutan, and Pakistan, television and radio are being used to promote the personal agendas of elected officials, rather than to inform and bring about social change for the common good of the people.

Political Heavyweights and Implications for Fragile Democracies

Russia and the USA are the main global superpowers responsible for the rise and fall of democracies in smaller nation states. To clarify this claim, one needs to see how those countries have earned the status of "global superpower." As countries with the largest military power, economic reach, and political influence, they emerged in the twentieth century as the greatest global superpowers following their diplomatic and military interventions in World Wars I and II, and during the Cold War period. Economic expansion and the ability to oversee the growth of democratic regimes were equally crucial for the USA's rise to world power status. Through international trade and cooperation, US values, beliefs, and cultural influences were conveyed to other countries (Mead 2002, p. 103). The USA's *soft power* was crucial in attracting immigrants to its territory (Nye 1990, p. 170). Further, the attractiveness of the Diversity Visa Lottery program (Ngwainmbi 2014), as well as the H-IB non-immigrant visa, tourist visa, and other initiatives of the US State Department and Department of Homeland Security, all designed to foster immigration and foreigners' staying in the USA, have made it a global cultural potpourri and economic superpower.

Russia's rise to power has been traced back to the eighteenth century with the defeat of Napoleon, followed by its spearheading of the defeat of Hitler and Nazi Germany in World War II. Other factors are that it has abundant territory, resources, and a large population (Peck 2016). However, Russia's continued engagement of the USA in a political drama for the last 70 years has made these countries leaders to be envied. From 1947, when the geopolitical, ideological, and economic struggle started between these two superpowers, to December 26, 1991, when the Soviet Union was dissolved, they have maintained their love–hate, untidy relationship on the world stage. In the second decade of the twenty-first century, Russia and the USA have remained important players in global security. Their vote at the UN Security Council has influenced outcomes in regions beset by conflicts, such as the Middle East, Africa, and Asia. For example, during the Syrian crisis in 2015, the BBC reported that Russia "blocked resolutions critical of Syrian President Assad at the UN Security Council and continued to supply weapons to the Syrian military despite international criticism."[13] In contrast, on the same issue the USA has supported Syria's main opposition alliance, the National Coalition against the Syrian government. The USA accused President Assad of responsibility for widespread atrocities and said that he must leave office. However, it agrees on the need for a negotiated settlement to end the war and the formation of a transitional administration.[14] The disparate decision making of the USA and Russia on critical matters affecting other countries has cemented their image and position as the exclusive global police or superpowers and global political pace setters.

However, Russia's potential interference in the US presidential elections, reported by CNN before and after voting on November 8, 2016, could drag both nations back into another Cold War quagmire. Russia's reported interference questions the validity of American democracy and may threaten the USA's future political influence among nation states that are grappling with democratic governance ideals. Those politically fragile nations could draw the wrong lessons from the political climate in the USA leading up to the presidential elections and the decision by the Electoral College to accept the results of votes that different observers believe were rigged. The sanctions imposed by the USA on Russia following the report completed by the Federal Bureau of Investigation (FBI) on December 12, 2016 confirm that even the democratic process in the most politically advanced countries, with high security, transparency tools, and a long history of conducting peaceful elections, could indeed be corrupt. According to well-informed sources, the US government, particularly the White House, was acutely aware of the Russian government's hacking of the Democratic Party's electronic communication systems and other covert activities that influenced the outcome of the presidential election. Since the USA did not immediately correct this problem, how then are countries recognized by the UN, World Bank, and the USA itself for having corrupt and fragile governments and with fewer election-monitoring resources supposed to conduct free and fair elections?

The Struggles of Emerging Democracies and Role of the UN

Formed on June 26, 1945, with the goal to allow states to live in peace with each other, unite nations to maintain security, and promote the economic and social advancement of all people, the UN has deployed peacekeeping forces to conflict regions. It stands for the "enforcement of the peace" and implementation of actions to promote "peaceful settlement" (Russell and Muther 1958, p. 232). As specified further in its Charter, the UN works to reaffirm the worth of humans, while promoting "social progress and better living standards of life in larger freedoms" (UN 1968, p. 3). In defense of those aims, the UN has some 48 agencies providing economic, social, environmental, and diplomatic support in most of its 193 member countries. The agencies provide technical assistance in the form of personnel and physical resources in the form of direct funds to local programs. For example, the United Nations Development Programme (UNDP) "advocates for change and connects countries to knowledge, experience and resources to help people build a better life," and finances programs to manage local elections and promote good governance in member countries, especially developing countries (emerging democracies). Its sister branch, UN Women, works for "gender equality" and the "empowerment of women; and the achievement of equality between women and men as partners and beneficiaries of development, human rights, humanitarian action and peace and security,"[15] among other activities. For its part, the United Nations Population Fund (UNFPA) "promotes the right of every woman, man and child to enjoy a life of health and equal opportunity."[16] In short, the UN agencies have been created to facilitate the lives of people and promote peace and social and economic development within and between countries.

However, for many decades world-renowned political scientists, sociologists, and economists have continued to provide measurable evidence showing that this organization is a tool of imperialist states and superpowers. For example, Dana Williams (n.d.) claims that extreme inefficiencies and undemocratic mechanisms are fundamental to the UN's organization. Public opinion in many parts of the USA on the question of land tenure along the Nile, particularly in respect to Gaza, has been, at best, split over the UN's role. Based on a poll regularly conducted by a non-aligned, non-governmental source called Debate.org, 64% of the global audience want the UN to be dissolved while 36% support its existence. Some observers have condemned Israel for defending itself when Hamas, the largest Palestinian military group, was in clear violation of international norms. According to a report published on its own website mfa.gov.il/MFA, the Israeli Ministry of Foreign Affairs on June 14, 2015 titled "The 2014 Gaza Conflict: Factual and Legal Aspects", the Israeli government accused Hamas of violating International law by launching rockets towards Israel from within the Gaza Strip. Not only did the UN turn a blind eye, it returned to the Palestinians weapons that were found in a UN school.[17] Recently, political figures have joined private citizens to call for the dissolution of the UN. In January 2015, US Senator Rand Paul did so during an interview on international cable news network MSBN, citing America's "huge" contribution "to foot the UN's bill" and terrorist attacks by developing countries.[18] Political pundits speaking on US television networks have also echoed the need to disband the organization, alleging bias against a main American ally, Israel. They have argued that the UN gangs up on one of their allies while doing nothing to stop the genocide in Syria.[19] Coupled with this position are more calls from political scholars,[20] and even some leaders of UN member countries have publicly decried what they term the dubious role of the organization.

During a UN plenary session on September 24, 2010, some world leaders argued that the UN has "evolved into a two-tier organization, reflecting the world divided into two groups, one with inherently laudable values, rights and liberties, and another that needed coaching on those principles."[21] Rwanda, said its president, Paul Kagame, seemed to have been relegated to the latter group, along with other developing nations: "Marginalized and disenfranchised, we are also considered chronic violators of our human rights."[22] The lack of accountability fosters the argument that the UN has not been a credible, relevant, and democratic organization.

Emerging economies and politically fragile states are set to operate on the dictates of the five permanent members of the UN Security Council, whose votes determine how the organization would respond to a political or economic crisis in another country or region. Whether it is because of their longevity as UN Security Council permanent members[23] and the power to veto UN Assembly measures or their position as the victors of World War II, China, France, the Russian Federation, the UK, and the USA control the peace process and the economic futures of non-council member states. With the exception of Sweden, Japan, and Italy, the other non-permanent Council members elected for two-year terms by the General Assembly who are currently serving on the Council are either heavily dependent on foreign assistance, struggling economically, or embroiled in some form of political crisis compared to the permanent member states. As such, those countries (namely, Bolivia, Senegal, Ethiopia, Egypt, Uruguay, Kazakstan, and Ukraine) are likely to continue requesting assistance from the UN as long as they remain members.

If we understand dependency as the concept that nations are not isolated, but rely on one another (Collins 2014) to maintain peace, we emerge with the consensus that the UN Security Council has the right intention to bring political stability to democratically fragile states. The functions of the UN Security Council include calls on member countries to apply economic sanctions and other measures not involving the use of force to prevent or stop aggression; take military action against an aggressor; investigate any dispute or situation which might lead to international friction; or recommend methods of adjusting such disputes or the terms of settlement.[24] However, the five permanent members whose votes have recommended and continue to indicate appropriate actions needed in other countries are the richest and most politically powerful countries in the world. As development scholars have clearly stated,[25] those "core states" are more powerful and productive than "peripheral states" (emerging democracies), and can, therefore, set the rules of economic exchange. "From this position of dominance," Craig Collins goes on, "they can impose a condition of unequal transfers of wealth, in trade, finance, and resource extraction upon the periphery"—the emerging economy/democracy.[26] We can, therefore, agree that rich countries only support poor ones on their own terms and that developing nations do not have the same bargaining power. Given its overwhelming influence in shaping the economies and political futures of younger nations and those countries struggling to practice democratic norms and values, the UN in general arguably does not operate in the best interests of all member countries. Therefore, the UN can be considered irrelevant, and emerging economies should look elsewhere for help.

The Dubious Nature of Foreign Aid Donors

Aligned with the controversial role of the UN in countries struggling to emerge from an economic slump and those beset by political upheavals is the well-documented rationale for the funding they receive from countries with healthy economies. A growing number of development analysts have explained why, despite decades of foreign financial support, many developing countries have not emerged from their economic quagmire. Major corporations or what can be called “economic empires” are driven by greed and they successfully execute plans to drain the resources of other countries by using “economic hitmen.” One of the characteristics of an economic empire is that it enforces its currency on the world. Countries that are heavily in debt are forced to sell their oil in dollars, which gives the empire more economic control. Such countries are controlled by “economic hitmen” whose role is to provide financial assistance to developing countries and do not expect the borrowing country to pay off their debt. A former Chief Economic Adviser to the World Bank, UN, IMF, US Treasury Department, and Fortune 500 corporations has revealed ways in which those organizations corrupt and destabilize developing countries and weaken their economic potential. In the bestselling book *Confessions of an Economic Hit Man*, John Perkins (2004) has shamelessly described how his economic projections convinced foreign governments to accept billions of dollars in loans from the World Bank to build dams, airports, electricity grids, and other infrastructure that he knew they could not afford. The bank gave the loans on condition that construction and engineering contracts went to US companies. When their governments failed to pay, “as was often the case, the U.S. or its henchmen at the World Bank or International Monetary Fund would step in and essentially place the country in trusteeship.”[27] They would dictate all actions, from the government’s spending budget to security agreements and even its UN votes. Perkins further claims that this is a clever way for the USA to expand its “empire” at the expense of citizens in developing countries. The hypocrisies of the so-called aid donors warrant the dissolution of international development organizations, including the UN, and the creation of new economic development agendas by local economists in each country. Also, a continuous sensitization of the local population by experts familiar with the intricacies of foreign aid is necessary. The sensitization can be achieved through a sustained information sharing campaign. Here, communication experts, economists, local leaders, and community group representatives can meet and plan ways of ways of sharing and utilizing important messages aimed at improving their local economy.

Community Relations and Global Markets

Community relations are constantly being redefined as more foreign citizens and businesses move into communities and share their values with the residents or practice their customs. This phenomenon or what this author calls ***intra-cultural proliferationization***, wherein external customs intermingle with local ones, also threatens the wellbeing of those within such communities, and forces them to relocate and inculcate values that may not be compatible with those taught by their ancestors.

Villagers in Ethiopia, Guyana, India, and other indigenous communities are being moved away from their farming and ritual areas to settlements provided by their governments, international organizations, and companies. That shows the evil face of globalization within emerging economies and what this author foresees as the ***dynamization*** of the poor by greedy (national and provincial leaders) and external forces (foreign governments and company executives). This author posits that foreign companies are eroding the economic capacities (residents, land, and water resources) and social values (religious traditions, familism, collectivism) of emerging economies with help from national governments. In other words, negotiations for the use of indigenous land and space between national governments and the executives of foreign companies without proper input from local leaders have led to the occupation of such space and the displacement of residents. This process has hence threatened and continues to threaten the social and economic security of the local community, which constitutes the majority of the so-called emerging democratic institutions.

Emerging Economies Versus Established Economies

Interactions between emerging nations and established ones in the "free world" leave some social scientists with the conclusion that democracy is a child of time: it never matures; instead, it is like the human body, which needs to be constantly fed with nutrients. In other words, both economically rich and developing countries have fractured democratic values for "young" countries where poverty causes massive corruption, and limited resources create the need for governments to restrict certain rights of their citizens (Shah 2011).[28] For rich, established countries, there are too many laws aimed at protecting individual rights, which exposes individuals to more violence and makes them vulnerable and insecure against the same infrastructures that have been created to protect them from harm. Thus, both small and big countries have to continue to build their democracies.

National Culture as a Deterrent to Economic Development

Overpopulation, corruption, prostitution, widespread infectious diseases, high infant and maternal mortality, and lack of access to primary healthcare are among the problems responsible for economic hardship and poverty in most countries in Africa, South America, and Asia, particularly India. Strangely, those factors slow socioeconomic development, in that governments and development agencies are bound to divert resources earmarked for other programs to tackle them. For example, an overpopulated community in any given developing country typically has many unemployed people and limited healthcare opportunities, which lead to widespread infectious diseases, poverty, and more crime. No matter how big a country's annual budget, the state cannot effectively manage its citizens if people do not have access to programs to train them to be self-reliant. Causes of overpopulation include the practice of polygamy (discussed further below), social policies that do not support contraception, early marriages, and cultural practices that foster high birth rates. In India and parts of Africa, international development organizations like the United Nations Development Fund (UNDF), the Joint United Nations Programme on HIV/AIDS (UNAIDS), the World Health Organization, and some missionary groups have failed to convince the country's lawmakers to adopt plans to distribute condoms among sexually active persons, or to encourage other planned parenthood programs. No African government has decried the collateral damage caused by polygamy and other factors responsible for high birth rates on the continent. Instead, the governments continue to solicit and accept foreign assistance for the social challenges engendered by overpopulation, recognizing that they cannot generate the necessary resources to address such complex, growing needs.

The Polygamy Question and Weak Emerging Economies

George Peter Murdock's *Ethnographic Atlas* (1981) stated that from 1960 to 1980, out of 1231 marital societies, 186 were monogamous (married to one person at a time), 453 had occasional polygyny (having more than one wife), 588 had more frequent polygyny, and 7 had polyandry (having more than one husband). The USA and Europe are the top monogamous societies in the world. The defining difference between those types of relationships is the sexual ideal that each embraces. In Africa, Islamic societies, and parts of Asia, as well as within the Mormon community, polygamy might be a deterrent to economic development. In many developing countries, people are trained to work with various government agencies. Their finances come from service to the state. Unfortunately, there are not enough jobs for everyone, especially when the work-fit younger population is outgrowing the adult working class.

Anthropologists have found that polygamy increases the labor supply within a kinship network and expands the range of a man's alliances to maintain or acquire a position of leadership. The fact that spouses in traditional polygamous marriages do not treat one another as equals (Strauss 2012, p. 524), while a central spouse has more control over the family than each peripheral spouse (p. 517), may be one of the reasons why democracy is hard to manage in such countries. However, because in a democratic state the law considers everyone to be equal, those practicing polygamy and polyandry may be resisting democratic reform in their countries. With an increase in democratic movements and improvements in the education of women and human rights protection initiatives fostered by the UN with support from national governments and non-governmental organizations (NGOs), polygamous practices are in decline.

UN Peacekeeping and efforts by UN Women aim to achieve equality between women and men as beneficiaries of development, human rights, humanitarian action, peace, and security. Margaret E. Galey has reported that the UN has been mobilizing women from all over the world to formulate strategies and objectives to achieve women's participation as full partners with men in all areas of decision making and to gain equal access to opportunities offered by their societies (Galey 1995a, b).

Economically powerful countries are not immune to the trappings of globalization and citizenship, as terrorist groups within and outside their borders have engaged the media to help them grow cells and utilize their citizens to carry out terrorist activities. After countries showcased their communities as safe havens for compassionate care by providing asylum for persons and families from other nations, recent bombings in France, Belgium, the UK, and the USA organized by Islamic terrorists that killed innocent people have forced those countries to reconsider their immigration policies (Ngwainmbi 2016, p. 2). In fact, members of the Republican and Democratic parties in the US Congress have spent a considerable amount of time debating measures to address the immigration of citizens from countries sponsoring state terrorism. Meanwhile, families from war-torn Syria seeking political asylum are being screened and selected, which challenges the notion of the West (Europe and North America) as the bastion of freedom and peace, according to media reports.

Emerging Economies

Data published by the *Economist*, Haver Analytics, and the IMF shows that among the 27 emerging economies from the Western and Eastern hemispheres, only two countries are in Africa (South Africa and Egypt), five in Europe (Hungary, Czech Republic, Russia, Turkey, and Poland), one in the Middle East (Saudi Arabia), six in Central and South America (Colombia, Mexico, Peru, Brazil, Argentina, and Chile), and the rest in Asia (Saudi Arabia. China, Indonesia, Singapore, Hong Kong, South Korea, Philippines, Thailand, Malaysia, Taiwan Pakistan, India, and Vietnam). The indicators used were inflation, interest and exchange rates, credit, current account balance, federal budget balance, and government debt.[29]

Questions remain unanswered about the role that diplomacy, and the local and international media, should play in mitigating democratization and promoting national economic growth.

To wit, political scientists, political communication scholars, and international relations experts still believe that institutional corruption in the public and private sectors and at a grassroots level, and unfair, unbalanced negotiations, are preventing countries from emerging as global economic players. Political scientists and human rights law experts point to difficulties in practicing Western-style democracy and the lack of will to promote local, traditional forms of democracy. Political and development communication scholarship shows gaps in information sharing among institutions and the lack of transparency and accountability by appointed officials.

Other concerns exist about the future of democracy that we can no longer ignore. Indeed, we can visualize the contexts in which some emerging economies in Africa, the Caribbean, South America, the Middle East, and Asia could chart their socioeconomic futures through progressive democratic practices.

The developmental history of today's liberal-democratic institutions demonstrates a clear parallel between liberal state practice and a global culture engineered by ICT. From a theoretical operational standpoint, liberal democracy has implications for today's policymakers interested in the political liberalization of newly declared "democracies" in Africa, Asia, and Central and South America. Economists have credited emerging markets for expanding the global economy. India, China, South Africa, Mexico, and minority communities such as black and Hispanic people in US urban areas have a renewed interest in economic exploitation. Among the debates taking place in developmental politics, we do not find clear solutions to the plight of the poor and the marginalized.

Some countries on the media "hit list" that have opened their markets to foreign competition have invariably been building accountability within the system. Russia as well as Central and Eastern bloc countries such as Croatia, Ukraine, Bulgaria, Poland and Hungary are seeing an increase in both domestic and overseas investment and attracting foreign companies, as well as at least three countries in Africa, Central and South America, the Middle East, and Asia having changed trade policies allowing foreign companies to invest within their national borders. However, with their severe economic problems such as the rising costs of products and services, low-paying jobs, and high unemployment, especially among young people, fragile states are at risk of becoming more dependent on foreign aid. There are also major environmental problems affecting those countries striving to move to the middle-income level that could prevent them from becoming self-reliant economies. These are air, land and sea pollution, deforestation, soil erosion, and mining caused by construction companies.

Conclusions

If we put together all the challenges presented in this chapter, we may agree that the psychology of a community should be well placed to help people respond to the challenge of their marginalization in constructive ways. We can cautiously draw the following conclusions:

(1) The social values of one country cannot be entirely or successfully applied in another country, because each country has its own challenges that are different from those in another country. In some cases, however, there are symbiotic challenges among neighboring countries.
(2) Emerging democratic institutions around the world face major problems in the area of social and economic security, due to the widespread use of affordable and easy-to-use information and communication tools.
(3) The governments of those countries that are simultaneously practicing democratic governance and implementing techniques for national and regional economic development are also struggling with rising crime rates, institutional terrorism, and a rapid erosion of cultural values.

Next Steps

It might seem unnecessary to suggest that social media use should be monitored in fragile states, as media are synonymous with freedom—democracy. However, if we consider that nations transitioning to democratic rule do not have the technical capacity to monitor terrorist activities and other issues that can pose a risk to national, transnational, regional, and global security, then we see the need for the control of data shared through wireless means.

Countries have to put their personal interests and differences aside and agree on a common agenda to establish sustainable peace among all nations and implement a joint strategy to end global terrorism. They must first consider the rights and freedoms of their citizens and align their information and immigration policies with prime national interests. In this context, we can praise the UK for having voted to leave the EU while citing resentment of EU immigrants from poorer countries and economically struggling countries as their basis for the Brexit vote.[30]

National sovereignty is necessary for the rehabilitation of social and economic institutions in rich countries, especially when citizens worry that their rights have been compromised, and resources have been given away to outsiders.

Civic education must move past the traditional state-centric framework, and search for ways that might lead to the meaningful integration of the idea of the global citizen, as Nabil Haddad and Keren Wang (2015) have argued. Put differently, before a village or nation is fully integrated into the world community, the best practices of both parties should be copied and implemented in a thorough manner.

Topics for Discussion

1. Summarize the negative and positive effects of changes in information and communication technology (ICT)—the internet, media, cable television, and social media—on emerging countries. Which is stronger, the negative or the positive results? Explain why.
2. Explain how emerging democratic institutions are related to the problem of social and economic security. Cite specific evidence from the chapter in your response.
3. How has the term "globalization" been redefined in our changing world?
4. How are terrorist groups using media? Discuss some recent examples of terrorist uses of media and the results.
5. According to this chapter, what are the contributions that media can make toward the development of democracy in emerging countries? Find some specific examples from current events to support your position.

Notes

1. Citizenship: Just the Facts Name Reading—ALEX, http://alex.state.al.us/uploads/31028/CitizenshipJusttheFactsStudent.pdf (accessed January 13, 2017).
2. GLOBALIZATION ISSUES—Emory Sociology, http://sociology.emory.edu/faculty/globalization/issues05.html (accessed January 13, 2017).
3. *Ibid.*
4. *Ibid.*

5. http://sociology.emory.edu/faculty/globalization/contact.html (retrieved April 24, 2016).
6. The Endangered Language Project is a web-based global initiative sponsored by Google and the Alliance for Linguistic Diversity.
7. Endangered Languages Project, http://www.endangeredlanguages.com/about/ (accessed January 13, 2017).
8. In a section on democracy and governance in Africa, a report made that argument in 1992 (Kpundeh 1992, ch. 5, https://www.nap.edu/read/2041/chapter/5). It still holds true in the second decade of the twenty-first century(Kpundeh 1992).
9. *Ibid., p. 32.*
10. http://web1.cnre.vt.edu/lsg/GEOG3104S10Web/Group6/INTRO/Introduction.html accessed January 13, 2017.
11. *Ibid.*
12. *Ibid.*
13. http://www.bbc.com/news/world-middle-east-23849587. Accessed 12/31/2016
14. *Ibid.*
15. See UN Women Mandate.
16. www.unfpa.org.
17. See http://www.debate.org/opinions/should-the-un-be-dissolved. The question of whether the UN should be dissolved is well discussed at www.Debate.org.
18. Steve Benson "Rand Paul looks to 'dissolve' the United Nations" http://www.msnbc.com/rachel-maddow-show. 02/08/15
19. "The U.N.—like the Galactic Senate—must be dissolved" on Fox News. Published December 28, 2016 http://redalertpolitics.com/2016/12/28/u-n-like-galactic-senate-must-dissolved-video/. Accessed 1-1-2017

    Read more at http://redalertpolitics.com/2016/12/28/u-n-like-galactic-senate-must-dissolved-video/#YgvttrldpsOHGr2l.99.
20. See, e.g., Brinkley (2013).
21. http://www.un.org/press/en/2010/ga10999.doc.htm. Accessed 1-1-2017. World leaders at the UN's 65th General Assembly were calling for Security Council reform.
22. *Ibid.*
23. The USA and the UK have been permanent members since 1946. France joined in 1958, China in 1971, Russia in 1991.
24. Functions and Powers of the UN Security Council. http://www.un.org/en/sc/about/functions.shtml. 1-1-2017
25. See, e.g., Craig Collins Dependency Theory: A Critical Review http://www.slideshare.net/CraigCollins2/dependency-theory-37376919. Accessed 1-1-2017

26. This author prefers the term emerging economy. See also Ngwainmbi *Reconstructing African Democracies for Development in Africa through Efficient Communication and Media Engagement, JDCS* (2014)
27. John Perkins' book, *Confessions of an Economic Hit Man* has received 1500 positive reviews online and is a *New York Times* bestseller.
28. Anup Shah Poverty Around The World (Nov. 12, 2011) http://www.globalissues.org/article/4/poverty-around-the-world. Accessed 1/3/2017
29. Seth Kaplan, Can Emerging Markets Handle Another Economic Shock? In www.fragilestates.com/2012/02/08.
30. According to the BBC coverage on June 24, 2004, 3 million non-British EU nationals live in Britain. Following the vote in the UK Parliament for Britain to leave the EU, once the exit deal has been agreed a citizen of an EU country may no longer have unfettered access to live and work in Britain, and new passport and residency rules will apply.

References

Amuwo, Kunle. 2002. Globalization, NEPAD, and the Governance Question in Africa. *African Studies Quarterly* 6 (3): 66–82.

Björn, Hettne, and Söderbaum, Fredrik. 1998. The New Regionalism Approach. *Politeia: Journal of Political Science and Public Administration*, 17 (3): 5–19.

Brinkley, Joel. 2013. "The Hypocrisy of the UN's Human Rights Council". *World Affairs Journal*, 25 Nov. http://www.worldaffairsjournal.org/blog/joel-brinkley/hypocrisy-uns-human-rights-council. Accessed 1 June 2017.

Burton, Mark, and Kagan, Carolyn. 2003. Marginalization: Community Prysholog. http://www.compsy.org.uk/Chapter13all.PDF. Accessed 29 Dec 2016.

Collins, A.Kristin. 2014. Illegitimate Borders: Jus sanguinis Citizenship and the Legal Construction of Family, Race, and Nation. *123 Yale Law Journal* 2134: 14–36.

Court, M. Pedro. 2001. The Impact of 'Globalization' on Cultural Identities. Pontifical Academy of Social Sciences. Acta 7. Vatican City., Italy. www.pass.va/content/dam/scienzesocial/pd/acta7-morande.pdf.

Detraz, Nicole, and Windsor, Leah. 2014. Evaluating Climate Migration. International Feminist. *Journal of Politics*. 16 (1): 127–146. http://sociology.emory.edu/faculty.

Galey, Margaret E. 1995a. Forerunners in Women's Quest for Partnership. In *Women, Politics, and the United Nations*, ed. Anne Winslow. Westport, CT: Greenwood Press.

Galey, Margaret E. 1995b. Women Find a Place. In *Women, Politics, and the United Nations*, ed. Anne Winslow. Westport, CT: Greenwood Press.

George Peter Murdock. 1981. *Atlas of World Cultures.* Pittsburgh, PA: University of Pittsburgh Press.

Haddad, Nabbih, and K. Wang. 2015. Participatory Global Citizenship: Civic Education Beyond Territoriality. *Journal of Self-Governance and Management Economics* 3 (1): 26–44.

Harrell, Andrew. 1995. Explaining the Resurgence of Regionalism in World Politics. *Review of International Studies* 21 (4): 331–358.

Jan Nederveen Pieterse. 2009. *Globalization and Culture: Global Mélange.* Lanham, MD: Rowman & Littlefield.

Joseph, S. Nye, Jr. 1990. Soft Power. *Foreign Policy* 80: 153–171. Available from http://www.jstor.org/stable/1148580. Accessed 11 Nov 2009.

Kpundeh, Sahr John (ed.). 1992. *Democratization in Africa: African Views, African Voices.* Washington, DC: National Academy Press.

Mead, W.R. 2002. Special Providence. New York: Routledge.

Meti, Vojay, P. K. Khandoba, and S. Guru. 2005. Social Media for Political Mobilization in India: A Study. *Journal of Mass Communication and Journalism.* doi:10.4172/2165-7912.100027.

Muggah, Robert. 2015. Preventing Fragile Cities from Becoming Failed Cities. *Fragile States.* http://www.fragilestates.org/2015/03/16/preventing-fragile-cities-from-becoming-failed-cities-by-robert-muggah/.

Nacos, Brigitte L. 2002. *Mass-mediated Terrorism: The Centrality of the Media in Terrorism and Counter terrorism.* Lanham, MD: Rowman & Littlefield.

Ngwainmbi, K. Emmanuel. 2004. Glocalization & Partnership for Change in Africa: Bridging the Digital Divide with Good Governance. *Columbia University International Affairs Online Journal.* www.ciaonet.org/wps/nge01.

Ngwainmbi, K. Emmanuel. 2007. NEPAD and the Politics of Globalization: Redefining Local Space, Group Dynamics, and Economic Development. In *Africa in the 21st Century: Toward a New Future*, ed. Ama Mazama, 221–257. New York: Routledge.

Ngwainmbi, K. Emmanuel. 2014. The US DV Visa Lottery Program and the African Experience: Cultural mediation or brain drain? *Journal of Development and Communication Studies* 3 (1): 35–57.

Ngwainmbi, K. Emmanuel. 2016. The Mediatization of Violence: A Model for Utilizing Public Discourse and Networking to Counter Global Terrorism. *Journal of Mass Communication and Journalism* 6 (3): 2–8.

Page, Sheila. 2003. *Developing Countries: Victims or Participants Their Changing Role in International Negotiations Overseas.* London, UK: Development Institute. London.

Peck, Michael. How Hitler Made Russia a Superpower. 2016. *The National Interest Magazine*, 18 June 2018. http://nationalinterest.org/feature/how-hitler-made-russia-superpower-16634. Accessed 31 Dec 2016.

Perkins, John. 2004. *Confessions of an Economic Hit Man.* New York: The Penguin Group.

Russell, B. Ruth, and Muther, E. Jeannette. 1958. A History of the United Nations Charter. Brookings Institution.

Shah, Anup. 2011. Poverty Around The World. Nov 12. http://www.globalissues.org/article/4/poverty-around-the-world. Accessed 1 Mar 2017.

Strauss, Gregg. 2012. Is Polygamy Inherently unequal? *Ethics* 122 (3): 516–544. doi:10.1086/664754.

Syria crisis: Where key countries stand. *BBC Online*, 30 Oct 2015. http://www.bbc.com/news/world-middle-east-23849587.

United Nations. 1968. Everyman's United Nations. A Complete Handbook.

United Nations Economic Commission for Africa (UNECA). 1996. Overview of Economic and Social Development in Africa. http://www.uneca.org/cfm1996/pages/overview-economic-and-social-development-africa. Accessed 18 Dec 2016.

Wade, Robert Hunter. 2004. Is Globalization Reducing Poverty and Inequality? *World Development* 32 (4): 567–589. doi:10.1016/j.worlddev.2003.10.007.

Williams, Dana. n.d. The United Nations Should Not Be Dissolved. http://danawilliams2.tripod.com/un.html. Accessed 1 Jan 2017.

Winslow, Anne. 1995. Forerunners in Women's Quest for Partnership. Women, Politics, and the United Nations, 1–11. Westport, CT: Greenwood Press.

World Bank Globalization. 2002. *Growth, and Poverty: Building an Inclusive World Economy*. New York: Oxford University Press.

World Bank. 2015/2016. Development Goals in an Era of Demographic Change. http://www.worldbank.org/en/publication/global-monitoring-report. Accessed 12 Dec 2016.

CHAPTER 2

Navigating the Development Aid Challenge: Toward a More Encompassing Framework

Jean-Claude Kwitonda

This chapter examines the conceptual issues that complicate the work of development and social change, especially in the global South. Within the context of international development, the rhetoric of securing development aid tends to evoke the notion of neoliberalism as either a hegemonic/top-down or bottom-up phenomenon. At the heart of the debate is the desire to democratize the development process; that is, to make sure that people's power undergirds the enterprise through participatory and bottom-up or grassroots approaches. Although the ideal of democratizing development projects advocated by political economists may be overlooking significant pitfalls, a discursive perspective seems to point to the possibility of establishing a more encompassing perspective.

Jean-Claude Kwitonda research interests include global neoliberalism, especially its various meanings. In this chapter, he suggests a way to redefine and understand neoliberalism.

J.-C. Kwitonda (✉)
Ohio University, Athens, OH, USA

E.K. Ngwainmbi (ed.), *Citizenship, Democracies, and Media Engagement among Emerging Economies and Marginalized Communities*,
DOI 10.1007/978-3-319-56215-5_2

This chapter takes into account the controversies of international aid and sensitivities that surround related concepts such as development and neoliberalism. Nevertheless, its central argument is that the divide between poststructuralists and political economists need not be deterministic. This central argument applies an unconventional theoretical lens (of neoliberalism as discourse) that merges the poststructuralist and political economist perspectives (Springer 2012). We can best understand the enterprise of foreign aid and its consequences for local beneficiaries through a dialectical process that binds bottom-up and top-down ways of thinking. In such contexts, the task of theorizing the benefits of aid is difficult: "It is one that necessarily involves reconciling the Marxian political economist perspective of hegemonic ideology with poststructuralist conceptualizations of governmentality, where policy and program along with state form approach fall somewhere in between" (Springer 2012, p. 137). Rather than its being a limitation, reconciling poststructuralist and political economist perspectives enriches our understanding of the workings of neoliberalism and its role in international development and related aid. This method of encompassing agreement does not purport to argue that those who choose either of the two perspectives are wrong or misguided. Rather, it argues that neoliberalism understood as discourse can assist in establishing a more sophisticated and inclusive framework between the two schools of thought that, in this context, may seem to be (essentially) disparate.

Dichotomous (Re)Conceptualizations of Development and the Role of Donor Agencies

The role of donor agencies has had a tremendous impact on the conceptualization and reconceptualization of development and related discourse (Storey 2000). International donor agencies tend to represent top-down perceptions associated with international aid. Hence, top-down approaches tend to trigger the need for (re)conceptualizing development projects based on grassroots, bottom-up ideas (Ugboajah 1985; Sastry and Dutta 2013). Although each perspective allows us to understand the consequences of international communication, the two patterns have led to polarities in the theory and praxis of international development. As a result, the field seems to be in a conceptual crisis (Escobar 2000a, b; Storey 2000; Waisbord and Obregon 2012).

Scholars who examined the role of media in the process of economic and social development heralded the passing of traditional societies (e.g., Lerner 1958). They identified the traditional personality of people in the so-called Third World countries as a key barrier to development (Williams 2003), seeing low self-esteem, absolute values, resistance to innovations, fatalism, and non-achievement as the main psychological components of the traditional personality (Williams 2003, p. 215). To develop, people in the Third World needed "to act and think in modern, western ways" (Wilkins 2000, p. 2). That is the dominant paradigm in international development discourse.

By the 1970s, scholars—most of them from the global South—felt skeptical about the prevailing paradigm. In fact, according to Williams (2003), although funds and efforts had been invested in modernizing poorer countries, there was weak economic performance between 1960 and 1970 in newly independent countries. Most notably, scholars like Escobar (1995) denounced the Eurocentric and imperialistic outlook embedded in the ill-fated modernization enterprise. Amid these critiques and controversies, the concept of participation emerged as a bottom-up and viable response to (top-down) Western modernization.

The participatory development turn emphasizes the need for the active participation and empowerment of local communities in the articulation of their requirements and strategies for the betterment of their social and economic status (Fals Borda and Rahman 1991; Waters 2000). Today, advocates of culture-based and participatory approaches present this paradigm as the solution to the imperialistic, neocolonial, and neoliberal tendencies associated with the modernization paradigm, as well as institutions perceived as perpetuating perpetuating such hegemonic patterns of power (Dutta 2004; Sastry and Dutta 2013).

Nevertheless, participatory approaches are known to have contradictions. For instance, scholars of international development studies find that participatory approaches to development are not immune to power, praxis, and ideological manipulations perceived in the dominant paradigm (Fals Borda and Rahman 1991; Rahman 1990; Waters 2000). Waters (2000) elaborates on this critique by arguing:

> Even though the new approaches may speak the language of empowerment, they do little to foster the social and political change that links local agents with higher levels of policy and decision-making. Assuming that participatory approaches are inherently more capable of generating social

> transformation is questionable because we simply have not seen a systematic analysis of how local agents engage with larger power structures represented by researchers and practitioners. (p. 93)

Also, the word *empowerment* connotes the subtitling of top-down attitudes. Who is empowering whom and from where is a question that should be answered by participation scholars and practitioners. Moreover, scholars who reflect on participatory approaches have found that the approach may be beset by non-trivial pitfalls that include neoliberal tendencies (Cornwall 2007; Leal 2007; Rahman 1990; Sachs 1991; Waisbord 2008) that culture-centered approaches want to avoid. For instance, Rahman (1990) noted that "participation has become a politically attractive slogan" (p. 202), arguing in addition that "the concept of involvement is serving the private sector and its supporters in the latest drive toward the privatization of development" (p. 203). Among other things, Rahman posits that the term has become a useful fundraising device for both local governments and non-governmental organizations (NGOs), who use it to secure donor funds.

Aid and the Divide Between Poststructuralism and Political Economy

There are valid concerns that development aid results from both local and extra-local dynamics in developing settings. For example, some scholars of African development note the lack of trust between African governments and the people at the grassroots (Ngwainmbi 2005; Rahnema 1990). For instance, Ngwainmbi (2005) points out that NGOs and major local companies "traditionally have better luck working with citizens [at] the grassroots level" (p. 307). Although the grassroots approach to development is desirable, some African case studies point to another complication, especially when international organizations are involved (Waisbord 2008). For example, referring to the case of Mozambique, Hanlon observes that governments of economically developed countries may use donations and NGOs to manipulate and advance their imperial, economic, and political agendas, or they may at least be perceived as bypassing governments to reach ordinary people directly, thereby weakening national governments. Aid in such cases has encompassing consequences regardless of whether one views it from a poststructuralist or political economist lens.

There is a similar dichotomy between the conceptualization of development and some intellectual movements such as poststructuralist and political economist perspectives. Escobar (2000a, b) provides an account of this link in his analysis of the three paradigms that have characterized the field of international development studies:

> These paradigms include individual and market-based liberal theories, currently resulting in neo-liberal development approaches that seem to dominate the policy field, production-based policy Marxist theories, which provide the foundation for dependency and world systems theories in the 1960s and 1970s, and which can be seen at play today in some neo-structuralist approaches; and finally language and meaning-based poststructuralist theories, which have in recent years enabled a new type of critique of development discourse and practices. (2000, p. 166)

Escobar also proposes that to tackle other theoretical orientations, questions should be asked at both top and bottom echelons of the development enterprise to address gaps that are between what he calls *sites of practices* and *the policy level*. As a result, Escobar suggests that this gap is at the heart of the social and epistemological crisis that has plagued the field of international development studies for many years now. He argues that "unless we question the development model significantly, which has to be accomplished at the policy level, we will not be able to transcend this social and epistemological impasse" (p. 165).

As it turns out, however, development discourse continues to revolve around the top-down/bottom-up dichotomy. There is the temptation to see the conceptualization of development projects as either diffusionist (i.e., top-down) or participatory (i.e., bottom-up). As a result, scholars of development studies have been grappling with this philosophical divide and a receding theoretical convergence (e.g., Waisbord and Obregon 2012). Political economy scholars present neoliberalism as a top-down hegemonic project, serving the interests of global capitalism most of the time under the guise of philanthropy (e.g., King 2008; Sastry and Dutta 2011, 2013).

On the other hand, scholars like Lemke (2002) and Ferguson and Gupta (2012), influenced by the Foucauldian notion of governmentality, perceive neoliberalism as a bottom-up phenomenon. Due to long-standing ontological and epistemological differences between Foucauldian and Marxian understandings of power and discourse, it is quite common to find an either/or dichotomy in studies that are influenced by either school (Springer 2012). Because of the controversial nature that characterizes grassroots development imperatives and donor agencies, as well as other differences from the poststructuralist/political economist dichotomy, the nature of international aid programs calls for a more encompassing way of understanding the difficulties and opportunities of international assistance and related discourse.

Neoliberalism and International Development Discourse

Marxian and Foucauldian perspectives are believed to be quite divergent, and this view has implications for studies involving neoliberalism. Springer (2012) creatively illustrates this divide with a rather provocative and seemingly oxymoronic title to his paper (i.e., "Neoliberalism as Discourse: Between the Foucauldian Political Economy and Marxian Post-Structuralism"), in which he argues that there is a false dichotomy in the contemporary theorizing of neoliberalism. By intentionally misplacing his adjectives—associating Foucault with political economy and Marx with poststructuralism—Springer surprises readers with the nonconformist combination.

As noted in earlier sections, a similar dichotomous way of thinking can exist in international development aid discourse. For example, political economist scholars who use Gramscian hegemonic lenses to analyze neoliberal framing of international development assistance and related discourse (e.g., international health campaigns) tend to posit neoliberalism in terms of power over, in the sense that donor agencies exercise *power over* aid recipients (Dutta 2006; Sastry and Dutta 2013). The latter scholars offer valuable contributions regarding public understanding of international development aid discourse and unequivocally state that "future scholarship ought to further examine the paradoxes and dialectics through which local actors and partners negotiate the global partnerships to carry out a politics of resistance both locally and globally" (Sastry and Dutta 2013, p. 37).

Dematerialized poststructuralism need not be the ultimate perspective, but one can argue that the specific context of international development aid warrants more than just a dominators/dominated understanding of power. Thus, viewing neoliberalism as discourse permits us to incorporate poststructuralist and political economist perspectives into the analysis of power, and to accommodate the dichotomy between dematerialized poststructuralism and Marxian political economics. Moreover, the call for a similar merger in the field of international development studies (and a reconceptualization of the role of the donor agency) has been around for more than a decade (Storey 2000).

Reflection on Culture-Centric Imaginations of Development Aid

Culture-centric frameworks are not immune to the internal contradictions that characterize human societies and cultures. Because of this, culture-centric concepts such as Afrocentricity (Asante 2003) may be less self-reflexive, especially given institutional tensions that constrain the bottom-up approaches to development and related aid (Waisbord 2008). Moreover, Young (2006) has critiqued Afrocentricity as having an idealized image of African cultures. However, cultural experiences such as gender oppression/patriarchy in Africa suggest that a lack of self-reflexivity and an exclusively Afrocentric outlook may not fully address the rationalities that facilitate neoliberalism. Under the guise of the transcendental subject, class divisions within the black community are suppressed and, in turn, advance the class interests of the elites (Young 2006, p. 33). Young finds that Afrocentrism, like dematerialized poststructuralism, seeks to suppress class, which is perhaps why Young wants to bring materialism back into cultural studies.

Some scholars consider Marxism and poststructuralism as forms of self-alienation and an inferiority complex that prompt, for example, black intellectuals (e.g., Asante 1993) to look for solace in Eurocentric concepts and experiences. Some African development scholars find that their use is rather a dilemma (Chukwuokolo 2009) and others, such as Ngwainmbi (2005), find that scholars may view the combinatorial use of Asiacentric, Eurocentric, and Afrocentric ideas as an encompassing and beneficial way of thinking about development. The section that follows takes this line of thinking further by considering the conceptual implications embedded in how and why neoliberalism thrives through the discourse it constructs in the context of communication and international development studies.

Aid as Discourse: Implications for Communication and Development Studies

While this chapter does not claim to have worked out the ontological and epistemological differences found in the field of international development and communication studies, the special context of international aid calls for a more encompassing way of navigating the discourse of development and related aid. This way of understanding the development aid challenge is important, because conceptual polarities have practical consequences vis-à-vis the ways in which development and related communication interventions are imagined and implemented. For example, in both elite and popular culture, there is some apprehension induced by the word "development"—mostly because of its association with modernization or Eurocentrism, whereby the so-called developing countries are reportedly trying to be like or catch up with the developed world. When the word *development* becomes impossible to avoid, some commentators prefer to use *traditional development* (e.g., Prahalad 2014) or *post development* (Escobar 2000a, b). Because most countries in the global South depend on aid from economically powerful countries, the meanings associated with the term *development* become difficult to wish away.

Precisely because development as a concept is infused with both poststructuralist and hegemonic aftertastes, scholars and practitioners who operate at the opposite ends of the two schools of thought may find themselves in different but overlapping semantic fields. For example, poststructuralists concerned with the practical consequences of language and meaning share grievances with political economists regarding the beguiling implications embedded in the discourse of development and related conditions such as development aid.

Some thinkers justify the importance of development aid through the rhetoric of *progress* and improvement. Attempts to render the term development by using alternative words such as sustainable de-growth, post development, or traditional development tend to sustain and reify the concept, allowing it to re-emerge as "a zombie concept that is alive and dead at the same time" (Gudynas 2011, p. 442). This discourse-based debate is indeed welcome. In particular, the debate should interest practitioners as well as scholars concerned with the work of communication and development, because the way we think about and communicate meanings is the way we often act. This way of thinking about discourse and its practical consequences, which Burke (1984) echoes, eloquently reminds us that concepts are ways both of seeing and of not seeing. In fact, these commendable efforts that seek to recast the idea of development should invite scholars to understand the concept of development (and related notions such as neoliberalism) as discourse. Such an orientation can boost theory and praxis, especially in this struggling but important field of international development and related communication studies (Storey 2000).

International Development Controversy and Neoliberalism

Evidently, the controversial concept of international development tends to evoke the idea of neoliberalism. Although neoliberalism is a fluid concept, most scholars agree on four lines of thinking. The first sees neoliberalism as *policy and program*. The latter concerns itself with issues such as privatization, deregulation, and liberalization (Brenner and Theodore 2002; Kelpies and Vance 2003; Martinez and Garcia 2000; Springer 2012; Ward and England 2007). The second line of thought sees neoliberalism as a state form, defined as a "process of transformation that states purposefully engage into remain economically competitive within a transnational playing field of similarly minded states" (Springer 2012, p. 136). The discourse of development aid is also involved with thinking about neoliberalism, namely, with considering neoliberalism as a hegemonic ideological project (Brenner and Theodore 2002; Klepeis and Vance 2003; Sastry and Dutta 2011, 2013). Other thinkers consider neoliberalism as governmentality (e.g., see Ferguson and Gupta 2012; Escobar 2000a, b; Lemke 2002).

Although the concept of governmentality and its bearing on neoliberalism were first developed mainly within the context of Western democracies by Foucault (1991), scholars such as Ferguson and Gupta (2012) extend it to non-Western settings such as Africa and Asia. Ferguson and Gupta (2012) contest hegemonic understandings of neoliberalism, which consider neoliberalism as an overarching, concrete, and powerful force that operates from above. Ferguson and Gupta's insights are rooted in their concept of transnational governmentality, since they see—in modern international relations and institutions—an increase in the de-satiation of traditional state power by the proliferation of what they call quasi-autonomous NGOs or civil society.

The Top-down Approach, Neoliberalism, and Democracy

Even though both top-down and bottom-up views of neoliberalism start from different places, they share a common concern regarding power and praxis in the international development challenge, especially the need for resistance and a place-based conceptualization of international development interventions (Escobar 2001; Sastry and Dutta 2011; Dutta 2004). Sastry and Dutta (2011), for example, contest top-down/neoliberal approaches by calling for more participatory and culture-based interventions. While this perspective is viable, advocates of culture-based interventions need to start looking into the great challenge posed by local variability and internal cultural contradictions.

Up to this point, however, development programs that apply for participatory programs (such as entertainment education) attract disagreement between scholars. For example, some researchers suggest that entertainment education has the potential to promote free communication (Jacobson and Storey 2004; Tufte 2001; Waisbord and Obregon 2012). Others, such as Dutta (2006), find that when international donors fund such programs, they serve to promote Western values through indirect ways, such as health interventions and related communication. Yet others, such as Waisbord and Obregon (2012), are nuanced about the nature of aid, simply choosing to state that "the reality of health aid programs, including communication experiences, is more messy and unpredictable than Dutta acknowledges" (p. 25).

Furthermore, advocates of participatory approaches assume that cultures in the global South are traditionally democratic and inherently bottom-up. However, most cultures in the global South can be said to have followed a more or less similar trajectory of power structures that do not lend themselves well to participatory (i.e., people's power) understandings. From absolute monarchical power to colonial and postcolonial dictatorships, one can argue that people in most global South settings have only been coping with if not internalizing normalized, top-down political cultures. Besides, there is more to revolutionary concepts of participation—such as the local and the grassroots, as opposed to neocolonial or globalizing hegemonies—than meets the eye. Most states in the global South are economically broke and are required by development agencies to hold regular elections to secure aid or survive debt crisis. Rahnema (1990) observes that since "governments have learned to control and contain participation, significant political advantages are often obtained through the ostentatious display of participatory intentions" (p. 202). Democratic ideals in such cases are skillfully hampered through corrupt electoral systems or the creation of a phantom civil society, such as what Ferguson and Gupta (2012) describe as GONGOS (government-organized NGOs).

Participation in Development Discourse

Participation is, in many ways, a very attractive paradigm and it owes its legitimacy to the failures of what is known today as traditional development. However, the celebration of participation in development discourse (which is almost always unquestioned) echoes Rahnema's (1990) critique, which asserts that the zeal constitutes "the last temptation of saint development." These questions and debates surrounding the concept of development need to be worked out through a self-reflexive process, because often factors that lead to the failure of development projects spring from both Western and global South dynamics. Because of discourses that operate through dichotomous reactions and the positive emotional energy that participation often commands, it may not be easy to critique the grassroots head on. However, failure to examine such discourses may impede a self-reflexive discussion regarding issues of corruption and other socioeconomic shortcomings, and effectively undermine the ideals of open dialogue and democracy that motivate participatory approaches. Ferguson and Gupta (2012) posit that the needed self-reflexivity can be accomplished by questioning both commonsense assumptions about the verticality of states as well as many received ideas of "community," "grassroots," and the "local" (1990). Hence, we cannot comprehend that neoliberalism cannot function solely as either bottom-up or top-down "by constituting an external and supposedly omnipresent neoliberalism. Otherwise, we neglect internal constitution, local variability, and the role that 'the social' and individual agency play in (re)producing, facilitating, and circulating neoliberalism" (Springer, p. 136).

The diversity of the conceptual framework of neoliberalism manifests care and concern on the part of people who study international development and related communication interventions. Scholars such as Fox (2012) find that "the passion with which new labels for health communication are developed and launched, makes it hard to build a field by the accumulation of evidence" (pp. 64–65). More scholars have been opening up debates about the possibility of dialectical and integrative approaches, particularly in areas that seek to examine the relationship between neoliberalism, international development, and the work of social change (Gilbert 2005; McCarthy and Prudham 2006; Papa et al. 2006; Raco 2005; Springer 2012). Springer (2012) finds practical value in problematizing frameworks that condition our understanding and constrain our self-reflexive capabilities. That constitutes a more encompassing way of apprehending neoliberalism and navigating the international development aid challenge. Therefore, it makes sense to consider Springer's call for flexibility and, most importantly, self-reflexivity, because "together they may assist in disestablishing neoliberalism's rationalities, deconstructing its strategies, disassembling its technologies, and ultimately destroying its techniques" (pp. 143–144). As a variegated and fluid concept (Cotoi 2011), one can use neoliberalism for many purposes, and its rationalities can manifest both local and extra-local realities. Indeed, endeavors that seek to engage neoliberalism in the context of development aid need not be dichotomous or construed as either top-down or bottom-up.

Conclusion

This chapter has explored conceptual dichotomies within the special context of international development and related aid. The latter context recasts these dichotomies as dialectical tensions that bind the institutional bureaucracy and rhetoric of securing donor funds to do the work of development internationally. Scholars have explored and outlined controversial but illuminating concepts such as neoliberalism and development and their polarizing consequences vis-à-vis theory and praxis. Because scholars of development studies and global social change express a need for convergence between such conceptual divides, it seems more pragmatic to posit development aid and related concepts as discourse. The latter outlook allows for a more encompassing understanding of the special context of international development aid (i.e., from a discursive perspective). Scholars and practitioners are therefore encouraged to continue the problematization of discourse and ways in which aid is used to justify development endeavors. While development continues to be a moving target in the global South, it will perhaps be necessary always to keep (re)examining development even when it happens.

Topics for Discussion

1. What is your definition of neoliberalism? Should emerging economies embrace it?
2. Expatriates, as well as development agencies in developing countries, tend to rely on the development paradigms and experiences from the region where they studied. Critics have complained that a state that applies multiple development theories causes confusion and underdevelopment. If you agree with this assessment, which unique approach should a country select and on what basis? If you do not agree, explain and support your position.
3. Should each country identify and implement its development approach to meet the conditions being set by the forces of globalization? Explain the reasons for your answer.
4. Do you agree that Africa's heavy dependence on foreign assistance is largely responsible for poverty, underdevelopment, and weak public institutions?

References

Asante, K. Molefi. 1993. *Malcolm X as a Cultural Hero and other Afrocentric Essays*. Trenton, NJ: Africa World Press.

Asante, K. Molefi. 2003. *Afrocentricity: The Theory of Social Change*. Chicago, IL: African American Images.

Brenner, N., and N. Theodore. 2002. Cities and the Geographies of 'Actually Existing Neoliberalism. *Antipode* 34: 349–379. doi:10.1111/1467-8330.00246.

Burke, K. 1984. *Permanence And Change*. Berkeley, CA: University of California Press.

Chukwuokolo, J.C. 2009. Afrocentrism or Eurocentrism: The Dilemma of African Development. *OGIRISI* 6:24–34. http://www.ajol.info/index.php/og/article/view/52333/40958.

Cornwall, A. 2007. Buzzwords and Fuzzwords: Deconstructing Development Discourse. *Development in Practice* 17: 471–484. doi:10.1080/09614520701469302.

Cotoi, C. 2011. Neoliberalism: A Foucauldian Perspective. *International Review of Social Research* 1 (2): 109–124. http://www.irsr.eu/issue02/07_Cotoi_p109-124.pdf.

Dutta, M. 2004. The Unheard Voices of Santalis: Communicating about Health from the Margins of India. *Communication Theory* 14 (3): 237–263. doi:10.1111/j.1468-2885.2004.tb00313.x.

Dutta, M. 2006. Theoretical Approaches to Entertainment Education Campaigns: A Subaltern Critique. *Health Communication* 20 (3): 221–231. doi:10.1207/s15327027hc2003_2.

Escobar, A. 1995. *Encountering Development: The Making and Unmaking of the Third World*. Princeton: Princeton University Press.

Escobar, Arturo. 2000a. Place Power and Networks in Globalization and Post Development. In *Redeveloping Communication for Social Change: Theory Practice and Power*, ed. K.G. Wilkins, 89–102. Oxford, England: Rowman & Littlefield.

Escobar, Arturo. 2000b. *Redeveloping Communication for Social Change: Theory, Practice, and Power*. Oxford: Rowman & Littlefield.

Escobar, Arturo. 2001. Culture Sits in Places: Reflections on Globalism and Subaltern Strategies of Localization. *Political Geography* 20: 139–174. doi:10.1016/S0962-6298(00)00064-0.

Fals Borda, O., and M.A. Rahman (eds.). 1991. *Action and Knowledge: Breaking the Monopoly with Participatory Action Research*. New York, NY: Apex.

Ferguson, J., and A. Gupta. 2012. Spatializing States: Toward Ethnography of Neoliberal Governmentality. *American Ethnologist* 24: 981–1002. doi:10.1525/ae.2002.29.4.981.

Foucault, M. 1991. In *The Foucault Effect: Studies in Governmentality*, ed. G. Burchell, C. Gordon, and P. Miller, 87–104. Chicago, IL: Chicago University Press.

Fox, E. 2012. Rethinking health communication in aid and development. In *The handbook of global health communication*, ed. S. Waisbord, and R. Obregon, 52–69. Malden, MA: Wiley.

Gilbert, E. 2005. The Inevitability of Integration? Neoliberal Discourse and the Proposals for a New North American Economic Space After September 11. *Annals of the Association of American Geographers* 95: 202–222. doi:10.1111/j.1467-8306.2005.00456.x.

Gudynas, E. 2011. Buen Vivir: Today's Tomorrow. *Development* 5 (4): 441–447. doi:10.1057/dev.2011.86.

Jacobson, T.L., and J.D. Storey. 2004. Development Communication, and Participation: Applying Habermas to a Case Study of Population Programs in Nepal. *Communication Theory* 14 (2): 99–121. doi: 10.1111/j.1468-2885.2004.tb00307.x.

King, S. 2008. *Pink Ribbons Inc: Breast Cancer and the Politics of Philanthropy*. Minneapolis: University of Minnesota Press.

Klepeis, P., and C. Vance. 2003. Neoliberal Policy and Deforestation in Southeastern Mexico: An Assessment of the PROCAMPO Program. *Economic Geography* 79: 221–240. doi:10.1111/j.1944-8287.2003.tb00210.x.

Leal, P. 2007. Participation: The Ascendancy of a Buzzword in the Neo-liberal Era. *Development in Practice* 17: 539–548. doi:10.1080/09614520701469518.

Lemke, T. 2002. Foucault, Governmentality, and Critique. *Rethinking Marxism* 14: 49–64. doi:10.1080/089356902101242288.

Lerner, D. 1958. *The Passing of Traditional Society: Modernizing the Middle East.* Glencoe, Ill.: Free Press.

Martinez, E., and A. Garcia. 2000. What is Neoliberalism? A Brief Definition for Activists. *CorpWatch.* http://www.corpwatch.org/article.php?id=376.

McCarthy, J., and S. Prudham. 2006. Neoliberal Nature and the Nature of Neoliberalism. *Geoforum* 35: 275–283. doi:10.1016/j.geoforum.2003.07.003.

Ngwainmbi, E. K. 2005. Globalization and NEPAD's Development Perspective: Bridging the Digital Divide with Good Governance. *Journal of Black Studies* 35 (3): 284–309. doi:10.1177/0021934704266080.

Papa, M.J., A. Singhal, and W.H. Papa. 2006. *Organizing for Social Change: A Dalectic Journey of Theory and Practice.* New Delhi, India: Sage.

Prahalad, C.K. 2014. Social Enterprise: Can it Succeed Where Traditional Development Has Failed? *The Guardian.* (2 Feb 2014). http://www.theguardian.com/global-development/poverty-matters/2014/feb/25/social-enterprise-succeed-traditional-development-failed.

Raco, M. 2005. Sustainable Development, Rolled-out Neoliberalism and Sustainable Communities. *Antipode* 37: 324–347. doi:10.1111/j.0066-4812.2005.00495.x.

Rahnema, M. 1990. Participatory Action Research: The "Last Temptation of a Saint". *Development Alternatives* XV: 199–226. http://www.jstor.org/stable/40644681.

Sachs, W. 1991. *The Development Dictionary: A Guide to Knowledge as Power.* London: Zed Books.

Sastry, S., and M.J. Dutta. 2011. Postcolonial Constructions of HIV/AIDS: Meaning, Culture, and Structure. *Health Communication* 26: 437–449. doi:10.1080/10410236.2011.554166.

Sastry, S., and M.J. Dutta. 2013. Global Health Interventions and the "Common Sense" of Neoliberalism: A Dialectical Analysis of PEPFAR. *Journal of International and Intercultural Communication* 6 (1): 21–39. doi: 10.1080/17513057.2012.740682.

Springer, S. 2012. Neoliberalism as Discourse: Between Foucauldian Political Economy and Marxian Post-structuralism. *Critical Discourse Studies* 9 (2): 133–147. doi:10.1080/17405904.2012.656375.

Storey, D. 2000. A Discursive Perspective on Development Theory and Practice: Reconceptualizing the Role of Donor Agencies. In *Redeveloping Communication for Social Change*, ed. K.G. Wilkins, 103–118. Lanham, MD: Rowman & Littlefield.

The World Bank. Development Goals in an Era of Demographic Change. http://www.worldbank.org/en/publication/global-monitoring-report. Accessed 12 Dec 2016.

Tufte, T. 2001. Entertainment-education and Participation. *Journal of International Communication* 7 (2): 25–51. doi:10.1080/13216597.2001.9751908.

Ugboajah, F.O. 1985. Oramedia in Africa. In *Mass Communication, Culture, and Society in West Africa*, ed. F.O. Ugboajah. London: WACC. Reprinted in A. Gumucio-Dagron & T.

Waisbord, S. 2008. The Institutional Challenges of Participatory Communication in International Aid. *Social Identities* 14 (4): 505–522. doi:10.1080/13504630802212009.

Waisbord, S., and R. Obregon. 2012. Theoretical Divides and Convergence in Global Health Communication. In *The Handbook of Global Health communication*, 9–33. Malden, MA: Wiley.

Ward, K., and K. England. 2007. Introduction: Reading Neo-liberalization. In *Neo-liberalization: States, Networks, Peoples*, ed. K. England, and K. Ward, 1–22. Malden, MA: Blackwell.

Waters, J. 2000. Power and Praxis in Development Communication: Discourse and Methods. In *Redeveloping Communication for Social Change*, ed. K.G. Wilkins, 89–102. Lanham, MD: Rowman & Littlefield

Wilkins, K.G. 2000. Introduction. In *Redeveloping Communication for Social Change: Theory, Practice, and Power*, ed. K.G. Wilkins, 1–4. Oxford, England: Rowman & Littlefield.

Williams, K. 2003. *Understanding Media Theory*. London: Hodder Arnold Publication.

Young, R. 2006. Putting materialism back into race theory: Towards a transformative theory of race. In *Race and the foundations of knowledge: Cultural Amnesia in the academy*, ed. J. Young, and J.E. Braziel, 32–45. Chicago: The Board of Trustees of the University Of Illinois.

PART II

Regionalism and the Mediated Global Civil Society

CHAPTER 3

The Impact of Regionalism on Democracy Building: An Examination of the Southern African Development Community (SADC)

Johannes Muntschick

The collapse of the bipolar world order after the end of the Cold War and growing globalization, with its multiple effects on the global economy and security, prepared the ground for the latest wave of regionalism. This phenomenon found expression in some new and renewed regional integration organizations in virtually every corner of the globe, particularly in the southern hemisphere.[1] It is quite surprising, however, that most of these "new regionalisms" (Hettne and Söderbaum 1998) mushroomed in the global South[2] and the world's peripheral and least

Johannes Muntschick's major research interests include regionalism inside and outside Europe, as well as statehood, conflicts, and war economies in Africa. In this chapter, he evaluates the work of the Southern African Development Community (SADC) and concludes that the organization has been only partially successful in helping emerging nations achieve democracy.

J. Muntschick (✉)
University of Mainz, Mainz, Germany

E.K. Ngwainmbi (ed.), *Citizenship, Democracies, and Media Engagement among Emerging Economies and Marginalized Communities*,
DOI 10.1007/978-3-319-56215-5_3

developed regions. The preconditions for regional integration, such as economic interdependence, political stability, state capacity, and governance, are often less advantageous in the global South compared to those in the more developed and politically rather stable northern hemisphere (Axline 1977; Hurrell 1995b; Hout and Meijerink 1996).

Most of these new regionalisms[3] seek to promote regional economic, security, and infrastructure cooperation as a strategy to foster socioeconomic development and to cope with global and regional challenges. However, only a few focus explicitly on building and advancing democracy or good governance in the region and its member states as part of a more comprehensive agenda on regional development (Hartmann 2008; van der Vleuten and Hoffmann 2010). This phenomenon is quite surprising, insofar as democratic rule in an international organization and its member states is said to be of benefit not only for international peace and individual freedom, but in particular for economic prosperity as well as peace and security in an entire region (Doyle 1983). Thus, a country's motivation to engage in building and advancing democracy is accordingly supposed to be rooted not only in idealism, but rather in clear rational choice considerations as well.

Even if countries and their ruling elites do not have the intrinsic motivation or experience difficulties in the process of establishing and stabilizing democracy, there is—at least from a political science perspective—general agreement that regional integration and related regional institutions can be useful measures to promote and strengthen democratic rule. The reason is that an appropriate institutional "lock-in" on a regional level implies committing member countries of a regional organization to specified norms and practices related to democracy or beyond (Keohane 1982; Moravcsik 1998).

The *European Union* (EU) serves as an example of the success of this mechanism, given the transformation of the formerly authoritarian and communist European countries to stable democracies in the course of their EU membership (Cameron 2007). Some regionalisms in the global South, such as the *Common Market of the South* (Mercosur) in Latin America, have made similar efforts toward spreading and enforcing democratic principles by institutional means. While not explicitly dedicated to building democracies, the *Association of Southeast Asian Nations* (ASEAN) in Asia followed a similar strategy of promoting good governance and human rights as part of its regional agenda (van der Vleuten and Hoffmann 2010).

Against the background of these observations, it is quite puzzling whether regional institutions or regional integration organizations do have a positive effect on promoting and strengthening democracy—that is, democratic rule—in their constituent states. To fill the research gap, this chapter turns to the global South and focuses on the African continent, which certainly represents an important part of the developing world.

Among the existing regional integration organizations in Africa, the *Southern African Development Community* (SADC) counts as one of the most realistic and promising examples of the new regionalism on the continent (Mair and Peters-Berries 2001; Weiland 2006; Adelmann 2012). Founded in 1992, the SADC has seen remarkable achievements—sometimes supported by external actors—in some regional integration projects over time (Muntschick 2015). Apart from the issues of the economy, security, and infrastructure, SADC's Common Agenda includes clear policies that aim to consolidate, defend, and maintain democracy (Oosthuizen 2006).[4] Regarding the research gap on the relation of regionalism and democracy, the key question in this chapter is: "Does regionalism in the SADC contribute to the democratization of the region and democratic rule in its member states?"

To give theory-driven answers to that question, this study provides a theoretical framework for the causal relationship between regionalism and the promotion/consolidation of democracy. Next, it analyzes the SADC's regional agenda and institutionalized policies on building and maintaining democracy, to clarify the organization's plans and stated regional conditions at the time of its institutionalization. By applying a before-and-after design and methods of rigorous process tracing, the study provides in the course of its empirical analysis a benchmarked evaluation of the organization's efforts in this respect. It concludes that the SADC has so far been only partially successful in the achievement of democracy using regional governance mechanisms.

Theorizing Regionalism and Democracy: An Uneven Relationship

Analytical explanations and profound answers demand in general a theory-driven analysis of the case under observation with respect to the observed phenomenon. This chapter is intended to provide a short overview of the state of research on regionalism and democratization. It also gives some food for thought on how to conceptualize an analytical framework that provides answers to the causal relation between institutionalized regional cooperation and the promotion/consolidation of democracy.

State of the Art and Research Gaps

Analyzing the relationship between institutionalized regional cooperation within the framework of regional integration organizations and their effects on building democracies within their member states is a paramount and current topic in political science. Not least since the end of the Cold War and the accession of several postcommunist countries to the EU, researchers are highly interested in whether and how regionalism contributes to the building of democracy and the stabilization of democratic rule—including democratic principles and values—in the member states concerned. Against this background, there is no doubt that political science research is also interested in gaining knowledge on whether similar mechanisms exist and work in regionalisms beyond Europe.

In the academic literature and current theoretical debate, most of the scientific research that deals with the relationship between regionalism and the manifestation or stabilization of democracy in participant states has so far focused on the well-known example of the EU. In this context, the phenomenon of *Europeanization*—for instance, the positive effects of European integration on domestic polity and policies—has sometimes been observed (Cameron 2007; Levitz 2010). This analytical concept focuses on the transfer of European values and has only been applied to analyze cases in Europe so far. Therefore, it seems questionable whether one can apply such a concept to a situation outside Europe.

In terms of empirical case-study research on the topic of this chapter, there exists only a very small academic literature with analyses on regionalisms beyond Europe (Hoffmann and van der Vleuten 2007). A recent article deals with the enforcement of democracy by regional organizations in the South (van der Vleuten and Hoffmann 2010), but most experimental works either focus only on the state of democracy in specific countries, or simply describe the institutional nature of regionalisms in general. Experts in area studies have written about many regionalisms in the South—and about the SADC in particular—and many of these works provide valuable empirical details, but they are, unfortunately, in most cases not very analytical and rather descriptive (Brinkmann 2000; Mair and Peters-Berries 2001; Stahl 2010).

Rational Choice and Institutionalized Regional Cooperation

Rational institutionalist theories on regional integration attribute institutionalized regional cooperation and the recent emergence of the new regionalisms in the global South basically to functional pressures and specific problematic situations in international relations (Keohane 1984; Zürn 1993). A specific understanding of regions and regionalism will be applied to make this theoretical approach favorable to the topic and the research question.

Regions will be conceived as supranational subsystems within the international system, whose constituents are states that are geographically close and share some degree of interdependence (Hettne 2005, p. 544). Following this understanding, a regionalism can be interpreted as a planned, multilateral, and state-led organization of interdependence within a confined geographical space that gives rise to a cluster of various, multidimensional, or specific regional cooperation projects and accompanying institutions (Stein 1982, p. 316; Bach 2003, p. 22). By this minimalist conceptualization, a multifaceted regional colossus such as the EU falls into the category of regionalism. In fact, we can interpret the EU as acting as a multilayered system of nested international cooperation projects and related institutions that deal with many cross-cutting issues (Gehring 1994, p. 216; Moravcsik 1998, p. 15).

According to the rationalist institutional school of thought and regime theory, the demand for international cooperation in any country is based on international or regional cooperation problems which arise from complex interdependence between states (Keohane and Nye 1977). Patterns of interdependence are not exclusively confined to the economic realm (e.g., trade relations or investment flows), but exist in virtually every issue area (e.g., security, migration). Rational utility-maximizing actors, considered here as the countries and their governments, will abstain from unilateral behavior and are invited to engage in institutionalized cooperation, provided that the (expected) gains and related net benefits surpass the payoffs of non-cooperation or an uncoordinated status quo (Keohane 1984, p. 15; Hurrell Hurrell 1995a).

Regarding regional integration, organizations represent the superstructure of formal institutions which are composed of member states and bound by their territorial dimensions. Institutions help to overcome regional cooperation problems by various means (Keohane 1982; Müller 1993). Institutions can reduce uncertainty by providing transparency and information. They help to extend the "shadow of the future" (Axelrod 1987, p. 11), offer an arena and framework for consultation, facilitate policy coordination, and ideally promote and reward cooperative behavior among their members. Thus, regional institutions can help to create a regional "club good" and achieve Pareto-superior outcomes for all countries involved. In the case of good performance, the regulative elements of a regional integration organization's institutions may add to the welfare, political stability, peace, and security of the respective region and its member states (Rittberger and Zürn 1990, pp. 90–91).

According to rationalist institutional theory (Keohane 1984; Zürn 1993), the relative power distribution among actors can significantly influence the emergence and design of institutionalized cooperation. An actor in a position of relative power (e.g., a local key country or hegemon) may decide to act in favor of (or against) a cooperation project and thus either significantly fuel or inhibit the cooperation process. While all actors are assumed to share the common interest in obtaining overall gains from collective action and collaboration, they nevertheless have self-centered and divergent preferences about the distribution of contingent costs and assets; that is, the relative gains. To achieve the individually best outcome, actors will consequently engage in negotiations over the institutional embedding and particular design of a cooperation project (Zangl 1994, pp. 284–287). These international negotiations are above all characterized by bargaining. A country's relative power distribution can be deduced from the character of the overall—and particularly issue-specific—patterns of interdependence between the countries involved. Patterns of asymmetry imply the availability of attractive unilateral policy alternatives and exit options for states (Keohane & Nye 1977, pp. 9–10, 268–270).

Referring to international relations on a regional level, states in a central position—that is, those on which others are dependent—occupy a relatively strong power position and consequently will be essential cornerstones in any regional organization (Moravcsik 1998, pp. 64–65). Therefore, any institutionalized cooperation agreement will finally reflect the relative power position of negotiators. Regional great powers therefore play a crucial role in the establishment and performance of regional integration and the governing institutions (Keohane 1988, p. 387; Zürn 1993, p. 70).

In sum, regionalism is the product of various institutionalized cooperation projects in different issue areas, be it regional agreements on the economy, on security, or even on shared democratic principles (Muntschick 2015, p. 40). States and their ruling governments become interested in institutionalized cooperation if these policies provide a regional "club good" that entails mutual benefits that surpass the status quo ante. In this context, regional powers have the best chance to influence the design of regional institutions according to their national interests. For regionalism to become effective, it is not only mandatory that the participant member states comply with regional agreements, it is also necessary that institutional performance is visible and measurable.

Effects of Regionalism on Democracy Building

Having explained the conditions under which countries pursue a process of regional cooperation and how regional powers can influence the institutional design of regional cooperation projects, we have to elaborate on their relationship to democracy and democracy building. This elaboration will be done by illustrating the concept of democracy and linking the latter in a causal relationship with regional institutions.

First, there is no single definition or undisputed concept of democracy,albeit hundreds of researchers and books have dealt with this important topic. Even the EU does not provide a precise definition of democracy if one looks at the organization's official documents and statements. According to many experts, democracy does exist in a state if that state allows first for political competition (in particular, free and fair elections in regular time periods) and second for political participation (i.e., having the right to vote and to be voted on). These two conditions form the core of democracy (Dahl 1971; Moravcsik 2003).

The Charter of Paris (OSCE 1990) specifies the abovementioned assumptions and declares:

> Democratic government is based on the will of the people, regularly expressed through free and fair elections. Democracy has as its foundation respect for the human person and the rule of law. ... Democracy, with its representative and pluralist character, entails accountability to the electorate, the obligation of public authorities to comply with the law and justice administered impartially.

Against the background of this widely recognized document, it becomes clear that democracy is more than simply elections. Modern understanding of democracy and democratic rule includes aspects such as human rights and the rule of law. The latter aspects should also be taken into consideration when analyzing the case of SADC and the organization's impact on democracy building in member states at a regional level. Adequate measures to evaluate the state and conditions of democracy in a country, for instance by an index, should therefore take these aspects into account using appropriate indicators or references.

However, how does regionalism take effect in democracy building? There has to be an institutionalized regional cooperation project that deals with the policy issue of democracy as a necessary condition. A regional treaty or protocol codifies the agreed objectives and "locks in" the participant countries' cooperative intention using common principles and guidelines, which should make it possible for all signatories to attain the desired objectives. Incentives and sanctions could be part of such a regional institution to oblige all participants to stick to it. In the case that one or more countries implement the institutional provisions and follow the rules, for example on democratic governance and democracy building, there should be visible effects at the national and regional level as a consequence.

The leverage model of international rule transmission assumes that the willingness of countries to implement an agreement's principles and provision—for instance on democracy building—depends to a high degree on the interests of the ruling elite (Freyburg et al. 2011; Lavenex and Schimmelfennig 2011). Since the governing elite's priority is assumed to be always to safeguard power, stabilize its ruling position, and stay in government, the interest of a country's ruling elite in implementing democratic principles and building democracy (e.g., according to the demands of a regional institution) depends on the political system and character of the government.

According to the experiences of the eastern enlargement of the EU, countries fall into three categories on their ruling elites' receptiveness to democratization (Schimmelfennig and Sedelmeier 2004; Vachudova 2005). There is a category of countries with governments that are favorably disposed toward democratic principles and democracy building. Analysts characterize those countries as having a strong degree of the rule of law or even common elements in the political system. Second, there is a category of countries with fragile political systems or unstable democracies where the ruling elites follow illegal practices to stay in power. Such countries are likely to implement democratic principles only insofar as doing so serves the governmental power and office of the ruling elites. Symbolic implementation without actual effects is liable to be observed under such conditions.

Autocratic countries with entirely non-democratic elites belong to the last category. The elites remain in office and critical government positions by being opaque and intimidating citizens. As such, there is no interest in following a regional institution's demand to implement democratic principles or build democracy, since this policy would inevitably lead to a regime change, which implies the government's—as well as the elite's—loss of power.

About the theoretical framework and the assumptions above on the causal mechanisms between regionalism and democratization, the central hypotheses of this chapter can be deduced as follows:

- The institutional design of institutionalized regional cooperation on democracy building depends on the interest of the country in a superior relative power position on a regional level (e.g., a regional great power).
- The effects and performance of institutionalized regional cooperation on democracy building depend to the highest degree on the interests of the ruling elites and the character of the political system of the countries involved. Autocratic government and lack of the rule of law offer grounds for refusal; (semi-)democratic government and rule-based political systems offer reasons for receptiveness.

The following empirical section takes these theoretical aspects into consideration when it focuses on analyzing the SADC and the organization's institutional effect on democracy building in its member states over time.

Democracy Building in the SADC: A Critical Appraisal

To analyze SADC's efforts and progress on democracy building, the following subsections give an overview of the organization, provide insights into SADC's institutionalized cooperation project on democracy building, and evaluate the organization's performance in that respect.

An Overview of the SADC as an Organization

Founded in 1992, the SADC is the successor organization of the *Southern African Development Coordination Conference* (SADCC), which has historical roots in the *Front Line States* (FLS) alliance. Both of SADC's predecessor organizations, established by black-majority-ruled countries in 1980 and 1974, respectively, had the objective of reducing economic dependence on South Africa and coordinating, among other things, the inflow of international donors' money in their struggle against the hostile apartheid regime(s) in the region (Khadiagala 2007).

Today the SADC consists of 15 member states[5] and covers an area of about 10 million km^2 with a population of at least 300 million inhabitants. Most of its member countries—except Botswana, Mauritius, the Seychelles, and South Africa—are classified as least or less developed. The *Republic of South Africa* (RSA), a SADC member country since 1994, is the only industrialized nation and counts as a regional hegemon because of its superior economic power and military strength (Odén 2000; Alden and Soko 2005). In 2001, an institutional overhaul transformed the fairly inefficient and decentralized character of the organization gradually toward more centralization. As a consequence, the former Sector Coordination Units were bundled into four directorates[6] and located at the SADC headquarters in Gaborone (Oosthuizen 2006). The SADC Secretariat, however, did not gain noteworthy additional executive competence during the reform process, and the SADC therefore remained a relatively intergovernmental organization. The only true supranational body, the SADC Tribunal, was substantially deprived of power at the demand of a majority of SADC state leaders in 2012.[7]

Since the mid-1990s, the organization has put a focus on economic integration. Not only is this a cornerstone of regionalism in the SADC, market integration also constitutes a major developmental strategy toward growth and socioeconomic prosperity (Oosthuizen 2006; Vogt 2007). The *Regional Indicative Strategic Development Plan* (RISDP) provides several guidelines on regional economic integration, which led to the successful establishment of the SADC Free Trade Area in 2008 (SADC 2004, 2008). The scheduled formation of the SADC Customs Union by 2010 has not been accomplished, however, due to external interference from the EU (Muntschick 2013).

Regional security cooperation in the SADC region is a significant issue of concern and experienced a major stimulus after South Africa joined the organization. In 1996, the SADC established its *Organ for Politics, Defence and Security* (OPDS) as a specific institution dealing with regional security cooperation and conflict management. After the OPDS's institutional reform in 2001, the SADC countries approved the *Strategic Indicative Plan for the Organ* (SIPO) in 2004, whose guidelines initialized the formation of a common SADC Standby Force in 2007. While the latter has been declared operational and is said to include about 4000 soldiers, there are doubts over whether the SADC Standby Force can be deployed, since its general logistics depot has not been built yet (van Nieuwkerk 2007; Nathan 2012).

Other important policy areas where institutionalized regional cooperation under the SADC umbrella takes place include infrastructure (e.g., electricity, water courses, and traffic routes), natural resources (e.g., forests, fishery, and minerals), culture, health, and legal affairs. More than 20 SADC protocols, charters, and memoranda of understanding give proof not only of the organization's cooperation efforts, but also of the member states' commitment to regionalism (Oosthuizen 2006, pp. 122–134).[8] While not all cooperation initiatives and agreements have been entirely implemented and proven successful so far (SADC 2012), these institutional dynamics nevertheless offer examples of the SADC being one of the most vibrant and dynamic regional integration schemes in Africa.

Demand for Democracy Building in the SADC Region

Philosophers and political scientists have argued since the time of Immanuel Kant (1724–1804) and the publication of his famous essay on "Perpetual Peace" that democracies do not principally wage war against each other (Kant 1917). According to Babst (1964), "no wars have been fought between independent nations with elective governments" during the period 1789–1941 (Babst 1964, p. 10). More than three decades later, Ray (1998) corroborates this observation and declares that the "empirical evidence for the proposition that democratic states have not initiated and are not likely to initiate interstate wars against each other is substantial" (Ray 1998, p. 43). According to this so-called democratic peace theory, any international or regional community made up of democratic states will enjoy eternal peace, stability, and prosperity as mutual distrust and threat cease to exist (Morgan 2013, p. 35). One can assume that this idea and related aspirations fuel a general demand for democratic rule in virtually every society and state that has the freedom to decide according to its own interests and destiny.

The SADC region and its countries faced some challenges to national security and political stability during the early and mid-1990s. These included among other things the risk of war and conflict among members, poor governance, the lack of democracy, and in some cases the troubled consolidation of democracy, as well as illegitimate elections and a lack of socioeconomic development (Matlosa 2004, pp. 9–10; Oosthuizen 2006 p. 284). Against the background of the uncertain regional situation, it is clear that there existed a regional cooperation problem on an SADC level throughout that time. Every single SADC country could reap the full benefits of improved political stability and security if all of the organization's member states became stable democracies and thus contributed to a process that would recall Kant's presumed state of perpetual peace (Khadiagala and Nganje 2015, p. 2). A common SADC institution such as an agreement or protocol could thus help to create a regional "club good" (i.e., a region of democracy and peace) which would facilitate Pareto-superior outcomes for all countries involved, unlike an uncoordinated status quo.

Besides the aforementioned structural demand factors from within the SADC region, it was external actors such as the *United Nations* (UN)and the *African Union* (AU) that fueled demand for institutionalized regional cooperation and democracy building in the SADC region. The UN handbook on human rights and elections of 1994, for example, aimed to promote democracy and human rights worldwide and set among other things some standards on free and fair elections. The AU Declaration on the Principles Governing Democratic Elections in Africa (adopted in 2002) bound the SADC member states to the principles of democratic, regular, free, and fair elections to consolidate the continent's nascent democratic governance and improve political stability (Matlosa 2004, pp. 11–12). The SADC countries embraced these international and continental provisions and incorporated the core principles into their organization's RISDP and SIPO agendas by 2004 (Matlosa 2005, pp. 3–5).

Based on those arguments, one should assume that there existed a structural demand—at least pro forma—to institutionalize common provisions on democracy building in every single SADC country, as long as this did not imply costs and risks for democracy-adverse national elites and governments. Implementation of and compliance with such regional institutions, of course, are a different matter.

Regional Cooperation and Institutionalization: The SADC Principles and Guidelines Governing Democratic Elections

The SADC member states' overall demand for democracy in the region, including idealistic motives, security reasons, or simply the economic benefits thereof, fueled the need to come to a regional agreement on the issue, and for a regional institution to "lock in" the joint position and provisions. With the SADC Parliamentary Forum and the SADC Electoral Commissions Forum[9] having worked on the development of common standards for elections in 2001 and 2003, the SADC countries formulated the SADC Principles and Guidelines Governing Democratic Elections with input from both bodies (Matlosa 2005, p. 5).

Before focusing on the contents of the SADC Principles and Guidelines Governing Democratic Elections, it is important to state that the character of interstate negotiations on this joint regional agreement remains, unfortunately, somewhat obscure. There is little information about which actors or countries had a significant influence on drafting the document's provisions, since everything was developed secretly, and without involvement of the supranational SADC Secretariat (Oosthuizen 2006, p. 303). There is strong evidence, however, that South Africa as regional hegemon took a leading role in strengthening democratic values and promoting democracy at SADC level in this respect. The post-apartheid administrations of Presidents Mandela and Mbeki regarded democracy and good governance in the SADC region as necessary conditions for political stability and economic prosperity in the whole of southern Africa, which was not least to the benefit of the national interests of a democratic South Africa itself (Khadiagala and Nganje 2015, pp. 3–10).

With the member states having agreed to pursue a path of cooperation toward strengthening democracy and good governance, including a common framework, the SADC Summit proceeded to codify and institutionalize the project and adopted the SADC Principles and Guidelines Governing Democratic Elections (in short, SADC election guidelines) by consensus in August 2004.[10]

The major objectives include, among others, to "promote and enhance adherence to the principle of the rule of law," to "promote the holding of regular free and fair, transparent, credible and peaceful elections," to "enhance electoral integrity by providing a basis for comprehensive, accurate and impartial observation of national elections" and to "promote electoral justice and best practices in the management of elections."[11]

Interestingly enough, part of the SADC election guidelines has been copied from the AU's guidelines without further modification (Oosthuizen 2006, p. 304). More important, however, is the fact that the SADC's regional cooperation project on democracy building deals to a greater degree with election observation than with implementing democratic rules or—at the least—election management (Matlosa 2004, p. 17).

Altogether, the SADC election guidelines are certainly an expression of the organization's member states' structural demand for regional peace and stability, which they aimed to achieve among other things by facilitating fair and democratic elections at a national level, according to regional standards and under regional surveillance. South Africa, the regional hegemon, was the driving force behind the process of institutionalization and exerted much influence on the guidelines' institutional design. The fact that Pretoria played a key role in forming the agreement confirms the first hypothesis of the theoretical parts of this work. Apart from this, the SADC election guidelines are not legally binding, as they do not constitute a formal treaty. However, the guidelines demand a commitment from the signatory states, insofar as they are the result of the SADC countries' public and official declaration to adhere to these provisions. Thus, citizens can hold the member countries and their governments accountable, especially since the guidelines are "made in SADC" and not imposed by a former colonial power or the like (Matlosa 2004, pp. 18–20).

To evaluate the performance and institutional effectiveness of regional cooperation within the framework of the SADC election guidelines on democracy building, the next section proposes a before-and-after analysis on the basis of several indicators to illustrate the relationship between regionalism and democratization, at least by correlation analysis.

Impact of the SADC Guidelines on Democracy Building on the Region and Its Member States

In parallel to the latest wave of new regionalism, a "third wave" of democratization took place on the African continent after the end of the Cold War and found expression in the transition of many former military regimes or one-party states into multi-party democracies—at least according to their constitutions. During the first few years, this democratization process was strongly welcomed and fueled a great optimism about the future of political and socioeconomic development in Africa. After 20 years, however, some disillusion has come about, since the process of democratization has neither been unidirectional nor led to flourishing and stable democracies all over the continent. Instead, several African countries have struggled with democratic rule and experienced democratic rollbacks or hybrid regimes with authoritarian leaders (Lynch and Crawford 2011, pp. 1–2). It was only with the independence of Namibia in 1990 and the end of minority rule and apartheid in South Africa in 1994 that one could speak of fundamental freedom in the region. During the years before the SADC election guidelines became subject to interstate negotiations and were finally institutionalized, the situation in the SADC and its member states was, according to Breytenbach (2002), as shown in Fig. 3.1.

In 2000 only Mauritius, South Africa, and Botswana had consolidated democracies with free and periodic elections, including satisfying political rights and civil liberties. Those countries enjoyed the best level of socioeconomic development at that time. A large number of SADC countries

Development Index (per capita and HDI)				
	High	N/A	N/A	N/A
	High medium		Seychelles	Mauritius South Africa Botswana
	Low medium	Swaziland	Namibia Lesotho	
	Low	DR Congo	Zimbabwe Zambia Angola & Tanzania Mozambique & Malawi	
		Autocracy	**Electoral 'Grey' Zone** **Democracy/Authoritarianism**	**Consolidation**
	Institutional and Freedom Index **(regular elections, political rights, civil liberties)**			

Fig. 3.1 Institutional and Development Index for SADC countries (2000)
Note: *HDI* Human Development Index

classified as electoral "gray" zones, however, were in a state of transition, with either embryonic or relatively stable democracies that were only partly free (regarding political rights and civil liberties) or lacked regular elections (Mentan 2009, p. 5). These SADC countries were likewise only in the middle range on socioeconomic development—a correlation that gives reasons to speculate whether there existed a causal relationship between the state of democracy and the level of development and welfare. Swaziland and the Democratic Republic of (DR) Congo, both least developed countries, counted as autocracies or blocked transitions at the turn of the millennium (Breytenbach 2002; Matlosa 2004). That is not surprising, because Swaziland was an absolute monarchy while DR Congo, sunk into civil war at that time, was ruled by a despotic president and warlords.

There is no doubt that there is a broad range of indicators and possible interpretations of how to classify countries according to their state of democracy, political freedom, and development. For this reason, Fig. 3.1 should serve as an illustration of the state of affairs and not as matters of fact set in stone. However, this particular categorization has been chosen because it reflects similar classifications and conclusions in the academic literature on the issue in a nutshell (Breytenbach 2007; Lynch and Crawford 2011).

With the adoption of the SADC election guidelines in 2004, one could expect a positive change regarding democracy building in the organization's member countries using institutionalized regional cooperation. Regional and national commitment to the SADC election guidelines should not only be reflected in the states' adherence to its provisions, but also in observable or measurable effects.

The Combined Index on Democracy (KID) serves the latter purpose perfectly, as it is a recognized indicator for evaluating the quality of democracy. The index is threefold and combines data series of the Freedom House Index (with a focus on political rights and civil liberties) with polity and governance indicators from the World Bank (Lauth 2015). A high index value (10) indicates a consolidated democracy with good governance, the rule of law, and exemplary political rights and civil liberties. A low index value (0), in contrast, indicates the opposite: autocratic rule, corruption, weak state institutions, and restrictive measures that nullify political rights and civil liberties.

Figure 3.2 gives an impression of how the state of democracy has changed in the SADC countries over time since the guidelines for elections officially came into effect in 2004.

Generally speaking, the index values do not depict significant positive changes regarding democracy building in most SADC countries. According to the graph, there are only two positive trends toward democratization in the whole region: the cases of DR Congo (from 2004 until 2014) and Zimbabwe (from 2008 until 2014). Virtually all other countries seem to stick to the status quo during the period observed, except Madagascar. In the latter case, the index on democracy depicts a deteriorating situation, as the index value dropped from 5.5 to 2.6 between 2008 and 2010 (only to recover to 4.8 by 2014). Altogether, according to this index, the SADC election guidelines seem to have had no considerable effect on improving democracy in

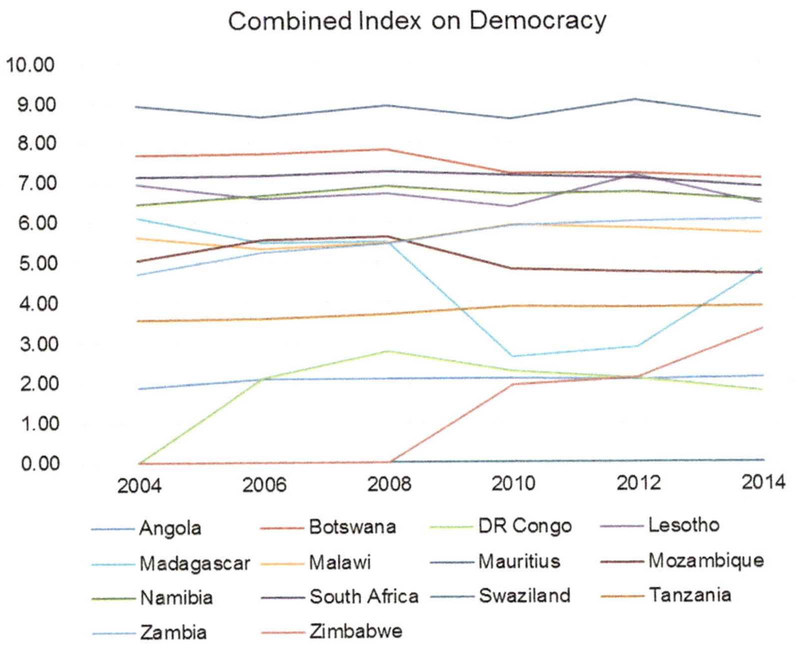

Fig. 3.2 Combined Index on Democracy for SADC countries (2004–2014)

the organization's member states, besides possibly DR Congo and Zimbabwe.

To cross-check and perhaps corroborate the information illustrated, consider the values of the Bertelsmann Transformation Index (BTI), which has a focus on 'Political Transformation' (Fig. 3.3).

Quite similar to the KID, the BTI values do not depict significant positive changes in most of the SADC countries under observation since the time the SADC adopted the guidelines. Four countries, however, do show an improvement toward democratic transition since 2003. Angola's path toward democratic transition has slowly gained momentum (the BTI value increased from 3.4 to 4.5). It was the same in DR Congo (the BTI value rose from 2.2 to 3.5) as well as in Zimbabwe (the BTI value increased from 3.4 to 4.4). The situation in Malawi improved at a higher level (the BTI value rose from 5.2 to 6.7). Virtually all other SADC members, however, remain more or less at status quo, with only oscillating index values. Madagascar, again, is an obvious exception, because its BTI value deteriorated from 6.4 in 2003 to only 4.4 in 2014. Summing up the evidence according to the BTI, the SADC election guidelines did not have a significant positive effect on improving democracy in the

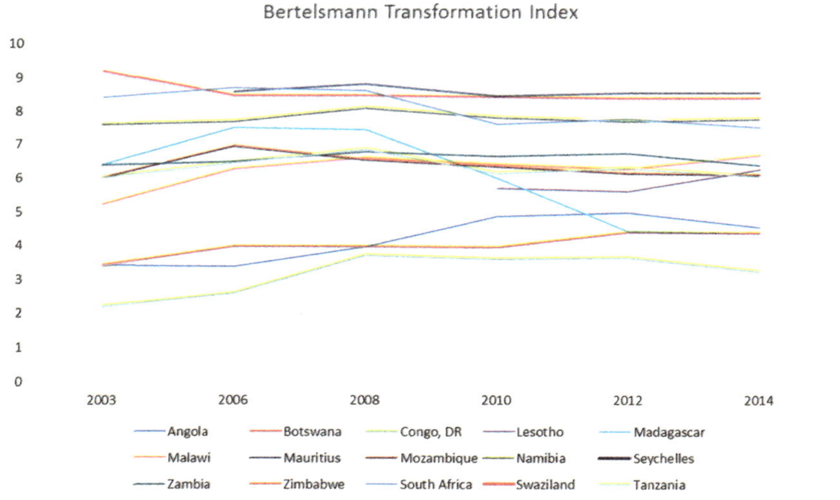

Fig. 3.3 Bertelsmann Transformation Index for SADC countries (2003–2014)

SADC countries under observation, besides possibly Angola, DR Congo, Zimbabwe, and Malawi.

There is no doubt that data from both of these indicators is to some degree selective and provides only a sketchy illustration of what SADC institutions contribute to democratization in the region and its countries. The SADC has undertaken several election observation missions in some member states, which have certainly had a positive impact as well. A detailed analysis of these missions, however, would go beyond the scope of this chapter.

Conclusion

The task of this chapter was to elaborate on whether regionalism has contributed to democracy building in the SADC region and the democratization of the organization's member states. It became apparent, at least from a theoretical perspective, that virtually all SADC countries should have had a preference for institutionalized regional cooperation to gain comprehensive socioeconomic benefits from a collective good such as a regional sphere of democracy. Therefore, it was a rational decision for all SADC countries to negotiate and adopt the SADC Principles and Guidelines Governing Democratic Elections in 2004, at least pro forma. The UN and the AU as external actors provided incentives—and a blueprint—for this endeavor. With democratic South Africa, the regional hegemon, being most interested in the SADC election guidelines, it did not come as a surprise that Pretoria had the most influence on the institutional design and provisions of those guidelines.

With the SADC election guidelines in place, it was a key task to find out whether the latter performed well and had any institutional effects in terms of contributing to democracy building in the SADC area and its member states. To show a positive correlation between regionalism and democratization, the chapter consulted data series and well-recognized indicators that measure democracy and democratic transition. The empirical evidence, however, was relatively disappointing. In sum, neither the KID nor the BTI provides sound evidence that the adoption of the SADC election guidelines had any significant positive impact on democracy building in the SADC region and its member states. Only 4 out of 15 countries appeared to show a slight improvement—from a relatively low level—on the path toward democratization and good governance from 2004 to the present: Angola, DR Congo, Zimbabwe, and

Malawi. One country, Madagascar, even experienced a democratic rollback during the period under observation.

The empirical observation based on the values of KID and BTI confirms the central assumptions of the leverage model and the second hypothesis of this work. It is quite evident that those countries that were either autocracies or fragile states with unstable electoral democracies before 2004 were relatively reluctant to implement and comply with the SADC election guidelines, to such a degree that noticeable positive effects occurred. It is therefore not surprising that improvements in democratization only took place at a very low level in Angola, DR Congo, Zimbabwe, and Malawi, and that the unsatisfactory status quo prevailed in countries that were part of the so-called electoral "gray" zone. Mauritius, Botswana, and South Africa, as consolidated democracies before 2004, were not only in favor of SADC's election guidelines, but of course retained their status as democratic countries after the adoption of the document.

In a nutshell, it has become clear that regional cooperation in the SADC region was successful insofar as the member states institutionalized an agreement adopting the SADC Principles and Guidelines Governing Democratic Elections and demonstrating in public their intention to adhere to its objectives and provisions. Regarding the organization's institutional performance and effectiveness, however, the SADC election guidelines have turned out to be dissatisfactory and a failure so far.

Topics for Discussion

1. How do we understand the concept of regionalism from a rational institutionalist point of view?
2. What are the possible effects of regionalism on democracy building in general?
3. What kind of regional organization is the SADC and what are its central goals?
4. If all SADC countries successfully implemented the principles of democracy indicated in the SADC document, would there be peace and security in that region?
5. What best practices can other parts of Africa and other emerging economies pick from the SADC?

6 Discuss whether institutionalized cooperation and regionalism are useful instruments to maintain and promote democratic rule in the countries involved in the SADC.
7 Discuss whether the SADC guidelines on democracy building have had an impact on democratization in the region and its member states.
8 What challenges can they learn from?

Notes

1. Well-known examples—to name just a few—include the Association of Southeast Asian Nations (ASEAN) in Asia, the North American Free Trade Agreement (NAFTA) in Northern America, the Caribbean Community and Common Market (CARICOM) in the Caribbean, the Common Market of the South (Mercosur) in South America, as well as the Economic Community of West African States (ECOWAS) and the Southern African Development Community (SADC) in Western and Southern Africa, respectively.
2. The South shall be understood in the sense of a "meta-region" that encompasses regions of predominantly non-industrialized, developing countries in the southern hemisphere (Söderbaum and Stålgren 2010, p. 2).
3. According to leading scholars, new regionalism can be understood as a "comprehensive, multifaceted and multidimensional process, implying the change of a particular region from relative heterogeneity to homogeneity with regard to a number of dimensions, the most important being culture, security, economic policies and political regimes" (Hettne and Söderbaum, 1998, p. 6).
4. Retrieved from: http://www.sadc.int/about-sadc/overview/sadc-common-agenda/ (11/10/2015).
5. Angola, Botswana, the Democratic Republic of the Congo (DR Congo), Lesotho, Madagascar, Malawi, Mauritius, Mozambique, Namibia, the Seychelles, South Africa, Swaziland, Tanzania, Zambia, and Zimbabwe.
6. Namely, Trade, Industry, Finance and Investment (TIFI), Infrastructure and Service (IS), Food, Agriculture and Natural Resources (FANR), and Social and Human Development and Special Programmes (SHDSP) directorates (Oosthuizen 2006, pp. 200–204).
7. Retrieved from: http://www.bdlive.co.za/world/africa/2013/01/28/sadc-tribunal-paid-the-price-for-threatening-states-authority (12/06/2016).
8. Retrieved from: http://www.sadc.int/documents-publications/ (12/11/2015).

9. In collaboration with the Electoral Institute of Southern Africa (EISA).
10. SADC (2004): Record of the Summit held in Grand Baie, Republic of Mauritius, 1–17 August 2004. Paragraph 5.4 (SADC 2004).
11. SADC (2004): SADC Principles and Guidelines Governing Democratic Elections. Retrieved from: https://eisa.org.za/pdf/sadc2015principles.pdf (SADC 2004).

Works Cited

Adelmann, Martin. 2012. *SADC—an Actor in International Relations? The External Relations of the Southern African Development Community*. Arnold-Bergstraesser-Institut: Freiburg.

Alden, Chris, and Mills Soko. 2005. South Africa's Economic Relations with Africa: Hegemony and its Discontents. *Journal of Modern African Studies* 43 (3): 367–392.

Andrew, W.Axline. 1977. Underdevelopment, Dependence and Integration: The Politics of Regionalism in the Third World. *International Organization* 31 (1): 83–105.

Axelrod, Robert. 1987. *Die Evolution der Kooperation*. München: R. Oldenbourg.

Babst, Dean V. 1964. Elective Governments—a Force for Peace. *The Wisconsin Sociologist* 3 (1): 9–14.

Bach, Daniel. 2003. New Regionalism as an Alias: Regionalisation through Trans-State Networks. In *New Regionalism in Africa*, eds. Andrew J. Grant and Fredrik Söderbaum, 21–30. Aldershot: Ashgate.

Breytenbach, Willie. 2002. Democracy in the SADC Region: A Comparative Overview. *African Security Review* 11 (4): 87–102.

Breytenbach, Willie. 2007. Democracy and development in the southern and eastern African regions. In *Monitoring Regional Integration in Southern Africa Yearbook*, ed. Anton Bösl, Willie Breytenbach, Trudi Hartzenberg, Colin McCarthy, and Klaus Schade, 94–117. Stellenbosch: Trade Law Centre for Southern Africa.

Brinkmann, Manfred. 2000. *Regionale Integration im Süden: Der MERCOSUR in Südamerika und die SADC im südlichen Afrika*. DBG Bildungswerk: Duisburg.

Cameron, David R. 2007. Post-communist Democracy: The Impact of the European Union. *Post-Soviet Affairs* 23 (3): 185–217.

Dahl, Robert A. 1971. *Polyarchy. Participation and Opposition*. New Haven, CT: Yale University Press.

Doyle, Michael. 1983. Kant, Liberal Legacies, and Foreign Affairs. *Philosophy & Public Affairs* 12 (3): 205–235.

Freyburg, Tina, Sandra Lavenex, Frank Schimmelfennig, Tatiana Skripka, and Anne Wetzel. 2011. Democracy Promotion Through Functional Cooperation?

The Case of the European Neighbourhood Policy. *Democratization* 18 (4): 1026–1054.

Gehring, Thomas. 1994. Der Beitrag von Institutionen zur Förderung der internationalen Zusammenarbeit: Lehren aus der institutionellen Struktur der Europäischen Gemeinschaft. *Zeitschrift für Internationale Beziehungen* 1 (2): 211–242.

Hartmann, Christof. 2008. Regional organizations and the promotion of democracy in Sub-Saharan Africa. In *Governance and Legitimacy in a globalized world*, eds. Rüdiger Schmitt-Beck, Tobias Debiel, and Karl-Rudolf Korte, 207–227. Baden-Baden: Nomos.

Hettne, Björn. 2005. Beyond the 'New' Regionalism. *New Political Economy* 10 (4): 543–571.

Hettne, Björn, and Fredrik Söderbaum. 1998. The New Regionalism Approach. *Politeia: Journal of Political Science and Public Administration* 17 (3): 5–19.

Hoffmann, Andrea R., and Anna van der Vleuten. 2007. Legitimacy and democracy in regional integration organizations: Closing or widening the gap? In *Closing or Widening the Gap? Legitimacy and Democracy in Regional International Organizations*, ed. Andrea R. Hoffmann, and Anna van der Vleuten, 193–202. Aldershot: Ashgate.

Hout, Wil, and Frits Meijerink. 1996. Structures in the International Political Economy: World System Theory and Unequal Development. *European Journal of International Relations* 2 (47): 47–76.

Hurrell, Andrew. 1995a. Explaining the Resurgence of Regionalism in World Politics. *Review of International Studies* 21 (4): 331–358.

Hurrell, Andrew. 1995b. Regionalism in Theoretical Perspective. In *Regionalism in World Politics: Regional Organization and International Order*, ed. Louise Fawcett, and Andrew Hurrell, 37–73. Oxford: Oxford University Press.

Keohane, Robert O. 1982. The Demand For International Regimes. *International Organization* 36 (2): 325–355.

Keohane, Robert O. 1984. *After Hegemony, Cooperation and Discord in the World Political Economy*. Princeton, NJ: Princeton University Press.

Keohane, Robert O. 1988. International Institutions: Two Approaches. *International Studies Quarterly* 32 (4): 379–396.

Keohane, Robert O., and Joseph S. Nye. 1977. *Power and Interdependence. World Politics*. Boston, MA: Little, Brown, and Company.

Khadiagala, Gilbert M. 2007. *Allies in Adversity: The Frontline States in Southern African Security, 1975–1993*. Lanham, MD: University Press of America.

Khadiagala, Gilbert M., and Nganje, F. 2015. The evolution of South Africa's democracy promotion in Africa: From idealism to pragmatism. *Cambridge Journal of International Affairs* (published online): 1–21.

Lauth, H.-J. 2015. Datensatz Kombinierter Index der Demokratie (KID), 1996–2014. Würzburg: Institut für Politikwissenschaft und Soziologie.

Retrieved from: http://www.politikwissenschaft.uni-wuerzburg.de/lehrbereiche/vergleichende/forschung_kombinierter_index_der_demokratie_kid/ (12/11/2015).

Lavenex, Sandra, and Frank Schimmelfennig. 2011. EU Democracy Promotion in the Neighborhood: From Leverage to Governance? *Democratization* 18 (4): 885–909.

Levitz, Philip. 2010. Why no Backsliding? The European Union's Impact on Democracy and Governance Before and after Accession. *Comparative Political Studies* 43 (4): 457–485.

Lynch, Gabrielle, and Gordon Crawford. 2011. Democratization in Africa 1990–2010: An Assessment. *Democratization* 18 (2): 275–310.

Mair, Stefan, and Christian Peters-Berries. 2001. *Regionale Integration und Kooperation in Afrika südlich der Sahara: EAC, ECOWAS und SADC im Vergleich*. Bonn: Weltforum Verlag.

Matlosa, Khabele. 2005. Democratization at the Crossroads. Challenges for the SADC Principles and Guidelines Governing Democratic Elections. *ISS Paper* 118. Retrieved from https://www.issafrica.org/uploads/Paper118.pdf.

Matlosa, Khabele. 2004. Managing Democracy: A review of SADC principles and guidelines governing democratic elections. Paper presented at the EISA Democracy Seminar Series, Johannesburg, South Africa, Oct 2004. Retrieved from https://eisa.org.za/pdf/DSS_matlosa2004.pdf.

Mentan, Tatha. 2009. *Democratizing or reconfiguring predatory autocracy? Myths and realities in Africa today*. Bamenda: Langaa Research and Publishing Common Initiative Group.

Moravcsik, Andrew. 1998. *The Choice for Europe: Social Purpose and State Power from Messina to Maastricht*. Ithaca, NY: Cornell University Press.

Moravcsik, Andrew. 2003. In defense of the 'Democratic Deficit': Reassessing Legitimacy in the European Union. *Journal of Common Market Studies* 40 (4): 603–624.

Morgan, Patrick. 2013. Liberalism. In *Contemporary Security Studies*, ed. Adam Collins, 28–41. Oxford: Oxford University Press.

Müller, Harald. 1993. *Die Chance der Kooperation: Regime in den Internationalen Beziehungen*. Darmstadt: Wissenschaftliche Buchgesellschaft.

Muntschick, Johannes. 2013. Explaining the influence of extra-regional actors on regional economic integration in Southern Africa: The EU's interfering impact on SADC and SACU. In *Mapping Agency: Comparing Regionalisms in Africa*, eds. Ulrike Lorenz-Carl, and Martin Rempe, 77–95. Farnham: Ashgate.

Muntschick, Johannes. 2015. *Regionalism and external influence: The Southern African Development Community (SADC) and the ambivalent impact of the EU on regional integration*, PhD Thesis, Otto-Friedrich-Universität Bamberg, Bamberg.

Nathan, Laurie. 2012. *The Community of Insecurity: SADC's Struggle for Peace and Security in Southern Africa*. Farnham: Ashgate.

Odén, Bertil. 2000. The Southern Africa region and the regional hegemon. In *National Perspectives on the New Regionalism in the South*, eds. Björn Hettne, András Inotai, and Osvaldo Sunkel, 242–264. London: Macmillan.

Oosthuizen, Gabriël H. 2006. *The Southern African Development Community: The Organization, its Policies, and Prospects*. Midrand: Institute for Global Dialogue.

Organization for Security and Co-Operation in Europe (OSCE) (1990): Charta of Paris for a New Europe. Retrieved from: http://www.osce.org/mc/39516?download=true (12/11/2015).

Ray, James L. 1998. Does Democracy Cause Peace? *Annual Review of Political Science* 1 (27): 27–46.

Rittberger, Volker, and Michael Zürn. 1990. Towards regulated anarchy in East-West relations: Causes and consequences of East-West regimes. In *International Regimes in East-West Relations*, ed. Volker Rittberger, 9–63. London: Pinter Publishers.

SADC. 2004. *Regional Indicative Strategic Development Plan*. Gaborone: SADC Secretariat.

SADC. 2008. *SADC Free Trade Area: Growth, Development and Wealth Creation*. Gaborone: SADC Secretariat.

SADC. 2012. *Desk Assessment of the Regional Indicative Strategic Development Plan 2005–2010*. Gaborone: SADC Secretariat.

Schimmelfennig, Frank, and Ulrich Sedelmeier. 2004. Governance by Conditionality: EU Rule Transfer to the Candidate Countries of Central and Eastern Europe. *Journal of European Public Policy* 11 (4): 661–679.

Söderbaum, Fredrik, and Patrik Stålgren. 2010. The EU and the Global South. In *The European Union and the Global South*, ed. Fredrik Söderbaum, and Patrik Stålgren, 1–11. Lynne Rienner: Boulder, CO.

Stahl, Bernhard. 2010. Die Gemeinschaft südostasiatischer Staaten (ASEAN): Erfolg und Probleme einer überforderten Institution. In *Multilaterale Institutionen in Ostasien-Pazifik: Genese—Strukturen—Substanz—Perspektive*, ed. Dirk Nabers, 17–53. Wiesbaden: VS Verlag für Sozialwissenschaften.

Stein, Arthur A. 1982. Coordination and Collaboration: Regimes in an Anarchic World. *International Organization* 36 (2): 300–324.

Vachudova, Milada A. 2005. *Europe Undivided: Democracy, Leverage, and Integration After Communism*. Oxford: Oxford University Press.

van der Vleuten, Anna, and Andrea R. Hoffmann. 2010. Explaining the Enforcement of Democracy by Regional Organizations: Comparing EU, Mercosur and SADC. *Journal of Common Market Studies* 48 (3): 737–758.

van Nieuwkerk, Anthoni. 2007. Organizational dimensions of security cooperation in the Southern African Development Community. In *Proceedings of the 2006 FOPRISA Annual Conference*, ed. Jonathan M. Kaunda, 99–127. Gaborone: Botswana Institute for Development Policy Analysis.

Vogt, Jörgen. 2007. *Die regionale Integration des südlichen Afrikas: Unter besonderer Betrachtung der Southern African Development Community (SADC)*. Baden-Baden: Nomos.

Weiland, Heribert. 2006. The European Union and Southern Africa: Interregionalism between vision and reality. In *Interregionalism and International Relations*, ed. Heiner Hänggi, Ralf Roloff, and Jürgen Rüland, 185–198. London: Routledge.

Zangl, Bernd. 1994. Politik auf zwei Ebenen: Hypothesen zur Bildung internationaler Regime. *Zeitschrift für Internationale Beziehungen* 1 (2): 279–312.

Zürn, Michael. 1993. Problematic social situations and international institutions: On the use of game theory in international politics. In *International Relations and Pan-Europe: Theoretical Approaches And Empirical Findings*, ed. Frank Pfetsch, 63–84. Lit: Münster.

Suggestions for Further Reading

Kant, Immanuel. 1917. *Perpetual Peace: A Philosophical Essay*, translated with Introduction and Notes by M. Campbell Smith, with a Preface by Professor L. Latta. London: George Allen and Unwin.

CHAPTER 4

The Role of Cyber Activism in Disambiguating the Cosmopolis and Discourse of Democratization

Jean-Claude Kwitonda

Public diplomacy, democracy, and democratization have become like an international law that tends to command a higher normative order than national legislation (Guilhot 2005). Even the idea of national sovereignty has become very fragile, as the promise of democratic principles is increasingly the national and international jurisdiction. In emerging and dependent economies, *democracy* and *human rights* are used almost interchangeably as hallmarks for international order, a requirement for deserving international development aid and securing regime legitimacy locally and internationally (Frank 1992; Guilhot 2005; Uvin 1999). Economic development, human rights, and democratic practices cannot exist independently of each other.

Jean-Claude Kwitonda's research interests include global neoliberalism, especially its various meanings. In this chapter he proposes cyber communications as alternative tools for a new form of global civil society and citizens' media.

J.-C. Kwitonda (✉)
Ohio University, Athens, Ohio, USA

E.K. Ngwainmbi (ed.), *Citizenship, Democracies, and Media Engagement among Emerging Economies and Marginalized Communities*,
DOI 10.1007/978-3-319-56215-5_4

Although countries in emerging economies have been holding regular elections, most countries have witnessed little or no significant improvement in human rights violations, personal lives, economic growth, or social or infrastructure development. Violence and political upheavals continue to take human lives and many people are led to undertake dangerous journeys to seek sanctuary in Western countries. Sometimes popular violent uprisings are backed by core nations against dictatorial regimes (e.g., the Arab Spring). Some commentators view international military interventions conducted or supported by core nations as a solution that will restore civic virtues in peripheral nations; others continue to see potential in acts of international public diplomacy and the spread of civic virtues (e.g., democracy) through the power and proliferation of electronic communication products. Thomas McPhail is one of the scholars who advocate the latter alternative and its promise of capturing the minds and hearts of people around the world through electronic communication. He argues that "spreading democracy around the world at the end of a gun simply will not work" (2010, p. 365). Further, McPhail asserts that "declaring people enemy combatants and putting them in jails like Abu Ghraib or Guantanamo not only does not work but increases recruitment of more radical enemies of the US and other core nations" (p. 365). Thus according to McPhail (2010), public diplomacy and electronic communication can benefit not only peripheral nations but also core nations.

This chapter is about the global relevance and role of cyber communications and world public diplomacy in the collective process of promoting and protecting democratic practices. As democracy per se is not a bad value, the purpose of this chapter is not to disparage the cosmopolitanism of democracy and related practices. Rather, the chapter seeks to build on McPhail's Electronic Colonization Theory to move forward theorizing about discourses, practices, and processes of the cosmopolitics of democratization.

This chapter begins by explicating the theoretical background and drawing on the historical context of global democratization and its discursive support. The theoretical and historical context section will also reveal the ambiguous techniques and discursive mutations of the democratization project. The second section will discuss current instances of global public diplomacy. The remaining sections will focus on the relevance of cyber communications vis-à-vis the historical background of the cosmopolitics of democratization, and reflect on cyber applications in engaging discursive practices of democratization and as tools of protest and citizens' journalism. The chapter will end with a conclusion reflecting on the potential of cyber communications and cyber activism in promoting civic initiatives.

Context

This chapter takes stock of the Electronic Colonization Theory (ECT) advanced by McPhail (2010), due to its potential to account for the effects of electronic communication and public diplomacy in the promotion of successful images and as an enabling tool for a global civil society. However, a discourse-centered framework will complement the premises of ECT, because such a framework possesses a unique ability to attend to the ambiguous and discursive mutations of global public diplomacy. McPhail (2010) calls this democracy. This section starts by reviewing the merits of ECT, before presenting its relationship to a discourse-centered framework in the context of cyber activism and cyber communications.

Electronic Colonization Theory

McPhail (2010) acknowledges that his ECT may strike people as a reincarnation of modernization theories (i.e., McPhail's paradox). However, he also points to the practical and realistic side of this framework, understood in the context of accounting for the promotion of popular attitudes and values—by spreading messages and mechanisms of choice (McPhail 2010). He explains that this process unfolds in an indirect manner through electronic media exposure and its creation of a *mental empire* as well as messages of public diplomacy:

> What appears to work is spreading mass media to other nations through a broad range of public diplomacy initiatives. The more foreign nations consume of modern communication, the more they will want to become like us. That is why some foreign nations and some religions ban or shun western media. They know it contains values and shows people enjoying freedoms. The internet is China's, Iran's and other authoritarian regimes' worst nightmare. (2010, p. 265)

In this unique context, ECT argues that Western media and their global appeal can displace national cultures that are undemocratic. McPhail (2010) also acknowledges that people who prefer globalization from below—or what he describes as *the imperialist and cultural purist camps*—may not like the premises of ECT. However, while cultural imperialism is not desirable, authoritarianism, wherever it happens, is not desirable either. Although authenticity and bottom-up approaches have supplanted the promises of the modernization paradigm, internal contradictions within the local (e.g., oppressive national governments) alienate citizens, prompting them to idolize Western norms.

Advocates of bottom-up approaches often assume that the authenticity of national cultures in non-Western settings can inherently guarantee fairness (good governance, and equal rights based on gender, ethnicity, class, or religion). However, history indicates that non-Western societies have followed almost the same trajectory spanning monarchical power to the colonial and ultimately postcolonial dictatorships, leaving people in those societies with some sociopolitical legacies that are not progressive.

The promotion of authentic, home-grown information systems invokes what McPhail (2010) calls development journalism/communication. Although the latter paradigm has the potential to counterbalance the imperial thrust of electronic colonialism and promote local agendas, development communication media are often propaganda vehicles for totalitarian and military regimes (McPhail 2010). Once again, the sociopolitical hardships unleashed by such unprogressive regimes may partly explain how and why the Western style of life appeals to people exposed to Western media products that are readily available thanks to electronic communication. It is mainly due to this that McPhail (2010) reminds us that people who live in repressive societies "over time and with increasing consumption of media fare … want to become like us. They want our clothes, lifestyle, and they see a good life that has escaped them" (p. 365). Progressive images in Western media are also reinforced by acts of public diplomacy, especially when leaders of core nations encourage governments in peripheral nations to abide by democratic values. For example, during a recent visit, then US President Obama encouraged Cuba to embrace democracy and respect for human rights. He had the same message during his visit to the African Union headquarters in Ethiopia in 2015, where he criticized African presidents who change constitutional term limits to extend their stay in power.

However, just like development communication that can be controlled by authoritarian governments, acts and messages of public diplomacy performed by representatives of core nations do not operate in a historical vacuum. International efforts often embrace different interests and policies at once, which results in notable contradictions (e.g., see Guilhot 2005). Cornwall (2007) reminds us about the importance of discourse in the pursuit of different goals and interests that sometimes contradict each other, because "when ideas fail, words come in handy" (p. 474). In other words, the impetus of the cosmopolitics of global democratization should be understood *as discourse*. The following section provides a brief background that clarifies not only the ascendancy of discourse, but also its relationship to the concept of global civil society in processes of globalization.

Global Public Diplomacy as Discourse

Due to inherent contradictions within and beyond local states, some scholars have been interested in the all-inclusive participation derived from the tenets of global civil society. Global civil society is defined as "the organized expression of the values and interests of society" (Castells 2008a, b, p. 78). According to Castells (2008a, b), the influence of the state and a genuine (i.e., functioning) civil society is the basis of democracy. Thus, understanding global public diplomacy as discourse is more attuned to the complexities and contradictions of global public diplomacy, because it is via this discourse-centered approach that citizen-led initiatives can be efficiently expressed through the space of global civil society.

This chapter reflects on cyber communications as a space for a new form of global civil society. As Castells (2008a, b) observes, "The process of globalization has shifted the debate from the national domain to the global debate, prompting the emergence of a global civil society and ad hoc forms of global governance" (p. 78). To understand the cosmopolitics of democratization and the role of cyber communications, one has to consider the historical context of global public diplomacy as well as the diplomatic relationships between governments in emerging economies and those in industrialized countries. For example, international development aid and related policies and programs bind relationships between the core and peripheral nations. Such policies and program often enforce values that have a universal appeal (e.g., democracy and human rights), resulting in the enforcement of what will, intersubjectively, become universal norms.

The relationship between core nations and emerging economies is often undifferentiated from other processes of globalization and its close referent of neoliberalism. Consequently, Larner, Heron, and Lewis (2007) reiterate Castells' (2008a, b) argument regarding processes of neoliberalization. They state that "part of the debate about the significance of neoliberalism has shifted in focus from domestic politics of a particular country case studies to globalizing processes driven by international institutions and actors" (p. 226). It is for the same reasons that contemporary theorizations on the relationship between core nations and emerging economies are now focusing on discourse rather than the effects of global neoliberalization (Castells 2008a, b; Guilhot 2005; Larner et al. 2007; Springer 2012).

Neoliberalism is a discourse because of its creative capability to mutate through discourses of public diplomacy enacted by representatives of international institutions (Kwitonda 2016). Such institutions include development aid institutions such as the Millennium Challenge Corporation (MMC), the World Bank, the United States Agency for International Development (USAID), and the International Monetary Fund (IMF). With the ascendancy of democracy as a universal value, more specialized institutions have established themselves as purveyors of international democratic practices. These include, for example, the International Foundation for Electoral Systems, the National Endowment for Democracy or Transparency International, and the Center for Democracy and Governance, established in 1994 and funded by the USAID, to name a few.

The role of the discourse deployed by these organizations has created mixed feelings about them because they are double agents (Guilhot 2005). It is perhaps the forces in these processes that have allowed neoliberalism to generate different understandings, because thinkers understand neoliberalism using mutually exclusive lenses—as either a hegemonic ideology, policy, and program, state form, or governmentality (Springer 2012). The following section explains how the different understandings of neoliberalism affect the cosmopolitics and discourse of democratization.

Participation, Discourse, Double Agents, and Democratization

The notion of involvement entails democracy. The various understandings of neoliberalism outlined above have given participation an original impetus. However, as shown elsewhere (Kwitonda 2016), development and related aid have so far proved to be discursive phenomena. Even the concepts of participation—as attractive as it sounds—may not be politically and linguistically innocent.

Initially, international development and related aid had a façade of being apolitical (they seemed to focus exclusively on the economic concerns of development). The focus appeared to be on economic *policy and programs* such as privatization, deregulation, or liberalization, or the depoliticization of policies and programs (see Brenner and Theodore 2002; Klepeis and Vance 2003; Springer 2012; Ward and England 2007). The World Bank and the IMF and their Structural Adjustment Programs (SAPs) have historically been the focus of most studies. Through its discursive disguise, neoliberalism managed to ensure that eligibility for SAP loans hinged on the adoption of neoliberal policies and programs while pretending to be apolitical. SAP loans failed partly because their top-down policies and programs did not take into account the unique interests of each country that received them.

In the wake of severe criticism leveled against these institutions and their SAPs, the institutions have transformed their top-down approaches to development by co-opting the concept of participation (Leal 2007). They achieved this by adopting the discourse of what once belonged to activists and dissenters in relation to SAPs. In particular, participation is part of the discursive reinvention by these two institutions, especially in the context of not only putting the blame for SAPs failures on recipient countries, but also countering "the ills of failed states and underdevelopment" (Guilhot 2005, p. 210). According to Guilhot (2005), participation was also motivated by the need to hold leaders of failed states accountable through the promotion of a vibrant civil society, transparent institutions, and participation.

That bold move of enforcing international norms put democracy makers in multifaceted circumstances, playing many roles at the same time. For example, they have had to address "not only macroeconomic fundamentals but also the whole political and legal order. The promotion of economic liberalization was successfully converted into the struggle for democratization" (Guilhot 2005, p. 191), reiterating the designation of double agents that has been used to refer to neoliberal institutions of international development. For example, despite claims to promote vibrant civil society, institutional transparency, and participation, there is evidence suggesting that the institutions behind SAPs sometimes prefer quasi-authoritarian regimes, because these appear to be more efficient in implementing SAPs and are immune to participatory pressures from the grassroots (Guilhot 2005). However, why did the participatory approaches run counter to the promotion of democracy when the two suggest the same purpose? The answer lies in the discursive game of global neoliberalization, as democracy and human rights sometimes imply a fight against communism.

Originally rooted in the radical pedagogy of the Brazilian, Marxist, and democracy educator Paulo Freire, participation can, in many ways, go against the capitalist, anti-communist world order (Leal 2007). Because of its appeal in the arena of international diplomacy and neoliberal policies, participation is never frontally opposed. Instead, through discourse, the notion of involvement has been *co-opted* by states and non-governmental organizations (NGOs) alike (Chossudovsky 2002; Leal 2007).

Participation is not only a threat to the hegemonic agenda of global neoliberalism, it is also a threat against national dictatorial regimes in peripheral nations. Those regimes are, in a sense, forced to hold regular elections to secure aid or survive debt crises (Rahnema 1990). As such, dictatorial governments use participation as a maneuvering tool and an attempt to steal the show. Rahnema (1990) observes that such governments "have learned to control and contain participation, and maintain political advantages through the ostentatious display of participatory intentions" (p. 202). For obvious reasons, these regimes cannot leave *the people's choice* to the *whim of the people.*

Consequently, the power of participation does not only involve repression in most dictatorial settings, it also allows global neoliberal policies to have the upper hand in matters of local policies, programs, and governance. Castells (2008a, b) calls this *the crisis of legitimacy*, as nation states need to navigate the interests of the nation in the global web of policymaking and public diplomacy.

Despite the careful use of discourse in world public diplomacy—coated with "glorious appearances of progressive struggles and solidarities" (Guilhot 2005, p. 30)—the efforts of nation states reflect some of the problems that motivated the Cold War (Gowan 2006). This refers to the tension that pitted the USSR against the USA (and its allies) in the scramble for global ideological influence.

The current war against international terrorism has amplified the need for solidarity at the expense of democracy. Such solidarity often takes the form of what Guilhot calls reliance on the politics of realism, which is, again, a legacy of Cold War strategies. Guilhot (2005) observes that "earlier, the antagonisms between the two superpowers ensured the success of realism as the main doctrine of foreign policy, which legitimated all kinds of accommodations with authoritarian regimes as long as they had chosen to side with 'the free world'" (p. 30). The recent report and Testimony of the Assistant Secretary for the Bureau of African Affairs, Linda Thomas-Greenfield, before the US Senate Foreign Relations Committee regarding US policy in Central Africa is a good example (Thomas-Greenfield 2017).

There are notable disparities in the testimony. It devotes considerable time to some countries that are deviating from human rights expectations in the region. However, the case of Burundi has become particularly interesting, especially among commentators who are sensitive to the history of the tension between communism and capitalism as two competing paradigms of global politics and influence (e.g., see Jones and Donovan-Smith 2015). Almost half of the 15-page document discusses the crisis in Burundi. It also details all the sanctions that have already been imposed on Burundi because its current president wants to stay in power longer than the expected 10 years. However, the report spends only two short paragraphs on Uganda, a country whose leader has been in power for more than 30 years. It is also ironic that the president of Uganda, Museveni, is mentioned as someone who has mediated the peace talks between warring factions in Burundi. It is important to remind readers that Museveni and his government have been a long-term ally of the USA.

This disparity seems to substantiate a pattern in international diplomacy, especially when it comes to the issue of term limits. "The west while referring to that issue in Burundi and other countries in the region, Jones and Donovan-Smith (2015) observe that the West's inconsistent stance on the issue recognizes that not all term limits are created equal" (8).

Jones and Donovan-Smith (2015) also suggest that the interest Burundi has stimulated among observers evokes traditional Cold War politics, reflected in the rivalry between Russia and China on the one hand as well as the USA-led alliance. They emphasize that Burundi's relationships with countries that have historically been perceived as communist are what lurks beneath the surface of the inconsistent Western pressure for democracy and human rights in the Great Lakes region of Africa: "Burundi's government is making a high-stakes bet: instead of Western donors, it is turning to China and Russia. Both countries have publicly supported the Nkurunziza regime, attending Conseil National Pour la Défense de la Démocratie–Forces pour la Défense de la Démocratie (CNDD–FDD) functions and issuing public statements. Their veto power in the Security Council precludes UN intervention and even discussion on the topic, stifled in May and August. Moreover, crucially, according to Burundian advisers, China is said to have pledged up to $25 million to fill holes in the country's aid-starved budget".

On the surface of governmental public diplomacy, no entity may detect these inconsistencies and compromises. For example, Mrs. Greenfield started her report with a neutral statement stating that "The U.S government has privately and publicly expressed its position that peaceful, democratic alternation makes for a healthy democracy" (p. 13). However, according to Guilhot (2005), these efforts constitute a significant contradiction in US democratization policies, because such policies point instead to "a conservative project built upon the confusion of national interests and universalistic values, which has consistently used the latter to further the former" (p. 30).

We can have the same view regarding the strategic relationship between the USA and Cuba, another communist country. Baker perceived the recent efforts at rapprochement between the two nations as attempts to remove the last vestige of Cold War hostilities. However, while visiting the island, Obama's message did not mention communism directly. Instead, it focused on freedom of expression, human rights, and democracy. The denotative meaning of communism as a value that is antithetical to liberty and democracy is not uncommon. For example, MacPhail (2010) suggests that one of the advantages of electronic colonization is to vanquish communism by the use of media products, because the latter are the central nervous systems of economic development, freedom, and choices, and hence of democracy. He asserts:

> This package also comes with democracy and free enterprise businesses. The East Germans learned all this by watching and listening to British and American shows, movies of all sorts, and music, from jazz to the Beatles. *Dallas* and *Dynasty* did more to undermine communism than all of the US propaganda campaigns. The same overall picture is also true of the other former communist countries which stampeded to become members of the open and democratic European Union after the end of the Shaw. (p. 365)

Based on the above quotation, communism implies a lack of democracy. It is important then to consider the discourse of public diplomacy, because this approach is suited to the challenges of understanding the many aims of public diplomacy. Obviously, each country prioritizes its own interests. One can have a better understanding of the definition of public diplomacy from Snow (2010): "public diplomacy seeks to promote public interests of the United States through understanding, informing and influencing foreign audiences" (Snow 2010, p. 90). However, the interests that motivate core nations tend to use an ambiguous discourse—one which is committed to collective solidarities toward progressive values on the one hand, and one that uses the struggle for democracy and human rights selectively against rogue states on the other.

In sum, it is these contradictory solidarities from within and without that limit the potential of bottom-up approaches to democratization and participation. Participation is thought to be a bottom-up buffer against the top-down tendencies of global neoliberalism (Brenner and Theodore 2002; Dutta 2004, 2006; Klepeis and Vance 2003; Sastry and Dutta 2011, 2013). As mentioned above, however, local leaders are also responsible for the weak status of democratic practices and institutions in emerging economies. Development aid is another force that works against grassroots initiatives, as it comes invariably with policy prescriptions that diffuse downward from donor countries.

This support conundrum invokes another line of thinking, which conceives of neoliberalism as governmentality. Governmentality invokes the promise of self-reliance when it aims to transform recipients of welfare and social insurance into entrepreneurial subjects who may be motivated to become responsible for themselves (Ward and England 2007, p. 13).

In other words, its objective is to facilitate the creation of *responsibilized* neoliberal subjects (Rose 1996) through *technologies of self* that, according to Ren (2005), they may use for self-formation. However, as many scholars have pointed out, this way of envisioning neoliberalism is not without contradiction, as less government does not necessarily entail less governance (Larner et al. 2007). As seen in preceding sections, however, in the absence of discursive and critical consciousness, there is a risk of appropriating the original promise of governmentality—just as neoliberal capitalist power co-opted the concept of participation.

Cyber Communications as a New Form of Education

The previous sections show that the cosmopolitics of democratization is carefully embedded in the specific language that once belonged to dissenters against global neoliberalism. This discursive mutation is not unprecedented. For example, throughout history, communication and information have been key sources of power and counter-power, of domination and social change. Moreover, the primary battle fought in society is over the minds of the people. Cyber communications have provided a new form of influencing public opinion (e.g., mass self-communication; for more details, see Castells 2007). According to Castells, most features of the new media (e.g., SMS, blogs, podcasts, wikis) are general and customizable, personal and mass formats of communication at the same time; hence the designation of mass self-communication.

These types of media are attuned to the nature of the cosmopolitics of democratization because they can engage the realm of discourse. Cyber communications have enabled a new form of socialized communication, what Castells calls *power making* and *mind framing*. There are two main ways in which cyber communications achieve this on the ambiguous nature of the discourse of international development in general and the promotion of democracy in particular.

First, in the context of public opinion and discursive practices, cyber communications provide support for the joint social production of meaning. This feature is important especially vis-à-vis the need to educate ordinary people who are often the target of political and international development concepts (e.g., democracy, participation).

For example, the idea of involvement has a close link to Cold War and neoliberal politics and policies. Cyber communications can be used to support the joint social production of meaning by, for example, disambiguating established buzzwords and fuzzy concepts such as participation or development. Since the idea of participation is also linked to the concept previously conceived by Freire (1970), cyber communications can be used to educate lay citizens to grasp their *classical conditioning* and *levels of consciousness* through a neo-Freudian approach to the pedagogy of the oppressed, because ordinary people often participate in their own oppression. Although discourse and discursive engagement may not seem to be relevant in the context of the practical field of development, the discourse has now been recognized as a precursor to practice because it fixes boundaries (Cornwall 2007).

This thought–action link is echoed in Castells' assertion in the context of cyber communications that "the Internet provides the essential platform for debate, their means of acting on people's mind, and ultimately serves as their most potent political weapon" (p. 250). The capacity of new media to engage in the battle over human minds is similar to McPhail's ECT. The accessibility of social media tools such as WhatsApp and Facebook in the developing world can be leveraged to disambiguate the ideologies, policies, and programs mentioned above that thrive on double standards. Furthermore, that this has enhanced the power of the new media points to its potential for assisting new forms of protest.

Cyber Communications as a New Movement of Protest and Public Opinion

In addition to being instrumental in the process of mind framing, cyber communications are also key platforms for cyber activism, collective organizing, and a *movement of public opinion* (Castells 2008a, b). Public opinion is important in the context of involving governments and NGOs, as the latter are far from what Guilhot (2005) describes as disinterested entities. In previous sections, we demonstrated that the relationship/solidarity between governments of core nations and governments in emerging economies is bound by interests that are sometimes counterproductive (e.g., military interests, neoliberal policies).

Even the ideals of most non-profit/non-governmental organizations that oversee the promotion of democracy around the globe rely heavily on funding that often comes from governments and for-profit organizations with strings attached. In fact, Castells (2008a, b) asserts that these organizations frequently "affirm values that are universally recognized but politically manipulated in their interest by political agencies, including governments" (p. 84). Thus, disinterestedness becomes compromised among international NGOs once regarded as representatives of an independent global civil society.

Additionally, the money used by such international NGOs must be justified; and so such NGOs usually end up toeing the political line of national governments, because donor governments do not want to lose legitimacy in the eyes of taxpayers. Consequently, both governments and the international NGOs they sponsor are looking for success stories. Coincidentally, governments in emerging economies need the same success stories to justify aid received from donor countries. Because of these conditions, many development organizations shy away from engaging in political issues (Waisbord 2008).

Most development projects are essentially based on political problems (e.g., lack of good governance, suppression of grassroots initiatives), as well as other social issues that require deep social transformation and social justice (e.g., gender, ethnic discrimination). Thus sometimes success stories associated with aid and political practices, such as holding regular elections, are nothing more than public relations performances aimed at impressing development donors.

Even when political issues are engaged, they are involved in particular ways which only reflect the politics of patronage between governments of donor countries and their military and political allies in emerging economies. Despite the impressive rhetoric and public performance of a free society, there is no significant improvement in emerging economies. As such, there is a need for some global civil society to fill this gap in the realm of public diplomacy and public opinion. In other words, there is a need for some global meta-communication to rehabilitate the ideals of world civil society.

Cyber communications enjoy unprecedented leverage in this regard in the sense that they are organizing tools of "ad hoc mobilizations using horizontal, autonomous networks of communication" (Castells 2008a, b, p. 86). Their strength lies in the fact that they are horizontal, and differ from the traditional top-down communication process. According to Castells, they are self-mass communication, and their interactive diffusion process can be "from many to many both synchronous and asynchronous". In particular, the movement of public opinion using horizontal and autonomous networks of communication seems to be somewhat beyond censorship (2007).

First, cyber communications are ideal tools for the movement of public opinion in both global and local contexts. Public opinion is important in contexts of dictatorships, because dictatorships have traditionally relied on the control of information, especially information that can shape foreign aid policies. Beyond narrowly defined political and security interests (e.g., maintaining militant proxies and political allies), the governments of donor countries are not necessarily interested in democratic practices in emerging economies, but they are, at least, sensitive to the concerns of their taxpayers and voters, who foot the bill for international aid.

As cyber communications constitute a new form of visibility (Thompson 2005), they can be used to speak directly to voters in donor countries, and this can put pressure on governments in those countries. That, in turn, can influence aid policies in the sense that the assistance can address genuine democracy. In other words, the issue of international aid makes the discourse and cosmopolitics of democracy a global challenge.

There are actual case studies that exemplify how cyber communications and cyber activism can shape a new form of civil protest on a global scale. For example, digital media fueled public outrage when a personal photograph taken by military staff in Abu Ghraib, a US-run prison in the suburbs of Baghdad, was leaked in the public domain. That influenced the photograph's reproduction in newspapers and on television (Thompson 2005), putting tremendous pressure on the Bush administration. The concrete outcomes of exposing hidden practices are summarized by Thompson (2005):

> In this world, making actions and events visible is not just the outcome of leakage in systems of communication and information flow that are increasingly difficult to control. It is also a clear strategy for individuals who know very well that mediated visibility can be a weapon in the struggles they wage in their day-to-day lives. (p. 31)

There are case studies that are particularly relevant in contexts of emerging economies such as sub-Saharan Africa, where dictatorial governments have co-opted or silenced independent media and NGOs. In particular, cyber communications have a unique ability to shape the agendas of both local and international media. Cyber communications have been used in mobilization for political change and global awareness, including and not limited to what happened in the Arab Spring, as well as in countries such as South Korea, the Philippines, Spain, Ukraine, Ecuador, Nepal, and Thailand. Castells et al. (2006) offer a detailed review. Because most governments in emerging economies depend on positive media reports in order to secure or sustain aid, the new media is likely to equip the grassroots with tools to capture and share information that can shape sociopolitical and economic undertakings in such contexts (Ngwainmbi 2000). That emphasizes the practical impact of global communication networks built around mass media. So, to a large extent, communication framing of the public mind in the network society has replaced political legitimacy (p. 258).

Myanmar (formally known as Burma) is another interesting case study for most countries under military dictatorships. It is, in fact, a case of cyber activism and citizens' journalism that effectively mobilized global awareness and solidarity (Castells 2008a, b; Mydans 2007). It all started as a students' movement against the Myanmar military junta using text messages (SMS) and e-mails, and posting daily blogs and notices on Facebook as well as videos on YouTube (Castells 2008a, b). As usual, the military junta resorted to violence against its people, but all the brutality was being captured using video on cell phones and was being uploaded to YouTube and social media (Mydans 2007).

The technological revolution spurred two actual changes. First, this shaped the agenda of both local and global media, because the uploaded images "were broadcasted back into Myanmar by foreign radio and television stations, informing and connecting a public that receives only propaganda reports from its government" (Mydans 2007, pp. 3–5). Second, this affected the relationship between the junta and its Chinese sponsors. Furthermore, the USA and the European Union put diplomatic pressure on the Burmese junta following the public outrage that was globally expressed using cyber communications (Castells 2008a, b).

Conclusion

This chapter has looked at the contribution of cyber communications to national democratic movements for democracy and democratization. It builds on the well-established theory of Electronic Colonization Theory (McPhail 2010) not only to acknowledge the potential of cyber communications, but also to show that scholars need to disambiguate the discourse of freedom and democracy. The discourse of public diplomacy itself tends to reflect the multifaceted nature of democratization.

The latter process catapults countries that are at the forefront of global governance into a double bind. As Guilhot (2005) observes, the role of these countries mutates discursively from being Cold War warriors to human rights activists. ECT does not recognize this discursive mutation, because it assumes that messages of public diplomacy diffused through electronic communication mean what they say and say what they mean. Public diplomacy between core nations and emerging economies becomes even more ambiguous when, for example, lenders apply sanctions against countries that may deserve the penalties in a selective manner.

The chapter discussed the reasons why there is a need to have an ad hoc form of communication that would assume the original meaning of global civil society by engaging in the ambiguous discourse that characterizes the cosmopolitics of democratization. Discourse is particularly crucial because, like other norms of international development, democracy is a political process, and any politics is media politics where the human mind is the real site of struggle.

Cases studies reviewed in this chapter show that cyber communications are effective tools when it comes to influencing the agenda of both national and international media, as well as public opinion and international development policies. Public opinion in the context of international relations is particularly critical for countries in emerging economies, as the latter will need legitimacy in a world where the control of information is becoming increasingly more difficult. Cyber communication products such as cell phone cameras have a unique ability to bypass established media in distribution via the various applications of Youtube, WhatsApp, Facebook, and other social media, which is why some commentators find cyber communications an epitome of citizen's journalism, especially in times of protest. As Mydans (2007, pp. 3–5) reported: "Today every citizen is a war correspondent." This kind of civil society is truly democratic.

Topics for Discussion

1. Can rural communities effectively utilize cyber communications to enhance democratization?
2. How can social media best be used to promote democracy in a fragile state or a marginalized community?

Works Cited

Brenner, Neil, and Theodore, Nik. 2002. Cities and the Geographies of 'Actually Existing Neoliberalism'. *Antipode* 34: 349–79, doi:http://dx.doi.org/10.1002/9781444397499.

Castells, Manuel. 2008a. The Information Age: Economy, Society, and Culture. In *The Rise of the Network Society*, Vol. 1. Oxford: Blackwell Publishers.

Castells, Manuel. 2008b. The New Public Sphere: Global Civil Society, Communication Networks, and Global Governance. *The ANNALS of the American Academy of Political and Social Science* 616: 78–93. doi: abs 10.1177/0002716207311877.

Castells, Manuel, Mireia Fernández-Ardèvol, and Araba Sey. 2006. *Mobile Communication and Society: A Global Perspective*. Cambridge: MIT Press.

Chossudovsky, Michel. 2002. *The Globalization of Poverty: The Impacts of IMF and World Bank Reforms*. London: Zed Books.

Cornwall, Andrea. 2007. Buzzwords and Fuzzwords: Deconstructing Development Discourse. *Development in Practice* 17: 471–484. doi:10.1080/09614520701469302.

Dutta, Mohan. 2004. The Unheard Voices of Santalis: Communicating about Health from the margins of India. *Communication Theory* 14: 237–263. doi:10.1111/j.1468-2885.2004.tb00313.x.

Dutta, Mohan. 2006. Theoretical Approaches To Entertainment Education Campaigns: A Subaltern Critique. *Health Communication* 20: 221–231. doi:10.1207/s15327027hc2003_2.

Frank, Thomas M. 1992. The emerging right to democratic governance. *The American Journal of International Law* 86: 46–91.

Freire, Paulo. 1970. *The Pedagogy of the Oppressed*, trans. and ed. M. B. Ramos. New York: Herder and Herder.

Gowan, Peter. 2006. Triumphing Toward International Disaster. *Critical Asian Studies* 36: 3–36. doi:10.1080/1467271042000184562.

Guilhot, Nicolas. 2005. *The Democracy Makers*. New York: Columbia University Press.

Jones, Cara, and Donovan-Smith, Orion. 2015. How the West Lost Burundi. *Foreign Policy*, 1–15. Retrieved on January 8, 2017, from http://foreignpolicy.com/2015/08/28/how-the-west-lost-burundi/.

Klepeis, Peter, and Colin Vance. 2003. Neoliberal policy and deforestation in southeastern Mexico: An assessment of the PROCAMPO program. *Economic Geography* 79: 221–240. doi:10.1111/j.1944-8287.2003.tb00210.x.

Kwitonda, J. Claude. 2016. Development Aid and Disease Discourse on Display: The Mutating Techniques of Neoliberalism. *Journal of Critical Discourse Studies*, 14. doi:10.1080/17405904.2016.1174139.

Larner, Wendy, Heron, Richard, and Lewis, Nicholas. 2007. Co-constructing "After Neoliberalism": Political Projects and Globalizing Governmentalities. In *Neoliberalization: States, Networks, Peoples,* ed. England Kim and Ward, 223–247. Malden, MA: Blackwell.

Leal, P. Alejandro. 2007. Participation: The Ascendancy of a Buzzword in the Neo-Liberal Era. *Development in Practice* 17: 539–548. http://dx.doi.org/10.3362/9781780440095.008.

McPhail, Thomas. 2010. *Global Communication: Theories, Stakeholders, and Trends.* Malden: Wiley-Blackwell.

Mydans, Seth. 2007. Myanmar Comes Face to Face with a Technology Revolution. *International Herald Tribune.*

Ngwainmbi, K. Emmanuel. 2000. Africa in the Global Infosupermarket: Perspectives and Prospects. *Journal of Black Studies* 304: 534–552.

Rahnema, Majid. 1990. Participatory Action Research: The "Last Temptation of Saint" Development. *Alternatives* XV: 199–226. Retrieved from http://www.jstor.org/stable/40644681.

Ren, Hai. 2005. Modes Of Governance In Neo-Liberal Capitalism: An Introduction. *Rhizomes,* 10. Retrieved from http://www.rhizomes.net/issue10/introren.htm.

Rose, Nikolas. 1996. The Death of the Social? Re-figuring the Territory of Government. *Economy and Society* 25: 327–356. doi:10.1080/03085149600000018.

Sastry, Shaunak, and Mohan Dutta. 2011. Postcolonial Constructions of HIV/AIDS: Meaning, Culture, and Structure. *Health Communication* 26: 437–449. doi:10.1080/10410236.2011.554166.

Sastry, Shaunak, and Mohan Dutta. 2013. Global Health Interventions and the "Common Sense" of Neoliberalism: A Dialectical Analysis of PEPFAR. *Journal of International and Intercultural Communication* 6: 21–39. doi:10.1080/17513057.2012.740682.

Springer, Simon. 2012. Neoliberalism as Discourse: Between Foucauldian Political Economy and Marxian poststructuralism. *Critical Discourse Studies* 9: 133–147. doi.org/10.1080/17405904.2012.656375.

Snow, Nancy. 2010. Public Diplomacy: New Dimensions and Implications. In *Global Communication: Theories, Stakeholders, and Trends*, ed. Thomas McPhail, 84–102. Malden: Wiley-Blackwell.

Thomas-Greenfield, Linda. 2017. Testimony of Assistant Secretary Linda Thomas-Greenfield Bureau of African Affairs, U.S. Department of State before the Senate Foreign Relations Committee U.S. Policy in Central Africa: The Imperative of Good Governance. United State Senate Committee on Foreign Relations. Retrieved January 2017 from http://www.foreign.senate.gov/imo/media/doc/021016_Thomas-Greenfield_Testimony.pdf.

Thompson, B., and John. 2005. The new visibility. *Theory, Culture & Society* 22: 31–51.
Uvin, Peter. 1999. Development aid and structural violence: The case of Rwanda. *Development* 42: 49–56. doi:10.1057/palgrave.development.1110060.
Waisbord, Silvio. 2008. The institutional challenges of participatory communication in international aid. *Social Identities* 14: 505–522. http://dx.doi.org/10.1080/13504630802212009.
Ward, Kevin, and England, Kim. 2007. Introduction: Reading neo-liberalization. In *Neoliberalization: States, Networks, Peoples*, ed. England Kim and Ward, 1–22. Malden, MA: Blackwell.

PART III

Television as Political Weapon: The Asian and African Experience

CHAPTER 5

The Changing Face of Television and Public Policy Implications in India

Srinivas Panthukala

Brief History

Television in India started in Delhi on September 15, 1959, with the help of a grant of US $20,000 from the United Nations Educational, Scientific and Cultural Organization (UNESCO) and equipment provided by the USA and the Phillips television company. The main purpose of television at that point was community development and education. An experimental television station was started in New Delhi to train personnel "to discover what television could achieve in community development and formal education," with a possible transmitter range of only 40 km^2. Members of 180 television clubs were also provided with free sets by UNESCO (Chatterji, 1991).

Among Srinivas Panthukala's research interests are television journalism and journalism studies. In this chapter, he calls for a more equitable and egalitarian development of television stations in India.

S. Panthukala (✉)
The English & Foreign Languages University, Hyderabad, Telangana, India

E.K. Ngwainmbi (ed.), *Citizenship, Democracies, and Media Engagement among Emerging Economies and Marginalized Communities*,
DOI 10.1007/978-3-319-56215-5_5

In the mid-1960s, Dr. Vikram Sarabhai, a visionary technocrat and founder of India's space program, began arguing in policymaking circles that a nationwide satellite television system could play a major role in promoting economic and social development. Sarabhai's initiative, a national satellite communication group, came into existence and through its recommendations, the Indian government approved a "hybrid" television broadcasting system consisting of communication satellites as well as ground-based microwave relay transmitters. Sarabhai envisaged the satellite component, which allowed India to leapfrog from very basic to state-of-the-art communication technology, undermined because of a lack of infrastructure (Singhal 2001). By 1967, the output had expanded to include farmer education programming in the rural areas of surrounding states. The station broadcast the program in a one-hour bulletin. From 1967 to 1975, authorities established relay stations in Bombay, Srinagar, Amritsar, Pune, Calcutta, Madras, and Lucknow. In this period, television in India was rather limited regarding its reach, scope, and programming.

In 1975, an experiment in satellite television called SITE (Satellite Instructional Television Experiment) was started in India, which was also the first time in the world. The Indian government provided funds, and the US National Aeronautics and Space Administration (NASA) offered scientific support to operationalize the project. Developmental programs for rural students, farmers, and women, and programs in science, health and hygiene, family planning, and national integration, were beamed to 2400 community television sets placed in six of the poorest states in the country: Bihar, Orissa, Madhya Pradesh, Rajasthan, Andhra Pradesh, and Karnataka.

Around the same time, for one year on an experimental basis, Kheda TV was started in 355 villages in the state of Gujarat, where authorities installed community television sets at milk cooperative societies. They also set up about 504 small 61 cm television sets for community viewing. A 1 kW television transmitter was installed in Pij to serve an area of 3000 km^2 of Kheda district. This transmitter received signals from the microwave receiver terminal located in Ahmedabad, about 45 km^2 away. The authorities then ensured the transmission of Kheda TV programs from a common SITE center and the Kheda studio at Ahmadabad. In Kheda TV the planners aimed at effecting behavioral changes among the rural poor. The main objective of this experiment was to bring development activities to rural people.

Between 1975 and 1977, television was monopolized by the state. In 1975, the prime minister of India, Indira Gandhi, imposed a state of emergency. At that time press freedom was suppressed, and broadcast media, including television, became a propaganda tool and mouthpiece of the Congress government. The television channel was separated from All India Radio (AIR) and was called Doordarshan. It started with a one-hour program running twice a week and moved eventually to today's telecasting of 24-hour news channels.

In 1977, the Varghese Committee, which had set up a trust called the National Broadcasting Trust for AIR and Doordarshan, submitted a report describing a complaint board with quasi-judicial powers, among other issues. In 1979–1980, Indira Gandhi's Congress government returned to power and shelved the Varghese Committee's recommendations. To this day, the recommendations have not been implemented and state television continues to function under the Ministry of Information and Broadcasting.

The broadcasting infrastructure expanded rapidly in the 1980s to support the Asian Games in New Delhi in 1982. This expansion took place under the supervision of Indira Gandhi's son Rajiv Gandhi, who was seeking to establish himself as a young and dynamic leader of modern India. The country's 18 television transmitters in 1979 had expanded to 176 by 1985. With this change, 80% of the urban population and 50% of the rural population came within range of a television signal. For the first time, the country introduced color television sets, leading to a dramatic change in the form and content of television. Soap operas, news and current affairs, and advertisements began to appear on television. Stations broadcast popular epic serials like the *Ramayan* and *Mahabharat* during this time. Television became a source of entertainment for the masses and a symbol of social status. It moved from local space to the global arena, and the state-owned television station became part of the global village[1] at the Asian Games through beaming satellite communication signals around the world.

After Asian Games, another big event, the hosting of the Commonwealth Games in October 2010, gave India the opportunity for the gradation of information and communication technology (ICT) about television and promotion of the discourse of television studies. The event also created an opportunity for action when private television channels exposed corruption and underdevelopment of slum areas in the capital city. This became an indication that the television revolution in India could have a wide impact on state and society.

In 1984 there were only 100 cable operators, a number that had risen to 60,000 by 1995. Now, there are at least 15,000 cable operators in Andhra Pradesh and the Telangana states alone. STAR televises 24-hour news in 38 countries through five channels, which the cable operators show to their subscribers. In addition, ZEE TV strengthened the cable system through its entry. By 1995 the cable operators could provide their service to 1.20 crore houses; now, their reach is more than 3.5 crore houses with 250 channels.

The entry of private channels subjected the cable network to a remarkable change. A change of technology on the one hand and an increase in the number of channels on the other stymied the cable operators and their investment increased heavily. At that juncture, smaller operators worked together and the number of cable operators declined. As the cable network operators began to emerge as an organized body, however, the number of multiple system operators (MSOs) increased simultaneously. These operators came under the umbrella of organizations like Siti Cable, In Cable, Hathaway, SCV, and RPG, and organized themselves. The MSOs were also successful in turning the operators into their co-agents and giving them the feed. Siti Cable evolved as the largest MSO in the country. In India, Mumbai is currently the leading market in cable use, followed by Delhi. Gujarat, Andhra Pradesh, Maharashtra, and Punjab have a deep-rooted cable network.

Cable TV channels also compete with satellite channels for ad revenue and income generation in the Telugu regions. At present, the operative cable television channels are C Channel, CITI Cable, Jagruthi TV, Janata TV, RK News, Deccan TV, TNN TV, Munsif TV, Ruby TV, and Metro TV. There is no uniform subscription policy for Cable and Satellite TV networks across the country. With the increase in paid channels, the subscription has increased with time.

Regarding income level, the government has introduced a Conditional Access System (CAS) to control illegal subscription collection from customers. As per this system, the customer at present has the option to buy a set-top box and select channels/packages and a cable operator for at least 40 free channels and Paid Channels for approximately 250 rupees for per month (approx.$4).

Conditional Access System (CAS) and DTH

In early 2000s, the authorities introduced CAS in the four metropolitan cities of Chennai, Mumbai, Delhi and Kolkata, but it gave rise to many disputes. Immediately there were elections, and CAS was put into cold storage. When the Congress Party gained political power, it focused on a direct-to-home (DTH) policy. If customers buy a Dishnet, they can watch 30 channels free of charge. Among these there are 18 Doordarshan channels. Since many channels have been showing an interest in joining DTH, Doordarshan is planning to increase the e-platform to 50 channels.

DTH appears to be more useful in rural areas. The advantage is that if customers invest once, they could enjoy the benefits lifelong and need not pay a subscription. However, the future of DTH depends on whether the client is ready to buy a receiver or not. It was necessary to disregard the cable operator system in the country, but if cable services are spreading through *convergence*, DTH would not be a successful alternative. Earlier, when CAS was introduced, there was an inadequate response from customers. Hence, there are doubts in the case of DTH too.

Some Indian channel networks are joining forces with different channels to offer different packages for a fixed subscription. The STAR, ZEE, and Sony packages are some examples of this kind of deal. In the Telugu, states of Andhra Pradesh and Telangana people pay to watch MAA TV, Gemini TV, Teja TV, and ETV, and they are increasing in number with the passing of time. In this type of system, channel management relies largely on cable operators, and the cable network in India has developed to establish itself like an organized private limited venture, which is dictating terms to private satellite channels.

Paid channels have crossed the national boundaries and started collecting subscription in dollars by launching channels in different countries for the benefits of non-resident Indians (NRIs). In the USA there are two relevant agencies working toward this end, Direct TV and the DISH Network. The former offers a package for US $29.99/88 channels and the latter for US $19.99/70 channels.

Channel owners rely on information related to the question of how many people watch which channel in selected cities, for rating purpose. The channel owners take the help of MSOs in selected cities in a state to improve program quality, and they do not hesitate to pay money for better ratings. Hence, cable operators have become important in these circumstances. "Convergence" is taking cable operators forward.

Experimenting with Television Broadcasting in Rural Communities

An innovative broadcasting experiment is underway in the rural, hilly hinterlands of Jhabua district in Madhya Pradesh state (Space Application

Center, 1996). The population of Jhabua is 85% tribal, with a literacy rate of 15%. The district is rich in natural resources, though its people are among India's poorest. Infant mortality rates are high, and transportation and communication facilities are poor.[2] The Development and Educational Communication Unit (DECU) of the Space Application Center (SAC) in Ahmedabad launched the Jhabua Development Communication Project (JDCP) in the mid-1990s (DECU also implemented the Kheda Communication Project).

The purpose of JDCP was to experiment with utilization of an interactive satellite-based broadcasting network to support development and education in rural areas. The authorities then installed some 150 direct-reception systems (a satellite dish, TV sets, video-cassette recorders [VCRs], and other equipment) in several Jhabua villages that received television broadcasts for 2 hrs every evening from DECU's Ahmadabad studio, delinked through satellite. Also, 12 talkback terminals were installed in each of the block headquarters to provide feedback and to report on progress. However, the SITE, Kheda, and Jhabua initiatives were continued just for a short while, although later programmers started educational programs for school children. To provide benefits to rural children through these programs, television sets were given to the schools. However, due to electricity problems, the schools were not in a position to use these facilities and in some areas there were no proper school buildings.[3] There could be various political and economic issues related to this non-usage of television as a media for the development of the country.

In 1990, foreign direct investment (FDI) occurred in mass media that ended the monopoly of state-owned television and led to a steady mushrooming of private television channels all over India. Ownership underwent a dramatic change as a consequence regarding form and content. From 2009 to 2011, the number of households owning television sets increased from 123 to 141 million. The number of households with cable or satellite television rose from 90 to 116 million. Between the years 2000 and 2011, 800 news and non-news television channels were registered all over the country. During this period, 500 news and non-news television channels had been officially recorded to broadcast generic or niche forms of news and entertainment television channels. By 2010, The direct-to-home (DTH) connections increased from 15–26 million people owned television sets (TAN India 2010). India has approximately 150 active news channels, the largest number in any country (Kohli-Khandekar, 2011). Since 2016, 150–200 channels have been awaiting permission from the Ministry of I & B for become operational.

Villagers used to pull out cots into the open area in front of their houses and drown themselves in chat until they went to sleep. Now, villagers stay awake till the early hours of the following day watching television programs, as some television networks actively broadcast the news in English, Hindi, and 12 other regional languages.

Private Satellite Television Channels and Liberalization, Privatization, and Globalization

Information has become a powerful player in the hands of capitalists, and it is the cause of the emergence of regional politics. Economically, politically, socially, and culturally, the conditions had matured in society so much so that by the time of globalization, private capitalists wanted to take the media industry into their own hands. Thus, the government was under pressure to privatize television channels and radio stations. Secondly, regarding ownership, the medium of television moved from simple reportage to strategizing to improve the lobbying capacity of capital with national forces. Regarding this development, one respondent interviewed for this study stated to this author:

> The mushrooming of television channels in India in general and especially in Telugu regions, the rise of cross-media ownership combined with political clout as embodied in Sun TV, ETV, the media landscape is complicated by business models and ethics that often corrode media practices. In this scenario, systemic corruption is evident in "private treaties" wherein the media–corporate interface leads to a confusing reportage that is a cross between advertisement and public relations copy. In today's dynamic media landscape then, media ownership is becoming an increasingly fluid proposition. (Krishna Reddy, 2013: Personal Interview)

An impressive variety of programs increased in number and Doordarshan (government-sponsored) television shows were the last alternative for the viewer. The Congress government took an interest in reviewing the Prasar Bharathi Bill of 1990 by setting up the Vardhan Committee in 1991, and the National Front government then moved one step forward to frame a National Media Policy. In 1995, the Ramvilas Paswan Committee made 46 recommendations, and the Prasar Bharathi Board was set up. In 1998, however, Pramod Mahajan, Information and Broadcasting Minister, announced that his government would scrap the Prasar Bharathi.

During the National Democratic Alliance (NDA) government, the Information and Broadcasting Minister felt that strengthening the Prasar Bharathi Bill would help Doordarshan to compete with private satellite channels. He considered that better programming and marketing could produce positive results by capitalizing on viewership, and set up a committee to reconstruct Prasar Bharathi. Doordarshan time and again proved that it could react to the needs of the new millennium. Now, it telecasts all the proceedings of Parliament, Rashtrapati Bhavan, and official sports events, as it possesses the rights and has gained the upper hand regarding rural viewership. Doordarshan helps bring reliable news to the population, disseminates information, and exchanges knowledge. It is able to occupy a prominent place in the Indian television industry as it is the only player with a vast terrestrial network across the country.

Cable Television Industry and Direct to Home (DTH)

Cable television entered the media industry when Doordarshan was flourishing. Video parlors used VCRs and video compact discs (VCDs) to show films to the public. The services were not expensive, and one could watch the latest films every day. Providers offered cable services at competitive subscription rates to apartment residents. A cable operator of a huge apartment played at least 75 films for the residents, and soon after there was one cable operator for two to three apartments. Through the new system of entertainment a cable network became a successful business enterprise.

The Rise of 24 × 7 TV News Channels

In most parts of the world, 24-hour news channels operate in a very crowded and highly competitive marketplace. Daya Thussu has argued that the Murdoch-owned 24-hour news channel Star News in India has diminished the quality of Indian television in the 2000s. He concludes that "the market, Murdoch, and Murdochization seem to have mitigated against a prospect where Indian journalism could assert itself on the world stage after the state's control of broadcasting was relaxed" (Thussu 2007). CNNI, BBC World, CNBC, Bloomberg TV, Fox News, Euronews, Russia Today, Al Jazeera and Al Jazeera International, Zee

News, NDTV India, NDTV 24 × 7, Sun News, PTV News, ARY News, Star News, CCTV9, Channel News Asia, and the ABS-CBN News Channel overlap in transnational reach and influence. In India, it is difficult to pin down the precise number of rolling channels because many news stations are offering rolling content and current affairs programs. Pradip N. Thomas (2010) has highlighted certain key issues such as media concentration, commodification, intellectual property, media policy and governance, audio-visual trade and informationalization, and the cross-sectoral digital economy.

Indian Media and Political Economy

The political economy of media has long-term issues which offer a critical point of thinking and views on mainstream media and its development in India. It raises questions about the nature of journalism and its relationship to democratic practices, such as regarding how media firms and markets operate. We can see the political character of the press regarding class, caste, gender, economic inequality, the communication policymaking process, and regulation. The political economy of the media also focuses on public and private broadcasting and the establishment of alternative media institutions and systems for the free flow of information in society. The media system in India has always been the beneficiary of massive subsidies. The largest media firms receive extraordinary subsidies ranging from monopoly licenses to television and radio frequencies, a monopoly on cable television, satellite television systems, copyright, and much more.

Corporate bodies, real estate agents, political party leaders, businesspersons, chit fund (savings) companies, liquor barons, seed companies, societies, trusts, journalist-managers, and sometimes stockholders often control media organizations in India, where there are no cross-media ownership restrictions. Everybody wants to start a newspaper; then they go on to start television news channels and FM radio stations. There is no diversity of content and creativity on the public agenda for pressurizing the state. Every channel has its own agenda and vested interest in launching television channels. It is not that the television news industry is profit making: it has only 13–15% of target rating point (TRP) ratings. However, 24-hour television channels are mushrooming. The TV news industry makes no profits, but it can create other profit-making options for the owner.

The promoters and controllers of media groups hold interests in many other business interests, often using media for the benefit of their business. There are a few instances of promoters who have used the profits from their media operations to diversify into other (unrelated) businesses. The growing corporatization of the Indian media shows how large industrial conglomerates are acquiring an interest in media groups. There is also an increasing convergence between the creators/producers of media content and those who distribute/disseminate that content.

In India's media landscape, the number of publications, radio stations, television channels, and websites is a reliable guarantor of plurality, diversity, and consumer choice. There were over 82,000 publications registered with the Registrar of Newspapers on March 31, 2011. There are over 250 FM radio stations in the country. The Ministry of Information and Broadcasting has allowed nearly 800 television channels to uplink or downlink from the country, including 300 that claim to be television channels broadcasting "news and current affairs." There is an unspecified number of websites aimed at Indians. In India, which still is home to the largest number of illiterates and poor and malnourished people on earth, there has been a breathtaking proliferation of mass media. It is, however, safe to say that the bulk of the press today represents something positive for the transformation of democracy. By its very nature, the press empowers and liberates. In a competitive system, the media act as useful instruments to check authority and promote the public good. Healthy doubt, questioning authority, humility, independence, pure anger at injustice, tolerance of difference, and respect for diversity are the hallmarks of Indian media. These are also the vital ingredients of a democratic society.

Conclusion

Today in India, there is a two-tier television communication system/process of broadcasting. On the one hand there is the mouthpiece of the state and the ruling party in the name of the state-owned media, Doordarshan and allied channels, which are under the control of Ministry of Information and Broadcasting. On the other is the private satellite channels, which are owned, managed, and controlled by the upper classes and capitalist-oriented people functioning in a top-down model. The number of television channels has grown exponentially; the ownership or monopoly of the state-run television has transferred from the state to the private sphere; the content of television has diversified; and advertising revenue and viewership have increased tremendously. Still, television is in the hands of the ruling government or the upper class or multinational corporations.

Today, there is no longer a monopoly of state control of television and there seems to be a plurality in this area. Television news channels, still serving the dominant political interests, ignore the interests of tribal groups, women, and the urban and rural poor. The media can meet the interests of these audiences only when ownership and production of television move into their hands in the form of community television. Though there are many challenges for community broadcasting in India, it is a goal worth pursuing. While the spaces on satellites are abundant, such channels are not able to fill the content and work the software.

Regional news television channels allow for more democratic space in comparison to national and international news and entertainment programs. The existing 18 diverse languages play a vital role in the dissemination of information, education, and entertainment, which is not discussed much in Western media theories and practices. Also, there is little discussion of television studies in India as compared to film studies. Not only is television dependent on the film industry and film-related texts for sustaining television medium, this also seems to be the case with television studies as well.

Topics for Discussion

1. Do you agree with the assertion that mass media will be a threat to the democracy, plurality, and social responsibility of the media in India?
2. How can the public prevent the corruption caused by media moguls who utilize the medium as a tool to promote personal interests?
3. Can the development interests of the poor population be better served by traditional media or by broadcast media? Give reasons for your answer.

Notes

1. The term 'global village' is associated with Canadian-born Marshall McLuhan's books *The Gutenberg Galaxy: The Making of Typographic Man* (1962) and *Understanding Media* (1964). McLuhan described how

the globe has been contracted to a village by electronic technology and the instantaneous movement of information from every quarter to every point at the same time (McLuhan 1964).

2. Jhabua Development Communication Project, Satellite. More at http://www.indianetzone.com/42/jhabua_development_communication_project.htm (accessed Jan. 11, 2017).

Bibliography

Acharya, Rabi Narayan. 1987. *Television in India: A Sociological Study of Policies and Perspectives.* Delhi: Manas Publications.

Agrawal, Binod.C and Mira.B Aghi. 1987. *Television and the Indian Child: A Handbook.* New Delhi: UNICEF.

Benjamin, Walter, Hannah Arendt, and Harry Zohn. 1970. *Illuminations.* London: Jonathan Cape.

Blog, Gaurav's. 2010. CommonWealth Games…UnCommonWealth Opportunities…. http://www.gauravblog.com.

Chakravarthy, N. 1986. *A Vision for Indian Television.* New Delhi: NAMEDIA.

Chatterji, P.C. 1991. *Broadcasting in India.* New Delhi: Sage Publications.

Cottle, S. and M. Rai. 2008. Television News in India: Mediating Democracy and Difference. *International Communication Gazette* 70, no. 1 (February 1, 2008): 76–96. doi:10.1177/1748048507084579.

Dasgupta, Paramita, Usha Ramachandra, and Ashita Allamraju. 2009. *Report on Cross Media Ownership in India.* Hyderabad: Administrative Staff College of India.

Dhawan, B. D. 1973. Television in India: Retrospect and Prospect. *Economic and Political Weekly* 8, no. 28 (July 14, 1973).

Ghose, Bhaskar. 2005. *Doordarshan Days.* New Delhi: Penguin, Viking.

Golding, O, and G, Murdock. 2000. Culture, Communications and Political Economy. In *Mass Media and Society*, ed. James Curran and Michael Gurevitch. New York: Oxford University Press.

Gupta, Nilanjana. 1998. *Switiching Channels: Ideologies of Television in India.* Delhi: Oxford University Press.

Herman, Edward S., and Noam Chomsky. 1988. *Manufacturing Consent: The Political Economy of the Mass Media.* New York: Pantheon Books.

Horkheimer, Max, Theodor W., Adorno, and John Cumming. 1997. *The Dialectic of Enlightenment (Verso Classics).* New York: Verso Books.

Kohli-Khandekar, Vanita, and Peter Mukerjea. 2006. *The Indian Media Business*, 2nd ed. Delhi: SAGE Publications.

Kumar, K.M. 2003. Mixed Signals: Radio Broadcasting Policy in India. *Economic and Political Weekly.*

Kumar, Keval J. 2005. *Mass Communication in India*, 3rd ed. India: Jaico Publishing House.

Majumdar, Boria. 2010. How the CWG Can Make or Break Doordarshan. http://www.friendsofprasarbharati.org/cwg.htm.

Mankekar, Purnima. 1999. *Screening Culture, Viewing Politics: An Ethnography of Television, Womanhood, and Nation in Post-Colonial India*. Durham: Duke University Press.

McLuhan, Marshall. 1964. *Understanding Media: The Extensions of Man*, 4th ed. London: Routledge & Kegan Paul.

Mehta, Nalin. 2008. *India on Television: How Satellite News Channels Have Changed the Way We Think and Act*. New Delhi: HarperCollins Publishers India, a joint venture with the India Today Group.

Mehta, Nalin (ed.). 2009. *Television in India: Satellites, Politics and Cultural Change*. London: Taylor & Francis.

Menon, Mridula. 2008. *Indian Television and Video Programmes: Trends and Policies*. New Delhi: Kanishka Publishing House.

Ministry of Information and Broadcasting. 1996. *Broadcasting Bill: Issues and Perspectives and Broadcasting Law for India*. New Delhi: Ministry of Information and Broadcasting. www.mib.nic.in.

Munshi, Shoma. 2009. *Prime Time Soap Operas on Indian Television*. New Delhi: Routledge India.

Pavarala, Vinod and Kanchan Kumar Mallik. 2007. *Other Voices: The Struggle for Community Radio in India*. New Delhi: Sage Publications.

Rajagopal, Arvind. 2001. *Politics After Television: Religious Nationalism and the Reshaping of the Indian Public; [Hindu Nationalism and the Reshaping of the Public in India]*. Cambridge, UK: Cambridge University Press.

Sarabhai, Vikram. 1969. Indian Television: Today and Tomorrow. *The Society for International Development conference*. New Delhi: The Society for International Development conference.

Sarabhai, Vikram. 1974. *Television for Development, Science Policy, and National Development*, ed. Kamla Chowdhury. New Delhi: Macmillan.

Sushil, K.S. 2006. *Globalization of Indian Broadcasting*. New Delhi: Raj Publication.

Telecom Regulatory Authority of India. 2013. *Technical Interoperability of DTH Set Top Boxes—2010*. New Delhi: Consultation Paper No.11: Telecom Regulatory Authority of India.

Thakurtha, Paranjoy Guha. 2012. Media Ownership Trends in India. Accessed 2012. www.thehoot.org.

The Working Group on Software for Doordarshan (PC Joshi Committee). 1985. The Communication Revolution—Towards Our Own Version. *An Indian Personality for Television*. New Delhi: Ministry of I&B, Publications Division.

Thota, Bhavanarayana. 2009. *Television Journalism*. Hyderabad: NextGen Media.
Thota, Bhavanarayana. 2008. *Telugu News Channels: Struggling for Survival*.
Thussu, D. K. 2007. The 'Murdochization' of News? The Case of Star TV in India. *Media, Culture & Society* 29, no. 4 (July 1, 2007): 593–611. doi:10.1177/0163443707076191.
Vilanilam, J. V. 1998. The Socio-Cultural Dynamics of Indian Television: From SITE to Insight to Privatisation. *Media Asia* 25, no. 26.
Vilanilam, J.V. 2005. *Mass Communication in India: A Sociological Perspective*. New Delhi: Sage Publications.
Vishweshwar Rao, P. L. 2007. News Papers Have Responsibility. *Round Table Conference on Media-Business: Regulating Line*. Hyderabad: AP Press Academy and Andhra Pradesh Union of Working Journalists.
Williams, Raymond. 1974. *Television: Technology and Cultural Form (Technosphere)*. London: HarperCollins Distribution Services.
Yashpal. 1978. The Crucial Decision. *Seminar* 232, no. Special Issue on "The Other TV".

CHAPTER 6

Television, Political Imagery, and Elections in India

Nagamallika Gudipaty

Private Television: Ownership and Politics

The private satellite television channels in India began to beam programs in the 1990s, bringing a whole new experience to Indian viewers; until then they were subjected to content wholly owned and produced by Doordarshan, the public broadcaster of the Government of India. Doordarshan, which held a monopoly over the airwaves until 1991, gave way to satellite and cable television channels that grew steadily in number.[1] The total number of private and government-owned TV channels doubled from 461 to 827 between 2009 and 2015 (www.mib.gov.in). Of these, news and current affairs channels account for more than 400 (www.mib.gov.in), which is roughly half of the total number of channels, an indication of the increased interest in news-based channels. The

Nagamallika Gudipaty's current research is in political communication and journalism studies. In this chapter, she discusses how media framing affects the audience's perceptions and attitudes about politicians and political parties.

N. Gudipaty (✉)
Hyderabad, Telangana, India

E.K. Ngwainmbi (ed.), *Citizenship, Democracies, and Media Engagement among Emerging Economies and Marginalized Communities*,
DOI 10.1007/978-3-319-56215-5_6

reasons seem more political than economic, as the maximum number of channels began operations either before the elections held in 2009 or before the next elections held in 2014. Though it is far more expensive to run a news channel than an entertainment channel and more costly to apply for a news channel license (Kumara, 12 July 2014), the number of news channels increased dramatically. According to the Telecom Regulatory Authority of India (TRAI), the net worth of a company has to be Rs 20 crore (US$3 million) to apply for a news channel license, while it is Rs 5 crore (US$0.76 million) for a non-news channel (Kumara 2014). It is also significant that in addition to businesses, political parties and persons with political affiliation own or control increasing sections of the media in India (Thakurtha 2012).

The non-political promoters and controllers of media groups hold interests in other firms as well, often using their media outlets to further their interests (Thakurtha 2012). Owning media organizations makes it easy to access political circles and government. Back in the 1950s and 1960s, the Tatas, Birlas, and the Jain[2] group owned the daily newspapers the *Statesman*, the *Hindustan Times*, and the *Times of India*, respectively.[3] They were synonymous with the corporate world, being the architects of modern industrial India, but for a while they were into the publication of newspapers for the proximity it provided to the political class, before they withdrew due to their own internal problems (Thakurtha 2012). Similarly, in the south of India, Ramoji Rao of the Eenadu group in Andhra Pradesh, who initially sold pickles under the brand name Priya, followed by ownership of a chit fund (savings) company, Margadarsi, which continues to flourish, forayed into media in the 1970s with the launch of the Telugu-language newspaper *Eenadu* (meaning "today"). Ramoji Rao is known for his close links with the government in the state from which he hails, Andhra Pradesh, as well as in the neighboring state of Telangana where his major business interests lie. The corporate houses recognize the power of private television channels to confer a legitimate profile in an increasingly uncertain political and regulatory environment. The media are perceived as active political collaborators due to the allegiances of their owners and editors to political parties. For politicians who own media and seek to influence voters, television, one of the prime channels to reach out to the electorate, has provided an excellent opportunity (Thakurtha 2012). Politics itself has become a business which needs constant media exposure. Almost every major national or regional party across India owns publications or radio and television channels or has some interest in them, which exposes the close links between media and politics. For example, one national party, the Communist Party of India (Marxist), has its own publications like *People's Democracy, The Marxist* at the national level,[4] and *Deshabhimani*, published by Chintha Printing and Publishing, *Kairali TV, and People TV* on a regional basis, apart from several weeklies and fortnightlies published from all the great cities and in various Indian languages (Ghatak and Thakurtha 2012). Sometimes family ties override party loyalties, as in the case of one Congress Party leader who controlled the News 24 Hindi News channel along with his wife, who happens to be the sister of the opposition party member. Between the two, they own other channels named Aapno 24 and E24, under BAG Films and Media in the television space, and Dhamaal 24 in the radio space (Ghatak and Thakurtha 2012).

Provincial Broadcast Media Ownership and Political Ambition

Zee News, a national Hindi channel, is owned by Subhash Chandra, who plans to stand for elections under the Bharatiya Janata Party (BJP) ticket. India TV is the property of Rajat Sharma, a sympathizer of the BJP. India News belongs to a member of the BJP and Reliance Industries, which bought the controlling shares in new channel CNN-IBN (CNN-Indian Broadcasting Network, now called CNN News 18), which led to the ousting of senior journalist Rajdeep Sardesai, known to be an opposer of the BJP's Narendra Modi. In the state of Tamil Nadu, the erstwhile leader of the regional opposition party, Dravida Munnetra Kazhagam (DMK), controls Sun TV, Sun News, KTV, Sun Music, Chutti TV, Sumangali Cable, Adithya TV, Chintu TV, Kiran TV, Khushi TV, Udaya Comedy, Udaya Music, Gemini TV, Gemini Comedy, and Gemini Movies.

He also controls the newspaper *Dinakaran*, as well as Suryan FM 93.5 and Red FM 93.5 in the radio space. Sun TV is controlled by Sun TV Network, Suryan FM is owned by Kal Radio, Red FM belongs to South Asia FM, and *Dinakaran* is the property of Kal Publications. Kal Radio and South Asia FM are, in turn, subsidiaries of Sun TV Network. The DMK party chief himself owns Kalaignar TV under the company of the same name (Ghatak and Thakurtha 2012). Similarly, the late

Jayalalitha, the erstwhile chief minister of Tamil Nadu and a member of AIDMK, had Jaya TV as her voice box.

In Telangana, the English daily *Deccan Chronicle*[5] is loyal to the Congress Party, while the daily *Eenadu* Telugu and ETV have strong political connections with the main opposition party, the Telugu Desam Party (TDP). Similarly, the Telugu daily *Sakshi* and Sakshi TV are owned and controlled by Y.S. Jagan Mohan Reddy, via Indira Television (Sakshi TV) and Jagati Publications, the holding company for the daily. Y.S. Jagan is a sitting member of the legislative assembly (MLA) in the state of Andhra Pradesh, and heads a regional political party, the YSR Congress Party (YSRCP), while *Namaste Telangana,* a Telugu daily, and T News are owned by the holding company Telangana Broadcasting, owned by K. Chandrasekhar Rao, the Chief Minister of Telangana. Not all media companies have direct links with politicians, as some choose the path of surrogacy, visible in the information filed with the Registrar of Companies (Ninan 2013). Some businesspeople either have a share in media companies or give their shares to media companies in exchange for favorable news. The Government of India warned stock investors against paying heed to the advice provided by business channels, as there was the danger of playing up an advertiser than providing genuine investment advice (Thakur 2013). One of the effects of such a symbiotic relationship in the realm of politics is to exploit the media, especially television, to create a larger-than-life image of themselves. The outcome of such framing can help win elections, despite the limitations of reality that dog politicians.

Using the techniques of framing, this chapter explores how two politicians—one at the national and the other at the regional level—are framed by the media. Prime Minister Narendra Modi's historic win in 2014 at the national level and Y.S. Jagan Mohan Reddy's win at the regional level in the state of Andhra Pradesh are examples of how television framed these politicians to create a favorable public opinion in the electorate, despite charges of corruption, nepotism, and communalism.

Theoretical Perspectives of Framing

Framing theory is understood as an extension of agenda setting, in the larger concept of media effects (Scheufele 1999). According to Weaver et al. (1998), agenda setting is concerned with the salience of *issues*, while frame setting or the second level of agenda setting is concerned with the salience of *issue attributes* (Scheufele 2000). In short, the frame is an emphasis on the salience of some aspects of a topic (Vreese 2003). Empirical studies show that the perceived importance of specific frames rather than salience is the key variable (Scheufele 2000). Broadly speaking, frames can be examined as the outcomes of journalistic norms or organizational constraints, which is called the sociological approach to framing research (Pan and Kosicki 1993). It is based on Heider (1944), attribution theory, and Goffman's (1974) frame analysis.

Heider (1944) assumes that individuals cannot understand the world fully in its complexity and so try to infer underlying causal relations from sensory information. He said that attribution is the link between observed behavior and a person who is considered to be responsible for his or her actions. Drawing on this, Iyengar (1991) argued that people try to make sense of political issues by reducing them to questions of responsibility. This can be responsibility toward social or individual problems, or societal responsibility at large. Goffman (1974) in his frame analysis says that individuals cannot understand the world fully and therefore every person actively classifies, organizes, and interprets life experiences to make sense of the world around him or her. Such experiences are dependent on schemes of interpretation called primary frameworks (Goffman 1974), which can be classified as natural and social. Natural frames identify events as physical occurrences or sensory experiences, taking quotes literally and not attributing any social forces to the causation of events. On the other hand, social frameworks view events as socially driven occurrences, which help to "locate, perceive, identify and label" (Goffman 1974) them with intentional goals and manipulations onrhetoric carried the day the part of other social players (people). Social frameworks are built on natural frameworks and the data interpreted, processed, and communicated is strongly influenced by these. In contrast, a psychological approach (Fischer and Johnson 1986) examines frames as individual means of processing and structuring incoming information (Scheufele 2000).

There are two concepts in framing: media frames and audience frames (Scheufele 1999), depending on the outlook. To Gamson, a media frame is a central organizing idea or story line that provides meaning (Gamson and Modigliani 1987). Frames are abstractions that work to organize or structure message meaning (Davie 2010). Media frames are part of the process by which individuals construct meaning. Building public opinion is part of the process whereby journalists develop and crystallize meaning in public discourse (Gamson and Modigliani 1989). Gitlin (1980) defines media frames as persistent selection, emphasis, and exclusion. In political events, the media actively set the frames of reference that readers or viewers use to interpret and discuss public events (Tuchman 1978) and "spin a story" (Neuman et al. 1992) using their professional knowledge and taking the pulse of the audience, keeping in mind their organizational alignment and limitations. In essence, the way something is presented to the public (called the "frame") influences the choices people make about how to process that information. Audience frames can then be defined as mentally stored clusters of ideas that guide individuals' processing of information (Entman 1993).

Frames can be identified through either an inductive or a deductive approach. While the inductive approach requires identifying the frames from the text, the deductive approach allows one to examine frames with a priori definitions. The inductive approach does not allow for generalization, unlike the deductive approach. There are rhetorical structures in news frames evident through symbolic devices like metaphors, exemplars, catchphrases, depictions, and visual images (Gamson and Modigliani 1989). In other words, media framing often manifests itself by the choice of some keywords, key phrases, and images that reinforce a particular representation of the reality and a specific emotion toward it, and the omission of other elements that could suggest a different perspective or trigger a different sentiment. It can also be observed that the journalist selects whom to quote, what to quote, and where this quotation will be located in the story.

News discourse may be perceived as employing these framing devices with effects on the audience (Cappela and Jameison 1997; Iyengar 1991; Norris 1995; Patterson 1993). The framing effect is one where salient attributes of messages render particular thoughts applicable, resulting in their activation and the use of evaluations (Price et al. 1997). Such frames may be issue-specific news frames which are related to pertinent or specific topics, or generic frames which transcend themes and can be identified in relation to various topics (Vreese 2002). Valkenburg and Semetko (2000) study using generic frames identified some common frames that occur in the news, like conflict frames, attribution of responsibility, economic consequences, human impact, and morality frames. According to Valkenburg and Semetko (2000), a *conflict frame* emphasizes the conflicts between individuals, groups, or institutions as a means of capturing audience interest. A *human interest frame* brings forth the human face or emotional angle to the presentation of an event, issue, or problem. An *economic consequences frame* reports events, issues, or problem regarding the consequences they will have for individuals, groups, a region, or a country. A *morality frame* puts the event, issue, or problem in the context of religious tenets or moral prescriptions. A *responsibility frame* presents an issue or problem in such a way as to attribute responsibility for its cause or solution either to the government or to the individual or group. Such frames help in "the perception, information processing, attitudes, decision making and behavior" (Vreese 2003) of individuals. Strategically framed news focuses on winning and losing, and also on the language of war, games, and competition, which contains performers, critics, and audiences. It focuses on candidates' style and perceptions and gives weight to polls and candidates' standings (Capella and Jamieson 1996). This theory is similar to Patterson's (1993) game frames, which refer to strategies and predictions of electoral success, emphasizing a candidate's position in the electoral race.

Using the above theoretical aspects of framing, this chapter analyzes two political leaders to determine the dominant frames that emerged during the last Indian general elections held in 2014. Both leaders were unique in their strategies, yet were successfully framed in the media. A generic frame analysis using some of Fairhurst and Sarr's (1996) rhetorical framing devices, like metaphor, stories, myths, legends, rituals, ceremonies, slogan, jargon, catchphrases, artifacts, contrast, and spin, was employed for the framing analysis.

Electioneering in India

A series of changes took place in the modes and methods of election campaigns in India, from the time of independence till the present. In the early days, campaigning was through public meetings, rallies, and door-to-door visits by political leaders and grassroots workers supporting the party (Karan 2009), which Norris (2007) classifies as the premodern style of campaigning, also witnessed across all nations. The current phase of election campaigns is understood to be characterized by the decline of traditional forms of party campaigning, such as local rallies and door-to-door canvassing, and by new developments like the growth of spin doctors and political consultants (Norris 2007).

A series of case studies has documented these trends in a range of established and newer democracies (Norris 2007). Such campaigns can be understood as the evolutionary processes of modernization that simultaneously transform party organizations, the news media, and the electorate (Norris 2007). In India, however, one can see that the traditional methods remain the primary mode, which the modern methods are integrated into, but do not displace. Though the national political parties use more modern approaches like political consultants and advertising, party websites, and social media, the regional parties work at the grassroots level, meeting their party workers and conducting door-to-door campaigns. However, newspapers and television are the media that are integrated into modern and traditional election campaigns at both national and regional levels.

The trendsetter for election analysis in India was psephologist Prannoy Roy, who began election analysis in the 1980s on Doordarshan, the public broadcaster, before the entry of private channels. He became a household name and later ventured into his own enterprise, New Delhi TV (NDTV), a 24/7 private news channel in English. Extensive election coverage began on private news channels like Zee TV and Sony for the first time in the 1990s (Karan 2009). Television became the mainstay for live election coverage from then on. Prominent television anchors were hired to provide media coaching to party spokespersons and influential political leaders (Karan 2009). Political analysts, journalists, and scholars anchored television programs to analyze trends with extensive poll data, voter perceptions, and swing factors that were understood by a steadily growing and more sophisticated audience across the country (India Today 2004). A new dynamic was introduced into the political process with 24-hour news, as politicians were visible on a daily basis. The politicians who were television savvy survived the new medium and knew they had to be in a mode of permanent campaigning with 24/7 coverage. The daily television camera symbolized the scrutiny of public opinion (Mehta 2009, p. 49).

Presentable and articulate party spokespersons became regulars in all television debates, offering opinion and comment on any issue. As "modern" forms of political campaigns created new necessities, the institutions had to mold their campaign strategies to suit (Reddy 2009, p. 232). Although the relevance of interpersonal communication continued, the soundbites and visuals of election speeches and road shows became a prominent part of all election strategies. The inclusion of opinion polls sponsored by print and electronic media furthered an interest in politics among the Indian electorate (Karan 2009).

Rajiv Gandhi, the then leader of the Indian National Congress (INC) party, was the first to hire professionals in 1984 to handle advertising for the general elections through the ad agency Rediffusion (Narayanswamy 2009). It was entrusted with planning the 1984 election campaign at the national level through press, posters, and speeches by Indira Gandhi (his mother and a former prime minister, who was shot dead prior to the elections) through audio cassettes distributed for free. The campaign also included showing short films on Indira Gandhi and Rajiv Gandhi in each village through mobile vans, as there was then no satellite television or internet.

Rajiv Gandhi's win in the parliamentary elections by a huge margin of votes (Karan 2009) was attributed to a sympathy vote, though the sympathy could be sustained with the help of audio and visual media. At the regional level, two chief ministers came to power for two consecutive terms using similar election strategies in the 1990s. Cassettes and short films showcasing their programs and achievements were distributed freely in villages by Narendra Modi, the then chief minister of Gujarat, and Chandrababu Naidu in Andhra Pradesh, both known for being media savvy. This was also the time when regional parties gained prominence, and the era of coalition politics came to stay. National parties like the INC and the BJP began to rely on their regional partners to garner votes in the states. It was the BJP that ushered in the era of social media in elections, with Modi's trending tweets becoming popular among the youth in the 2014 elections.

The political affiliations of most channels in India are public knowledge, while a large number of channels (over 800) provide multiple viewpoints to the discerning audience. However, media as an information source during elections is only secondary for the marginalized class, as it is welfare schemes and other beneficial programs, apart from social factors like caste, religion, and community, that determine their loyalty. Through a complete information overload, it is the opinion leaders and cue-givers that influence the electorate. Television acts as a reinforcer of the public image of the party and leader if she or he can cleverly mold it into a continued point of influence using sentiment and rhetoric. If the editorial content is under the control of owner-politicians, it has a multiplier effect.

In pre-television days, the politicians' rhetoric carried the day. For instance, in 1990 the then president of the BJP L.K. Advani held a dramatic road show called a "rath yatra" (a chariot campaign where a mobile van was converted into a motorized chariot) in North India, traveling 10,000 km by road from Somnath in Gujarat to Ayodhya traversing (L.K. Advani's website 1990). The idea was to evoke memories of India's glorious past using religion as a powerful tool to help lay a solid basis for the rightist BJP's future. The yatra paid rich dividends, and the BJP rose to prominence despite the limited reach of television at that time. The yatra was covered in brief news bulletins by the public broadcaster Doordarshan, as there were no private channels present. Though the road show followed the traditional form of political campaigning, it had a great impact on the 1991 general elections. Two decades later, in 2011, Advani undertook another rath yatra in a bid to highlight the corruption of the then ruling Congress Party. However, in the changed media sphere, the yatra, though covered by several channels, did not impress the electorate. Advani's waning charm, similar charges of corruption against the leaders of his party elsewhere in the country[6] as he was leveling against the Congress Party, no clear strategy for rebuilding a favorable image in a changed political atmosphere, and media conditions meant that it evoked little or no interest among the electorate.

It was Modi who was the man to be reckoned with by that time. He took oath as the chief minister of the state of Gujarat in 2001 and over the next two decades built his image assiduously as the architect of the future India, being sworn in as prime minister of India in 2014. The media played a major role in his long journey of ups and downs. His image took a beating in the media after the 2002 riots in Gujarat, six months after he became chief minister. He was charged with actively abetting the arson and killing of thousands of Muslims. In the next decade and a half, he recreated his image as the man who heralded a new India using public relations professionals and spins doctors via a media sympathetic to the party and the person. His long-term strategy, which began in 2012 through the efficient use of social media and traditional media, culminated at the time of the 2014 general elections, paying rich dividends.

Another case is the strategic use of the television channel Sakshi, owned by Y.S. Jagan Mohan Reddy, MLA and leader of the opposition party in the state of Andhra Pradesh. He was the son of the popular former chief minister of Andhra Pradesh, Y.S. Rajasekhar Reddy, who had died following an air crash 6 months after being elected to power for a second consecutive term. Right from the inception of his channel just before the state elections in 2009, Y.S. Jagan used his channel to create a wave of sympathy after his father's death through "odarpu yatras" or "consolation trips" to reach out to the families grieving for his father's death. Several other yatras or road shows using his mother and sister followed. These road shows were televised on his channel and went a long way in creating and sustaining his people-friendly political image.

However, television or any media alone would not have succeeded in fashioning these pictures without the traditional campaigns and rallies. While the media allow for framing larger-than-life images during the "permanent campaigns," it is the rallies and road shows before elections that help in reinforcing the images of these politicians.

Methodology

The present study used a random selection of ten election campaign speeches and road shows of two politicians, Narendra Modi and Y.S. Jagan Mohan Reddy, from the election coverage uploaded on YouTube on the announcement of elections in March 2014 until the end of the final round of elections in May 2014. Some elements differed in the coverage of both the politicians. All of the speeches by Modi, as the prime ministerial candidate in the Hindi language, were covered live on all national channels, with subtitles in English in English news channels. Y.S. Jagan's speeches were also covered live and found space predominantly on his channel Sakshi TV (in Telugu), while other avenues covered his rallies along with other political party leaders. The dominant images that emerged from the analysis of the coverage of these two politicians could be understood through the use of visuals and rhetoric (metaphors, exemplars, contrast, spin, and other devices), and how such images were reinforced in the minds of the audience with a positive spin.

Media frames have a multiplier effect due to the unlimited time accessed by these politicians, given the nature of ownership of television channels as previously discussed. Since television is still the most popular medium in India, the impact of this audiovisual medium is at maximum compared to other media and forms of communication used in the campaigns. The news channels owned by and sympathetic to the two leaders gave them continuous coverage over the period. While Modi used the media strategically to get constant coverage through channels sympathetic to him, Y.S. Jagan got coverage on Sakshi, which was his channel long before elections were announced. At the time of the elections, Modi's election rallies and road shows were aired live on some of the prominent channels and in press owned by loyal supporters who wanted to build him up as India's savior (Mishra 2015). Similarly, Y.S. Jagan's channel Sakshi covered his election rallies and road shows under the garb of "consolation trips" right from its inception. As these leaders were unique in their own ways, all the social frames present in the study cannot be generalized.

Analysis

Case 1: Building Narendra Modi's Image

A Brief Background

Modi's ascent to the post of chief minister of the state of Gujarat in 2001 coincided with the Western rhetoric of "global war on terrorism,"a view that aligned with that of the rightist Hindutva-based BJP (Jose 2012). In 2002, five months after he took the oath as chief minister, one of the worst communal riots in India broke out in Gujarat, an alleged "reaction" to the attack by Muslims in Godhra (in the state of Gujarat) on a group of Bajrang Dal activists (a wing of a predominant radical Hindu group called the Vishwa Hindu Parishad or VHP) who were traveling on a train. The Gujarat riots were the first explosion of communal violence to play out in real time on live television (Jose 2012). The active involvement and abetment by the ruling BJP[7] during the riots led to a vertical split in the party, with the hardliners supporting Modi and moderates against him. The detailed coverage in the media with vivid pictures and graphics on television had a devastating effect on the nation as well as on Modi's image. He was an unwelcome figure internationally, with several countries including the UK[8] and USA refusing him entry.

The first reinvention of Modi as a pro-business and development man began in 2008 when he welcomed one of the leading businesspeople in India, Ratan Tata, to put up his car plant in Gujarat. Within weeks of the plant's inauguration in June 2010, both Ford and Peugeot approached Gujarat, seeking plots to build their factories, since Modi promised several incentives.[9] This was covered widely in the media (Jose 2012). Modi held international business summits annually, inviting investors across the world to invest in his state. These initiatives were widely publicized in the media and helped to project him and his state as a fast-growing economic "model state" in India. Modi's government relentlessly provided the media with positive stories of efficient administration, rapid construction, and economic growth (Jose 2012), though the reality according to the statistics was different from that projected.[10]

Modi's transformation into a statesman began in 2010 as a precursor to his ambition to be the prime minister of India. The conversion of his image was powered by a sophisticated public relations campaign, but the spin was based on some facts like his capable administration and lack of interest in money, unlike the majority of politicians in India. However, his interests lay elsewhere—in power—which appealed to many people who viewed him as a strong leader who could lead the nation. Since his appointment as chief minister in 2001, he had won two subsequent state elections in Gujarat, each with a two-thirds majority. Known to be a man with an extreme nature, his passion for getting to the top drove him single-mindedly.[11] Given his complex personal background and the extensive and intense campaign, it is not easy to cover all aspects. The predominant frames that made the transition from a chief minister of a state to the prime minister of a nation are analyzed here.

Framing Narendra Modi

The Numbers Game

The game frames (Patterson 1993) were predominant in the election campaign coverage, as the media constantly mentioned the number of seats won by each party, the losses of other party leaders, the margins by which a candidate won or lost, or the huge difference between winner and loser. The emphasis on the number of seats won by the BJP under Modi's leadership, with visuals and graphics to reinforce the numbers, was a constant reminder of the Modi factor in the win. One clear strategy was his "Mission 272+" exhorting his party cadre to win more than 272 seats along with their allies. In the final tally, all channels emphasized the historic nature of the win, as the "282 seats that the party won in the 2014 general elections was on its own [meaning without any allies] becoming the largest single party to come to power at the national level after 25 years." This was attributed to Modi and his leadership. Another predominant frame that recurred was the number of rallies he covered before and during elections. He took part in "437 big rallies, participated in a total 5827 public interfacing events and travelled over three lakh kilometers [190,000 miles] across 25 states during the elections," which no other leader did. He was seen as pro-business (due to his business summits in Gujarat), and a significant amount of money that was donated and spent by the party added to his worldwide acceptance. A large fraction of his election funding was from NRIs who supported Modi: "The Bharatiya Janata Party as a political party was funded by leading industrialist-capitalist-corporate of the country with huge amounts exceeding 10,000 crores [1,00,000 million USD]." Though this was far above the Election Commission's stipulations, none of the media raised a query.

"NaMo" and Nationalism

With a slogan that closely resonated with US president Barack Obama's campaign, **Na**rendra **Mo**di—NaMo for short—led India to believe that he was "NaMo—the change that India needs." NaMo is also a Sanskrit word meaning "salutation," a fall back on Hindu tradition. The BJP is identified as a right-wing Hindutva party and Modi as a conservative leader given his moorings in Rashtriya Swayam Sevak (RSS), a nationalist Hindu group. Nationalism is a recurring theme in all his election speeches, which are laced with Hindu mythology and love for the land. A great orator, his election speeches began with greeting the motherland, "*Bharat Mata ki Jai.*" His party slogan was very straightforward and catchy, "*Ab Ki Bar, Modi Sarkar*" (this time round, it is Modi's government), even for the non-Hindi-speaking population. Similarly, a musical video that was the party anthem was titled "My promise to this land, I will not allow this country to perish." Such traditional symbolism recreated pride in the nation's past, while Modi was seen as the heir to such a rich legacy. In contrast, the Congress Party was headed by Sonia Gandhi, whose Italian ancestry made her the "other," as the mental images of her origins were reinforced by her struggle with a foreign tongue while addressing rallies in Hindi. With each election rally, the spirit of nationalism in the new form of "Hindutva" gained ground among the electorate, with Modi being the natural leader. One of his speeches was punctuated with "My idea of India…" 19 times, a clear rhetoric that framed him as a visionary whose aim was to bring back past glory.

The Disciplinarian

According to Henry Kissinger, the task of a leader is to "get his people from where they are to where they have not been." Modi promised just that as a leader capable of bringing about a positive change for the nation. The Congress Party, mired in scams under a "silent" prime minister, Manmohan Singh, was framed as "weak" in contrast to the impeccably attired, well-groomed Modi, with a confident demeanor and excellent oratory skills. The most prominent frame was that of Modi against the "rest," as he was portrayed as a one-man army. His announcement as the prime ministerial candidate of the BJP made it easy for people to recall his face. Moreover, he was compared to Sardar Vallabhai Patel, the first Home Minister of an independent India, whose resolve to unite the entire country immediately post-independence earned him the epithet "the iron man of India"—a metaphor that when ascribed to Modi struck a chord with the people. Modi declared that it was "not luck but hard work" that would bring the change he desired, a frame that clearly defined him as a person who is committed to his work.

The Common Chai Wallah:

Another prominent frame to woo the common man was derived from Modi's humble ancestry. As a child, he served tea (*chai walla* in Hindi) in his uncle's tea shop, which made an instant connection with the man on the streets, unlike his Congress Party counterpart Rahul Gandhi and his family, often projected as "royal" and privileged. This led to the creation of an original cultural context, where *chai pe charcha* or "discussion over tea" became part of Modi's electoral campaign. The contrasting imagery was not lost on the electorate, as these debates did not happen in local shops but were telecast in 3D format and streamed live in webcasts for the entire country to watch. In one of his speeches he cleverly used his *chai wallah* background to ask the audience, "Do you want to vote for someone who sells the country or someone who sells tea?" The Congress Party had lost faith among the electorate and was already burdened with an anti-incumbency factor, having served for two consecutive terms, providing a sharp contrast.

Modi's framing as a person with humble beginnings and a disciplined life over other attractions were not lost on the electorate either. For instance, the projection of his mother, a retired school teacher, taking an auto rickshaw to vote, and Modi receiving his mother's blessings in her humble abode, were top stories on every channel. There were debates about his marital status, as it was under wraps for a long time. In fact Modi ran away from home the day he was married at the age of 16 as per the social customs of his caste. He never looked back or accepted his wife. Until his marital status was disclosed during the elections, however, he was projected as a *sanyasi* or someone who renounced this world and all materialism, probably to prove his RSS identity. There was a shift in the narrative after the declaration of his marital status, as his brother compared Modi to "Buddha," who left his wife to renounce the world. Modi was elevated to a godlike status, as a selfless person rather than as a man who abandoned his wife and did not acknowledge her.

The larger-than-life image of Modi took on epic proportions when, bearing a striking similarity to the narrative on his website, a comic published by Gujarat-based Rannade Prakashan and Blue Snail Animation laid out a glossy compilation of stories on Modi's childhood. Titled *Bal Narendra* (child Narendra), the comic describes how a young Modi frees a trapped bird, brings home (and subsequently releases) a young crocodile, and jumps into a lake to save a drowning friend, among other spectacular feats. There was no way to ascertain the authenticity of the story as no author was named (Katyal 2014).

"The Development Man"

The main plank on which Modi built the myth of a change agent for development was the "Gujarat model," advanced under his leadership as a sort of panacea for India's problems. Burdened with the image of the man behind the riots of 2002, Modi resurrected himself successfully through the projection of his home state Gujarat as a model state for the development of the rest of India. The indicators that showed otherwise were not highlighted anywhere in his campaigns. His pet themes of attaining independent power through the use of alternative energy (solar) sources and rooting out corruption struck a chord with all the electorate. Two major issues of concern were the numerous scams in which several leaders and ministers of the Congress Party were involved, and continuing farmers' suicides. Modi's assurance that he would end both made him a strong leader that could lead the nation out of its crisis.

Case 2

Y.S. Jagan Mohan Reddy used an entirely different strategy to woo the audience. While Modi was the man who meant business, Y.S. Jagan used a more emotional approach to frame himself as a man wronged and backstabbed by his party. He is the MLA and present leader of the opposition party in Andhra Pradesh.

Electioneering in Andhra Pradesh

In Andhra Pradesh, media and politics were intrinsically associated from the 1980s when the then charismatic Telugu film hero NT Rama Rao (NTR) floated his own political outfit, the Telugu Desam Party (TDP), which stressed the "pride" of being a Telugu, bringing him to power within nine months of the birth of his party. *Eenadu*, a Telugu daily, and ETV from the same house provided the perfect platform for the regional party led by Rao with a growing and politically active audience (Reddy 2009). Each passing election witnessed a spurt of television channels in Andhra Pradesh that explains how intricately the prospects of the media industry are linked to the political markets (Reddy 2009). For instance, between the election years 2004 and 2014, more than a dozen channels were launched. 2014 was also a watershed in the history of Andhra Pradesh as the state was divided into Andhra and Telangana. Almost all channels serve both the Telugu-speaking states.

The 1980s and 1990s were the eras of the TDP, while it was the Congress Party that was in power from the 2000s until the country bifurcated in 2014, due to the diligent efforts of Y.S. Rajasekhar Reddy, or YSR as he was popularly known, the chief minister of Andhra Pradesh in 2004 and 2009.[12] In his inimitable style of dressing in the *dhoti* (the traditional attire of rural farmers in India), he crisscrossed the state on foot to reach out to the people a year before the elections and continued until the elections. His yatras (walkathons) evoked an enthusiastic public response (Jaffri 2004) as YSR endeared himself to the common man. This strategy was later used by his son Y.S. Jagan Mohan Reddy, who was on constant yatras to win the support of the people, which were regularly telecast on his television channel Sakshi. YSR paved the way for the entry of his son, who was elected as a Member of the Legislative Council (MLC) for the first time in his tenure.

A Brief Background to Y.S. Jagan

In September 2009, 6 months after he took over as chief minister for the second time, YSR died in an air crash. However, before that, his son Y.S. Jagan, who was in the Congress Party at that time, campaigned for the party across the state for the May 2009 elections. He launched a huge publicity campaign through his newspaper (begun in 2008) and TV news channel Sakshi (meaning "witness"), which started operation in March 2009. As the state's two biggest newspapers—*Andhra Jyothi* and *Eenadu*—ran stories exposing government corruption, Sakshi took on the opposition and highlighted the government schemes (Sahi 2009). Soon Sakshi became the biggest opposition yet for the Congress Party, as Y.S. Jagan's ambitious journey to succeed his father as the next chief minister of Andhra Pradesh failed. His plan of being the unanimous choice to succeed his father did not get the approval of Congress Party high command Sonia Gandhi, which led him to quit the Congress and start his own party, the Y.S. Rajasekhar Reddy Congress Party (YSRCP). Y.S. Jagan undertook road shows, meeting people at the grassroots level, similar to his father's strategy to bring to the people the wrongs done to him and his family, covered extensively on his channel Sakshi TV.

Like Modi, Y.S. Jagan had to contend with a negative image after he was implicated and arrested for possessing a disproportionate amount of assets made in a short span of five years, during his father's tenure as the chief minister of Andhra Pradesh. The Central Bureau of Investigation (CBI) alleged that he made quid pro quo arrangements with leading corporates to fund his newspaper and television channel, among several other activities. These deals made him one of the richest politicians in India, owning several businesses in mining and real estate. He was arrested during one of his rallies. With Y.S. Jagan in jail, the mantle fell on his mother and sister to campaign for his party, creating sympathy votes. While the coverage on other channels abated once Y.S. Jagan was arrested,[13] his TV channel Sakshi gave 24/7 coverage to his party's campaign with his mother and sister in charge. The old widow and the young sister came out to plead with voters to bring victory to Jagan *Anna* (elder brother), thereby drawing an emotional bond with the electorate. Massive rallies held in every small village and mandal (subdistrict) drew huge crowds, as reported on Sakshi TV. The predominant frame that emerged in the mother–sister combination was that of "women of the house" brought to the streets due to the evil machinations of the

Congress Party. While the entire electorate saw it as a conspiracy against Y.S. Jagan, the coverage on Sakshi also gave no scope for the electorate to wonder about his unaccounted-for wealth.

Soon after Y.S. Jagan was released on bail after 10 months, he continued with his campaigns until the 2014 elections. The interim period after YSR's death and the bifurcation was one of chaos and disturbance. Two chief ministers changed during this time, while the demand for a separate state of Telangana grew louder, resulting in the center acceding to the request in 2014. Y.S. Jagan contested the election from the residual Andhra state, where his chief rival was Chandrababu Naidu of the TDP. Naidu subsequently won the elections, with Y.S. Jagan becoming the leader of the opposition party with the second highest number of seats won.

The framing of Y.S. Jagan can roughly be divided into two phases between 2009 (when his father died) and 2014 (when a separate state was declared). In the first three years the psychological frames dominated, while in the last two years it was sociological frames. An analysis of the frames that emerged will make clear the changes.

Building Y.S. Jagan Mohan Reddy's Image

Phase 1

"Odarpu Yatra" or Consolation Tour

The pretext for Y.S. Jagan's road shows was unique in the initial days after his father's death. That death in a helicopter crash supposedly sparked off suicides and heart attacks in at least 60 persons in the various districts of the United Andhra Pradesh (www.rediff.com 2009), which was widely reported on Telugu television channels. There is a different debate altogether regarding the authenticity of this claim, but at this juncture, it will be analyzed in the context of framing only. Y.S. Jagan used this to embark on "Odarpu Yatras" or the "Consolation Tours" to console all those who lost Someone in their families in the aftermath of his father's death. These frames established his concern for the electorate who loved his father (and therefore could not accept his death). The connect was reinforced through a highly emotional frame, since he adopted his father's picture with petal showers as the logo of his TV channel. Visuals of Y.S. Jagan in the presence of old people or children against the backdrop of poverty-stricken thatched houses, and an enthusiastic crowd surrounding him captured the picture of a young man setting aside his loss and reaching out to the grieving masses. These frames directed at the poor and women had the desired effect, as they were the two largest vote pullers in the by-elections held in 2011 and 2012. The Sakshi channel built a loyal viewership with positive political vibes in response to the continuous bleeding-heart coverage that it gave to Y.S. Jagan (Shaw 2012). The visuals, songs, and background music in the coverage of the Odarpu Yatras created an overall cinematic experience that captured the public's imagination. The background songs are often takes on popular film songs, creating an immediate connection with the common man who is familiar with such songs. The superimposed images of YSR and Y.S. Jagan meeting the crowds and merging with them furthered the impression of special effects with both the father and son being one with the crowd.

The Wronged Man

Y.S. Jagan's speeches pitted him against the Congress Party as a wronged man fighting for justice (since he was not made the chief minister of Andhra Pradesh after his father's death) versus the powerful enemy. He framed himself as the natural heir to carry on the work of his father. Visuals of old ladies blessing him and babies being thrust into his hands for him to bless helped to create a larger-than-life image. The frames that were set up through his sad yet smiling face showcased him as a Catholic Christian who was wearing the crown of thorns for his father, similar to Jesus Christ, Son of God, who sacrificed his life for his people. Framing Y.S. Jagan in this manner firmly established him as the leader of the masses. His strongly worded speeches are often bordering on insult, lambasting the Congress for insulting the memory of his father, and these were repeatedly telecast. His statements, reiterated in his campaign speeches and broadcast regularly, made Y.S. Jagan out to be the messiah who could continue the many schemes[14] his father had begun. Through the strategic use of his channel, he appropriated the schemes of the Congress Party and made them his own—and presented them as a legacy passed on by his father.

The visuals of Y.S. Jagan giving his trademark grim smile and a "Namaste," greeting old women or embracing them affectionately, carrying babies and kissing them, contribute to the way his political image is being nurtured to make it theatrical and cinematic. Y.S. Jagan has proved that it is not always about being a politically correct leader, but also an actor both political and otherwise, being constantly in the public eye.

Phase 2

The period of uncertainty before the announcement of the new state led to heartburn and disillusionment with the Congress Party in both regions of the country. By 2014, after bifurcation, the enemy changed from the Congress Party to the TDP, as the trend became apparent that it was the latter that would be the main opposition party as the time for elections approached. The Congress Party, which was held responsible for the bifurcation, did not win a single seat in the elections.

The Loved Son/Brother

Y.S. Jagan's strategy during elections did not change much, as he continued to use the death of his father to create sympathy. To that extent, his campaigns followed a similar pattern as in Phase 1. Unlike the opposition leader Naidu, who ruled Andhra Pradesh for two terms before he lost to YSR, Y.S. Jagan has no administrative experience. His trump card is his father, who was a successful chief minister. However, Y.S. Jagan strategically delinked the party, Congress, from the man, YSR. In the final run-up to elections, the media frames that emerged followed a familiar pattern except for minor differences. The shadow of his father never left his speeches. Y.S. Jagan always prefixed references to his father with "late leader and beloved leader" and began all his speeches by referring to the work that his father had done.

In many ways, the frames of the "wronged man" continued, laced with an emotional connection with the audience as a "loving son/brother" of the larger YSR family (meaning the people of the state). Y.S. Jagan's round-the-year visibility through his channel lent credence to his image as someone who is one among the masses. He was a crowd puller with his oratorical skills and attracted huge crowds.

Conclusion

As Price et al. (1997) mention, the framing effect is one where salient attributes of messages render particular thoughts applicable, resulting in their activation and use in evaluation. The analysis makes clear that the cognitive effect on the audience is activated through the various media frames, resulting in a particular evaluation of the two leaders. With the distinct possibility of media content being largely influenced by its political owners, the dominant media frames led to the building of positive images of Modi and Y.S. Jagan. The negatives were absent or minimized. For instance, CNN-IBN, a national news channel in English under the Network 18 group, was critical of Modi and the party chief Amit Shah under its founder editor Rajdeep Sardesai. Both were accused in the 2002 riots and subsequently declared innocent by the highest court in the country, after the elections. Soon after the elections, the channel was bought by Reliance Industries, whose proximity to Modi was known, but whose business ethics were questioned. Consequently, Sardesai resigned while CNN turned pro-Modi in its coverage. Such news rarely changed the perception of the majority, who continued to believe in Modi mainly due to the strong influence of positive media frames.

With the 2002 riots taking a back seat and the development agenda in the foreground, the messages produced special frames where Modi's image was transformed into a visionary and a savior, from that of the man responsible for the genocide in Gujarat. Similarly, from being one of the richest politicians sent to jail for disproportionate assets, the media created frames that made Y.S. Jagan one whose interest lies in the welfare of the poor.

Strategic frames imposed on and by the press lacked context, as the leaders' speeches telecast live highlighted the opponents' failures and their sincerity to the cause. Being powerful orators, they made news even as the media lent positive frames to these leaders. The audience made their evaluation based on the conditions before the elections (social frames) as well as on the promises made by the politicians (original frames). For instance, in the case of Y.S. Jagan, people thought that he was being targeted, as they knew that all politicians were corrupt and he was no exception. Imprisoning him was seen as harassment rather than justice being meted out. The strategically cultivated images were devoid of the highly arbitrary nature of Modi and Y.S. Jagan, who were known to be the only decision makers at the helm of affairs, with no second-rung leaders in their respective parties. Such images rarely appeared in the media frames and were conveniently backgrounded by the electorate. The individuals became the party as the person was identified with the party. The party agenda became secondary to the leaders themselves.

The public relations agency that Modi hired actively set frames of reference that readers or viewers could easily interpret. Most discussions on social media and public events, which were constantly telecast, centered on the issues raised by Modi and Jagan, thus setting the media's agenda. The stories that Modi spun using mythological interventions and those of Y.S. Jagan using his father's reference to enhance their images and ideology set the frames of references (Neuman et al. 1992). Modi's highly attended rallies focused on the nationalistic spirit, with promises to usher in a change for the better, while Y.S. Jagan's popularity at the state level led to his pledge to bring back the golden rule of his father. Ironically, Modi did not have any experience as a national parliamentarian, since he had served as the chief minister of one province, and Y.S. Jagan was an MLC/MLA with no administrative experience. However, they came across as formidable opponents to all political parties and leaders with experience. In a way, their inexperience made them more acceptable to the electorate, who were skeptical of past governments. Both used the media extensively for their campaigns. While Modi used social media to reach out to youth, Y.S. Jagan relied on his television channel to reach out to the masses.

The differences lie in the way they strategized their campaigns, using unique framing techniques. Modi's dominant media frame was like a star on the distant horizon, untouched by corruption and family ties (seen as the cause of corruption in India). His starched Nehru jacket and neat appearance, waving to the crowds from a distance, set him apart from the commoners who looked up to him. Y.S. Jagan, on the other hand, was predominantly framed as a family member, one among the common people (he was referred to as Jagan *Anna* or brother), addressing "mothers, fathers, brothers and sisters" at the beginning of all his campaign speeches. Dressed in casual clothes and in most frames seen mingling with the crowds, Y.S. Jagan comes across as a commoner in contrast to Modi. This was in keeping with his father's image as a pro-poor chief minister.

In conclusion, a strong correlation exists between particular media frames with unlimited access to television time and content, and the construction of positive media images aided by electoral conditions and media-savvy strategies, which can influence the electorate's decision-making process. This can win elections and get leaders elected.

Topics for Discussion

1. Should national governments in emerging economies rely more on strategic networking or the media for rapid positive change?
2. Who should influence the media agenda during election campaigns, the electorate or the politicians?

Notes

1. For more information on the evolution of satellite news channels in India, see Mehta (2009).
2. The Tatas, Birlas, and Jains are considered the pillars of modern India, recognized as some of the greatest entrepreneurs who laid a strong foundation for the very growth of Indian industry through their singular efforts. Apart from being founders and leaders of various industries in numerous sectors like automobiles, steel, education, and others, the publication of newspapers has been one common feature of these entrepreneurs right from pre-independence days. Newspapers were seen as strong weapons of defiance in the British era and later on as a source of influence with the government of India. The newspapers started by these groups are still among the top 10 largest-circulation English dailies in India today.
3. See Ninan (2012) 'Ownership Worries', Livemint, June 6 for more information on media ownership. Also see Thakurtha (2012).
4. A specialist in international affairs and foreign affairs in the National Defense Division of the Congressional Research Service stated in 2015.
5. T. Venkatram Reddy, nephew of Congress MP T. Subbirami Reddy, has a substantial media empire comprising *Andhra Bhoomi, Deccan Chronicle, Asian Age,* and *Financial Chronicle*, which are held under Deccan Chronicle Holdings (of which TVR holds 21%). The *Asian Age* was started with onetime Congressman M. J. Akbar, Venkatram Reddy, and the now discredited Suresh Kalmadi.
6. The then chief minister of Karnataka, Yeddyurappa, had to resign on charges of corruption. Karnataka is the only state in the south where the BJP is in power.
7. There were several instances reported of complicity of the police in the riots. One gruesome incident in a colony called the Gulbarg Society was recorded where a former Congress MP, Ehsan Jaffri, was attacked and killed. "He must have made over a hundred phone calls for help," narrated Jafri's wife, Zakia. He called the Gujarat director-general of police, the Ahmedabad police commissioner, the state chief secretary, and dozens of others, pleading for their intercession. A witness who survived

the carnage later told a court that Jafri even called Narendra Modi: "When I asked him what Modi said, [Jafri] said there was no question of help, instead he got abuses." Word of Jafri's frantic calls for help even reached Deputy Prime Minister L.K. Advani in Delhi: a BJP insider close to Modi, who was with Advani on February 28, told me that the BJP leader had even called Modi's office himself to ask about Jafri. By 2:30 p.m., the mob had broken through the gates of the housing society, and a flood of men converged on Jafri's home. Women were raped and then burned alive; men were made to shout "Jai Shri Ram" and then cut to pieces; children were not spared. According to records later submitted in court, Jafri was stripped and paraded naked before the attackers cut off his fingers and legs and dragged his body into a burning pyre. The official police report indicates that 59 people were murdered in the Gulbarg Society, though independent inquiries put the number at 69 or 70. Jafri's wife and a few others who had locked themselves in an upstairs room survived.

8. http://thewire.in/2015/11/17/when-mr-modi-went-to-london-15802/.
9. Reddy's election declaration of 2004 included tax returns showing his assets at US$0.92 million, out of total family assets of US$1 million. In April 2009, he revealed total assets of US$770 million, and by 2011 this has allegedly increased to US$3.65 billion.
10. For instance, Modi projected Gujarat as a power-excess state, and almost every big-picture story about the "Gujarat miracle," from *Business Today* to the *Sydney Morning Herald*, highlighted this fact. But farmers' unions were protesting for almost a decade that their electricity needs were not being met, and government statistics show that the share of power diverted to agriculture fell from 43 to 21% between 2000 and 2010. More than 375,000 farmers were still waiting for electricity connections for their irrigation pumps. Similarly, though Modi presented Gujarat as the clear leader among Indian states in attracting foreign direct investment, it ranked fourth among states on this measure between 2000 and 2009, and in 2011 fell to sixth place, after Maharashtra, Delhi–National Capital Region, Tamil Nadu, Karnataka, and Andhra Pradesh; Maharashtra has FDI inflows almost nine times greater than Gujarat.

    Data from the Planning Commission showed that in spite of Gujarat's economic growth, the state lags behind even Bihar, Uttar Pradesh, West Bengal, and Andhra Pradesh in rates of poverty reduction. According to the 2011 India Human Development Report, Gujarat also scores poorly on several social indicators, with 44% of children under 5 suffering from malnutrition, worse than in Uttar Pradesh.

11. "Modi only thinks of winning—and winning all the time," a former chief minister of Gujarat said. "Other politicians can imagine that they will someday lose, and plan accordingly. But this attitude may get him into trouble, because in the future he can only be at one of the extremes: either he will be prime minister or he will go to jail. If I live long enough, I would be surprised to see him anywhere else—it has to be one or the other" (source: Caravan Donthi, Praveen, The Takeover, The Caravan, May 1, 2012).
12. YSR's victory run continued unabated, as he became the first Congress chief minister of Andhra Pradesh in three decades to get a successive second term when he won the assembly elections in 2009. Incidentally, he was also the state's only chief minister ever to complete a full five-year term. His Congress Party won 33 of the state's 42 constituencies—four more than in 2004—giving Andhra Pradesh the distinction of sending the largest number of Congress MPs from any state to the 15th Lok Sabha. YSR also won 158 of the Assembly's 294 seats. When film star Chiranjeevi launched the Praja Rajya party (PRP) in August 2008, triggering speculation that he could challenge YSR, the chief minister immediately began a comprehensive public relations campaign publicizing his various welfare steps, the most notable being the massive irrigation projects worth over Rs 1 lakh crore to provide water to some 10 million acres of agricultural land.
13. There was a lot of speculation about his arrest, with a "will he, won't he" type of possibility, as the CBI and the government took all precautions to ensure that the case was strong enough for his arrest. This speculation lasted for almost a week, with all media giving coverage to his imminent arrest.
14. Several welfare schemes like Indiramma Housing, Arogyasri, a pension scheme for the old, and others were initiated by the Congress Party when YSR was the chief minister of Andhra Pradesh. Although some of these schemes were initiated during NTR's tenure, they were discontinued by Naidu as they left the coffers empty. They was restarted by YSR, which made him popular among the masses.

References

Cappella, J., and K. Jamieson. 1996. News Frames, Political Cynicism, and Media Cynicism. The Media and Politics. *The Annals of the American Academy of Political and Social Science*, 546: 71–84. Sage Publications in association with the American Academy of Political and Social Science. URL: http://www.jstor.org/stable/1048171.

Cappella, J., and K. Jamieson. 1997. *Spiral of cynicism. The press and public good.* New York: Oxford University Press.

Davie, G. 2010. *Mass Communication theory: From theory to practical application* http://masscommtheory.com/. Accessed 22 Nov 2015.

Donthi, Praveen.The Takeover. *The Caravan: A Journal of politics and culture.* May 1, 2012. http://www.caravanmagazine.in/reportage/takeover-0/2#sthash.Z15GAdPl.dpuf. Accessed 22 Dec 2015.

Entman, R. 1993. Framing: Toward clarification of a fractured paradigm. *Journal of Communication* 43 (4): 51–58.

Fairhurst, G., and Sarr R. 1996. *The Art of Framing.* Managing the language of leadership. San Francisco: Jossey-Bass.

Fischer, G. W., and Johnson E. J. 1986. Behavioral decision theory and political decision making. In *Political Cognition: The 19th Annual Carnegie symposium on cognition*, ed. Richard R Lau and David O. Sears, 55–65. Hillsdale, NJ: Lawrence Erlbaum Associates.

Gamson, W. A., and Modigliani, A. 1987. The changing culture of affirmative action. In *Research in political sociology* ed. R. G. Braungart and M. M. Braungart. 3: 137–177. Greenwich CT: JAI Press.

Gamson, W. A., and A. Modigliani. 1989. Media discourse and public opinion on nuclear power: A constructionist approach. *American Journal of Sociology* 95: 1–37.

Ghatak, Aditi Roy, and Thakurtha. 2012. *Politics and media control.* www.thehoot.org. June 30. http://www.thehoot.org/media-watch/media-business/politics-and-media-control-6046. Accessed Sept 2012

Gitlin, T. 1980. *The whole world is watching: Mass media in the making and unmaking of the new Left.* Berkeley: University of California Press.

Goffman, E. 1974. *Frame Analysis: An essay on the organization of experience.* New York: Harper and Row.

Heider, F. 1944. Social perception and phenomenal causality. *Psychological Review* 51 (6): 358–374.

India Today. 2004. Elections special. *India Today Group* 9 (24): 33–170.

Iyengar, S. 1991. *Is anyone responsible? How television frames political issues.* Chicago: University of Chicago Press.

Jaffri, Syed Amin. 2004. The'perpetual dissident' finally becomes CM. May 13. www.rediff.com, http://www.rediff.com/election/2004/may/13ysr.htm. Accessed 8 June 2012.

Jose, Vinod, K. 2012. The Emperor Uncrowned. The rise of Narendra Modi. *Caravan: A Journal of politics and culture.* March 11. http://www.caravanmagazine.in/reportage/emperor-uncrowned.

Karan, Kavita. 2009. Political Communication in India. In *A Political Communication in Asia*, ed. Lars Willnat, and Annette Aw, 191–215. New York, NY: Routledge.

Katyal, Ritika. 2014. From Chaiwallah to Chief Minister: Modi's eventful journey. *The South Asian Channel*. June 25. http://foreignpolicy.com/2014/06/25/from-chaiwallah-to-chief-minister-modis-eventful-journey/.Accessed 2 July 2015.

Kumara, Prasanna. 2014. How much does it cost to set up a TV channel in India? *Quora*. July 12. https://www.quora.com/How-much-does-it-cost-to-set-up-a-TV-channel-in-India.

L K Advani website. 1990. 'Ram Rath Yatra' September—October 1990. http://www.lkadvani.in/eng/content/view/449/295/. Accessed 15 May 2012.

Mehta, N. 2009. *Television in India: Satellites, politics and cultural change*, 2nd ed. New Delhi: Routledge.

Mishra, Pankaj. 2015. Narendra Modi: The divisive manipulator who charmed the world? *The Guardian*. November 9. http://www.theguardian.com/world/2015/nov/09/narendra-modi-the-divisive-manipulator-who-charmed-the-world?CMP=share_btn_fb.

Narayanswamy, Harihar. 2009. Do popular ad campaigns win elections. *Economic Times*. May 27. http://articles.economictimes.indiatimes.com/2009-05-27/news/27638366_1_political-advertising-campaigns-general-election. Accessed 22 June 2012.

Neuman, W.R., M.R. Just, and A.N. Crigler. 1992. *Common Knowledge*. Chicago: University of Chicago Press.

Ninan, Sevanti. 2013. Surrogate media ownership. In Opinion. www.thehoot.org. November 2. http://www.thehoot.org/media-watch/opinion/surrogate-media-ownership-7142.

Norris, P. 1995. The restless searchlight: Network news framing of the post-cold war world. *Political Communication* 12: 357–370.

Norris, P. 2007. A virtuous circle, Political communication in post-industrial societies. In *The Political Communication Reader* ed Ralph Negrine and James Stanyer, 111–115, NY: Routledge.

Pan, Zhongdang, and Gerald M. Kosicki. 1993. Framing Analysis: An approach to news discourse. *Political Communication* 10: 55–75.

Patterson, T. 1993. *Out of order*. New York: Knopf.

Price, V., D. Tewksbury, and E. Powers. 1997. Switching trains of thought: The impact of news frames on readers' cognitive responses. *Communication Research* 24: 481–506.

Reddy, Krishna G. 2009. Forging Public Opinion: The Press, Television and electoral campaigns in Andhra Pradesh In *The Indian Public Sphere: Readings in Media History*, ed. Arvind Rajagopal, 228–244. New Delhi: Oxford University Press.

Sahi, Ajit. 2009. Eating The Cake And The Cherry. *Tehelka Magazine,* May 30. http://www.tehelka.com/story_main41.asp?filename=Ne300509eating_the.asp. Accessed 6 June 2012.

Scheufele, D.A. 1999. Framing as a theory of media effects. *Journal of Communication* 49 (1): 103–122.

Scheufele, D.A. 2000. Agenda Setting, Priming and Framing revisited: Another look at cognitive effects of political communication. *Mass Communication and Society* 3 (2 and 3): 297–316.

Shaw, Padmaja. 2012. More or less news. Posted/Updated on September 11. www.thehoot.org, http://www.thehoot.org/media-watch/media-business/more-or-less-news-6255. Accessed 15 Sep 2012.

Thakur, Aditya. 2013. Top 7 Indian Channels That Are Owned By Politicians! August 21. http://hillpost.in/2013/08/top-7-indian-channels-that-are-owned-by politicians/95166/comment-page-2/

Thakurtha, Paranjoy. 2012. Media ownership trends in India. Posted/Updated on July 03. www.thehoot.org. Accessed 10 Sep 2012.

Tuchman, G. 1978. *Making News: A construction of reality.* New York: Free Press.

Valkenburg, Patti M., and Holli A. Semetko. 2000. Framing European politics: A content analysis of print and television. *Journal of Communication* 50 (2): 93–109. doi: 10.1111/j.1460-2466.2000.tb02843.x.

Vreese, de, C.H. 2002. *Framing Europe: television news and European integration.* Amsterdam: Aksant Academic Publishers.

Vreese, de, C.H. 2003. Television reporting of second order elections. *Journalism Studies* 4: 183–198.

Weaver, D., McCombs M., and Shaw D.L. 1998. Agenda-setting research. Recent developments in place and focus. Paper presented at the annual convention of the World Association for Public Opinion Research, St. Louis, MO.

www.mib.gov.in. Total no. of TV channels permitted as on 29.12.2015. TV channels authorized for uplinking from india = 732. Ministry of I&B. http://mib.nic.in/writereaddata/html_en_files/tvchannels/status_at_a_glance.pdf. Accessed 16 Aug 2015

www.rediff.com Andhra Pradesh is in shock: YSR's death leads to a spate of suicides. Last updated on September 04, 2009. http://news.rediff.com/report/2009/sep/04/sixty-people-lose-lives-in-ap-after-ysr-death.htm. Accessed 6 May 2012.

CHAPTER 7

Media Exposure of Corruption and the Re-Election Chances of Incumbent Parties in Africa

Mavuto Kalulu

Information is widely recognized as a cornerstone of good governance and an important tool in the fight against corruption (World Resource Institute 2012). As of 2014, 13 countries in Africa had adopted freedom of information (FOI) laws (Odinkalu and Kadiri 2014). In the absence of such laws, most people rely on the media for information about their governments. It is not surprising that the African Union (AU) Convention on Preventing and Combating Corruption recognizes the importance of the press by explicitly obliging member states to provide "the right of access to any information

Mavuto Kalulu is an economist whose research interests include public choice and political economies, especially corruption and its effect on the electoral process in developing countries. In this chapter, he concludes that information about corruption does not affect the re-election chances of incumbent parties and offers a possible reason for this situation.

M. Kalulu (✉)
University of Central Arkansas, Conway, AR, USA

E.K. Ngwainmbi (ed.), *Citizenship, Democracies, and Media Engagement among Emerging Economies and Marginalized Communities*,
DOI 10.1007/978-3-319-56215-5_7

that is required to assist in the fight against corruption and related offenses" (African Union 2003).The media, therefore, has the potential to shape public opinion both positively and negatively, depending on who is in control of it and what their motive is. Indeed, information that is disseminated through the different media plays a critical role in any democratic processes.

However, there is a tendency for ruling parties in Africa to control the media through the state's monopoly on the issuance of licenses, and in some extreme cases through intimidation of already existing media houses. In countries where the main broadcaster is state controlled, those in the opposition are left to complain about the unfairness of the press, but sadly when they get a chance to assume power they make little progress to improve the situation.

As economic agents, parties in authority want to have strong control of the media to use it as a propaganda tool. Their objective is to stay in authority and enjoy all the benefits that accompany controlling state institutions. However, this comes at a huge cost to the nation as a whole, because people are left to make decisions based on incomplete or outright wrong information. The elected governments are, therefore, less likely to reflect the wishes of the citizens.

This chapter discusses whether or not information influences the decision-making process of African voters. Answering this question will assist international and local democratic institutions to better engage African voters in the democratic process. To respond to this question, we utilize presidential elections in Africa. We specifically examine the re-election chances of incumbent parties' presidential candidates when information on corruption is made available to voters by the media. We find that in Africa, information on corruption has no effect on election outcomes.

Motivation

A large volume of empirical literature shows that corruption has a negative effect on economic growth, resulting in high poverty levels. Mehmet Ugur (2014) conducted a meta-analysis based on 596 estimates reported in 72 empirical studies, and concluded that corruption has a negative and genuine effect on growth in low-income countries. About 85% of the studies report estimates that show a negative effect of perceived corruption on economic growth. Transparency International defines corruption as the abuse of public resources for private gain. Paolo Mauro (1995) finds that the main channel through which corruption affects the poor is through its effect on economic growth. Corruption lowers investment and hence slows down economic growth. Pak Mo (2001) finds that corruption has a negative and significant relationship with human capital, measured by the average years of schooling in the population over age 25. Vito Tanzi and Hamid Davoodi (1998) find that corruption negatively affects the quality of public investments. Sanjeev Gupta, Hamid Davoodi, and Erwin Tiongson (2001) examine the effect of corruption on the quality of public healthcare provision, and find that child mortality rates in highly corrupt countries are about one-third higher than those in less corrupt countries.

Despite the evidence that corruption is detrimental to the wellbeing of the poor, people still engage in corruptive practices, causing some to wonder whether corruption might be beneficial. Samuel Huntington (1968, p. 69) argues that in over-centralized, dishonest bureaucracies, political bribes and kickbacks can help cut through the bureaucratic red tape and improve government efficiency. Francis Liu (1985) shows in a formal model that corruption can efficiently reduce time spent in queues. Another reason some view corruption as beneficial hinges on the key economic assumption that self-interest enhances prosperity because competition ensures that a product is purchased by those who value it the most; thus firms that are willing to pay more in bribes are awarded contracts (Liu 1985). However, as Johann Lambsdorff (2001) argues, this type of invisible hand may not exist when private actors deal with the government to provide products to the state or to demand publicly controlled services. This study views corruption as bad for the majority of people not directly involved in corruptive activities, and as detrimental to economic development.

If corruption negatively affects voters, voters should punish incumbent parties for corruption by voting them out of office. It is not uncommon, however, to see corrupt incumbent parties re-elected in Africa. In 2010 Chad, for example, was ranked the third and eighth most corrupt country in Africa and the world, respectively, and yet in the 2011 presidential elections the incumbent party's candidate was re-elected (Transparency International 2010). Across the empirical literature, the results on the effect of corruption on election outcomes are mixed. For example, in Brazil's mayoral elections, Claudio Ferraz and Frederico Finan (2008) find that voters punish corrupt officials by withdrawing their vote; while in Italy's legislative elections, Eric Chang and Miriam Golden (2004) conclude that there is no significant difference in the re-election chances of corrupt officials and non-corrupt ones. However, the existing literature has focused on developed countries, except for Ferraz and Finan (2008) who conducted a country-specific study in Brazil. Another exception is Stefan Krause and Fabio Mendez (2007), who combine developed countries and developing countries from South America.

The current study adds to the literature by focusing only on Africa, where almost the whole continent is plagued with the problem of corruption. Transparency International's 2015 Corruption Perception Index (CPI) reveals that 40 out of Sub-Saharan Africa's 46 states have a serious problem with corruption (Tikum 2016). Also, the anti-corruption agencies in Africa tend to be less trustworthy, because they tend to have limited to no autonomy. A 2011–2013 Afrobarometer survey found overwhelming skepticism about anti-corruption measures in Africa, with 56% of respondents in 34 African countries indicating that their country was "fairly bad" or "very bad" at countering corruption. Only 35% said their governments had done "well" or "very well" (Tikum 2016).

The intertwined nature of the causes of and solutions to corruption makes the fight against corruption through anti-corruption agencies harder, especially in emerging democracies. The very people who are corrupt are the very people who influence the appointment of the heads of such agencies. Also, the agencies tend to have no budgetary independence or secured tenure for senior management, which leads to bottlenecks and biases in prosecutions. It may indeed be in the interest of a corrupt government to keep these agencies deliberately weak so that staff can continue to reap the benefits of corruption without paying the electoral consequences. Exposing corruption may be risky in such an environment due to inadequate legal protection for the whistleblowers, in a system that is very protective of the politicians in the incumbent party. In democratic nations, elections may, therefore, offer opportunities for voters to express their attitudes toward corruption without directly being labeled whistleblowers. However, Barry Rundquist, Gerald Storm, and John Peters' (1977) model suggests that voters may vote for a corrupt incumbent party because they are uninformed or misinformed about the extent of corruption and its consequences for their wellbeing. Voter access to information in Africa may be an important element in explaining the re-election of corrupt incumbents.

Radio broadcasts are a more important source of information to the rural masses in Africa than is television or the internet. The levels of per capita income in developing countries make it difficult for people in the countryside to purchase televisions and computers and to access the internet in their homes. Also, the lack of electricity in the countryside makes it harder to own appliances like televisions and personal computers. According to the World Bank in 2015, only 24% of the population of Sub-Saharan Africa has access to electricity, compared to 40% in other low-income countries. Furthermore, apart from high power tariffs, the power supply is also unreliable. African countries experience power outages on average 56 days per year (World Bank 2015). It is highly likely, therefore, that people in rural areas get informed mostly through radio broadcasts, because radios are affordable and can easily be powered by batteries or by solar and manual (wind-up) means. Thus the analysis of voter information about political corruption should explicitly include radio. Unfortunately, for this study we could not find data on the number of radios per household for the period in which we are interested. As a solution, we measured access to information using the number of cellular subscribers per 100 of the population as a proxy. An alternative was to use the number of internet users per 1000 of the population. It is more likely that people in rural areas will own cellular phones than computers and an internet service. Moreover, people can easily recharge their phone batteries at shopping centers, where some individuals may not have access to electricity.

Scope of the Study

Using a data set compiled from various data sources, this study models the re-election chances of an incumbent party's presidential candidate as a function of corruption, information variables, and various control variables. (A detailed specification of the econometric model is provided in a subsequent section). Corruption is measured by the Corruption Control Index (CCI) produced by Daniel Kaufmann of the Natural Resource Governance Institute (NGGI) and Aart Kraay of the World Bank Development Research Group. The key questions that this study seeks to address are (1) whether voters in African countries punish incumbent parties for corruption; (2) whether voters' access to information enhances the re-election chances of incumbent parties in Africa; and (3) whether information about corruption changes the response of electors. A key innovation of this study is to include a term for the interaction of information variables and corruption, allowing one to analyze the effect of information dissemination on the re-election chances of incumbent parties' presidential candidates. Establishing whether the accessibility of information matters can guide institutions set up to fight against corruption in the way they should disseminate information about corruption in Africa.

This study attempts to make three other contributions to the election corruption literature. First, it assesses the re-election chances of incumbent presidents using a set of African countries only. The extant literature is limited to developed countries. Second, electoral fraud in developing countries is included in the model as an explanatory variable. If electoral fraud plays a role in altering voters' preferences, the omission of the variable has grave consequences for the reliability of the estimates. In most African countries, election outcomes are disputed because of alleged electoral fraud. In the Kenyan 2007 elections, for example, the opposition refused to accept the election results, claiming that the Electoral Commission of Kenya (ECK) manipulated the results for the incumbent party's candidate. Similarly, in the 2013 Kenyan elections, the losing candidate again challenged the results in court. The third contribution of this study is the inclusion of voter turnout as an explanatory variable, which the other studies do not do.

The rest of the chapter is organized as follows: the next section reviews the literature; the following section discusses the data; the fourth section discusses the methodology and the results; while the final section concludes and proposes a future direction.

Corruption and Economic Growth

Despite the evidence that corruption is detrimental to the wellbeing of the poor, people still engage in corruption. This constant practice has caused some theorists to wonder whether corruption might be beneficial. This section provides a brief review of studies that have investigated the effect of corruption on society and have found a negative impact on the wellbeing of citizens.

Using a sample of 67 countries, Paolo Mauro (1995) finds that the main channel through which corruption affects economic growth is by lowering the investment rate. He concludes that a one standard deviation increase in the corruption index is associated with an increase in the investment rate by 2.9% of gross domestic product (GDP). He uses an older corruption index provided by Business International (BI). Many other studies that use other indices of corruption support Mauro's findings. Stephen Knack and Phillip Keefer (1995) use data from the Political Risk Service's International Country Risk Guide (PRS/ICRG). Aymo Brunetti, Gregory Kisunko, and Beatrice Wader (1998) use the corruption index from the World Bank and the University of Basel.

Shang-Jin Wei (2000a) detects a significant negative impact of corruption on foreign direct investment (FDI). Johann Lambsdorff and

Peter Cornelius (2000) show an adverse impact of corruption on FDI for African countries. Other studies that find similar results include those by Beata Smarzynska and Shan-Jin Wei (2000), Witold Henisz (2000), Shang-Jin Wei (2000b), George Abed and Hamid Davoodi (2002), Jonathan Doh and Hildy Teegen (2003), and Stephane Straub (2008).

With regard to the quality of the services provided, Vito Tanzi and Hamid Davoodi (1998) examine the effect of corruption on the quality of public investments, while Sanjeev Gupta, Hamid Davoodi, and Erwin Tiongson (2001) support them with a study that examines the effect of corruption on the quality of public healthcare provision. These studies provide evidence that corruption negatively affects economic growth and human wellbeing, directly or indirectly. Of particular importance to the current study is the voting behavior of citizens when the public officials running for re-election are perceived to be corrupt. A considerable scholarly effort in public choice has been devoted to studying the relationship between corruption and voter turnout, but not so much on the corruption–election outcome relationship. The next section discusses studies that investigate the turnout–corruption relationship.

Corruption and Voter Turnout

Gökhan Karahan, Morris Coats, and William Shughart (2006) tested the hypothesis that government corruption increases voter participation rates by analyzing the results of the 1987 county supervisor elections in the 82 counties in the state of Mississippi. Their findings show that turnout is higher in counties where the incumbent was corrupt than in those where the incumbent was not. Their explanation is that public corruption leads to increased competition for public office, because of opportunities to earn bribes and other forms of unlawful compensation, which raise the returns for holding office. Higher payoffs for holding office increase the intensity of consumption for voters. This growing demand for votes drives the corrupt candidates to mobilize people to come out and vote. In the African context, the increased effort might include politicians bribing voters. Robert Fatton (1986) argues that such a link between corruption and voter turnout exists because Africans are embedded in a network of relationships in which patrons bribe citizens to participate in elections.

Gökhan Karahan, Morris Coats, and William Shughart (2006) recognize that the demanders of votes (candidates) play a crucial role in mobilizing voters. While their view is that mobilization stems from politicians' effort, others contend that mobilization is a result of disgruntled voters seeking to remove corrupt leaders from office. Michael Bratton, Robert Mattes, and Emmanuel Gyimah-Boadi (2005) argue that citizens want clean and accountable governments, and if they do not find transparency and effectiveness, they may turn out in large numbers to cast a protest vote. Kris Inman and Josephine Andrews (2009) find that citizens in Senegal tend to show up in higher numbers when faced with corrupt governments.

The essence of politicians engaging in electoral engineering, however, is to mobilize voters to vote for them so that they can win elections and continue maximizing the benefits of holding office. While politicians hope that campaigning increases voter turnout, to the extent that elections are not rigged outright they have no control over what happens in the polling booth. This is where the current study departs from those that seek to investigate the turnout–corruption relationship, by focusing on the re-election–corruption relationship instead.

Corruption and Election Outcome

Erik Chang and Miriam Golden (2004) investigate the fate of members of the Italian lower house in the first 11 postwar legislatures (1948–1994) using survival analysis techniques and logistic regressions. They find that judicial allegations of serious transgressions significantly lower the probability of re-election by 7%. However, when they look at the legislatures separately, they find that voters punish members of the legislative assembly for serious wrongdoing by not voting for them in only 2 out of the 11 postwar legislatures. Their results show that 51% of those charged with serious wrongdoing get re-elected to national office, compared to 58% of their honest counterparts, leading Chang and Golden (2004) to conclude that corrupt officials are not severely punished by voters. The major difference between their study and the current one is that their study is country specific, while the present research is cross-country. Another country-specific study that supports Chang and Golden (2004) is that by Stevens Reed (1999). He finds that Japanese legislators lose only a few percentage points over their previous vote shares when they are indicted or convicted of corruption; 62% of legislators convicted of corruption over the period 1947–1993 were subsequently re-elected.

Other country-specific studies have established that voters do punish corrupt public officials. John Peters and Susan Welch (1980) assessed the electoral impact of corruption on accused candidates in the US House of Representatives from 1968 to 1978. They isolated and determined the degree to which specific corruption allegations diminished the electoral success of candidates. In their study, they considered the victory or defeat of allegedly corrupt candidates and examined the impact of corruption charges on both electoral turnout and the percentage of votes received by the accused candidates. Their results show that not only do a significant number of accused candidates get defeated at the polls or resign before risking defeat, but accused candidates also suffer a significant loss of votes in re-election bids. Overall, candidates accused of corruption appear to suffer a loss of 6–11% from their expected vote.

Another cross-country study that supports Peters and Welch (1980) is by Claudio Krause and Frederico Mendez (2007). They evaluated the question of whether voters reduce their support for an incumbent whenever they perceive an increase in corruption. Their sample includes 28 countries and 93 election periods covering the period between 1995 and 2007. Their sample includes European and North and South American countries. They use the Corruption Perception Index (CPI) for their measure of corruption. The dependent variable in their model is the gain (or loss) in the share of votes received by the incumbent party on the previous election. The difference between the current study and that by Krause and Mendez (2007) is that the former focuses on African countries only, while the latter combines developed and developing countries. Another difference is that this study tests the effect of corruption information on re-election chances. Furthermore, it uses a categorical variable, re-election, as the dependent variable. This study also uses the change in the CCI instead of the change in the CPI.

Controlling for both economic and political variables, Krause and Mendez (2007) find that a perceived rise in corruption in public office is effectively punished by voters in an election. Furthermore, they find strong evidence that voters punish corrupt practices more in the parliamentary form of government than the presidential form of government. The reasoning behind this is that in regulatory systems, voters perceive corruption as an individual flaw, while for parliamentary regimes, voters view the entire party as being corrupt. They also find that corruption is punished more severely in newer democracies than in established ones.

In conclusion, studies that use the change in the share of votes as the dependent variable seem to suggest that voters punish corrupt officials by withdrawing support (Peters and Welch 1980; Ferraz and Finan 2008; Krause and Mendez 2007). Those that use categorical dependent variables seem to establish that voters do not punish corrupt officials. To reconcile the two, one can conclude that the loss of the share of votes for corrupt officials may not be significant enough to make those corrupt officials fail to be re-elected.

Media and Corruption in Africa

As an example of the role that the media plays in providing information revealing corruption, James Jarso (2010) explains the role that the Kenyan media played in exposing numerous multimillion-dollar financial scams. He explains that even though Kenyan law is silent on the role of the media in the fight against corruption, the Kenyan media has made remarkable achievements in the fight against corruption through four major fronts: "as a whistleblower; in piling pressure on government officials to account for their corrupt acts and omissions; in public education (dissemination); and in investigative journalism" (Jarso 2010, p. 33).

The Kenyan media exposed the Goldenberg scandal, where the company Goldenberg International collided with Kenyan government officials to claim money for the re-export of gold and diamonds. Through the export compensation scheme initiated by then President Daniel Arap Moi to encourage exports in Kenya, government officials benefited by paying the company Goldenberg International 35% more than the enterprise's actual foreign earnings (Warutere 2005).

Another scandal that was exposed in Kenya was the Anglo-Leasing scam, which is alleged to have started under the presidency of Daniel Arap Moi and continued under that presidency of his successor, Mwai Kibaki (World Bank/UNODC 2004). The media exposed the fact that government officials were awarding contracts to phantom firms which did not honor the contracts. This was a way of looting the government's financial resources.

As can be seen, the media has the potential to expose corruption. It is imperative to have a free press so that such scandals are revealed to help voters make informed decisions in their choice of president. Aymo Brunetti and Beatrice Weder (2003) discuss various indices of corruption and how they relate to press freedom. They find that a higher degree of press freedom is associated with less corruption.

Data Description

This study uses data from 50 elections in 30 African countries over the period 2000–2011. The sample period was determined by the availability of data. The CCI was first compiled in 1996. Since we are interested in the change in the index between two election cycles, the first set of data generated for this variable is for the year 2000. Data for electoral fraud is only available up to 2012, limiting the sample size for this study.

Re-Election

Re-election is a dummy variable that takes the value of 1 if the incumbent party's presidential candidate wins an election and 0 if not. Thus, to be assigned the value of 1, the winner must either be an incumbent president or be from the same party as the incumbent when the incumbent is not allowed to contest. Most democratic nations place a constitutional limit on the number of terms a president can serve. So, the incumbent does not contest after completing the maximum number of terms provided for by the constitution. The highest number of terms varies from one to an open-ended arrangement like in the case of Zimbabwe, which does not impose a limit on the number of terms. From Table 7.1, it can be seen that in 80% of the elections in the sample, the incumbent party's presidential candidate as re-elected. The data for re-election was obtained from three main sources, the Electoral Commissions of the various countries, Psephos: Adam Carr's Election Archives, and the Center on Democratic Performance (CDP).

Voter Turnout

Voter turnout can be measured as the number of voters that turn out to cast a vote as a percentage of registered voters or as a proportion of the voting age population (VAP). Using the number of registered voters as the denominator leaves out eligible voters who may not have registered to vote, while using VAP includes those who do not qualify to vote, such as non-citizens. The current study uses the former, but it would be

Table 7.1 Descriptive statistics on dependent and independent variables

Name	*Definition*	*Mean*	*Std. Dev.*	*Min.*	*Max.*
Re-election	1 if re-elected and 0 if not	0.800	0.404	0.000	1.000
Δ in corruption control	Calculated from change in CCI	0.0296	0.337	−0.560	1.060
Cellular	Subscribers per 100 of population	30.359	26.174	0.690	96.190
Press freedom	Higher number means more freedom	42.860	15.637	12.000	74.000
Turnout	% of vote divided by registered voters	62.599	14.088	36.240	97.510
Electoral fraud	1 if election fraudulent and 0 if not	0.460	0.503	0.000	1.000
Level of democracy	Higher means more democratic	3.020	4.283	−5.000	10.000
% Δ in GDP per capita	Change between two elections	10.740	16.648	−47.000	63.000
# of challengers	# of opposition presidential candidates	6.280	6.034	1.000	24.000
Same candidate	1 if sitting president runs and 0 if not	0.660	0.479	0.000	1.000

interesting to test whether the results would change if VAP were used instead. Table 7.1 shows that the mean turnout in African countries is 62.6%.

It is important to note that different countries use different voting systems for presidential elections. Some countries use the plurality system, while others use the majority system. The majority system requires a runoff when no candidate reaches 50% plus 1 of the votes. In the case of a runoff, this study uses the second-round (runoff) turnout, because that is the round where the winner is determined. The data sources for turnout are the African Elections Database, Psephos: Adam Carr's Election Archives, the CDP, the Institute for Democracy and Election Assistance (IDEA), and the Electoral Commissions in the respective countries.

A priori, there is no way of knowing the direction of the influence of voter turnout on election outcomes. If a large turnout is a result of one side being able to mobilize its base and new voters, then that party may stand a better chance of winning an election. In some countries, for example, access to remote areas may require many resources, and the incumbent may have an advantage over the opposition because the incumbent can use government resources to campaign in those areas. The increase in voter turnout may increase the incumbent's chances in this case, but still, there is no guarantee that the electorate will vote for any particular candidate, since the voting is done secretly. Bernard Grofman, Guillermo Owen, and Christian Collet (1999) argue that a higher voter turnout may be bad news for the incumbent party, because core voters usually differ from peripheral voters. Peripheral voters are defined as those who do not like the status quo. Therefore, the more involved the peripheral voters become, the worse the incumbent party will fare in a fair election. The expected sign for voter turnout is, therefore, inconclusive.

Corruption Control

Corruption is defined as the abuse of entrusted public power for private gain. Examples include bribing of public officials, kickbacks in public procurement, or embezzlement of public funds. The plan in this study was to use the CPI compiled by Transparency International (TI).

However, for sample size considerations, an alternative measure, the CCI, was used instead. The CPI was first compiled in 1995, and most of the African countries did not get a score until the early 2000s. Also, in 2012 the scaling of the index was changed from a 0 to 10 scale to a 0 to 100 scale. Because the variable of interest is the difference in corruption levels between election cycles, using CPI generated only 27 elections in Africa. A simple correlation between the two variables (change in CPI and change in CCI) yields a correlation coefficient equal to 0.055, which is statistically significant at 1%. Furthermore, according to Anja Rohwer (2009), unlike CPI which measures corruption in the public sector, CCI not only captures corruption in the public sector, it also includes corruption in industry.

The CCI captures perceptions of the extent to which public power is exercised for private gain, including both petty and grand forms of corruption, as well as "capturing" of the state by elites and private interests (Ugur and Nandini 2011). The score ranges from −2.5 for weak control of corruption to 2.5 for strong control of corruption. Thus, a bigger positive score is an indicator that voters perceive public officials as more corrupt, while a bigger negative score (in absolute value) suggests the opposite. This study uses the change in CCI between two elections to measure corruption by a particular ruling party, so that only the level of corruption is measured and that can be attributed to the incumbent during the period between two election cycles.

By its very nature, corruption is deliberately hidden, making gathering information problematic. Other studies have used the number of prosecutions in a country as a measure of the level of corruption. Johann Lambsdorff (2008) argues that the number of prosecutions does not reflect actual levels of corruption but the quality of prosecutors. With regard to validity, Anja Rohwer (2009) states that the World Bank uses a combination of different data sources in the construction of the CCI.

Electoral Fraud

It is not uncommon for the defeated candidate to refuse to accept the outcome of an election, citing electoral fraud as the cause of the defeat. In the 2012 Ghanaian elections, for example, the opposition candidate refused to accept the results, claiming that they were manipulated for the incumbent. In Malawi, no major losing candidate had accepted defeat since 1994, when Hasting Kamuzu Banda conceded to Bakili Muluzi. Kenya is also an interesting case. In 2007, the opposition, led by the candidate Raila Odinga, claimed that the elections were rigged for the incumbent. The accusation resulted in an ethnic conflict that left over 1000 people dead. For the 2013 election, to avoid a repeat of the 2007 events, an independent body, the Independent Electoral and Boundaries Commission (IEBC), was hired to conduct the election. The losing candidate did not accept the results, arguing that the failure of the biometric machines, which led to a manual count, was a deliberate ploy to manipulate the results for the winner. The matter was resolved in the Kenyan Supreme Court for the IEBC.

Electoral fraud is, therefore, one of the control variables in this study, but measuring it is not easy because of its covert nature. Moreover, people may question the motive of complainants, since they have an interest in having the results overturned. This study utilizes a measure compiled by the World Bank political database, which rates elections as free and fair or fraudulent. A fraudulent election takes the value of 0 while a free and fair election takes the value of 1. Using this measure of fraud has the advantage that it is available over the period of this study, and it is from an outside source, which supposedly has no interest in influencing the outcome of elections directly.

However, the measure assigns 0 to countries where opposition parties are officially and constitutionally banned or where irregularities are not mentioned.

Level of Democracy

The availability and quality of democratic institutions can influence the outcome of an election. This study uses the democracy standards of a country to control for the quality of institutions, on the premise of a positive relationship between the degree of democracy and the quality of those democratic institutions. The Polity IV index is used to measure a country's level of democracy. Ranging from -10 for extreme autocracy to +10 for the most democratic, the Polity IV index measures democracy by the competitiveness of political participation, competitiveness of executive recruitment, openness of executive recruitment, and constraints of the chief executive. A score of +10 indicates a strongly democratic state; a score of −10 indicates a strongly autocratic state. This variable is listed in the Polity IV dataset as *polity*. One weakness of the index is that it does not distinguish between a monarchy and a single-party regime. However, for this study that is not a problem, because the countries included in the study have indexes ranging from −6 to 10. The mean democracy variable is 3.02, an indication that the African countries in the sample are not very democratic.

Level of Competition Faced by the Incumbent

A fragmented opposition increases the chances of an incumbent getting re-elected. Having a large number of opposition candidates may even be part of the incumbent's strategy to divide the opposition. With government resources to use, the incumbent can sponsor smaller parties in opposition strongholds to increase the chances of winning the election. The number of opposition candidates is used as a proxy to measure the strength of opposition the incumbent faces. On average, in Africa there are six presidential candidates running against an incumbent. Just like voter turnout, it is important to note that some countries require a 50% + 1 majority to win an election, so the number of challengers is reduced to one in the runoff. The major data source for the number of challengers is Psephos: Adam Carr's Election Archives.

Economic Performance as Measured by Change in GDP Per Capita

Research has shown that economic conditions shape electoral outcomes. Michael Lewis-Beck and Mary Stegmaier (2000) explain that good economic performance keeps parties in power, and bad performance cast them out. Their findings are founded on the premise of economic voters who hold the government responsible for the state of the economy. The present study uses the percentage change in real GDP per capita between two elections to capture how well an incumbent performed economically. In developed countries, the unemployment rate plays a crucial role in informing the electorate on the economic condition of a country. The unavailability of unemployment data in Africa leaves per capita GDP as the best indicator of economic performance. The reason for using the percentage change in per capita GDP is the idea that in considering whether to re-elect an incumbent, voters consider how well off they were before the incumbent came to power and how much their lives have improved. The mean change in real GDP per capita in Africa is 10.74%, indicating an improvement in economic performance on average. The data for GDP per capita was obtained from the World Bank.

Amount and Quality of Information

The amount and quality of information made available to the voters play a role in determining the electoral outcome. If the incumbent is corrupt, it is to his/her advantage if the corruption is not exposed. The media therefore plays a major role in influencing the election outcome through the type of information that is disseminated. For the majority of poor people in rural areas, radio is the best means through which information is passed. Instead of using the number of radios per 1000 of population to measure access to information, this study uses the number of cellular subscribers as a proxy for the amount of information. Also, the press freedom index is used to control for the ease with which reporters can disseminate information. The interaction between the data variables and corruption is included in the analysis to allow for the examination of voters' response when information on corruption is provided to them. The mean of the number of cellular subscribers per 100 of population is 30, indicating that at least 30% of the people in Africa have access to information (via a cellular service). The mean press freedom in Africa is 42.86. Data on the number of cellular subscribers per 100 of population was gathered from the World Bank, while data on freedom of the press was collected from Freedom House. Freedom of the press is measured on a scale of 0 to 100, with lower numbers implying more freedom. In this study, however, we transformed the scale so that bigger values imply more freedom of the press. This was done to allow for a natural interpretation of our results.

Power of Incumbency

An incumbent president has an advantage over his/her competitors because he/she is already known and can also use government resources for the campaign. Incumbent presidents can easily disguise a political function as a state function and, in the process, use public resources to finance their campaigns. Also, the voters already know the incumbent president, so it is easier for the ruling party than its competitors to sell its candidates. To control the power of incumbency, this study uses a dummy variable taking the value of 1 if the ruling party features a sitting candidate and 0 if the incumbent party changes its presidential candidate.

Estimation Results

The dependent variable in this study, re-election, is categorical. The estimation method is the probit maximum likelihood estimator (MLE). We specify four different models that are distinguished by the variables that are included in the estimation, as seen in Table 7.2. All the models are well specified, as evidenced by Wald chi-square statistics that are greater than 30. Because most of the dependent variables are potentially related to one another, we check for multicollinearity. The correlation coefficients in Table 7.2 indicate that the dependent variables do not pose a problem of multicollinearity. The biggest coefficient in absolute value is 0.536 for the correlation between free press and democracy.

Table 7.3 provides results for the probit estimation method. Models 1 and 2 include the number of cellular subscribers per 100 of population as a proxy for access to information. In Model 2, the number of cellular subscribers interacts with control of corruption. The interaction ensures that voters have access to information on corruption. In Models 3 and 4, freedom of the press is used introduced to capture how freely the media can disseminate information. In essence, the freedom of the media is used as a measure of the quality of information to which voters

Table 7.2 Probit estimation (dependent variable = re-election)

	Δ in CCI	*Cellular*	*Free press*	*Turnout*	*Fraud*	*Democracy*	*Δ in RPGDP*	*Challengers*	*Same candidate*
Δ in CCI	1.000								
Cellular	0.028	1.000							
Free press	0.019	−0.114	1.000						
Turnout	0.058	0.105	−0.141	1.000					
Fraud	−0.017	−0.065	−0.209	0.001	1.000				
Democracy	0.060	−0.164	0.536	−0.235	−0.373	1.000			
Δ RPGDP	0.0273	−0.179	0.093	0.160	−0.074	−0.142	1.000		
Challengers	−0.169	0.090	0.062	−0.033	0.387	−0.088	0.075	1.000	
Same candidate	0.023	0.199	−0.271	0.069	−0.015	−0.405	0.009	0.140	1.000

Table 7.3 Probit estimation (dependent variable = re-election)

	(1)		*(2)*		*(3)*		*(4)*	
	Coeff.	*AME*	*Coeff.*	*AME*	*Coeff.*	*AME*	*Coeff.*	*AME*
Change in corruption control	0.528	0.061	0.092		0.639	0.072	2.954	
	(0.964)	(0.117)	(1.333)		(0.912)	(0.112)	(2.912)	
# of cellular subscribers per 100 pop.	−0.038***	−0.004***	−0.036***		−0.038***	−0.004***	−0.030**	
	(0.011)	(0.001)	(0.011)		(0.012)	(0.002)	(0.014)	
Cellular* change in corruption control			0.020				0.025	
			(0.026)				(0.033)	
Press freedom					0.013	0.002	0.010	
					(0.023)	(0.026)	(0.026)	
Press freedom* change in corruption							-0.060	
							(0.044)	
Turnout	N	N	N	N	N	N	N	
Electoral fraud	N	N	N	N	N	N	N	N
Democracy	Y	Y	Y	Y	Y	Y	N	N
Change in GDP per capita	N	N	N	N	N	N	N	N
# of challengers	Y	Y	Y	Y	Y	Y	Y	Y
Same candidate	Y	Y	Y	Y	Y	Y	Y	Y
Wald chi² (k + 1)	36.39		30.07		33.54		34.76	

Robust standard errors in parentheses
***p < 0.01, **p < 0.05, *p < 0.1
n = 50

AME = average marginal effects, N = not significant, Y = significant are exposed. A free media allows for information to be relayed to the electorate without fear of persecution. Just like Model 2, Model 4 introduces the interaction between corruption and the data variables. Also included in Table 7.3 are the marginal effects of the variables that do not interact.

Not included in Table 7.3 are the marginal effects of corruption and the information variables, which are interacted and require a separate calculation. These are reported in Table 7.4. In all four estimated models, there is no evidence that corruption affects the re-election chances of an incumbent party's presidential candidate. This finding is different from others who have found that voters do punish incumbents for corruption, such as Krause and Mendez (2007), Ferraz and Finan (2008), and Peters and Welch (1980). Similarly, this is contrary to studies by Chang and Golden (2004) and Reed (1999) showing that corruption positively affects the re-election of corrupt leaders. Our results show that voters do not consider corruption in determining for whom to vote.

Access to information, as measured by the number of cellular subscribers, is significant in all four models that were estimated. Models 1 and 3 show that the average marginal effect of access to information on the re-election chances of an incumbent party's presidential candidate is −0.004. This implies that the re-election chances of an incumbent party's presidential candidate are reduced by 0.4%.

Table 7.4 Marginal effects of interaction variables

	Fraud = 1			*Fraud = 0*		
Model	*(2)*	*(4)*		*(2)*	*(4)*	
	*Cellular *corruption*	*Cellular *corruption*	*Press freedom *corruption*	*Cellular *corruption*	*Cellular *corruption*	*Press freedom *corruption*
Same candidate = 1	−0.0005 (0.0015)	−0.0013 (0.0038)	0.0004 (0.0017)	−0.0010 (0.0019)	−0.0041 (0.0050)	0.0013 (0.0048)
Same candidate = 0	−0.0026 (0.0115)	−0.0081 (0.0426)	0.0026 (0.0141)	−0.0051 (0.0082)	−0.0225 (0.0286)	0.0072 (0.0238)

Robust standard errors in parentheses

***p < 0.01, **p < 0.05, *p < 0.1

Even though the control variables of electoral fraud, turnout, and change in GDP per capita have the expected signs, they are insignificant in all the models. Democracy is significant in all but three models. This variable shows that the more democratic a country is, the lower the re-election chances of an incumbent. The other two control variables, namely number of challengers and same candidate, are significant in all the models. If one more candidate decides to run for the presidency, the re-election chances of the incumbent party's presidential candidate increase by about 2%. The additional candidate splits the opposition vote, allowing the incumbent party's presidential candidate an easier path to victory. It is not surprising, therefore, that the ruling party can use this as a strategy to retain power by sponsoring smaller parties in the opposition strongholds to increase the chances of winning re-election. Such parties usually disband or end up joining the ruling party after the elections.

Fielding a sitting president is advantageous for the incumbent party. The results show that the likelihood of an incumbent party winning re-election is about 21% higher if the incumbent party fields a sitting president than when the party changes its presidential candidate. Holding everything else constant, a sitting president is already well known and therefore easier to sell than a different candidate. This may explain why after serving the maximum number of terms allowed for by the constitution, some ruling parties try to manipulate the constitution to allow the same candidate to run for office. In Zambia in 2002, for example, the incumbent president sought to change the constitution to run for a third term but failed. Similarly, in Malawi in 2004, the incumbent party made two attempts to manipulate the constitution to allow for an open term and later to a third term, but failed in both attempts.

In Models 2 and 4, interaction terms are introduced to test the response of voters when the information variables interact with corruption. The idea is that the interaction term will capture the effect of the media being able to disseminate information on corruption (Model 2) and also being able to expose corruption freely without fear (Model 4). The estimated marginal effects of information about corruption are shown in Table 7.4. Recall that there are two dummy variables that have to be accounted for.

The results in Table 7.4 show that in Africa, regardless of whether the elections are free or not and irrespective of whether the incumbent is contesting or not, information on corruption has no effect on the election outcomes. The result may seem puzzling considering that one expects voters to react to such information. These results must, however, be interpreted with caution, considering that accessibility to information was measured by a proxy (number of subscribers per 100 of population). Mavuto Kalulu (2014), using the number of radios per 1000 of population, finds some evidence that when voters are provided with information on corruption, the incumbent's chances are reduced.

Conclusion

This study set out to answer three questions: (1) whether or not voters in Africa punish incumbent parties for corruption; (2) whether voters' access to information through the media enhances the re-election chances of incumbent parties; and (3) whether or not information on corruption has an effect on the re-election chances of incumbent parties. The study employed a probit model to analyze the three questions, with re-election (taking the value of 1 if the incumbent party is re-elected and 0 if not) as the dependent variable. A key premise of this study is that corruption, defined by Transparency International as the abuse of public resources for private gain, negatively affects the economic wellbeing of citizens. A brief review of studies that found that corruption affects economic growth through a negative effect on investment has been provided in the current study. The current study finds that (1) in Africa corruption has no effect on the re-election chances of incumbent parties; (2) access to information as measured by a proxy (number of cellular subscribers per 100 of population) reduces the re-election chances of incumbent parties; and (3) when corruption is interacted with the information variables number of cellular subscribers per 100 of population and freedom of the press, there is no effect of corruption information on the re-election chances of the incumbent.

One of the challenges encountered in the study is the dearth of data in Africa. Finding data for a measure that captures voters' access to information is problematic. Since rural areas receive most of their information through radio, the number of radio broadcasters would have been a better measure compared to the number of cellular subscribers. Unfortunately, such data is not easily available.

Another challenge is the unavailability of an objective measure of electoral fraud. This study uses an indicator from the World Bank political institutions database, which categories elections as free and fair or not free. Interestingly, despite the claims of electoral fraud by the losers and sometimes independent observers, electoral fraud does not have an effect on the outcome of elections. This is another area that will require further investigation. One possibility is to check at constituency level for voter turnout that is close to or over 100%.

Despite this weakness, the major takeaway from this study is that access to information is necessary. Thus, the government and other stakeholders must prioritize voters' easy access to information. However, there is a need to investigate further why there is no response by the electorate when information on corruption is presented to them. Maybe voters in Africa view corruption differently than we would want to imagine. One possibility is that with or without corruption, they never experience any improvement in their wellbeing. Another option is that corruption is so embedded in the system that it does not matter who wins an election, they will not change anything.

Future areas to which this study could be extended include studying the effect of corruption on the re-election chances of members of parliament in Africa. The challenge at the moment is a lack of information on lawmakers who are convicted of corruption. This may be due to the ineffectiveness of the legal system, or it may be because those who engage in corruption are from the party in power and are, therefore, being protected by the system.

Topics for Discussion

1. Can rural voters rely on the media to make decisions on whom they want to elect?
2. How can the media in fragile states eliminate corruption by public officials?
3. To what extent is the media in developing regions capable of exposing institutional corruption?
4. How can voters have access to information on the re-election chances of incumbent parties in Africa?
5. How can the media work with voters to ensure that the right candidates are elected to public office?

References

Access to Information Gains Ground. World Resource Institute. April 3, 2012. Accessed Dec 18, 2016. http://www.wri.org/blog/2012/04/access-information-gains-ground-africa.

Abed, George T., and Hamid R. Davoodi. 2002. Corruption, Structural Reforms, and Economic Performance. Governance Corruption and Economic Performance, ed George T. Abed, and Sanjeev Gupta, 489–537. Washington: International Monetary Fund.

Africa-Fact Sheet: The World Bank and Energy in Africa. The World Bank. http://ideas4development.org/medias/2015/07/M3640N-3-39n@ilo-org_20150714_121049.pdf.

African Union Convention on Preventing and Combating Corruption. African Union. Accessed Dec 18, 2016. http://www.eods.eu/library/AU_Convention%20on%20Combating%20Corruption_2003_EN.pdf.

Bratton, Michael, Robert B. Mattes, and Emmanuel Gyimah-Boadi. 2005. Public Opinion, Democracy, and Market Reform in Africa. Cambridge: Cambridge University Press.

Brunetti, Aymo, and Beatrice Weder. 2003. A Free Press is Bad News for Corruption. *Journal of Public Economics* 87 (7): 1801–1824.

Brunetti, Aymo, Gregory Kisunko, and Beatrice Weder. 1998. Credibility of Rules of Economic Growth: Evidence from a Worldwide Survey of the Private Sector. *The World Bank Economic Review* 12 (3): 353–384.

Chang, Eric, and Miriam Golden. 2004. Does Corruption Pay? The Survival of Politician Charged with Malfeasance in the Postwar Italian Chamber of Deputies. Unpublished paper, Michigan State University and the University of California at Los Angeles.

Corruption Perceptions Index. 2010. Transparency International Annual Report. Accessed Dec 18, 2016. http://www.transparency.org/cpi2010/results.

Daniel Arap Moi/Anglo Leasing Case. 2004. Stolen Assets Recovery Initiative. The World Bank and United Nations Office on Drugs and Crime. Accessed Dec 18, 2016. http://star.worldbank.org/corruption-cases/node/18485.

Doh, Jonathan P., and Hildy J. Teegen. 2003. Private Telecommunications Investment in Emerging Economies-Comparing the Latin American and Asian experience. *Management Research: Journal of the lberoamerican Academy of Management* 1 (1): 9–26.

Fatton, Robert. 1986. Clientelism and Patronage in Senegal. *African Studies Review* 29 (4): 61–78.

Ferraz, Claudio, and Frederico Finan. 2008. Exposing Corrupt Politicians: The Effects of Brazil's Publicly Released Audits on Electoral Outcomes. *Quarterly Journal of Economics* 123 (2): 703–745.

Grofman, Bernard, Guillermo Owen, and Christian Collet. 1999. Rethinking the Partisan Effects of Higher Turnout: So what's the Question? *Public Choice* 99 (3–4): 357–376.

Gupta, Sanjeev, Hamid R. Davoodi, and Erwin Tiongson. 2001. Corruption and the Provision of Health Care and Education Services. In *The Political Economy of Corruption*, ed. Arvind K. Jain, 111–141. London: Routledge.

Henisz, Witold J. 2000. The Institutional Environment for Multinational Investment. *Journal of Law Economics and Organization* 16 (2): 334–364.

Huntington, Samuel P. 1968. *Political Order in Changing Societies*. New Haven: Yale University.

Inman, Kris, and Josephine T. Andrews. 2009. Corruption and Political Participation in Africa: Evidence from Survey and Experimental Research. *Midwest Political Science Association*, 3–6.

Jarso, James F. 2010. Media and the Anti-Corruption Crusade in Kenya: Weighing the Achievements, Challenges, and Prospects, The. *Am. U. Int'l L. Rev.* 26: 33.

Kalulu, Mavuto. 2014. Corruption and Re-election Chances of Incumbent Parties in Developing Countries. *Journal of Development and Communication Studies* 3 (2): 511–527.

Karahan, Gökhan R., Morris R. Coats, and William F. Shughart. 2006. Corrupt Political Jurisdictions and Voter Participation. *Public Choice* 126 (1–2): 87–106.

Knack, Stephen, and Phillip Keefer. 1995. Institutions and Economic Performance: Cross-country Tests Using Alternative Institutional Measures. *Economics and Politics* 7 (3): 207–227.

Krause, Stefan, and Fabio Méndez. 2007. "Corruption and Elections: An Empirical Study of a Cross-section of Countries. *Economics and Politics* 21 (2): 179–200.

Lambsdorff, Johann G., and Peter Cornelius. 2001. Corruption, Foreign Investment, and Growth. *The Africa Competitiveness Report* 2000: 70–78.

Lambsdorff, Johann G. 2001. *How Corruption in Government Affects Public Welfare: A Review of Theory*. No. 9. The university of Goettingen, Department of Economics.

Lambsdorff, Johann. 2008. The Methodology of the Corruption Perceptions Index. Transparency International. Accessed Dec 18, 2016. http://www.icgg.org/downloads/Methodology_2008.pdf.

Lewis-Beck, Michael S., and Mary Stegmaier. 2000. Economic Determinants of Electoral Outcomes. *Annual Review of Political Science* 3 (1): 183–219.

Liu, Francis T. 1985. An Equilibrium Queuing Model of Bribery. *Journal of Political Economy* 93 (4): 760–781.

Mauro, Paolo. 1995. Corruption and Growth. *The Quarterly Journal of Economics* 110 (3): 681–712.

Mo, Pak H. 2001. Corruption and Economic Growth. *Journal of Comparative Economics* 29 (1): 66–79.

Odinkalu, Chindi, and Maxwell Kadiri. Making Progress on Freedom of Information in Africa. Open Society Foundations. Aug 14, 2014. Accessed Dec 18, 2016. https://www.opensocietyfoundations.org/voices/making-progress-freedom-information-africa.

Peters, John G., and Susan Welch. 1980. The Effects of Charges of Corruption on Voting Behavior in Congressional Elections. *American Political Science Review* 74 (3): 697–708.

Reed, Stevens R. 1999. Punishing Corruption: The Response of the Japanese Electorate to Scandals. In *Political Psychology in Japan: Behind the Nails which Sometimes Stick out (and Get Hammered Down)*, ed. Ofer Feldman. Commack: Nova Science.

Rohwer, Anja. 2009. Measuring Corruption: A Comparison between the Transparency International's Corruption Perceptions Index and the Worldwide Governance Indicators. *CESifo DICE Report* 7 (3): 42–52.

Rundquist, Barry S., Gerald S. Storm, and John G. Peters. 1977. Corrupt Politicians and their Electoral Support: Some Experimental Observations. *American Political Science Review* 71 (3): 954–963.

Smarzynska, Beata K., and Shang-Jin Wei. 2000. *Corruption and Composition of Foreign Direct Investment: Firm-level Evidence*. No. w7969. National Bureau of Economic Research.

Straub, Stephane. 2008. Opportunism, Corruption and the Multinational Firm's Mode of Entry. *Journal of International Economics* 74 (2): 245–263.

Tanzi, Vito, and Hamid R. Davoodi. 1998. Corruption, Public Investment, and Growth. In *The Welfare State, Public Investment, and Growth*, ed. Hirofumi Shibata, and Toshihiro Ihori, 41–60. Japan: Springer.

Tanzi, Vito, and Hamid R. Davoodi. 2001. Corruption, Growth, and Public Finances. In *The Political Economy of Corruption*, ed. Arvind K. Jain, 89–110. London: Routledge.

Tikum, Njoya. 2016. To Fight Corruption, Africa must Explore Innovative Solutions. United Nations Development Programme in Africa. March 28, 2016. Accessed Dec 18, 2016. http://www.africa.undp.org/content/rba/en/home/blog/2016/3/28/To-Fight-Corruption-Africa-Must-Explore-Innovative-Solutions.html.

Transparency International. How do we Define Corruption. Accessed June 13, 2017. https://www.transparency.org/what-is-corruption/#define.

Ugur, Mehmet. 2014. Corruption's Direct Effects on Per-capita Income Growth: A Meta-analysis. *Journal of Economic Surveys* 28 (3): 472–490.

Ugur, Mehmet, and Dasgupta, Nandini. 2011. Evidence on the Economic Growth Impacts of Corruption in Low-Income Countries and Beyond. London: EPPI-Centre, Social Science Research Unit, Institute of

Education, University of London. http://eppi.ioe.ac.uk/cms/LinkClick.aspx?fileticket=wrCtuggn-IQ%3d. Accessed April 16, 2017.

Warutere, Peter. 2005. The Goldenberg Conspirancy: The Game of Paper, Gold, Money and Power. *Institute for Security Studies Papers* 117: 16.

Wei, Shang-Jin. 2000a. How Taxing is Corruption on International Investors? *Review of Economics and Statistics* 82 (1): 1–11.

Wei, Shang-Jin. 2000b. *Corruption, Composition of Capital Flows and Currency Crises*, vol. 2429. Washington: World Bank Publications.

PART IV

Marginalized Communities and the Challenge of Democracy in the US, Africa, Central, and South America

CHAPTER 8

The Impact of Governmental Strategies on Black Political Discourse Groups: Voices Heard from the Black Panther Party to the Black Lives Matter Movement

Ashlie Perry

The Civil Rights Movement: With Liberty and Justice for All

On the surface, the youthfulness and anger echoed by the Black Power movement appeared to be the polar opposite of the Civil Rights movement. Frustrated with housing and job discrimination, poverty and police brutality, the Black Power movement in the 1970s called for armed and sometimes violent resistance to the major social structures in the USA.

Ashlie Perry's research interests include identity politics, terrorism, collective action, gendered crimes, and political psychology. In this chapter, Perry uses the social strain/relative deprivation theories and backlash theory as a framework to assess the impact of policies on collective action and the mobilization of contentious groups after a backlash in the USA.

A. Perry (✉)
Endicott College, Beverly, MA, USA

E.K. Ngwainmbi (ed.), *Citizenship, Democracies, and Media Engagement among Emerging Economies and Marginalized Communities*,
DOI 10.1007/978-3-319-56215-5_8

The movement was discontented with the non-violent Civil Rights movement that sought to include everyone, and instead asserted that black people needed to urge for justice specifically for people of color:

> In order for nonviolence to work, your opponent must have a conscience, the United States has none … What Martin Luther King's contribution to us was not nonviolence which most people talk about, because that couldn't be … He told us how to face the enemy without fear and this is crucial in every struggle, because the job of the enemy is to just make the people afraid of their shadows, the shadows of the enemy. And the terrorist groups in America, the racist groups really had our people terrified, there is no question about that. If one is incapable of solving that political struggle through constitutional means, the logical extension is the gun; that is a law of history. (Stokely Carmichael in Svensson 1997)

Like the Black Lives Matter campaign that began after 2010, the Black Power movement addressed the killing of young, unarmed black men. During the Black Power movement, the members' discontent was fueled by deaths including those of Mack Charles Parker and Emmett Till, the latter a 14-year-old accused of whistling at a white woman in 1955. He was brutally murdered by a lynch mob; although the attackers were known, none of them was charged (Coleman 2012). For the Black Lives Matter campaign, the shooting and killing of Trayvon Martin sparked the dialogue for the exclusive focus on justice for black lives.

Trayvon Martin was a 17-year-old African American male walking home from the local convenience store when he was shot and killed by a neighborhood watchman in Sanford, Florida in 2012 (Lawson 2012). The highly publicized trial noted the racial undertone of the case: the presumption that Martin would not have been shot if he were not an African American. The neighborhood watchman, George Zimmerman, went on trial for Martin's murder, but was found not guilty by a jury of his peers. The Zimmerman case sparked protest, anger, applause, and speculation from many people about the judicial process. As with the 1955 murder of Emmett Till, the case represented more than the death of Trayvon: the numerous deaths of unarmed black men, the value of black lives, police brutality and the institutional policies that surround it (Lawson 2012). The murder of Trayvon Martin sparked the hashtag #blacklivesmatter on Twitter. The anger and frustration felt by many people after the trial were encapsulated in the viral movement that quickly became a national spotlight on inequities in the social structures of the USA; this movement would later become the Black Lives Matter campaign (Black Lives Matter n.d.).

Modern-day activists in the Black Lives Matter campaign can use platforms like Twitter and Facebook to spread the news about protests and marches. Most importantly, the Black Lives Matter movement has encouraged the videotaping of police profiling and of brutality, to make authorities accountable for any excessive force used. Similarly, but not to the same extent, the Civil Rights movement was able to capture excessive strength and policies toward people of color with the aid of the media. During the Civil Rights movement, activists were spit on, beaten, and jailed. Brute and excessive use of force were utilized by police officers when handling unarmed, peaceful protestors.

Photography and modern media supported the claims of the Civil Rights and Black Power movements that local and state police were authorized to use excessive force when dealing with unarmed civilians. Photographers pictured marchers having dogs unleashed on them or being beaten in the streets without provocation, and of an unarmed Martin Luther King, Jr., arrested for sitting at the whites-only counter. Regardless of the era, both movements attempted to challenge governmental interventions, or the lack thereof, through common political discourse. The Civil Rights and Black Power movements did not form in a vacuum; the political discourse groups were the byproduct of a longstanding issue of perceived injustices in the USA for people of color. A history of slavery, a nation built on a century of race supremacy, and institutional means of controlling black bodies have left their mark on the USA. This chapter investigates the context in which black collective groups mobilize to voice concerns about black lives and justice for all.

Relative Deprivation and Social Strain

Two major theoretical concepts frame this chapter. First, Smelser's social strain theory is coupled with Magnarella's theory of relative deprivation. Smelser's (1962) theory of social strain is utilized for the historical analysis of sociocultural and political factors that are thought to affect collective group activity.

Social strain theory suggests that collective action can occur under certain conditions. Smelser's theory places emphasis on the societal factors that prompt collective behavior (Locher 2002). He asserted that collective actions, like protests and social movements, become violent when structural opportunities present themselves. Politics, national strategies, economics, resources, ideology, media, and audiences all play a role in the transition to collective violent action. In the transition from the Civil Rights movement to the Black Power movement, the ideology of equality remained the same, but the strategy of excessive brute force prompted the call for "self-defense."

The second main approach used is the theory of backlash/blowback. Blowback occurs when a national security state, in this case the USA, makes decisions that ultimately create tensions and problems within a population, either within its home boundaries or abroad (Boggs 2013). Political discourse and the backlash are a reaction to the sense of "lost or threatened" power from the disadvantaged in an attempt to regain what is perceived to be lost. The known linkages to the Klu Klux Klan (KKK) and local governmental authorities, the lack of convictions in cases of the lynching of black people, and televised arrests of non-violent protestors supported the call for violent protest.

As Sharp (1973a) noted, when political leaders respond to corporate groups, particularly non-violent groups, with excessive force it often has unwanted consequences. The targeted group can become more united and increase its support to better challenge the leader. This occurs when there are martyrs and when previously neutral individuals join forces with those who experienced the repressive intervention (Sharp 1973b). From the story of Emmett Till to that of Trayvon Martin, the debate over justice for murdered black men has sparked black political discourse groups in the USA to organize and demand justice. It is the governmental interventions in such groups that largely influence their trajectory. In the 1960s, the official response included brute force and special teams to eradicate black "extremist" groups. In the 2010s, the governmental response to the death of black civilians at the hands of the authorities appears to be lacking, as no indictments have been made in cases of police brutality.

From Protests to Black Power

The struggle over the morality of treating one "race" as inferior to another began during slavery and continued into the Civil Rights movement in the USA. The ideology of superiority that propelled slavery continues to plague modern US thinking and prevents an institutional place for change (Fields 1990). The movements were the byproduct of a history of racial discrimination and biased policies at the state, local, and federal levels.

During the latter part of the 1950s, the Civil Rights movement employed several strategic, organized non-violent tactics, including boycotts, strikes, sit-ins, and attempts to integrate public places. However, during the 1960s, the "Year of Africa," several African nations gained independence from colonial powers, while many peaceful protestors still challenged the US government for the right to sit anywhere on a bus. The Year of Africa also marked the transition from the non-violent Civil Rights era to the Black Liberation/Black Power movement.

It became apparent to political activists committed to non-violence that the Civil Rights movement was a long-term objective. It was also clear that non-violent techniques utilized during the movement were not equally used by the US government, as they were met with brute force. Many student organizations and churches were at the helm of activities. In April 1963, a group of non-violent Christian student protesters were met with brute force by the Alabama police. Police released dogs on the crowd, physically abusing students; they also used high-powered water hoses. Journalists captured the later iconic images of the Civil Rights movement worldwide and the brute tactics employed by local authorities: physical abuse, the use of dogs, and high-pressure water hoses. In 1964, activists passing through Mississippi were arrested by the deputy sheriff, who then released them to members of the KKK; all three men were beaten and murdered (Southern Poverty Law Center n.d.).

The Civil Rights Ideology

An incorrect and binary view of the Civil Rights movement's ideology gives the impression that it suddenly "shifted northward and became more urban, angry and less deserving of public support after 1965" (Burrell 2012, p. 137). The swiftness with which Black Power became an acceptable ideology in more urban settings, and overall during the latter part of the Civil Rights movement, was attributed to the continued poverty, the incongruences felt from the liberalist approach, and the discrimination that blacks in America continued to believe occurred (Burrell 2012).

The Civil Rights Act, the Voting Rights Act, and the 11246 Executive Order starting Affirmative Action, all dating from 1965, did not end the poor living conditions or lack of political and educational opportunities. African Americans were still disenfranchised, and the Civil Rights Act did little to change what was happening on the ground. Discrimination that was present in society continued to fuel a weary population and created additional tension among minorities (Burrell 2012). Persistent police brutality and discriminatory practices in hiring made the struggles of the Civil Rights movement seem in vain.

Before his assassination in 1965, Malcolm Little, known as Malcolm X, went from being a silent observer of the early 1960s Civil Rights movement to becoming a boisterous voice in the Black Power movement. He supported involvement in the Black Liberation movement and urged for the fight for human rights versus civil rights. The Federal Bureau of Investigation (FBI) worked with its Nationof Islam (NOI) informants to "neutralize" Malcolm X (DiEugenio and Pease 2003). It submitted harsh letters to Elijah Muhammad, feigning an origin from Malcolm. After his hajj to Mecca, Malcolm began to rethink his separatist stance, but was assassinated in February 1965. The New York Police Department (NYPD), FBI, and the Nation of Islam were major components in the assassination (DiEugenio and Pease 2003).

On April 4, 1968, Martin Luther King, Jr. was shot and killed while standing on the balcony of a hotel in Memphis, Tennessee, by a "well-dressed white man" (Martin Luther King Shot n.d.). James Earl Ray pleaded guilty to shooting King, but two weeks later recanted his statement. The court upheld its decision to deny Ray a trial eight times. Coretta Scott King advocated for Ray to have a trial, in an attempt to establish the facts about those involved in the murder (Death of Judge 1969; DiEugenio and Pease 2003). The assassination was shrouded in conspiracy theories of government involvement and a systematic attempt to remove opponents of the US government.

Donald Wilson, a principal witness in the King assassination trial, removed and preserved artifacts from the scene that in 1999 were used as evidence of foul play. Judge W. Preston Battle, the first judge on the case, stated on record during the trial that James Earl Ray could not have acted alone based on the evidence presented in the case (DiEugenio and Pease 2003). Ray was sentenced to 99 years for King's assassination, even though it was clear that he was aided in the crime.

After Ray's sentencing, Battle noted that he, like many citizens at the time, was perplexed by the assassination, the further involvement beyond Ray, and the gun used (Judge Battle Dies 1969). Suspicion of conspiracy and an outside intervention by the FBI in King's murder arose quickly in many parts of the African American community. Evidence and the lack of proof suggested that it was likely that Ray did not act alone but was assisted, as he himself suggested, by the US government.

Battle acknowledged the accusations of a conspiracy surrounding King's assassination, but noted that Ray confessed to the act with a "sound mind" (Judge Battle Dies 1969; Death of Judge Entitles Trial 1997). It was not until 1999 that it was officially found that "foul play" had occurred on the part of an outside agency. However, the US government failed to determine which agency was involved.

During the wake of the transition from the Civil Rights movement (1954–1964) to the Black Power movement (1964–1972), the Black Panther Party for Self-Defense formed in Oakland, California. It comprised mainly college students/graduates. In 1967, the Student Nonviolent Coordinating Committee (SNCC) and the Black Panther Party (BPP) formed an alliance, due to their kindred ideology, and began the international struggle for enslaved Africans and African Americans (Spero 2008). In that same year, the BPP removed "for Self-Defense" from its name and began the socialist aspect of its ideology (implementation of social programs geared at free education, healthcare, and criminal services). The extremist ideology that pushed for "revolutionary violence" was rooted in community activism and the attempt to remove violent policing from black neighborhoods (Kirby 2011).

While the BPP encourage Black Americans to buy from Black owned business in their respective communities, police brutality within the community continued, validating the organization's claim for physical self-defense against the police (Newton 1973). Recruitment into, and support of, the BPP increased as it positioned itself as a community organization. The death of Malcolm X, a proponent of self-defense, and King mobilized many African Americans into the Black Liberation movement. These assassinations offered the BPP an additional venue to express its frustrations and gain community support. It used various tactics to show its frustration with the government of the USA, local police, and over the war in Vietnam. The group's tactics included rallies, armed protests, and firing at police officers. Police, under the false pretenses of members of the BPP, were called to a location and bombarded with firepower by the group (Courtney 1969).

The Central Intelligence Agency (CIA) and local police authorities used brute force to arrest and expel members of the BPP in 1969. BPP members Fred Hampton and Mark Clark were killed during a police raid in Chicago, while in their beds, contrary to the original report released by the local authorities. Several BPP members were injured and killed during the raids; the government response prompted harsher response tactics by the party. The Weather Underground formed in 1969 as well, in response to the US involvement in Vietnam and domestic policies toward African Americans. The deaths of Hampton and Clark sparked the Weather Underground into violent action since the group believed that the government was engaging in the sanctioned killing of black Americans (Green and Siegel 2003).

The BPP was experiencing increasing economic and organizational problems by the early 1970s. Members involved in organized crime (Black Guerilla Family), the loss of key members to death or jail over the expansion of the organization's territory, clashing beliefs between members like Eldridge Cleaver and Huey Newton, and lost community support all became part of the group's demise (Carson and Carson 1990). With the assistance of the FBI and the US government (including the police), by the mid-1970s many of the leaders of the BPP were in exile, dead, or in prison.

A special division within the FBI was created to counter "black" extremism, the Counter Intelligence Program (COINTELPRO), a government intervention formed at the federal level. The division was established to eradicate the threat of black political discourse groups using different tactics: espionage, bombings of the BPP headquarters, manipulation of members, and even murder. It is noted that at the time when COINTELPRO against "black extremism" began, both Malcolm X and Martin Luther King, Jr. were assassinated.

Collective Action in the USA

The Dynamics of Collective Action in the United States (DCA) is a database that specifically observes any form of collective action in the USA. According to the DCA, there were 22,952 forms of collective action in the USA between 1960 and 1995. It observed that the number of collective action events in the USA increased in the 1960s to peaks in 1965 ($N = 1051$) and 1969 ($N = 1006$) and then decreased until the mid-1970s. There was a rise in events again in 1979 ($N = 897$). Figure 8.1 shows the distribution of collective action events.

As can be seen from the figure, collective action in the USA increased during the time of the Civil Rights and Black Power movements. The peaks of protests in 1965 and 1969 coincide with the assassinations of King and Malcolm X. However, the decrease at the close of the 1970s coincides with the demise of the BPP. The CIA and local police authorities used brute force to arrest and expel members of the party in 1969.

Fig. 8.1 Beginning year of collective action in the United States: 1960–1995

Social Strain in the Civil Rights and Black Power Movements

Social strain theory and relative deprivation theory are utilized to identify the social conditions that aid in the transition from perceived grievances to collective action/black political discourse groups in the USA. Social strain factors (see Table 8.1) include external factors, group's ideology/ goal, type of movement, size of campaign, and the "last straw" event. External factors include the historical, cultural, and contextual factors previously outlined in the case analysis.

In September 1963, four girls were killed in an Alabama church bombing as retaliation for the non-violent student protest that had occurred there (Spero 2008). The SNCC increased its militant ideology and picketed the United Nations (UN) in response to the deaths. Stokely Carmichael, a future leader of the BPP, organized rallies in the South as a member of the SNCC. There was an effort to address the grievances of African Americans at national and local levels. Documents later revealed that the FBI investigated the incident but made no arrest, under President Hoover's advisement, and that the facts of the case were not appropriately disseminated to concerned parties.

A political figure accepted in both white and black areas, King was a symbol of the non-violent ideology. The FBI denied any involvement in his death, but was forced to acknowledge that the COINTELPRO program had targeted King during its investigations of black extremists. With

Table 8.1 Social strain factors in the civil rights and black liberation movements

	Social strain factors
Movement's ideology/goal	Civil rights, economic and political equality (including nationalist, socialist, separatist, and conservative perspectives)
Group's ideology/goal	Economic and political equality
Type of movement	Reform (civil rights), revolutionary (black Llberation)
Type of organization	Nationalist/separatist, communist/socialist
External support	Diaspora to African movements and vice versa, Weather Underground, British Diaspora
Length of movement	1950s–early 1980s
Length of organization	1960s–1980s
Tipping point	Assassination of Martin Luther King, Jr. and the murder of Emmett Till

direct orders from J. Edgar Hoover, FBI agents wrote officially documented letters to King advising him to kill himself. The 1968 assassination marked the "last straw" event for the liberal movement for equality: the voice of the non-violent, Gandhi-inspired resistance was murdered without another charismatic non-violent leader to take his place.

Infrastructural Conditions Leading to Discontent

Infrastructural circumstances in the USA continued to be a source of discontent. After the emancipation proclamation, economic and political opportunities for African Americans continued to be scarce. From the "grandfather" clause that prevented fair voting to sharecropping practices that made many African Americans into modern-day indentured servants, living conditions for many created discontent with the American political system.

The BPP's 10 Point Plan outlined the group's grievances and the economic and social disparities that it identified in American society, listing the structural changes that led to discontent. The lack of adequate housing and employment opportunities for people of color, the disproportionate number of poor and black people fighting in Vietnam, and the lack of trial by a "jury of peers" were structural factors that needed to change. Most notably, the BPP demanded the freedom and power to determine black people's destiny. The Weather Underground supported the point of ending American aggression (wars) and joined in an alliance with the BPP. The organization aided the BPP in several bombings and attacks.

Insufficiencies of the Infrastructure Not Corrected

The end of World War II sparked a new form of activism that addressed grievances beyond the Supreme Court and took petitions to the international community, mainly the UN. As petitions and requests went unheard, African American leaders began the Civil Rights movement to foster public and political audiences in the USA and abroad.

Although the Civil Rights movement utilized non-violent techniques, the US government responded to protests with brute police force. Additionally, its response to the request for equal rights was slow and calculated. After a decade of protests, coupled with beatings, bombings, lack of infrastructural change, and the excessive use of police brutality, the Black Liberation voice emerged. The idea of self-defense and an armed resistance became appealing to individuals who found the pacifist approach lacking. Black civilians found themselves at the helm of a revolution that did not require them to expect to be beaten. The Black Power movement called for them to be active agents for change and to use violence like their opponents. The boldness of the BPP encouraged others to follow their armed example. Charles Drew, as noted by Fergus (2009), relayed the sentiment of emboldenment by the militant group:

> When rumors surfaced that the Klan was going to shoot in the house of big niggers, I went to the sporting store ... I said, "I want a rifle ... because I understand that the Ku Klux Klan is gonna be coming through my neighborhood this weekend, and I'm not going to get on the floor anymore" ... When I saw [the Panthers] stand up against the landlords, the police and the Klan with those guns ... I attribute that courage to Larry Little and the Panthers.

Formation of Ideologies Revolving Around Discontent

Unlike the Civil Rights movement, the Black Power movement called on the young, frustrated, secular, urban, and poor to create change in their neighborhoods. The movement embraced "blackness" (i.e., wearing afros) and promoted being a self-sufficient movement without the reliance on, or alliance with, any white counterparts. Chants like "Black is beautiful, Free Heuy P. Newton" emphasized one side of the black campaign for rights, unlike its predecessors. Black people urged for self-determination and did so by the use of violent force and community activism. Continued frustration with the lack of support from the US government and the UN suggested to the leaders of the time that non-violent tactics were becoming obsolete.

The frustration created a space for more extreme ideologies that began to call for territorial separation from the USA and self-defense while in the country. Malcolm X's nationalist ideology urged for human rights and became popular in the early to mid-1960s. His organization, the Organization of Afro-American Unity (OAAU), and the SNCC were leading more aggressive campaigns by the mid-1960s.

Violent Action Manifests Itself

The political and social conditions in the USA between the 1950s and 1970s created a space for extremist ideologies, after several failed attempts to address grievances institutionally. In 1965, the USA passed several forms of legislation that ushered in the end of the Civil Rights movement. However, the lack of change in society, continued poverty, and police brutally allowed the transition into the Black Liberation and Black Power movement. By the end of the 1960s, many African Americans were urged to arm themselves and "fight back." Political leaders like Stokely Carmichael advocated armed resistance. In one of his speeches, he noted the link between politics and violence: "Political power grows out of the barrel of a gun, and the Negro must get that gun" (Courtney 1969).

Carmichael, a member of the BPP, echoed the voice of the Black Liberation movement by appealing to the frustration that many African Americans felt. The assassinations of both King and Malcolm X continued to draw suspicion about government involvement.

Summary

From the start of racial slavery in America to the Black Power/Black Liberation movement of the 1960s, people of African descent campaigned, petitioned, and institutionally attempted to reduce the inequalities in the USA. As early as 1857, with the Dred Scott ruling of "separate but equal" in the case of different races sharing a train, people of color attempted to address social injustices legally. Perceived grievances ranged from inequality in housing and job opportunities to police brutality, mobilizing black Americans to advocate social change.

Several institutional attempts were made to secure civil rights before and during the Civil Rights movement. The use of petitions and non-violent tactics slowly gave way to the voices of the armed Black Liberation movement. The assassinations of both King and Malcolm X enraged the black community. Coupled with the lack of change at the fundamental level and the official response to brute force, tactics used by the Black Power/Black Liberation movement included confrontations with police and riots; a notable change from the Civil Rights activist responses to the use of police force.

The BPP is often thought to have sprung from the Civil Rights movement as a violent black political discourse group with little community involvement or commonalities with the Civil Rights movement. Brute force used by the police during the 1950s–1960s peaceful Civil Rights movement created a backlash, infuriating many African Americans and sparking the Black Liberation movement. The ideology that prevailed during the Civil Rights movement (i.e., Malcolm X, SNCC, Congress of Racial Equality, etc.) continued into the Black Liberation movement. The ideology of the Civil Rights movement included the request for civil liberties and equal opportunities for African Americans and other groups of people of color. During the Black Liberation movement, the ideology continued to focus on civil liberties and equality of opportunity, but non-violence was no longer the tactic of choice. The Black Liberation/Black Power movement called for black power swiftly, and by any means necessary. Continuing the theme of equal opportunities, especially politically and by any means necessary, the BPP emerged during this time.

The Black Lives Matter Movement: Stop Killing Us

The fervor and frustration of the Black Power movement were quelled by the end of the 1970s. A small resurgence of a black issue movement was felt in the early 1900s, mainly after the Rodney King beating, discussed shortly. However, the same fervor and frustration of the Black Power movement were directly drawn on by the Black Lives Matter campaign, calling for justice for black lives. Some 50 years after the Civil Rights movement, black Americans continue to protest for the end of police brutality and institutional inequalities:

> When we say Black Lives Matter, we are broadening the conversation around state violence to include all of the ways in which Black people are intentionally left powerless at the hands of the state. We are talking about the ways in which Black lives are deprived of our basic human rights and dignity. (BlackLivesMatter.com n.d.)

The Black Lives Matter campaign attributes its beginnings to the Trayvon Martin–George Zimmerman trial that occurred in 2012. The Zimmerman case was based on the defense that Zimmerman adhered to the "stand your ground" policy found in Florida. The discussion of "defending" and feeling "threatened" are terms that have resurfaced in explanations about the shooting of unarmed black men and police brutality.

In 1992, riots erupted in Los Angeles, California, after four police officers were found not guilty of charges of assault with a deadly weapon and excessive use of force by a policeman, in a high-profile case (Rodney King Bio n.d.). Rodney King, a motorist pulled over by the Los Angeles Police Department (LAPD), was beaten on camera after a high-speed chase in 1991. The defense attorneys moved the trial from Los Angeles to a predominantly white suburb. The officers were found not guilty by a majority white jury. The Los Angeles riots resulted in an estimated US$1 billion in property damage (Rodney King Bio n.d.). The Department of Justice later found two of the officers guilty of infringements of civil rights. The other two officers were found not guilty. King was awarded US$3.8 million for the injuries he sustained. The lack of charges against the police sparked fresh anger among black Americans about the criminal justice system and the rights of black people.

Police brutality and the excessive use of force by officers continue to be a long-standing tension between communities of color and the police/criminal justice system. By the time the Martin–Zimmerman trial became part of mainstream media, Trayvon had become a symbol of inequalities in the criminal justice system.

Emergence of a Movement

One of the underlying concepts of the Zimmerman case, and in the USA generally, is the idea that black victims provoke their own deaths or assaults. The belief that the victim acts in a way to warrant the outcome of an incident is largely applied to black male victims. In the case of Martin, the fact that he was wearing a hoodie and was in the "wrong" neighborhood was used by defense lawyers to support the claim that he was suspicious and a threat. This justification was based on the idea that Martin, not the civilian with a gun, was responsible for his death by being suspicious/threatening. This notion has been applied in several cases in the past where black people were accused of being "uppity," "whistling at a white woman," or simply "out of place," as was asserted for Martin (Lawson 2012). Abuses ranging from police brutality to lynching have used this underlying belief to justify institutional inequalities and vigilante justice.

The "guilty by default" notion not only rouses perceived injustices in the black community, but also trickles down into the legal system when determining the guilt of the accused. The criminal justice system is marred with instances of social injustices, including mass incarceration, wrongful convictions, and racial profiling (Lawson 2012).

The wrongful conviction of many black males is supported by the exoneration rates of the Innocence Project, an advocacy group of lawyers who help prove that discrimination is present in the criminal justice system. This group highlights the number of men wrongly sent to prison. The mass incarceration rates are heavily skewed toward people of color: African American males are incarcerated 6.7 times more than white males (Walker et al. 2012). Statistically, African Americans account for 12.1% of the US population, but 42% of the prison population (Walker et al. 2012; Seiter 2013). Such discrepancies in sentencing showcase institutional inequalities. Racial profiling, including the once controversial "stop and frisk" policy, disproportionately targeted men of color. Despite the known and documented cases of racial inequality in the criminal justice system, the "guilty by default" mentality continues to prevail as a commonly accepted truth and has an impact on the availability of equal/fair due process (Lawson 2012).

The ability of the defense, and Zimmerman, to successfully make the case that he felt "threatened" by an unarmed young black male perpetuated the "guilty by default" norm. Martin had not committed a crime for Zimmerman to investigate. Furthermore, there was not a suspect description in the area that Martin fit, nor was he near the scene of a crime; he did not appear to be an *actual* threat. In short, the message that resounded from the case was that Trayvon Martin was responsible for his own death because he was "out of place" and threatening. This is a message that has been repeated in other trials favoring police officers and vigilante civilians in regard to causing harm to black bodies. African

Americans and many in the black/brown communities related this to Martin's case, as it was a long-standing grievance (Lawson 2012).

The Black Lives Matter campaign grew from the frustration at perceived civil injustice and the dismissal of the notion that race was not a major factor in Martin's fate. Martin's death and Zimmerman's freedom sparked a movement unsatisfied with the message that black lives do not matter, especially in the eyes of the legal system.

The Rise of Discourse

The death of Trayvon Martin served as a catalyst for the Black Lives Matter hashtag and the internet discussion of social reform. However, it was the shooting of Michael Brown, another young black man, which drew the discourse from the web and placed it on the streets of Ferguson, Missouri.

Brown was an 18-year-old unarmed black male who was shot by Officer Darren Wilson in August 2014. Brown fit the description of a suspect in a theft at a convenience store who was seen on camera footage taking the cigarettes. The factual accounts vary beyond the camera in the convenience store: Wilson and some eyewitnesses allege that Brown attempted to take his gun and he then fired shots; other eyewitness accounts suggest that Wilson tried to pull Brown into the car and then fired shots. What is known is that Wilson left his vehicle and pursued Brown on foot. Brown turned to face Wilson, and was then shot several times in the chest and body (Harris and Edwards 2016).

Brown's body, covered by a sheet, became a symbolic tipping point for black Americans regarding the use of force (Harris and Edwards 2016). Wilson shot a total of 12 rounds at Brown (New York Times n.d.). Witness accounts range from saying that Wilson shot Brown in the back as he fled to Brown surrendering after he turned to face Wilson. Regardless of the process, Brown was shot and killed over a pack of cigarettes. The images of his body went viral, and frustration and anger grew in various parts of the country.

Before Brown's shooting, brown and black citizens of Ferguson felt unfairly targeted by the police department. A report conducted after the death found that the Ferguson Police Department was responsible for numerous constitutional violations, including the use of racial slurs, excessive use of Tasers, targeting the poor, and handcuffing individuals without probable cause. The grievances of the Missouri community in the 2000s echoed those in California in the 1960s. In the case of Martin, Zimmerman was not found guilty; Wilson was not even indicted for the death of Brown (Harris and Edwards 2016).

A combination of frustration with the police, the death of another young black male, and the repeated message of "guilty by default" sparked a string of protests in Ferguson that spread throughout the nation. The internet community of activists that shared the hashtag #blacklivesmatter now called for a physical presence on the streets. Trayvon Martin, Michael Brown, Freddie Gray, Eric Garner, and many other black men killed by excessive police force created and continue to fuel the Black Lives Matter movement.

Social Strain Factors in the Black Lives Matter Campaign

As with the Civil Rights and Black Power movements, Black Lives Matter has outlined its "guiding principles." The BPP stated its purpose through a 10 point plan; the Black Lives Matter uses 13 guiding principles to affirm its agenda. The guiding principles include, but are not limited to, diversity, globalism, restorative justice, being unapologetically black, transgender affirming, having collective value, focusing on black women, establishing black villages, empathy, building black families, queer affirming, loving engagement, and intergenerational (Black Lives Matter n.d.).

A guiding principle of the Black Lives Matter movement highlights the lack of black voices in the criminal justice system and the need for reform in policing practices. By not subscribing to the call to diffuse the topic to "All Lives Matter," the movement points to the general human strain factor that all lives are not treated equally in the American social space (Black Lives Matter n.d.). The goal of restorative justice hopes to permeate beyond the criminal justice system and intends to debunk the delegitimizing myths about black people as "guilty by default" or as individuals without a right to discourse (i.e., All Lives Matter). Refusing to accept social pressure to include "All Lives" mirrors the stance of the BPP to address black lives only (Table 8.2).

Table 8.2 Social strain factors in the black lives matter movement

	Social strain factors
Movement's ideology/goal	Civil rights, humanizing black lives, social and political equality
Group's ideology/goal	Social and political equality, involving various aspects of "black lives" and the humanizing of black lives/bodies
Type of movement	Reform and ethnic pride
External support	LGBT community, other black activist groups, black Diaspora
Length of movement	Three years
Length of organization	2012–current
Tipping point	Deaths of Trayvon Martin and Michael Brown

Note As the Black Lives Matter movement is in its infancy, this table reflects the information to date

Infrastructural Conditions Leading to Discontent

The black community has frequently echoed the notion that excessive and brute force has led to a disproportionate number of people of color killed by the police, leading to further discontent with the US government. In recent years, the black community has called on the Department of Justice to release statistics about the number of people killed by police every year. Repeatedly, the Department of Justice has not been able to supply the data either to refute or to support the claim that black Americans are shot and killed at a rate higher than their counterparts. Despite a call for mandatory reporting of deaths to the federal government, the USA continues to lack a comprehensive way to account for civilian deaths at the hands of officers. This infrastructural failure was acknowledged at a level as high as the former Attorney General Eric Holder, who said: "We lack the ability right now to comprehensively track the number of incidents. … Fixing this is an idea that we should all be able to unite behind" (The Guardian 2015). Nevertheless, institutional changes were not made. Promises of institutional change followed immediately after Brown's death, but a mandate to report civilian deaths was not installed before Holder's departure from the position. The suggestion to amend the current practice and solidify a more accountable system has largely been ignored, especially after the violent protests in Ferguson and Baltimore were quelled.

The FBI currently uses a system of "voluntary responses" to track justifiable deaths by police officers (The Guardian 2015). Independent groups, such as journalists at UK newspaper *The Guardian* and Killed By the Police, try to fill the data void by collecting data from crowd-sourced information (http://killedbypolice.net/). *The Guardian*, also inspired by the protest surrounding Michael Brown's death, began collecting data in an attempt to add to the discussion about the excessive use of force and policing in black communities (The Guardian 2015). It estimates that between 2005 and 2012 some 1100 police departments out of 18,000 reported justifiable killings.

Data collected by The Counted project, researched by a journalist at *The Guardian*, found that in 2015 a total of 1136 people were killed by the police, representing an increasing trend; the data was collected via crowdsourced information (see Figs. 8.2, 8.3, and 8.4). Caucasian Americans killed by police accounted for nearly half of the

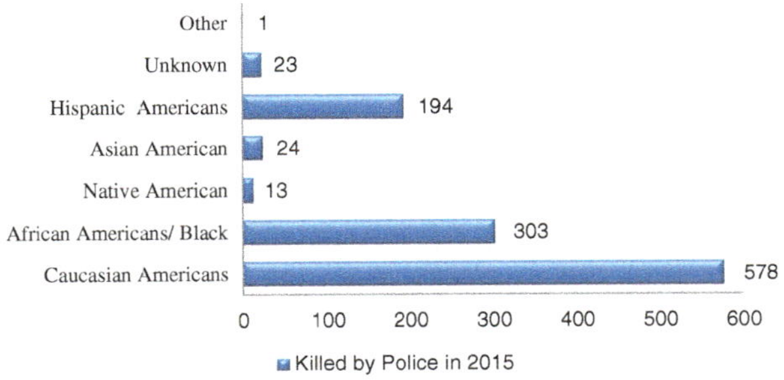

Fig. 8.2 Individuals killed by the police in 2015. *Source* The Guardian (2015)

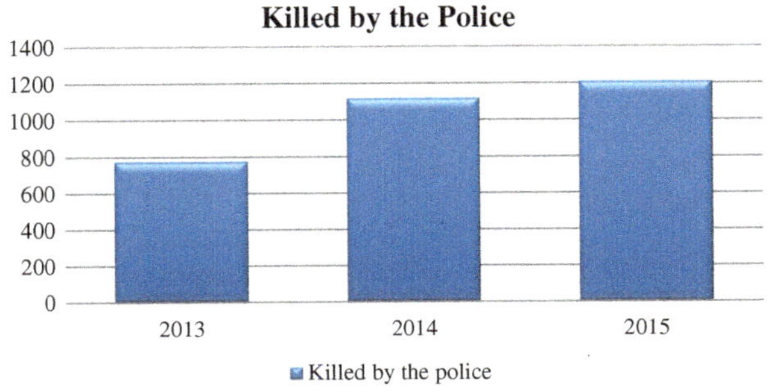

Fig. 8.3 Individuals killed by the police 2013–2015. *Source* http://killedbypolice.net/

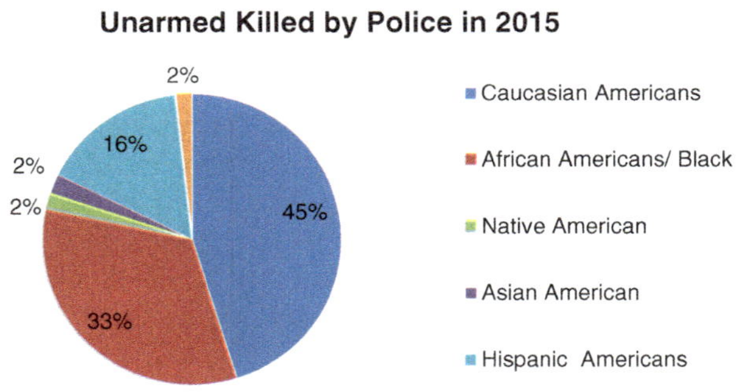

Fig. 8.4 Unarmed individuals killed by police in 2015, by race. *Source* The Guardian (2015)

dead (N = 578) at 45% of the total number. This rate is slightly lower than the proportion of Caucasians in the USA, around 62% of the overall population, but still somewhat consistent with The Counted's data findings. In contrast, African Americans/blacks accounted for 33% of the unarmed civilians killed by police between 2013 and 2015, even though African Americans make up only 13% of the total US population.

Insufficiencies of the Infrastructure Not Being Corrected

After the protest in Ferguson, groups like the Black Lives Matter movement and other civilians began to report instances of police mistreatment to mainstream media more so than in the preceding years. This reporting is aimed at debunking the dialogue that police brutality happens at the hands of a "few bad apples," and stressing that it is more of a systemic issue. For instance, on April 9, 2015, a 25-year-old black man died while in police custody. He was arrested in Baltimore, Maryland, and was alive and responsive. After a 45 min van ride, Freddie Gray arrived at the jail with severe injuries, from which he died from a week after his arrest (Lee 2015). The tension in Baltimore between police and the black community was high even before Gray's death. As with the Los Angeles riots in 1992, the protest after Martin's death in 2012, and that after the 2014 killing of Michael Brown, an infuriated group of Baltimore natives protested in the streets.

Gray's story highlights many of the grievances echoed in both the Black Liberation and Black Lives Matter movements, that social, economic, and political equalities still exist in America. Gray grew up in an impoverished neighborhood in Baltimore. His family received a "lead check" after he and his siblings showed side effects of living in an apartment that was not de-leaded and suitable for children to inhabit; an unfortunately common phenomenon for some inner-city children. Gray was four grade levels behind his peers in reading skills and comprehension and had a history of selling drugs (Hermann and Cox 2015). When one of the officers spoke at the beginning of the trials in 2016, he asserted that the consensus in the van was that Gray was "feigning" sickness to avoid being booked for lockup. They decided to ignore his plea for help. The "guilty by default" myth has an underlying tone that Gray was a criminal, a young male, and that his actions led to his demise, not the actions of the officers. None of the officers involved in the case was indicted for Gray's death.

Justice for Some

On January 2, 2016, a group of armed ranchers took over the Malheur National Wildlife Refuge (Welch 2016). The armed and law breaking ranchers were not assumed "guilty by default" like the aforementioned cases of unarmed black men and women. Unlike Trayvon Martin, Ammon Bundy and his followers disobeyed the law and were armed when doing so. The ability of the defiant armed ranchers to give interviews, engage in negotiations, and openly break the law with limited backlash from law enforcement solidified the grievances of black political discourse groups.

In stark contrast to the unarmed protestors in Ferguson and Baltimore, the media depicted the armed men as "occupiers" and not mob members. They were also able to talk to negotiators and express their ideology. The US government decided to deploy the National Guard on unarmed Black Lives Matter protesters, but not on the armed men in Oregon. "Did I miss the call for the National Guard in Oregon? I recall them in Ferguson and Baltimore," said Roland Martin via Twitter (Welch 2016).

It did not take long for black Americans, social media, and many others to recognize the stark contrast in approaching armed Caucasians who were breaking the law and unarmed black men. "Admit it. If the armed

Oregon militia were black or Muslim, they'd all be dead by now," commented Michael Moore, also via Twitter (Welch 2016). The Black Lives Matter movement was branded as deviant and its members arrested for trespassing at political campaign rallies, while armed and trespassing ranchers were deemed to be "occupiers" by the media (Welch 2016).

Summary

The grievances that black political groups are expressing in the twenty-first century echo those of the Civil Rights and Black Liberation movements. The Black Panther Party grew out of the Civil Rights movement, but police brutality sparked the "self-defense" campaign that led to violent discourse. The Black Liberation movement, unlike the Civil Rights movement, focused on the needs of black Americans and the injustices faced by that group.

The Black Lives Matter campaign openly cites the Black Liberation movement as one of its models for black empowerment, specifically focusing on the needs of people of color (Black Lives Matter n.d.). To assume that the social movements of the twentieth century are not in some part ingrained in the current political discourse would be a disservice to both movements. As Patrisse Cullors, co-founder of Black Lives Matter, commented: "[The BPP] made 'black' a word to be proud of … Their legacy is about challenging a narrative that our black lives do not matter, that actually what is true and honest is that we know best what we need to live our lives" (Weise 2016).

The Martin/Zimmerman case symbolized the treatment of blacks in America and the official response that seems to support, if not justify, action against black bodies. The "stand your ground" policy was used by the defense to suggest that feeling "threatened" is grounds for murder. The delegitimizing myth that black people are dangerous and are criminals adds a layer of complication when addressing the intersection of race and law. The message received by the black community was that black lives do not matter, the legal system does not support justice for all, and it is the duty of black Americans to make others feel "safe." The "guilty by default" principle used to support social and political inequalities is what sparked the Black Lives Matter campaign (#blacklivesmatter) on Twitter.

Another similarity in the Black Liberation and Black Lives matter movements are the reformation aspect. Both movements chose black political discourse to express the need for systemic reform, institutionally and within the black community. The BPP sought to encourage black people to embrace their "blackness" and focus attention on their political and social needs. Black Lives Matter expands on the notion of embracing "blackness" and seeks to include the LGBT (lesbian, gay, bisexual, and transgender) community in the discussion about black lives. Tipping points for both movements include the killing of a young black male, Emmett Till during the Civil Rights movement and Trayvon Martin for Black Lives Matter.

The Black Lives Matter movement is still in the early days of formation. Unlike its sometimes armed predecessor, the Black Liberation/ Power movement, Black Lives Matter attempts to use social media to draw awareness to cases of police brutality and inequalities in the legal system. The deaths of several black men in the last five years due to police brutality, excessive use of force, or vigilante justice have passed without accountability, supported by legal decisions not to indict those parties involved. The issue of social and political justice seems to be a continued cycle of discontent in the USA. The future of the Black Lives Matter movement and any subsequent protest group could largely be quelled or exacerbated by official responses to grievances.

Topics for Discussion

1. How are the Black Liberation movement and the Black Lives Matter movement similar?
2. What are some differences, other than the time frame, that stand out to you about the tactics or approaches of the two groups?
3. Do you think more social movements like these are likely to happen? Why or why not? Which type of movement, the Black Liberation movement or the Black Lives Matter movement, is more likely to occur?
4. What can governments do, in terms of policy or strategy, to quell such political discourse groups?
5. Should anything be done to appease these groups? Dismantle them?
6. What is a backlash theory and how does it apply to the events described in this chapter?

Works Cited

Biography. Rodney King Biography. Last modified 23 June 2015. http://www.biography.com/people/rodney-king-9542141#acquittal-and-resulting-riots.

Black Lives Matter. Black Lives Matter. Accessed 12 Dec 2015. http://blacklivesmatter.com.

Boggs, Carl. 2013. *Masters of War: Militarism and Blowback In the Era of American Empire*. London: Routledge.

Bruinius, Harry. For Black Lives Matter, MLK's Activism Isn't the Only Way. *Christian Science* Monitor, January 18, 2016. Accessed 11 Feb 2016. http://www.csmonitor.com/USA/Society/2016/0118/For-Black-Lives-Matter-MLK-s-kind-of-activism-isn-t-the-only-way.

Burell, Kristopher. 2012. Where from here? Ideological Perspectives on the Future of the Civil Rights Movement, 1964–1966. *The Western Journal of Black Studies* 36: 137–148.

Buchanan, Larry, Ford Fessenden, K. Rebecca Lai, Haeyoun Park, Alicia Parlapiano, Archie Tse, Tim Wallace, Derek Watkins, and Karen Yourish. What happened in Ferguson? *New York Times*, August 10, 2015. Accessed 19 Feb 2016. http://www.nytimes.com/interactive/2014/08/13/us/ferguson-missouri-town-under-siege-after-police-shooting.html?_r=0.

Carson, Clayborne, and David M. Carson. 1990. The Black Panther Party. In *Encyclopedia of the American Left*, ed. Mari Jo Buhle et al. New York: Garland Publishing.

Coleman, Jeffrey Lamar. (ed.). 2012. *Words of Protest, Words of Freedom: Poetry of the American Civil Rights Movement and Era*. Duke University Press.

Courtney, Kent. 1969. Are These Cats Red? The Black Panthers: An expose of a Communist front Which is Engaging in Guerilla Warfare Against High Schools and Universalities. *Conservative Society of America* 23. Michigan State University Library Archives. https://archive.lib.msu.edu/DMC/AmRad/thesecatsred.pdf.

Death of Judge Entitles Trial. 1997. New York Times, September 3. Accessed 08 Nov 2013. http://www.nytimes.com/1997/09/03/us/death-of-judge-is-said-to-entitle-james-earl-ray-to-a-new-trial.html.

DiEugenio, James, and Lisa Pease (eds.). 2003. *The Assassinations: Probe Magazine on JFK, MLK, RFK and Malcolm X*. Port Townsend: Feral House.

Fergus, Devin. 2009. *Liberalism, Black Power, and the Making of American Politics, 1965–1980*. Athens: University of Georgia Press.

Fields, Barbara Jeanne. 1990. Slavery, Race and Ideology in the United States of America. *New Left Review* 181 (1): 95–118.

Green, Sam and Siegel, Bill. 2003. The Weather Underground Film produced by The Free History Project, Inc.

Harris, Duchess, and Sue Bradford Edwards. 2016. *Black Lives Matter*. Minneapolis: ABDO Publishing.

Hermann, Peter, and John, Cox. 2015. A Freddie Gray Primer: Who Was He, How Did He Die, Why Is There So Much Anger? *The Washington Post*, April 28. Accessed 13 Feb 2016. www.washingtonpost.com/news/local/wp/2015/04/28/a-freddie-gray-primer-who-was-he-how-did-he-why-is-there-so-much-anger/?utm_term=.e462b52b675e.

Judge W. 1969. Preston Battle Dies; Presided Over the Ray Trial. *New York Times*, (31 March). Accessed 08 Nov 2013. http://jfk.hood.edu/Collection/White%20%20Files/King%20Jr%20Martin%20Luther/MLK%20490.pdf.

Kirby, Ryan. 2011. The Revolution Will Not Be Televised: Community activism and the Black Panther Party, 1966–1971. *Canadian Review of American Studies* 41: 25–62. Accessed 23 June 2015. doi:10.1353/crv.2011.0001.

Lawson, Tamara Francita. 2012. A Fresh Cut in an Old Wound–A Critical Analysis of the Trayvon Martin Killing: The Public Outcry, the Prosecutors' Discretion, and the Stand Your Ground Law. *University of Florida Journal of Law and Public Policy* 23: 271–310. Accessed 23 June 2015.

Lee, Trymaine. New Revelations in Events Leading Up To Freddie Gray's Death. *MSNBC News*, September 27, 2015. Accessed 14 Oct 2016, www.msnbc.com/msnbc/new-revelations-events-leading-freddie-grays-death.

Locher, David A. 2002. *Collective Behavior*. Prentice Hall: Upper Saddle River, New Jersey.

Martin Luther King Shot Dead. *BBC News*, (n.d.) Web 13 February 2012. Retrieved from http://news.bbc.co.uk/onthisday/hi/dates/stories/april/4/newsid_2453000/2453987.stm.

Newton, Huey. 1973. *Revolutionary Suicide*. New York City: Random House.

Preston Battle Dies, Judge W. New York Times, September 1969. Accessed 08 Nov 2013. http://jfk.hood.edu/Collection/White%20%20Files/King%20Jr%20Martin%20Luther/MLK%20490.pdf.

Seiter, Richard. 2013. *Corrections: An Introduction*, 2nd ed., New Jersey: Pearson Prentice Hall.

Sharp, Gene. 1973a. *The Politics of Nonviolent Action, Part One: Power and Struggle*, ed. Mariana Finkelstein. Boston: Porter Sargent Publishers.

Sharp, Gene. 1973b. *The Politics of Nonviolent Action, Part Two: The Methods of Nonviolent Action*. Boston: Porter Sargent Publishers.

Smelser, Neil J. 1962. *Theory of Collective Behavior*. New York: Free Press.

Southern Poverty Law Center. Civil Rights Martyrs. Accessed 12 Jan 2012. https://www.splcenter.org/what-we-do/civil-rights-memorial/civil-rights-martyrs.

Spero, Andrea M. 2008. *African American Freedom Struggle Timeline: An International Perspective*. Web. 10 March 2013, The Martin Luther King, Jr.

Research Institute at Stanford University. Retrieved from http://mlk-kpp01.stanford.edu/.

Svensson, Birgitta. 1997. *God is Angry: The Black Power Movement.* Sweden: Sveriges Television.

The Guardian. 2015. The Counted: People Killed by the Police in the United States. Last modified December 2015. https://www.theguardian.com/us-news/ng-interactive/2015/jun/01/the-counted-police-killings-us-database.

Walker, Samuel, Cassia Spohn, and Miriam DeLone. 2012. *The Color of Justice: Race, Ethnicity, and Crime in America.* Cengage Learning.

Weise, Elizabeth. 2016. Black Panther Party's Legacy of Black Power Endures. *USA Today,* February 1. Accessed 14 Feb 2016. http://www.usatoday.com/story/news/nation-now/2016/02/01/black-panther-party-legacy-black-power/79041002/.

Welch, Matt. 2016. What Black Lives Matter and the Oregon Ranchers Have in Common. *The reason,* March. Accessed 23 May 2016. http://reason.com/archives/2016/02/01/what-black-lives-matter-and-th.

Suggestions for Further Reading

Black Lives Matter Network. (n.d.). http://blacklivesmatter.com/about/.

Edwards, S.B., and D. Harris. 2016. *Black Lives Matter.* Minnesota: ABDO Publishing.

Wright, N. 1967. *Black Power and Urban Unrest: Creative Possibilities.* New York: Hawthorn Book.

CHAPTER 9

The Mediatization of Violence: A Model for Utilizing Public Discourse and Networking to Counter Global Terrorism

Emmanuel K. Ngwainmbi

Background

One cannot discuss terrorism today without associating it with particular countries and the media, particularly television and newspapers. In fact, in recent years stories about terrorism are not only part of international news coverage, they arguably construct their coverage in order to instill

---

Emmanuel K. Ngwainmbi's current research interests include raising awareness of the ongoing worldwide discussion and debate about the important and imperative topics of globalization and multiculturalism and their impact on society. His writings address the impact of the media on cultures and interagency efforts on governance, peace building, peace keeping, election preparation, cultural exchange, child mortality reduction, information management in fragile states, climate change and environmental protection, gender, and youth programs.

E.K. Ngwainmbi (✉)
Matthews, NC, USA

E.K. Ngwainmbi (ed.), *Citizenship, Democracies, and Media Engagement among Emerging Economies and Marginalized Communities*,
DOI 10.1007/978-3-319-56215-5_9

fear and bring a sense of urgency to the audience. In the course of their reporting plan, television networks have made ISIS, Boko Haram, and al-Qaeda household names, even among children.

According to international scholars, social scientists and research institutions involved with the study of homeland security, terrorists can use one or a variety of resources to execute the attacks such as bombs, explosives, dynamite, fake weapons, firearms, vehicles with explosives such as car or truck bombs, incendiary weapons, nuclear sources, or sabotage, equipment. Terrorist attacks in Asia, the USA, Europe, Africa, or the Middle East can be said to be largely exploited by the media for the benefit of their operational efficiency, information gathering, recruitment, fundraising, and propaganda schemes (Nacos 2002a, b). Other scholars contend that technologies have improved the capability of groups and cells in the areas of proselytizing coordination, security, mobility, and lethality (Baylis and Smith 2014). In short, information technology has strengthened coordination among terrorist groups and increased their engagement with the media to transmit their message to the world's public.

Television networks compete in their coverage of "breaking news" about terrorist attacks, as reporters with the help of rolling cameras present grueling images of people maimed and communities bombed, instigating fear or a sense of threat in viewers. In the same vein, terrorists could be perpetrating violence as a way of communicating a political message to a larger audience (Nacos 2002a). By sharing pre-recorded tapes with media networks or putting out press releases claiming responsibility for massive bombings of civilians, terrorist group leaders use the media as a forum to promote their political agenda. A shift in their social media strategy from the heyday of al-Qaeda's operations in Iraq and Afghanistan in the 1990s to the operations of ISIS networks in European, Asian, Middle Eastern, and African cities and communities between 2012 and 2016 suggests that the media has become a vehicle for transmitting terrorists' social, political, and cultural agenda.

From late 2004 through early 2008, al-Qaeda produced numerous low-quality, amateurish videos featuring battle triumphs in both Afghanistan and Iraq, as well as pronouncements from its leaders, Osama bin Laden and Ayman al-Zawahiri, exhorting young Muslims to jihad. The videos, presumably produced on inexpensive video cameras and then uploaded to the internet from cafés in Pakistan and elsewhere, were nonetheless a powerful reminder to the West that al-Qaeda's agenda to defeat the "far enemy" remained operational (Veilleux-Lepage 2016). Years of painful and expensive US and allied operations may have silenced al-Qaeda's core, but then, rising from another quarter, al-Qaeda in the Arabian Peninsula metastasized in Yemen, dragging the Western focus away from Afghanistan and Iraq (Veilleux-Lepage 2016). Boko Haram, operating in Nigeria, Chad, and northern Cameroon, and other terrorist groups in Libya, Mali, and Mumbai are a sharp reminder that such a movement is not only directed at the "far enemy" (the USA and the West); it is a global phenomenon without a specific goal. The recent bombings in upscale neighborhoods in the USA and hotels in Burkina Faso and Mali where security cameras are common reflect the fact that terrorists have different agendas, the most important being to bring the world's attention to their existence.

Before describing terrorism in terms of the role played by television, newspaper, and social media tools such as Facebook, websites, and online interest group platforms, in order to determine the media's role in prioritizing the subject of terrorism in its international coverage, it is necessary first to review the operational meanings of terrorism.

Interpretations of Terrorism

Three new trends appear to be emerging that have an impact on the relationship between the media, terrorists, and governments: anonymous terrorism, more violent terrorist incidents, and terrorist attacks on media personnel and institutions (Perl 1997). We define terrorism based on the social orientation of the group involved. Alex Schmid and Albert Jongmann (1988) have compiled an important study using 109 different definitions of terrorism. The media presents a view that is different from that of the policymaker, the public, or the media researcher. To understand these differences in terrorism, a definition of the term is required.

"Terrorism" is synonymous with "publicity" and "public fear" in recent times, in that it encompasses the use of violent acts to frighten people in the aim of achieving a political goal. The notion of terrorism presented by television networks differs from that of lawmakers and the general public in countries where terrorist activities have taken place. Gruesome images of real-time terrorist acts splashed across television screens and graphic videos of beheadings filmed by ISIS and released on the internet suggest that communication and sharing information or knowledge on violence can trigger more attacks. In fact, there is now evidence that the media coverage of terrorist attacks is linked to a greater number of attacks. Research has found that sensationalist media coverage of acts of terrorism results in more such acts being committed (Doward 2015). Michael Jetter (2014), a professor at the School of Economics and Finance at Universidad EAFIT in Medellin, Colombia, notes that there has been a dreadful increase in the number of terrorist attacks around the world in recent years. In his analysis of 60,000 terrorist attacks between 1970 and 2012, Jetter found an exponential increase in their number, with the total number of casualties from terrorist attacks in the past 15 years having soared from 3387 to 15,396. This increase in the number of deaths is a result of terrorist organizations receiving extensive media attention, as Jetter (2014) revealed in an interview with the *Guardian*. The Global Terrorism Database listed 1,395 attacks in 1998, a figure that rose, reaching a record high of 8,441 in 2012. Further, according to the National Consortium for the Study of Terrorism and Responses to Terrorism, a university-based research and education center comprised of an international network of scholars committed to the scientific study of the causes and human consequences of terrorism in the United States and around the world, the number of attacks dropped to about 1,600 by October 2015 (https://www.start.umd.edu/gtd).

Forms of terrorist attacks include armed assault, assassination, bombing and explosion, facility infrastructure attack hijacking, unarmed assault, hostage taking using barricade, or suicide. In fact, suicide missions receive significantly more media coverage, which could explain their increased popularity among terrorist groups. More multiple attack modes such as skyjackings display longer cycles than simpler models like threats and hoaxes or bombings (Sandler and Enders 2004). More significantly, both attack modes get more attention from media networks around the world than suicide missions, in that they are more unpredictable, and require extensive and time-consuming journalistic investigation.

Another interpretation of terrorism comes from the political sphere. US President Donald Trump, who has a background in business, not politics or diplomacy, promised in his election campaign to place a ban on all Muslims entering the USA, accusing the religious group of promoting terrorist acts against American citizens. Throughout the American presidential election campaign in 2015 and 2016, candidates and pundits appeared on television and shared their philosophy on how to prevent ISIS from infiltrating the USA. During televised debates and one-on-one interviews, they presented terrorism as the foremost problem facing America, and rolled out their plans to end terrorism. Trump's message may have boded well with voters because he was elected President by vowing to impose the aborted ban on particular entrants to the US, among other promises to protect Americans against terrorism in general. According to all the main news networks in the USA and abroad and statements issued by the chairman of the Republican National Committee, Trump may have defeated other candidates with his message about the banning of Muslims from entering the USA. Coupled with this notion is the perception that many Muslims are dangerous people, prone to destroying Christianity, the majority of whose adherents live in Europe and the Americas. A Pew Global Attitudes Project survey of more than 90,000 people in 50 nations, including many Arab and majority Muslim countries, reveals that Muslims still have a negative view of Americans and the USA continues to face enormous challenges regarding its public image in Arab and Muslim countries (Kohut 2005). Kohut further reports continuing anti-Americanism in the region and aversion to US policies driving events such as the war in Iraq, the war on terrorism, and US support for Israel, and the general perception that the USA has failed to consider the interests of countries in Middle East when it acts in the international arena. Similarly, the US public's concern about terrorism has surged, and positive ratings of the government's handling of terrorism plummeted following the terrorist attacks in Paris and San Bernardino, California. The Pew Research Center (2015), which focuses on US politics and policy, has found that attitudes to terrorism and security, as well as perceptions of whether Islam is more likely than other religions to encourage violence, have indeed not changed. It is not clear whether people judge others based on what they have seen on television and from other visual news sources and social media platforms or exclusively on pre-existing stereotypes.

Terrorism, Governments, and the Media

Terrorists, governments, and the general public have different perspectives on the functions, roles, and responsibilities of the press. As stated earlier, terrorists need publicity to promote their cause, and since the media tends to report all sides of a story, they expect segments of the public to have a favorable understanding of their message. Simply put, terrorists see the media as their ally. Terrorists may seek to control smaller news organizations through funding. For governments, the media defends national interests when covering terrorist events; it should serve as the eye of the government and defend public programs designed to counter terrorist plots and actions. People maintain differing and often opposing perspectives of the media depending on their level of education and political views. Perl (1997) has pointed out that such perceptions drive individual behaviors during terrorist incidents, often resulting in tactical and strategic gains, or losses, to the terrorist operation and the overall terrorist cause. The challenge to the national and press community is to understand the dynamics of terrorist enterprise and to develop policy options to serve the government, media, and societal interests.

To find the right policies that can serve government, media, and community interests, we need to assess the impact of terrorism on nations through the media lens.

Mediatized Terrorism and Its Impact on Global Communities

The impact of terrorism has been magnified through the media's ability to disseminate news of such attacks instantaneously throughout the world (Laqueur 1999; Bloomberg et al. 2004; Monahan 2010). Krueger and Malečková (2003) emphasize that "the intention of terrorists [is] to cause fear and terror among a target audience rather than the harm caused to the immediate victims." For their part, some scholars focus on how governments, security forces, and terrorist groups seek to manipulate the news, including by legal means and formal and informal government censorship (Norris et al. 2004). Brian Monahan (2010) demonstrates how the "9/11" terrorist attack by Islamic extremists on several American cities on September 11, 2001, which killed more than 3500 citizens and destroyed infrastructure, supposedly in retaliation for the war in Iraq, has been transformed into a morality tale centered on patriotism, victimization, and heroes. One can understand the mindset of the American people in utilizing a tragic day to remember people killed on American soil through an act of terror, for the American spirit is built on turning a negative into a positive experience.

Media representation of the 9/11 attack has raised serious concerns about the state of the hitherto secure nation, the USA. The Pew Research Center, a non-partisan, non-advocacy public think tank that informs the public about the issues, attitudes and trends shaping America and the world in a poll conducted between December 8–13, 2015 among 1,500 (http://www.people-press.org/2015/12/15). Adults found that 29% of Americans cite terrorism (18%) or national security (8%) as the most important problem facing the country, and 83% regarded ISIS as a major threat to the well-being of the USA, up from 67% in 2014.

The incident in 2001 did not only create fear and insecurity among citizens: it enhanced the American belief in hope and solidarity. However, this notion does not apply in the context of Nigeria, Somalia, Chad, Syria, Iraq, Afghanistan, or other countries where terrorist acts are common and media coverage tends to damage community spirit. Simply put, the television and newspaper articles in those countries focus on the number of weekly and monthly attacks and less on the efforts being made by civic groups to combat terrorism. In 2017, there has been a pervasive concern about Islamic terrorism across the United States and Europe. Jacob Poushter's survey of Americans and Europeans published on the Pew Research Center website May 24, 2017, shows that prior to the bombing Monday night that left 22 people dead in Manchester, England, most people in Europe and North America had a ubiquitous feeling about Islamic extremism. The polling conducted across 12 countries from February through April, 2017, said they were at least somewhat concerned about extremism in the name of Islam in their countries, including 79% who said this in the UK itself. And across the 10 EU countries surveyed, a median of 79% were concerned about Islamic extremism, while only 21% were not concerned; meanwhile, 72% in the US were very concerned (http://www.pewresearch.org/fact-tank/2017/05/24). It is very likely that those concerns stem from live images of destruction accompanied by news media coverage. One is more likely to see images of destroyed structures and deserted areas on international television than those of authorities discussing plans to address terrorism. Reporting terrorism equally curbs press freedom, not only in countries with fragile political systems, but in those seeking to maintain a strongman image among their allies and enemies.

Convergence of Terrorism and Low-Income Countries

While new media has focused its attention on the ISIS bombings of selected European and American cities, terrorist groups have been spreading their influence in low-income countries. There are social and economic reasons for this spread. Socially, through recordings that it prepares and disseminates on the internet, ISIS explains that its acts aim to bring global attention to Islam and that it is raging jihad—a war against the opponents of Islam. Whether or not there is sufficient evidence to support this claim, we know that ISIS has been recruiting young people from Algeria to Pakistan. Al-Qaeda in the Islamic Maghreb region and other terrorist groups stationed in Syria, Iraq, and Afghanistan have not only influenced local extremist organizations such as Boko Haram, al-Mulathamun Brigade, Ansari, and Ansar al-Shari 'an in Benghazi, they have also spread into smaller communities due to brainwashing. Bergen and Schneider (2014), CNN's national security analyst who is a vice-president at the New America Foundation and a professor at Arizona State University, has stated that three other groups—al-Mujahidin in the Arabian Peninsula, in Libya, and in Yemen—have also recorded statements of allegiance to ISIS, which ISIS broadcasts online. ISIS now controls the eastern Libyan city of Derna, not far from the Egyptian border. The expansion of its geographical reach in Islamic regions has been enhanced by schools where young people are indoctrinated to destroy humanity with the promise that their acts of violence are an honor to Allah. Young Muslims and disenchanted people in both western and eastern hemispheres have been exposed to audio and video messages disseminated online.

Observers of the terrorist crisis have claimed on various media channels that ISIS has been winning the war on terror, citing its access to substantial funding and easy recruitment of new followers as the rationale for this claim. Bergen and Schneider (2014) has remarked that partnering with ISIS makes sense from an economic perspective for many organizations, especially the smaller militant groups. These groups rely on resources from larger ones to survive and to recruit sympathizers.

Since ISIS became a global security threat, various articles from Reuters, Associated Press, Agence France International, TASS (the Russian News Agency), the Latin American Union of News Agencies (ULAN), Al Jazeera, and the African News Agency (ANA) have all reported that ISIS has been spreading its message online, mainly by posting photos and statements to highlight its military strength and territorial advances. According to web-based data mining software, a large number of pro-ISIS tweets originated in Saudi Arabia, Kuwait, and other Gulf countries (Faisal Irshaid 2014). A BBC journalist who filed a report from the Middle East found that ISIS provides extensive details on its Twitter feed of its operations, including the number of bombings, suicide missions, and assassinations it has carried out, and of checkpoints and towns that it controls.[1] However, the most significant reasons that terrorism has spread in low-income countries are the following:

- Many recruits are disillusioned, and they come from poor backgrounds and are less educated or unemployed.
- Girls are targeted and recruited as bombers because Islamic families still consider them less valuable than men, and ISIS offers their families a fee in exchange for the girls.
- The military in low-income countries is not as equipped as the terrorist groups that easily infiltrate their territory.
- There is a lack of programs in some countries, and of resources in poorer countries, to fight terrorism.

Media Role in Spreading Terrorism

Terrorists use different types of media as an information instrument to generate publicity and draw attention to their cause, particularly among Islamic extremists. They are known to exploit television, radio, or the internet because they realize that these instruments are valuable resources in instilling fear within a community or winning the hearts and minds of the populace (Lumbaca and Gray 2011). It has been revealed that videos produced by terrorist groups, especially ISIS, are highly doctored and rife with special effects. A radical US-based political organization called Counterpunch has reported that ISIS has its own 24-hour TV channel and merchandise that it is marketing as a corporation or even government does. In an article posted on http://www.counterpunch.org/, Ben Norton (2015) explains how the media has helped ISIS to spread its propaganda. He argues that the media created paranoia among Americans by basing its allegations most often simply on what ISIS itself says. This is evidenced in a CNN poll conducted in September 2015, in which 90% of Americans indicated that they believed that ISIS poses a threat to the USA. However, Norton (2015) adds that the media failed to emphasize that many of the failed "ISIS-linked" terrorist plots in the West involve undercover police informants and provocateurs. That presupposes not just media bias, but a deliberate attempt to induce fear among people in a particular community and provoke the government to take action to protect its citizens from harm.

Terrorist propaganda is spreading not only in electronic sources; downloadable print materials produced by Islamic extremists have played a role as well. Leftist terrorist groups, such as al-Qaeda in Iraq and leading thinkers in the "global jihadist movement," have authored some books as well. *Announcement to the People of the Birth of the Islamic State,* authored by Uthman bin Abd al-Rahman al-Tamimi, is a book that provides justification for al-Qaeda's establishment of the Islamic state of Iraq (Kimmage and Rodolfo 2007, p. 24). By making the books available for download, the authors aim to reach as many readers as possible.

Further, world governing bodies like FIFA and the UN that collectively utilize media outlets to entertain most people and influence the course of world politics and international diplomacy have not adequately exploited those channels to curb the spread of terrorism.

Impact of Terrorism on Democratization

It is understood around the world that terrorists' main goal is to prevent the transition from an authoritarian democracy or semi-democracy to an authoritarian political regime where the barrel of a gun is the law. Clearly, this ideology negates the norm that countries around the world have been striving to address for decades and centuries. In fact, citizens and leaders of various countries, with the help of foreign powers, especially countries with strong military programs and political institutions, have been working on democratizing their nations. These countries are encouraged by the notion that an environment in which people are free to channel their thoughts and expectations through the individuals they elect is more conducive to live in than one in which they are totally controlled.

Experts have produced convincing evidence that democratic regimes rarely go to war with one another. They have also observed that democracies are much less susceptible to civil wars and internal armed conflicts than are non-democratic regimes (Piazza 2014) and that global interests would be advanced if there were more democracy in the world (Lynn-Jones 1998). Moreover, democracies share norms that preclude wars among themselves. Put differently, liberal ideologies do not provide justification for wars between liberal democracies (Brown et al. 1996). Those arguments are predicated on the stance that peace promoted internationally benefits the world in the long run. Strikingly, various acts of violence, a form of terrorism, occur in all democratic environments as well. Democracies face major dilemmas when confronting acts of violence which fall under the rubric of terrorism. Although the recent focus on international terrorism has had an unprecedented impact on national-level policy, with implications for both mature and emergent democracies, the problem of how terrorism can be addressed without undermining the very foundations of the democratization process has social scientists scrambling to find a suitable answer. It is not easy to eliminate terrorism without compromising democracy. In fact, the key challenge to democratic governments when faced with terrorism is defending the security of their citizens while upholding their rights and freedoms. The test of a strong democracy is when its government sets policies and actions to protect citizens' rights while ensuring their security. However, in a liberal country, anti-terrorism laws check the balance of the rights and freedoms of citizens against some restrictive measures that are necessary for a positive outcome. Legislation could, ironically, have a greater negative impact on citizens than could terrorist networks.

Let us take the case of the Israeli government, which enacted a Prevention of Terrorism Ordinance (PTO) in 1948 following terrorist attacks. In an important paper on the impact of terrorism on democracy in Israel, Eunice Buhler (2010) has found that the PTO legislation not only strikes a balance between liberal civil liberties and protection against the constant threat of terrorist attacks, it also adds to the quality of Israel's democracy by providing confidence and reducing fear in society (p. 63).

There is an uneven cost of managing terrorism, with fragile states having to pull resources from other critical areas of national security to address emergencies involving terrorists within their countries and on their borders. For example, the infiltration of Boko Haram, an Islamic group in Nigeria, into Niger, Chad, and Cameroon since the start of 2016 forced these countries' leaders to dispatch more troops to protect their borders. Broadcast and online media reports in those countries revealed that militants killed many soldiers who were trying to free men, women, and children captured by the terrorists. One can only imagine the cost of relocating citizens and rehabilitating released prisoners in those low-income countries. It would be a mistake to compare that situation to one in New York, where mere knowledge of a terrorist plot has officials hiring thousands of personnel and mobilizing the military and police departments to protect sensitive areas. This imbalance in the allocation of resources is only one of the major difficulties in combating transnational terrorism.

The Difficulty in Combating Global Terrorism

Since the terrorist attacks on September 11, 2001, the fight to end terrorism worldwide has become a key topic in discussions among country leaders. It was, in fact, an agenda item at the United Nations (UN) General Assembly in both 2015 and 2016. At the UN's plenary session, which was broadcast around the world, the USA and Israel accused some Arab countries of sponsoring terrorism, making it difficult for accusers and accused alike to discuss strategies for eliminating terrorism. Further, diplomatic arrangements have failed to produce positive results.

Political action groups and media pundits have claimed that some rich countries are arming violent terrorists in the Middle East as part of their geopolitical strategy to overthrow heads of state they do not like. The crises in Tunisia, Egypt, Libya, Iraq, and Syria that led to the overthrow of these countries' leaders included the arming of local and regional groups that engaged the military. According to the Center for Research on Globalization, the US Central Intelligence Agency (CIA) warned the US president that "funding extremists rebels doesn't work" and that French terrorists who murdered the cartoonists in Paris apparently had just returned from waging war against the Syrian government, where they may directly have obtained US weapons and training" (http://www.globalresearch.ca).

Terrorists take advantage of loopholes in national privacy laws. For example, in the USA it is illegal to tap private telephones and other handheld information equipment. A warrant is required to search someone's home, even if an individual has prepared bombs and other tools to commit terrorist acts in the privacy of that home. In Belgium, terrorists completed plans that culminated in the bombing of Brussels airport. Media reports showed that the police could not intervene overnight when the terrorists were plotting because of a clause in the privacy law. According to the document produced by the Belgian Privacy Commission entitled "Protection of Personal Data in Belgium," "it is prohibited to collect, register or ask to disclose sensitive data related to race, political opinions, religious or philosophical beliefs, trade-union membership, health, sex life, prosecutions or criminal or administrative convictions (http://www.privacycommission.be). Anyone doing so is punishable by a 550 to 550,000 euro fine and, in the case of recidivism, with a three-month to two-year imprisonment" (http://www.privacycommission.be).

Some countries have less stringent immigration policies, particularly in obtaining a visa, residency, or citizenship status. An immigrant in the USA on a permanent residency status or a holder of a "green card" can apply for citizenship after at least three years, when his/her background is verified to make sure there is no criminal record. EXPATICA, a web-based instructional guide to French citizenship and permanent residence explains that anyone who wishes to live in France long term or permanently, may be eligible to apply for French permanent residence or French citizenship after five years of living in France, although this time is reduced in certain cases such as being married or parent to a French national (http://www.expatica.com/fr). "The five-year residency requirement is reduced to three years if you are joining a family member who already has permanent residence, or if you are the parent of child with French nationality with temporary residence. Anyone who meets the conditions of French citizenship via birth also has right to permanent residence" (http://www.expatica.com/fr). Although the application for French citizenship requires a criminal record certificate, the law may be perpetrating violence, in that resources are often limited to ensure a flawless background check. Moreover, some of the persons with dual citizenship status (who come from poor countries) often commit crimes in their country of birth that are not known or recorded in their adopted country. Without a common database available to security and immigration authorities in both countries, criminals and persons with radical views are allowed to live on French soil and use French documents to travel abroad at will. No doubt hundreds of jihadists trained in terrorist fields abroad are French citizens, as Al Jazeera, CNN International, Reuters, and BBC have reported since the London bombings on July 7, 2005. According to a report posted by iNews 24 on 11/17/2015, France has listed more than 10,000 people suspected of being radicalized or potential security threats, including homegrown assailant (http://www.i24news.tv/en/news/international/europe). With some 81, 905 French security forces keeping an eye on 10,500 persons on the State Security list known to have links to Islamic groups as reported by the French Ministry of Justice and Le Figaro-France's popular daily newspaper- (Peter 2016), it is clear that the media is collaborating with the French government to tackle pervasive problem of terrorism.

European media often publish conflicting reports about the proliferation of terrorism in Europe. They covered different angles of the gruesome incident, thereby sensationalizing terrorism instead of serving as the gatekeeper of community peace. For instance, when a Paris café was bombed on November 13, 2015, Germany's *Bild am Sonntag* (a widely read Sunday newspaper) raised questions about the security of Europe's borders, while the front page of the *Daily Telegraph* in the UK focused on how two men had entered Europe with false passports, posing as refugees. In their report of the unfolding terrorists attack in the French capital on Friday November 13, 2015, Isabelle Fraser and Barney Henderson stressed that 8 terrorists were dead, and "Black-clad gunmen attacked at five sites in the centre of the city and at the Stade de France, in the north at around 9.30pm local time". They pointed out that the attack happened just 24 hours after news broke that a drone strike in Syria was thought to have killed British terrorist Jihadi John" (http://www.telegraph.co.uk/news/worldnews/europe/france/11995543/Paris-shooting). Reporting on the attack, *Bild* quoted German intelligence sources as saying that two suspected terrorists posing as Syrian refugees seeking asylum were allowed onto European soil by Greek officials and were supposed to take part in the Paris attacks. Justin Huggler, filing his story from Berlin on February 14, 2016, states that Austrian authorities declined to comment on the new claims. The inconsistency in the coverage of the terrorist incident and the lack of commitment by authorities to share intelligence makes it difficult for public officials in the European Union (EU) to have reliable data to combat terrorism.

Allies and countries affected by terrorist acts are not sharing information on potential terrorists and related behavior, allowing terrorists to cross borders, recruit vulnerable people, and commit terrorist acts. The US Senate has made this claim. In a report published on the Breitbart news network on December 12, 2015, Ian Hanchett quoted Texas Representative Will Hurd as saying that America's European allies are not providing the US government with the information it needs to keep terrorists from American shores (http://www.breitbart.com/video/2015/09/08). This is one reason why the House of Representatives passed legislation tightening up the Visa Waiver program, which allows citizens of specific "friendly" countries to travel to the USA for tourism, business, or while in transit for up to 90 days without having to obtain a visa. The problem with this allocation is that some citizens from friendly countries are capable of carrying out terrorist acts.

European countries where terrorist attacks have been common in the last 5 years do not share data on suspected terrorists partly because of language problems. For example, the police and customs officers do not understand the language or cannot communicate with their counterparts in another country, which makes tracking the movements of suspected terrorists a challenge. In addition to not sharing information, the EU has few internal border checkpoints, making it easier for terrorists to cross borders without being detected. Frontline's investigative reporter Oriana Zill (2017) has revealed that terrorists in the Al Qaeda network travel the world using fake passports and other illegally obtained documents with no difficulty. Zill, the reporter famously known for her report titled "Hunting Bin Laden", specialized Al Qaeda terrorist groups in the US, Canada and Europe alter and supply passports to the terrorist network that are used by its operatives (http://www.pbs.org/frontline).

And based on the number of terrorist incidents in Europe in the last few years, it seems that the terrorist groups find it easy to obtain Schengen passports and gain access into Europe and subsequently the US than to other countries. Canada, France, Germany, Belgium and the UK have become easy targets for terrorist attacks. With with the Schengen Borders Code established by the EU that provides member states the capability to temporarily reintroduce border control in the event of a serious attack or threat against internal security, potential terrorists can easily drive from France to Germany to Belgium without border or immigration control. With the Visa Waiver program in place and immigration control when leaving Europe and arriving in the USA, terrorists with fake passports have still entered the United States and other counties due to the lack of proper surveillance and coordination.

Challenges in Controlling Information Technology to Combat Terrorism

Given that information can be easily transmitted to large numbers of people to influence their thinking and actions, terrorists have successfully used handheld devices to reach their fellow members, recruit other terrorists, and train them in various ways of carrying out successful acts. Given that prepaid phones and SIM cards can be purchased without identifying oneself, and messages transmitted via computers can be encrypted, intelligence units in most affected countries have not been able to track the operations of terrorists. The latter have become more skilled, concealing their URLs and making tracking the origin of the message more difficult. Some governments have implemented a law under which vendors document the identity of the SIM card purchaser.

For example, in Germany and South Africa, SIM cards are only sold to persons who can show proof of residency, and a government-issued identification, such as a driver's license or passport, is required. That measure can limit the chances of terrorists having a SIM card; however, it is not possible to control their access to a phone.

Following the exodus of civilians fleeing the war in Syria and hardship and poverty-stricken young people from Africa flooding to European borders, there is increased fear of mass immigration and homegrown terror. Ian Traynor (2016), the reporter for The Guardian's documentation of refugee activity on the German, France and Luxembourg borders in January 2016 reveals there was free travel uncontrolled travel across those borders for many months.

Further, it is difficult to control immigrants (refugees, terrorists, etc.) in Europe due to its free travel inter-nation policy that became fully fledged in in 1995. The ID-free travel zone rule that requires a person to have a Schengen passport or in some cases to drive a vehicle with "green dot stickers" on the windshield into any one of the 26 countries of the European continent may be partly responsible for the spread of terrorist acts. With only one form of identification that allows free access across the border, a terrorist can commit an offense in many countries or coordinate a series of activities without being easily detected using encrypted chat apps, messaging app telegram, and a software known as PGP (Pretty Good Privacy), well known for end-to-end encryption. Since there is no difference between "military grade encryption" and "consumer encryption" anyone can post encrypted messages publicly that may not be accessible to any national, regional or international intelligence group, including the National Security Agency (NSA), Central Intelligence Agency (CIA), Bundesnachrichtendienst (the Federal Intelligence Agency of Germany), or the Direction Générale de la Sécurité Intérieure, the French agency in charge of domestic counter-terrorism and counter-espionage intelligence. Unless the EU and US change their immigration policy, particularly with respect to border control, those regions are likely to face more grave security problems.

The Complex Relationship Between Facebook and Global Privacy

Following the release of Facebook and Twitter to the public, millions of users have taken to the excessive use of such systems, to share personal as well as professional data. Unedited and encrypted data has been transferred to interest groups by members across national borders, forcing governments to review their communication laws. Any national supervisory authority has an obligation to ensure privacy protection for its citizens. For countries like Belgium, where Facebook has an actual establishment, the need to oversee privacy protection for its citizens cannot be undermined. According to the Commission for the Protection of Privacy, there is a total misunderstanding between Facebook and the Belgian government in that Facebook was violating Belgian law by tracking non-users on its site. Facebook argued that because its headquarters were in Ireland, not Belgium, it only needed to comply with Irish law. Facebook has refused to recognize either the application of Belgian legislation or the Belgian Privacy Commission, arguing that applying the law and ensuring competent jurisdiction over the tracking of traffic and activity on Facebook accounts is illegal. With the "tracking through social plug-ins" in force, Facebook as well as internet users are affected in both Belgium and Europe more generally, which has had citizens complaining publicly and advocating for greater privacy. For its part, the Belgian Privacy Commission had not issued a ruling on Facebook's policies regarding users up till June 2015, which could have given terrorist networks access to the information-sharing medium and offers them the freedom to target certain groups, facilities, institutions, and individuals.

An *MIT Technology Review* report (2012) that Facebook can collect market-related information, such as tracking activity, by using a "Like" button that allows people to indicate with a click that they are interested in a brand, product, or piece of digital content, makes us wonder why makers of the medium have not invented a mechanism to track terrorist activity. Simonite (2012) foresees that Facebook might sell insights to data mined from its storehouse. This could compromise agreements with users and regulators to maintain their privacy. With more than one billion users of Facebook in different countries, national security is bound to be breached, particularly for those countries without the tools to control or protect information flow.

Conclusions

Terrorism has reshaped the public agenda, both at home and abroad, and the media has a double standard when it comes to reporting terrorism. Perceived as the main informant on terrorist activities, so far the media has in a subliminal way projected terrorist episodes against

Americans and some Western communities as the product of a religious sect—ISIS and al-Qaeda—whereas poverty, dependency, youth unemployment, illiteracy, segregated educational methods, local customs, and other socioeconomic problems that have not been successfully managed by world governing bodies such as FIFA and the UN for many decades are greatly responsible for the spread of terrorism globally. For example, as the only world football governing body that brings together all nations and people and raises billions of dollars funds through ticket sale, broadcast fees, and other initiatives, FIFA has capitalist proclivities to maximize revenue from organizing the World Cup tournament and other regional football events. Because the sport brings together people from all political, cultural and moral backgrounds, including terrorist networks, FIFA's governing body has the capacity to access global media to promote initiatives in regions torn by conflicts, foster economic development, and lift countries out of poverty. But FIFA focuses on utilizing the media mainly to organize footballing events and raising money. The media, policymakers, and citizens in affected countries have a mutual interest in ensuring that terrorist groups do not manipulate the media into promoting their agenda and violent activities. The media also want to become efficient watchdogs against terrorism and expect policymakers to play a fundamental role in bringing a rapid end to terrorism. Hence, the governments and media executives have to work on a plan to tackle homegrown and international terrorism.

The rapid spread of terrorism into wealthy and developing countries, into urban as well as rural communities, and into secure environments as well as expensive infrastructures, has certainly brought more attention to world leaders and big business. Terrorism has also led to a bigger investment in national security, especially among wealthy countries with relatively advanced democratic practices and strong institutions, such as the USA, Germany, Britain, France, and Spain, which have much to lose if attacked. There the budget to combat terrorism has increased dramatically; in the case of the USA, more money has been spent over the last 15 years on reducing internal and external terrorism than on education. Smaller countries are at greater risk of not being able to defend themselves because they have limited financial and technical resources. Most of their borders are not secure, which makes it easier for terrorists to enter their space and cause destruction with little resistance, or to recruit and train more terrorists, as daily press reports in Nigeria, Mali, India, Pakistan, and other countries with weak institutions show. For example, in the April 24, 2017 editions of the Guardian (newspaper of Nigeria) and The Observer, Patience Ibrahim and co-writer Andrea C. Hoffmann offer a vivid and compelling account of trauma and survival (http://www.theguardian.com/world/boko-haram). Kenya's The Star and South Africa's The Citizen covered the Paris terrorist attack for several days after the incident. Business Daily, (another Kenya paper) published the French satirical magazine's cover about Islam and terrorism. There are often write-ups about terrorism and related issues on the front or back pages of Chadian, Cameroonian and Ghanaian online newspapers. The BBC Africa news (http://www.bbc.com/news/world/africa) usually posts a story weekly or bi-weekly on the same topic.

Toward a Global Policy Against Information Sharing on Terrorism

This author posits that global terrorism can be eradicated mainly through information sharing among intelligence centers around the world and between the media and governments. This includes access to databases on existing and potential terrorists by all approved intelligence officers, constant training of security forces on terrorism, and prompt reporting of alleged terrorist plots. The fight to end terrorism must not be left in the hands of world governing bodies such as FIFA or the UN, as member states have no mechanism for monitoring or evaluating their work. Moreover, the UN plan to end terrorism is vague and difficult to implement. Based on its counter-terrorism plan posted on the UN website, the world governing body for peace seeks to:

- address conditions conducive to the spread of terrorism,
- prevent and combat terrorism,
- build states' capacity and strengthen the role of the United Nations, and
- ensure human rights and the rule of law.

Those pillars, presented as priorities, require the full support and commitment of all member states. Full support includes design, adoption, and implementation of policies to be respected by all countries, including those described as "rogue states." Moreover, cooperation by all countries is required in providing funding to counter and eliminate terrorism. The UN plan does not explain how it intends to monitor the prevention of terrorism or sustain the capacity of states to combat terrorism. Moreover, since its formation in 1945, the UN's capacity-building programs have not brought any long-term results, even for its socioeconomic initiatives in many countries. We can only expect the status quo when it comes to preventing or countering terrorism.

Further, to build state capacities, member states have to be united. They have to agree on a common modus operandi. However, diplomacy between Western countries and some Asian countries on this question has not been successful. Syria, Iran, and Saudi Arabia are considered harbingers of terrorist groups by the US and several Western nations, which creates tensions and makes it difficult for both parties to come up with a common agenda to ensure that human rights and the rule of law are respected.

Terrorism must not be countered only through the use of military action by coalition forces or the publicized showcasing of the deployment of such forces to affected regions. The constant spread of terrorism from the Middle East to other areas, despite or based on intense media coverage, shows that media reporting of terrorism has not helped in curbing the global nightmare. Also, televised speeches by European and American leaders have had no effect on terrorist cells, mainly because the terrorists believe they would be martyrs if killed in combat. Hence, different approaches are needed to suppress the proliferation of terrorism around the world. Arguably, the best approach is for all countries to have a database where all passengers heading to another country must be fingerprinted and have their names entered in a worldwide database, ensuring that authorities at all entry points can detect documented terrorists. In addition:

- Documented terrorists should be extradited to the country where they committed the crime.
- Information on terrorist groups and their movements should be shared instantaneously.
- All European countries should have a common policy with the USA and African and Arab countries for searching the homes of suspected terrorists. In Belgium, for instance, the law does not allow law enforcement personnel to search homes after certain hours. The "gap" in that law allows suspects to plan terrorist acts during those hours, as noted regarding the bombings at Brussels airport in April 2016.
- Intelligence sources should recruit computer hackers to track the operations of terrorist groups.

Lastly, reporters on assignment and other informants should have a secure mechanism for sharing "secret" information with government intelligence sources. It is not advisable for current or former officers to speak to the press about counter-terrorism techniques if governments want to expedite the process of ending global terrorism.

Topics for Discussion

1. Should the media be a watchdog to protect the community from terrorist acts? If so, in what ways can the media serve as a community watchdog against terrorism?
2. Should public officials as well as security forces speak to the press about tactics to confront or tackle terrorism?
3. Why do terrorists need the media?

NOTE

This chapter was published in the *Journal of Mass Communication and Journalism 6: 302* (2016), and is used with permission from the editor. Some sections have been modified for this book.

1. The footage showing heavily armed ISIS members, which was posted on a web platform in the Middle East, has inscriptions in Arabic. Irshaid (2014) says: "Alongside the Islamic State in Iraq and the Levant's [ISIS's] battlefield successes in northern Iraq, the group has deployed a sophisticated social media strategy that is redefining its propaganda." http://www.bbc.com/news/world-middle-east-27912569 accessed January 13, 2017).

Works Cited

Baylis, J., and Smith, S. 2014. *The Globalization of World Politics: An Introduction to International Relations*, 4th ed. NY, New York: Oxford University Press.

Bergen, P., and Schneider, E. 2014. Why ISIS is spreading across the Muslim world, CNN Report. http://www.CNN.com. Accessed November 19, 2014.

Bloomberg, S.B., Hess, G.D., and Orphanides, A. 2004. The Macroeconomic Consequences of Terrorism. *Journal of Monetary Economics* 51(5): 1007–1032.

Brown, M., S. Lynn-Jones, and S. Miller (eds.). 1996. *Debating the democratic peace*. Cambridge, MA: The MIT Press.

Buhler, E. 2010. The Israeli Prevention of Terrorism Ordinance and its Impact on the Quality of Democracy. *Stanford Journal of International Relations*, vol. XI, no. 2: 58–63 (Spring 2010).

Doward, J. 2015. Media coverage of terrorism 'leads to further violence'. The Observer. August 1. https://www.theguardian.com/media/2015/aug/01/media-coverage-terrorism-further-violence. Retrieved July 6, 2017.

Fraser, I. and Henderson, B. 2015. Paris shooting: Terrorists attack French capital – as it happened on Friday Nov 13. The Telegraph of London. http://www.telegraph.co.uk/news/worldnews/europe/france/11995543/Paris-shooting. Retrieved July 6, 2017.

Hanchett, R. 2015. GOP Rep Hurd: Border Wall 'Most Expensive' and 'Least Effective' Way to Do Border Security. September 8. http://www.breitbart.com/video/2015/09/08/gop-rep-hurd-border-wall. Retrieved 16 May 2016.

Ibrahim, P., and Hoffmann, C. A. 2017. A Gift from Darkness review – harrowing account of a Boko Haram kidnapping. The Guardian and The Observer. http://www.theguardian.com/books/2017. April 24. Retrieved June 17, 2017.

Irshaid, Faisal. 2014. How Isis is spreading its message online, BBC News June 19, 2014. http://www.bbc.com/news/world-middle-east-27912569 Accessed January 13, 2017.

Jetter, M. 2014. Terrorism and the Media. Discussion Paper No. 8497. The IZA research network (September 2014) ftp.iza.org/dp8497.pdf.

Kimmage, D., and Rodolfo, K. 2007. Iraqi Insurgent Media: The War of Ideas and Images. http://realaudio.rferl.org/online/OLPDFfiles/insurgent.pdf.

Kohut, A. 2005. Arab and Muslim Perceptions of the United States. The Pew Research Center. (November 10, 2005). Also available at http://www.pewresearch.org/2005/11/10/arab-and-muslim-perceptions-of-the-united-states/.

Krueger, A. B., and Malečková, A. 2003. Education, poverty, and terrorism: Is there a causal connection?. *Journal of Economic Perspectives* 17, 4: 119–144.

Laqueur, W. 1999. *The New Terrorism: Fanaticism and the Arms of Mass Destruction*. New York: Oxford University Press.

Lumbaca, S., and H.D. Gray. 2011. The media as an enabler for acts of terrorism. *Global Security Studies, Winter* 2 (1): 45–54.

Lynn-Jones, M. S. 1998. *Why the United States Should Spread Democracy. Discussion Paper,* 97–07. Center for Science and International Affairs. Massachusetts: Harvard University. March 1998.

Monahan, A.B. 2010. *The Shock of the News Media Coverage and the Making of 9/11.* New York: New York University Press.

Nacos, B. L. 2002a. *Mass-Mediated Terrorism.* Lanham, Maryland: Rowman and Littlefield.

Nacos, B. L. 2002b. "Terrorism, the Mass Media and the Events of 9–11." *Phi Kappa Phi Forum* 82 (2): 13 (Spring 2002b).

Norton, Ben. 2015. How the Media Helps ISIS Spread its Propaganda. *Counterpunch tells the facts, names the names.* http://www.counterpunch.org (May 8, 2015). Accessed January 13, 2017.

Norris, P., M. Kern, and M. Just. 2004. *Framing Terrorism: The News Media, the Government, and the Public.* New York: Routledge.

Perl, F.R. 1997. Terrorism, the Media and the Government: Perspectives, Trends, and Options for Policymakers. http://digital.library.unt.edu/ark:/67531/metacrs419. Accessed January 15, 2017.

Peter, L. 2016. How France is wrestling with jihadist terror. http://www.bbc.com/news/world-europe. July 28. Retrieved June 17, 2017.

Piazza, James. 2014. Democracy and Terrorism: A Complex Relationship. *The International Relations and Security Network.* (May 14, 2014) http://www.isn.ethz.ch/Digital-Library/Articles/Detail/?id=179658 Accessed January 13, 2017.

Poushter, J. 2017. Majorities in Europe, North America worried about Islamic extremism. The Pew Research Center. May 24. http://www.pewresearch.org/fact-tank/2017/05/24/. Retrieved June 17, 2017.

Sandler, T., and W. Enders. 2004. An economic perspective on transnational terrorism. *European Journal of Political Economy* 20 (2): 301–316.

Schmid, A., and A. Jongman. 1988. *Political Terrorism: A New Guide to Actors, Authors, Concepts, Data Bases, Theories and Literature.* Amsterdam: Transaction Books.

Simonite, T. 2012. What Facebook Knows. *The MIT Technology Review.* (June 13, 2012) http://www.technologyreview.com. Retrieved May 22, 2016.

The National Consortium for the Study of Terrorism and Responses to Terrorism. Sponsored by The Department of Homeland Security (DHS) and the University of Maryland. http://www.start.umd.edu/about/about-start.

The Pew Research Center. 2015. Views of Government's Handling of Terrorism Fall to Post-9/11 Low. December 15. http://www.people-press.

org/2015/12/15/views-of-governments-handling-of-terrorism-fall-to-post-911-low/. Accessed June 17, 2017.

Traynor, I. 2016. Is the Schengen dream of Europe without borders becoming a thing of the past? January 5. http://www.theguardian.com/world/2016. Accessed June 6, 2017.

Veilleux-Lepage, Y. 2016. Paradigmatic shifts in Jihadism in cyberspace: The emerging role of unaffiliated sympathizers in Islamic State's social media strategy. *Journal of Terrorism Research*, 7 (1): 36–51. doi:10.15664/jtr.1183.

Zill, Oriana. 2017. Crossing Borders: How Terrorists use fake passports, visas, and other identity documents. In Frontline, http://www.pbs.org/frontline. Accessed June 17, 2017.

CHAPTER 10

The Assassination of Journalists in Mexico: A Product of Criminal and Electoral Competition

Jose Luis Velasco

In the early twenty-first century, Mexico became one of the most dangerous countries for journalists, a contrast with the progress that freedom of the press had made in previous decades, when the country was also experiencing a broader process of democratization.

The aggressions toward journalists covering stories in Mexico have obvious negative consequences for democracy. For instance, they encourage the revival of censorship and self-censorship, which impoverish public debate, and thus the quality of democratic competition.

One should ask, therefore, why a formally democratic system is unable to protect its journalists, and thereby the freedom of its press. At first thought, the answer would seem obvious: because Mexican democracy

Jose Luis Velasco is a full-time researcher at the National Autonomous University of Mexico. In this chapter he analyzes the causes and effects of the many assassinations of journalists in Mexico and offers suggestions for a solution.

J.L. Velasco (✉)
Ciudad Universitaria Coyoacán, Mexico City, Mexico

E.K. Ngwainmbi (ed.), *Citizenship, Democracies, and Media Engagement among Emerging Economies and Marginalized Communities*,
DOI 10.1007/978-3-319-56215-5_10

operates in an adverse social context dominated by violent organized criminals. Yet is this problem only contextual? Is democracy merely a *victim* of such violence, or also one of its causes?

This chapter aims to answer those questions. However, the information about this type of topic tends to be murky and is often mixed with indeterminate amounts of concealment, disinformation, manipulation, and sheer fantasy. To deal with the problem, the chapter relies on a variety of publicly available documents: domestic and international reports on aggressions toward journalists, published testimonies of reporters, and official diagnoses by Mexican government institutions. This diversity would seem to create problems of its own. Sources, if sufficiently diverse, may give contradictory accounts of particular facts, making the separation of truth from falsity impossible.

This problem may be turned into an advantage if one tries to identify only patterns and trends, as this chapter does. When the addition of many partial accounts reveals a reasonably clear pattern, an important characteristic of the phenomenon has been identified.

A Virtuous Circle

Freedom of the press progressed in Mexico at the turn of the twenty-first century, due in large part to the dismantlement of the main traditional forms of government control and censorship. For example, the notorious official monopoly on printing paper production and distribution began to break down in the late 1980s and was finally abolished in 1998, with the privatization of the state-owned company charged with this task.[1] Similarly, penalties for defamation (often used against critical journalists) were progressively relaxed—though the most decisive step in this direction did not take place until 2007, when imprisonment was eliminated from the list of those penalties in the federal penal code.[2]

The creation of new media also advanced freedom of the press in Mexico, mostly in the printed press. To be sure, independent media always found some tolerance in the Mexican political system, but their existence was mostly short and precarious. However, since the late 1970s, several independent newspapers and magazines—some fiercely critical of government policies and conservative social values—managed to thrive as well as survive. These include *Proceso* (founded in 1976), *Reforma* (1993), and *La Jornada* (1984). Facing greater competition, even traditionally complacent media—for example, *El Universal* and *Excélsior*—became more open to public debate.

Other types of media grew as well. The number of radio stations increased from 554 in 1973 to 1750 in 2015 (Guerrero 2010, p. 260; IFT 2015); consequently, news programs grew in number, duration, and quality (Guerrero 2010, p. 260). Even the TV industry—though only two networks still controlled virtually the entire private-sector market—experienced some opening, with more news programs of better quality. Of course, the internet and digital social networks diversified the media considerably.

With less government control, newer media, and more competition, freedom of the press and the quality of public debate improved in various senses. Thus, to cite but one among several possible indicators, the country's "freedom of the press" score, as estimated by an influential watchdog, systematically improved at the close of the twentieth century, moving from 60 in 1993 to 36 in 2003 on a scale ranging from 0, "freest," to 100, "least free" (Freedom House 2016).

This progress was part of a broader movement toward democracy. Mexico's post-revolutionary regime, established in the late 1920s, was an autocratic, one-party-dominant one. Its opening began, at least at the formal level, with the political reform of 1977. Among other things, this reform facilitated the formation of new political parties, increased official support to opposition parties, and widened the opposition's access to the legislature. The process was quite slow. However, by 1994, after several rounds of elections and institutional reforms, the country had a competitive three-party system. The culminating moment came in 2000, when the official party, known as the PRI, lost the presidency. The overall product of this process was an electoral democracy endowed with an intricate web of legal and institutional safeguards and featuring much strong and often fierce competition among parties and candidates.

Paralleling this movement toward electoral competitiveness is a process of pluralization that gradually transformed the formal structure of power of the country. In the post-revolutionary regime, the PRI directly or indirectly occupied most positions in all branches and at all levels of government. However, the situation changed when it lost its two-thirds majority in the Chamber of Deputies in 1988 and its absolute majority in 1997. With some delay, a similar change took place in the Senate. As the PRI lost its monopoly on seats, the legislative branch overcame its subordination to the executive, transforming itself into a genuinely independent power. Similarly, constitutional reforms in 1994 and 1996 significantly strengthened the judiciary. Moreover, in 1989 the official party's monopoly on state governments was broken. In late 2000, parties other than the PRI ruled 13 of Mexico's 32 states. A similar process of pluralization took place in state legislatures and municipalities. On the whole, this process severed the partisan links that in fact, though not quite in right, subordinated state and local governments to the president.

Although not as clearly, political rights, civil liberties, and human rights also registered some important progress. Voting-related rights showed significant improvements: as outright electoral fraud all but disappeared, citizens in effect became able to choose among several competing options. In contrast, the improvement of other civil and political rights was slow and uncertain. Despite many legal and institutional reforms, including the creation of national and statewide human rights commissions, the record on human rights was even less encouraging; extra-judicial executions, forced disappearances, torture, and other human rights violations remained common in several areas of the country.[3]

The interaction between these two processes—the growing freedom of the press and the transition to a competitive political regime—seemed to form a genuinely virtuous circle. Democratization encouraged the expansion of the liberty of the media, and the latter, in turn, facilitated the advance of political pluralism. Thus, the political reform of 1977, which, as noted, inaugurated the process of electoral democratization, included a short but seminal addition to Article 6 of the constitution: "the right to information will be guaranteed by the state" (Segob 1977). Many other legal changes, especially those related to access to public information, were added later. The result was that despite several surviving limitations, the access of political parties and candidates to the media (printed, radio, and TV) became more equitable and pluralized (Guerrero 2010, pp. 279–294).

Drug Violence

As the twenty-first century moved on, that circle began to lose many of its virtues. One of the most dramatic manifestations of this decay was the assassination of journalists, a development that turned Mexico into one of the world's most murderous countries for people in this profession. These murders took place in the context of organized crime and the official fight against it. Hence, to understand these assassinations, it is necessary to explain first, at least in general terms, the crisis of drug violence that erupted in the country practically at the beginning of the twenty-first century.

The most visible part of this violence was the high number of so-called executions—homicides attributed to organized criminals, particularly to members of drug-trafficking organizations, most of which were committed with blatant brutality. Significantly for the topic of this chapter, data about these crimes comes mainly from newspapers and magazines, especially *Reforma*, *El Universal*, *Milenio*, *La Jornada*, and *Zeta*. Of these, the *Reforma* data series seems to be the most complete and systematic. Another primary source is the database created by the National Human Rights Commission (CNDH 2008, pp. 3–8), which brought together information from newspapers and government agencies. A third source is the Homicides Allegedly Related to Organized Crime Database (HRDO), published by the Mexican presidency (2011).

According to the *Reforma*, CNDH, and HRDO data series, there were between 34,542 and 43,642 drug-related executions from 2001 to 2010.[4] This means that on average, between 9 and 12 people were executed every day during this decade. Moreover, the number of executions grew consistently during the period. The largest annual increases in the total number of drug-related homicides took place in 2005 (32%), 2008 (at least 92%), and 2010 (at least 59%). The average number of daily executions multiplied by 14 during the period: "only" 3 Mexicans were executed every day in 2001, compared to as many as 42 in 2010. The incidence of executions also grew in another sense: in 2001 there were "only" 1.1 executions for every 100,000 Mexicans, compared to as many as 13.6 in 2010, which means that the rate of incidence of executions multiplied by 12 during the period.

Although, as elaborated below, data on drug violence became less abundant and reliable in subsequent years, it is quite certain that the number of executions decreased in 2012. While it began to grow again in 2014, in 2015 it was still below its 2011 peak (Mendoza Hernández and Mosso Castro 2014).

While information about this topic is notoriously unreliable, it is clear that most of these homicides were perpetrated by drug-trafficking organizations as they competed for control of the illegal drug market. To illustrate this point, one can note that the geography of drug-related executions largely coincides with that of the illicit drug market. Thus, most of these homicides were committed in the state of Tamaulipas and, particularly, Nuevo Laredo, which according to the US National Drug Intelligence Center is "the most lucrative smuggling corridor along the U.S.–Mexico border" (NDIC 2009, p. 6), and the state of Michoacán, particularly the area close to Lázaro Cárdenas, the country's most important port for freight transport and the most important point of entry for pseudoephedrine and other synthetic drug precursors. There is Ciudad Juárez, another major transit point between Mexico and the USA, with a long tradition in smuggling of people and illicit goods and also the headquarters of Mexico's most powerful drug organization in the 1990s, the so-called Golden Triangle. Further, there is the mountainous zone straddling the states of Sinaloa, Durango, and Chihuahua, which is the main drug-cultivation area of the country; Tijuana, another major connecting point between Mexico and the USA; and the state of Guerrero, home to the country's second most significant drug cultivation area.[5]

However, although this violence resulted, above all, from the competition among drug-trafficking organizations, it also killed many government officials (especially local police officers) and civilians uninvolved in the illegal drug business. Among the latter, there is a small but peculiarly well-documented category: journalists.

According to the most comprehensive available record, from 2000 to late 2015, 107 journalists were assassinated and 20 were forcibly disappeared (CNDH 2015b).[6] Not surprisingly, the organization Reporters without Borders (2015) classifies Mexico as "the Western Hemisphere's deadliest country for journalists."

This development has an obvious negative impact on the quality of democracy, since it impoverishes public debate and therefore the quality of political competition. To illustrate this situation, one can cite, once again, the country's "freedom of the press" score mentioned above: after improving for more than a decade, it began to deteriorate after 2003; by 2014, the gains of the previous 20 years had been completely erased (Freedom House 2016).

Criminal and Political Struggles

Why did Mexico become such a deadly place for journalists? The obvious culprit is organized crime. However, is this the whole truth—or at any rate, most of it?

Available data suggests that many of the 127 journalists who were assassinated or forcibly disappeared between 2010 and 2015 were, indeed, the victims of organized criminals. Thus, addressing themselves to the Zetas—one of Mexico's most dynamic drug-trafficking organizations—Journalists without Borders (2013, p. 20) affirmed: "using violence, you were instrumental in helping to make Mexico the continent's most dangerous country for journalists forcing local news operations to practice self-censorship and journalists to go into exile by your abuses." Less dramatically, CNDH noted that criminal organizations "have imposed a climate of terror and despondency in some states of the country, establishing, with the power of force, non-constitutional limits to the exercise of the freedom of expression and information" (CNDH 2013, p. 21). The location of casualties confirms these accusations. The four states with the most journalists assassinated or disappeared (Veracruz, Tamaulipas, Guerrero, and Chihuahua), which together account for almost half of these casualties, are indeed major theaters of drug violence.

Moreover, it is not hard to see the general motive behind the correlation of drug trafficking and aggression toward journalists. As previously argued, Mexican drug-trafficking organizations use violence as a tool in competition for markets and routes. However, this violence is more than a tool: it is also a semiotic, even an esthetic product. Thus, Gledhill (2014, p. 520) affirms: "In Mexico's drug wars violence is communicative: decapitated and dismembered corpses are used, along with banners placed on bridges, to send messages to the enemy and the population in general." Another author has argued that, in Mexico's drug violence, many homicides are "stylized": "The style of drug killings forms a semiotic system of 'inscribed' bodies subject to endless interpretation by cartel members and observers" (Campbell 2009, pp. 28–29). In other words, drug trafficking organizations use violence not only to eliminate their enemies, but also to produce messages and spectacles for each other, for the government, and for the rest of society.

However, criminals are not alone in this respect. Government forces have also actively contributed to the spectacle. This contribution has often taken the form of so-called joint operations. Since mid-2005, the federal government has repeatedly sent thousands of soldiers, marines, and federal police agents, backed by local forces, to confront drug traffickers in the states and regions where criminal violence seemed most threatening.[7] These operations have had a limited impact on the armed capacities of criminal organizations and, in fact, have often exacerbated the violence that they ostensibly sought to combat.[8] However, whatever their practical impact, they have been great spectacles: they have obviously tried to impress criminals, the Mexican public, and often also the US government, showing, in the most determined way, that the state is set on confronting violent offenders.

A second modality is the perpetration of spectacular massacres. This expedient has been mostly used after 2012, with at least three major cases documented in the press: Tlatlaya (June 2014), Apatzingán (January 2015), and Tanhuato (May 2015). The military and police forces participating in these massacres have apparently been ordered to "operate massively" in the nighttime to "kill criminals" (Centro Pro 2015, p. 21). However, although the executions themselves are perpetrated at night, the bodies of the victims—all of whom are officially referred to as "criminals"—are afterward displayed for public consumption. Thus, like the joint operations mentioned above, these massacres obviously aim to show to offenders and the public alike that the authorities are in deadly earnest about their fight against violent criminals.[9]

In response to this spectacular use of official force, criminals have often mounted their own counter-spectacles. A brief reference to the tactic known as "warming up a place" can illustrate this point. In most cases, proper joint operations, however massive they may seem to be, are obviously not vast and powerful enough to eliminate or at least immobilize all the relevant criminal organizations. This means that however impartial the authorities may wish to appear, in practice the official fight against violent organized criminals is necessarily selective. Taking advantage of this situation, criminal organizations often try to manipulate that selection, each of them seeking to direct the forces of the state away from itself and toward its rivals. One way to do this is to launch particularly vicious attacks, preferably against obviously innocent people, in the territories controlled by rivals, so as to provoke a public outcry and, therefore, compel the government to send its troops there.[10] This tactic, as is evident, cannot function unless the attack receives extensive press coverage.

Thus, the fight among criminal organizations and between them and the state can be seen as an intricate flux of messages and spectacles. Moreover, many of these messages and spectacles can reach their intended audience only through the press. Therefore, control of the press and journalists becomes critical—and murderous. As a desperate newspaper editor said: "If you do not print a narco message from one group, they will punish you. Alternatively, the other side will punish you if you do publish it. Alternatively, the government will punish for printing anything. You do not know where the threat is going to come from" (quoted in Wilkinson 2009).

Perhaps more significantly, in this context journalists become not only carriers of messages and reproducers of the spectacle, but also part of the message or spectacle itself. Criminals would kill a journalist not only to eliminate someone who was not willing to convey (or, on the contrary, conceal) certain information, but also to produce a message or spectacle with that much killing. This is why, in many cases, the bodies of assassinated journalists are not just thrown away but displayed in horrible ways, with the obvious intention to impress rival traffickers, the government, the general public—and other journalists.[11] In this way, the aggressions toward journalists have become part of the larger spectacle of criminal violence.

It would be a mistake to believe that drug traffickers and other organized criminals are the only great murderers of journalists. Again, the location of these murders provides a useful clue in this respect. The geography of drug violence and that of aggression toward reporters, while roughly similar, show significant mismatches. Thus, Veracruz accounts for 15% of the journalists assassinated and 20% of those disappeared, but for less than 2% of total organized-crime homicides reported by the official HRDO database. The case of Oaxaca, the fifth state with most journalists assassinated or disappeared, is roughly similar.[12]

This clue is confirmed by available reports on the topic. Thus, CNDH affirms that aggression toward journalists comes not only from criminals but also from corrupt and abusive "power groups and public servants" (CNDH 2013, p. 40). The information compiled by a specialized watchdog, Article 19, is more precise. Of the almost 400 instances of aggression toward journalists that this organization registered in Mexico in 2015, "41.5 were perpetrated by public officials" (Article 19 2016, p. 141).

It seems quite clear, therefore, that politicians—not only drug traffickers and other organized criminals—are major predators of Mexican journalists. Obviously, politicians may provoke, facilitate, or even directly perpetrate aggression toward journalists for a variety of reasons, like corruption, political repression, or counter-insurgency. However, why did they apparently become more prone to kill journalists precisely when criminals also did so?

Of course, it is difficult to disentangle the responsibility of criminals and that of politicians. However, although such disentanglement may be crucial to clarify specific cases, dwelling on it too much may obscure, rather than elucidate, the general pattern. Perhaps what matters most is not to determine which of those instances of aggression were perpetrated by organized criminals and which by politicians. For criminal struggles and political competition do not take place in mutual isolation: they often interact, and this interaction may have lethal consequences.

The combination of political and criminal competition can take several forms. One of them, perhaps the deadliest, is what could be called "dark alliances" between law enforcement authorities and drug-trafficking organizations, especially their criminal enforcement apparatuses. For drug criminals, the primary purpose of these alliances is straightforward: to use "the authorities as a weapon against rival cartels" (Stratfor 2012a). From the side of the authorities, apart from personal greed—an important but obvious factor—there is an apparently more respectable rationale. This can be illustrated by quoting a report written by the US Tijuana Consulate ("Post") in 2009, when two factions (one of them headed by Teodoro García Simental, "El Teo") were fiercely fighting for control of the Tijuana drug-trafficking organization (AFO). Referring to the municipal public security secretary, Lieutenant Colonel Julián Leyzaola, the document affirmed:

> Since coming to office six months ago, Leyzaola has fired some policemen with links to AFO lieutenant "El Teo". It is tempting to see Leyzaola as the good guy fighting the corrupting influence of the drug cartels. Unfortunately, though, the picture is a bit murkier. According to some Post contacts, Leyzaola has gone after "El Teo's" allies with such enthusiasm only because he made a "look the other way" agreement with one of "El Teo's" rivals within the AFO. He may believe that the only way to bring peace to the city is to defeat the undisciplined "El Teo" faction in favor of the faction which he believes will be more discreet in conducting its business. (US Tijuana Consulate 2009)

These dark alliances are particularly dangerous for law enforcement officials. Thus, in his analysis of police reform in Mexico, Sabet (2012, p. 12) noted: "While many [police officers] are believed to have been killed for their opposition to criminal groups ... it is believed that much more died because of their complicity in organized crime." Corrupt law enforcement personnel are killed either by the enemies of their criminal allies or by their allies themselves, especially when the latter feel betrayed or deserted. For example, according to a secret US Embassy cable, "the crackdown on police corruption has put compromised police officials in the position of either being prosecuted or breaking their established agreements/arrangements with the cartels. Hence, some of those who presumably choose the latter course are being punished brutally" (US Mexico City Embassy 2009).

Evidence of participation in dark alliances can be found at practically all levels of the law enforcement apparatus. However, for obvious reasons, access to the higher echelons of this apparatus is almost monopolized by the most powerful drug-trafficking organizations. This has been particularly the case for the so-called Pacific Cartel, which, according to Stratfor (2012b), "frequently provides U.S. and Mexican authorities with intelligence about its cartel enemies rather than taking direct military action against them." Not surprisingly, when a powerful criminal organization like this one splits up, violence visits even the uppermost—and usually safest—positions in the law enforcement hierarchy: the highest-ranking officials are forced to take sides and, when they do so, are likely to be punished by the disfavored faction. Something like this happened in 2008 and 2009, when the Beltrán Leyva faction broke away from the Pacific Cartel and several high-ranking functionaries at the Ministry of Public Security, including the head of the Federal Police, were killed in the subsequent struggle (see, for example, Padgett 2008).

A second major form in which the struggles of drug criminals and politicians combine consists of electoral alliances. As long as the PRI monopolized access to public office, opposition parties could boast of being untainted by drug corruption, simply because nobody took the trouble to buy them off. However, with the advent of political pluralism, this situation changed drastically. At first this change may seem anomalous: since citizens may be expected to punish parties and candidates that cooperate with criminals, competitive elections may be seen as a powerful shield against such alliances. However, at the same time elections provide a new field for the interaction of criminals and the authorities. It is not only that, as some authors have argued, electoral competition discourages politicians from acting together against drug criminals

(O'Neil 2009). More decisively, traffickers can provide politicians with resources that may be critical in tight electoral races, and some politicians from virtually every political party have rushed to take advantage of such remedies.

Perhaps the most obvious of such remedies is money. Revealingly enough, political parties themselves recognized that illegal drug money creates a strong temptation, too strong for them to withstand, and therefore repeatedly requested electoral authorities to "shield electoral processes from any organized crime influence." Responding to those requests, in late 2008 the Federal Electoral Institute approved a series of guidelines to "reinforce" the oversight of party and candidate finances (IFE 2009). However, for the next round of federal elections, held in 2012, the clamor from the public and politicians had become even louder, and the IFE was asked to update and reissue those guidelines (IFE 2012).

These temptations seem to be particularly strong at municipal and state level, where party finances and legal oversight mechanisms are weak. Thus, according to one analyst, "The risk that organized crime contributes money to control local elections is a pressing reality" (Curzio 2010, p. 104). Illegal drug money has suggested itself even in the highest electoral arenas. Among several possible examples, one can cite the case of the PAN (National Action Party) candidate in the 2012 presidential contest, who reportedly had received the support of people working for one of the most aggressive drug-trafficking organizations, known as Zetas (Carrasco Araizaga 2012). By investing in electoral races, drug traffickers obviously hope to acquire political resources that they can then put to use in their struggles against each other or the authorities. In this way, illegal drug money can bolster drug violence. Money itself is a neutral resource: it can be used for both peaceful and violent purposes.

However, drug-trafficking organizations have a second resource, one that is inherently violent and can also be critical in electoral races: armed force. Such force has often been directed against candidates, some of whom have been prevented from campaigning in particular sectors, while others have been ordered to stay out of the race altogether or, in extreme cases, have been killed. That force has also been directed against citizens, some of whom have been illegally prevented from voting, have been instructed to vote for certain candidates, or have been forcibly mobilized for certain candidates and parties. By using their armed force in these ways, drug traffickers have sought to make themselves into electoral censors, with the right to preselect or veto candidates, or to function like compulsory electoral machines. In either case, they have given their preferred candidates an advantage that might have proven critical in hotly contested electoral races.[13]

The struggle of drug traffickers and the competition of politicians may overlap in several other ways. However, these two—dark and electoral alliances—suffice to illustrate how that intersection may result not only in the criminalization of political competition, but also in the politicization of criminal struggles. To the extent that this intermixing takes place, criminal conflicts are fought in the political arena while political contests are played out in the criminal world. This does not only undermine the legitimacy of political competition and the efficacy of official anti-crime policies; it also extends the reach of criminal struggles and thereby exacerbates, instead of mitigating, the competitive violence emanating from the illegal drug market.

Some of these political–criminal alliances, at some moments, need to make themselves clearly visible to the public. Alternatively, they may need to conceal themselves and expose the alliances that oppose them. Whatever their preferences and the needs of the moment may be, they usually need to manipulate information about themselves and their rivals. This means that they normally need to mislead, buy off, threaten, kill, or abduct journalists. Thus, the interaction of criminal and electoral competitions magnifies the risks that each of them, separately, entails for journalists and the press.

More generally, this means that electoral democracy has not been a passive victim of criminal violence. By interacting with criminal competition, electoral pluralism itself has become a powerful cause of that violence—violence that, being often communicative, is often directed against those who control access to audiences.

Official and Corporate Responses

It would be unfair to say that government authorities and media companies have been insensible to the plight of journalists. Indeed, the Mexican government has taken several measures on this matter. One of these measures has been to set up law enforcement institutions specifically targeted at this problem. Thus, in February 2006, the Attorney General's Office (PGR) established a prosecutorial unit specializing in crimes against journalists, known as FEADP (PGR 2006). Four years later, this unit, now known as FEADLE, was somewhat upgraded by placing it under the direct control of the attorney general and by authorizing it to prosecute crimes against freedom of expression (PGR 2010).

Another measure is the creation of preventive and protective institutions. The most decisive step in this respect was the enactment, in June 2012, of the Law for the Protection of Human Rights Defenders and Journalists (LPDDHP). Months later, fulfilling the provisos of this law, the government established a so-called Protective Mechanism. This Mechanism is very ambitious: its stated objectives are "to implement and operate" preventive, protective, and urgent measures to guarantee "the life, integrity, freedom and security" of journalists and human rights defenders, through the cooperation of federal and state-level authorities. Interestingly, although the Mechanism is part of the Interior Ministry, it is governed by a nine-member body including four representatives of civil society organizations; four of the other members come from the federal government and one from CNDH (LPDDHP, arts. 1 and 5).

However, despite these institutional innovations, the aggression toward journalists has continued unabated. A good, although of course incomplete, indicator of the frequency of those instances of aggression is the number of complaints received by CNDH for alleged violations of the human rights of journalists. After dropping from 83 to 69 from 2009 to 2010, the number reached an unprecedented level (98) in 2011 and 2012 (CNDH 2013, p. 4).

Perhaps more to the point, the authorities have not shown much capacity to investigate and prosecute this aggression. According to data compiled by CNDH (2015a), only 11% of the instances of aggression registered from 2000 to 2015 were legally punished. The creation of a specialized prosecutorial unit does not seem to have alleviated this problem. Thus, of the 378 inquiries that FEADLE initiated from mid-2010 to mid-2013, 210 were dropped due to "legal incompetence," only 47 were taken to court, and just 1 resulted in a sentence. Many causes have been cited to explain this impunity, among them the lack of cooperation from local authorities, the large number of procedural deficiencies in the investigations, and the official reluctance to admit that aggression toward journalists had been motivated by their professional activities (CNDH 2013, pp. 46–48).

The preventive and protective institutions did not fare much better. As practically all of its observers agree, the Mechanism has not got close to its ambitious goals; even the minister of the interior reportedly acknowledged this failure (Cabrera 2014). According to an independent report, in its first two years of existence the Mechanism received almost 200 requests for protection, most of which—"approximately 157"—failed to receive the urgent attention that they demanded (WOLA 2015a, p. 4). Hence, "Human rights defenders and journalists have been left waiting many months for their particular situation to be analyzed and for measures to be granted, with no emergency protections provided during the delay" (WOLA 2015b, p. 3). Among the reasons most often cited for these failures are the massive turnover of personnel, lack of staff, insufficient funding, and lukewarm cooperation of local governments (WOLA 2015a, pp. 1–4).

Not only does the failure of protective and prosecutorial institutions leave aggressors free to murder and terrorize journalists at will, it also justifies or encourages censorship. At first, when the country's drug violence started to grow massively, media coverage of it was ample, almost florid. After 2006, when the government enthusiastically embraced the fight against organized crime and drug trafficking, it became almost chaotic. Even some respectable media published weekly body counts.[14]

However, it did not take long for this enthusiasm to cool. Perhaps the most significant step in this respect took place in 2011, when several influential media outlets published an "Agreement for the Media Coverage of Violence." Noting that "organized crime, and the terror that it has managed to propagate, is threatening the fundamental liberties of society" and the lives of journalists, the document called on the media to avoid "spreading information that endangers the viability of official actions and campaigns against organized crime or the lives and families of those who combat it" (Acuerdo 2011).

These calls for self-censorship coincided with a turn in the government's approach to organized crime. This turn was particularly visible after the inauguration of the Peña Nieto administration, in December 2012. Accusing its predecessor of exacerbating drug violence by paying too much attention to it, the Peña Nieto government seemed determined to downplay the matter (Mexican Presidency 2013, pp. 32–34). This approach called for a change in information policy. Therefore, although the government denied that it was imposing any form of censorship, it acknowledged that it had "made a pact with civil society organizations about how to provide information" on organized crime (Osorio Chong 2013, p. 55).

In practice, this new government communication policy had two main components. One was to suppress or under-report information about violence. Thus, not only did the government refuse to publish data on drug-related executions, official homicide statistics were also massaged to under-estimate the incidence of that crime.[15] One sign of this manipulation is the evolution of manslaughter, as compared with that of murder, in official statistics. After staying unchanged for many years, the officially registered number of complaints about non-intentional killings suddenly began to grow in 2012, exactly when that of intentional killings began to decrease (ONC 2014, p. 11, 16). Unless someone shows why Mexicans became more careless exactly when they became less aggressive, the only reasonable explanation for these changes is that increasing numbers of murders were reclassified as manslaughter. The result of manipulations like this is that, as international observers have noted, "A decreased emphasis by public authorities on the subject of violence and crime may not reflect actual decreases in commissions of violent crimes in fact" (Heyns 2014, p. 6).

A second component of the new government communication policy was to tighten the control of the media. Often, this enhanced control was performed with sheer force. Thus, physical aggression toward journalists, as documented by a watchdog, became more frequent after 2012—as did the proportion of such instances that were committed by government officials (Article 19 2015, pp. 15–17). Other forms of control were subtle but probably no less effective. One of them was the selective allocation of government publicity. Thus, a comprehensive analysis of the subject concluded: "Far from promoting accountability, official publicity in Mexico is a tool for indirect censorship that rewards or punishes the media according to their editorial lines, the information that they carry and the opinions that they form and propagate" (Article 19-Fundar 2015, p. 73). The accumulated effects of these soft and hard measures were so strong that sometimes even influential, mainstream journalists felt their pressure (see, for example, Loret de Mola 2015).

At first sight, these attempts at censorship and self-censorship seemed successful. From late 2012, there was an apparent decrease in the coverage of violence. Weekly body counts all but vanished from the pages of respectable newspapers. Even particularly deadly clashes were scarcely mentioned in the press (Seco 2013).[16] There is no evidence that censorship contributed to the decrease in that violence, which (as previously noted) after a two-year reduction seems to have bounced back in 2014. Nor did it apparently do much to stop the aggression toward journalists. Nor, finally, could it be expected to keep criminal violence away from public view for any considerable length of time. After all, many of these violent deeds are not inert products, which the media can freely decide to pick up or ignore. On the contrary, they are purposefully attractive, which means that if one media outlet refuses to publish them, others will quickly seize on them—or the perpetrators themselves will publish them in their own outlets. For, as the Committee for the Protection of Journalists noted, organizations like ISIS in Syria and Mexican drug traffickers "are not merely producing videos; they are acting as competing media outlets. ... In the days when the media exercised an information monopoly, journalists could collectively choose to exclude certain voices. Today, that power is gone" (CPJ 2015, pp. 25, 34).

In sum, the protective, prosecutorial, and censoring measures implemented by the government and media companies were clearly insufficient. This should not be surprising: while those measures may have been useful in some specific cases, they did nothing to address the interaction of criminal and political competition that, as argued above, makes it critical for both organized criminals and politicians to manipulate information—and therefore to mislead, corrupt, threaten, and assassinate journalists.

Conclusion

The assassination of journalists dramatically illustrates the deterioration of freedom of the press in Mexico. It is tempting to attribute most of this phenomenon to the increased power and aggressiveness of organized criminals. If that attribution were correct, electoral democracy would be one more victim of criminal violence. That is not the case, or at least not the whole of it. Electoral and criminal forms of competition are not separate; their combination, at least under present circumstances in Mexico, generates powerful forces against journalists and the press.

Therefore, perhaps it is not too exaggerated to say that the assassination of journalists in Mexico is a consequence of the growth of electoral democracy in a society that produces too many criminals eager to kill and be killed in the struggle for illegal opportunities. This means that while it is important to improve the institutions that protect the freedom of the press and the lives of journalists, something more is needed. For, if the previous analysis is correct, the best way to protect journalists in this context is an indirect one: to moderate criminal and political competition and to reduce the social production of violent drug traffickers.

These are daunting tasks, requiring audacious measures and involving many deeply controversial issues. However, they are indispensable if the good relation between freedom of the press and democratization is to be reconstructed.

Topics for Discussion

1. What are the causes of the assassinations of journalists in Mexico? What are the effects of these murders? What does the author set forth as possible solutions? Do you agree that these actions could solve the problem? Why or why not?
2. Should the government of each country share its policy for prosecuting those who assassinate a journalist in another country?
3. Would it be appropriate for a fragile government to censor the content of newspapers, television, or social media networks if it determines that the material being disseminated has a negative impact on that country's development objectives?

Notes

1. On the role that this company (known as PIPSA) played in the newspaper industry, see Zacarías (1996). On the official launching of the privatization process, see Segob (1998).
2. Yet this penalty persisted in many state-level codes and continued to be seen as a serious threat. As late as 2013, the National Human Rights Commission (CNDH) noted: "legal offenses like defamation, insult and slander have become the most frequently used legal means against supposed abuses of free expression. ... the mere existence of these legal figures indirectly restricts freedom of expression, since they convey the threat of fine or prison for those who allegedly insult or offend a public servant" (CNDH 2013, p. 20).
3. For a more detailed account of the evolution of electoral competition, political pluralism, civil liberties, and political and human rights as part of Mexico's electoral democratization, see Velasco (2005, pp. 19–24), on which the three previous paragraphs are based.
4. The *Reforma* data appeared on the following dates: January 2, 2006; January 8, 2007; January 7, 2008; January 1, 2009; January 1, 2010; and January 1, 2011.
5. Data about the geographical distribution of drug-related executions come from the *Reforma* and HRDO databases.

6. The data on homicides covers from April 2000 to October 2015; that on disappearances covers from April 2005 to October 2015.
7. According to a military report, from 2006 to 2012 the federal government launched 437 such operatives (SEDENA 2012).
8. One way in which this exacerbation may have happened is the following: "the success of President Calderon's aggressive anti-crime campaign ... has led to the arrest of important cartel leaders and narrowed the operating space of criminal gangs ... As a result, criminal gangs are now often in the control of more erratic and violent subordinates, leading to more killings and less predictable behavior" (USDS 2009, p. 441).
9. Among such exemplary massacres, the best-documented one is that of Tlatlaya. On this case see, among many others, Ferri 2014, CNDH 2014, and Centro Pro 2015.
10. A high-ranking federal official defined this tactic, in a peculiarly elliptical way, as "an attempt to augment the security forces in certain spaces, thus affecting the people who, in principle, have greater control or presence in the *plaza*" (Gómez Mont 2010).
11. Among many examples, see PGJ 2011.
12. According to CNDH 2013, Oaxaca accounts for 8% of journalists killed or disappeared, but "only" 1.25% of all HRDO homicides.
13. For a dated, but quite illuminating, overview of these and other forms of interaction between competitive elections and criminal competition, see Hernández Norzagaray (2010).
14. Perhaps the most famous was *Reforma*'s "execution meter" (*ejecutómetro*).
15. Indeed, however, the effort to suppress information on this matter started during the previous administration. In a significant step, the official HRDO database was suspended in 2011 and the information was classified as confidential (Lizárraga 2012).
16. Perhaps the greatest exception to this trend was *Zeta* Magazine, published in Tijuana, which kept recording and publishing drug-related executions.

Works Cited

Acuerdo para la Cobertura informativa de la Violencia (Acuerdo 2011). Available online: http://www.unesco.org/new/fileadmin/MULTIMEDIA/HQ/CI/CI/pdf/media_standards/Art%2019%20memorandum%20on%20the%20mexican%20draft%20federal%20act%20Acuerdo_Medios_23_marzo_2011.pdf. Accessed 15 Jan 2016.

Article 19. 2015. *Estado de Censura*. Mexico City: Article 19.

Article 19. 2016. *M.I.E.D.O. (Medios, Impunidad, Estado, Democracia, Opacidad)*. Mexico City: Article 19.

Article 19-Fundar. 2015. *Libertad de expresión en venta: Acceso a información y censura indirecta en publicidad oficial*. Mexico City: Article 19-Fundar.

Cabrera, Rafael. 2014. El mecanismo de protección a periodistas es un fracaso, reconoce Gobernación. *Animal Político*. April 4. Available online: http://www.animalpolitico.com/2014/04/gobernacion-prometio-modificar-mecanismo-de-proteccion-de-periodistas-rsf/#axzz2yJk0WLTP. Accessed 22 Feb 2016.

Campbell, Howard. 2009. *Drug war zone: Frontline dispatches from the streets of El Paso and Juárez*. Austin, TX: University of Texas Press.

Carrasco Araizaga, Jorge. 2012. Los Zetas en Veracruz: Los tentáculos corruptores del cártel se extienden hasta Vázquez Mota. *Sin Embargo*. June 18. Available online: http://www.sinembargo.mx/18-06-2012/266630. Accessed 25 Feb 2016.

Centro de Derechos Humanos Miguel Agustín Pro Juárez (Centro Pro). 2015. "Tlatlaya a un año: la orden fue abatir." Mexico City: Centro Pro.

Comisión Nacional de los Derechos Humanos (CNDH). 2008. *Informe especial sobre el ejercicio efectivo del derecho fundamental a la Seguridad pública en nuestro país*. Mexico City: CNDH.

Comisión Nacional de los Derechos Humanos (CNDH). 2013. Recomendación General no. 20 sobre agravios a periodistas en México y la impunidad imperante. Mexico City: CNDH.

Comisión Nacional de los Derechos Humanos (CNDH). 2014. Recomendación No. 51/2014 sobre los hechos ocurridos el 30 de junio de 2014 en Cuadrilla Nueva, comunidad San Pedro Limón, municipio de Tlatlaya, Estado de México. Mexico City: CNDH.

Comisión Nacional de los Derechos Humanos (CNDH). 2015a. Comunicado de Prensa CGCP/328/15. Oct. 30. Available online: http://www.cndh.org.mx/sites/all/doc/Comunicados/2015/Com_2015_328.pdf. Accessed 20 Feb 2016.

Comisión Nacional de los Derechos Humanos (CNDH) 2015b. Comunicado de Prensa CGCP/351/15. Nov. 23. Available online: http://www.cndh.org.mx/sites/all/doc/Comunicados/2015/Com_2015_351.pdf. Accessed 20 Feb 2016.

Committee to Protect Journalists (CPJ). 2015. *Attacks on the Press 2015 Edition: Journalism on the World's Front Lines*. Hoboken, N.J.: Wiley.

Curzio, Leonardo. 2010. Elecciones y seguridad. In *Atlas de la seguridad y la defensa de México 2009*, ed. R. Benítez Manaut, A. Rodríguez Sumano and A. Rodríguez Luna." México City: CASEDE.

Ferri, Pablo. 2014. Exclusiva: testigo revela ejecuciones en el Estado de México. *Esquire Latinoamérica*. Sept. 17. Available online: http://www.esquirelat.com/reportajes/14/09/17/esxclusiva-esquire-Testigo-revela-ejecuciones-ejercito/?cq_ck=1410990831177. Accessed 21 Feb 2016.

Freedom House. 2016. Freedom of the Press. Detailed Data and Subscores (1980–2015). Available online: https://freedomhouse.org/sites/default/files/FOTP2015%20Detailed%20Data%20and%20Subscores%201980-2015.xlsx. Accessed 15 Feb 2016.

Gledhill, John. 2014. Indigenous autonomy, delinquent states, and the limits of resistance. *History and Anthropology* 25 (4): 507–529.

Gómez Mont, Fernando. 2010. Conferencia de prensa que ofreció el Secretario de Gobernación, Fernando Gómez Mont. Available online: http://calderon.presidencia.gob.mx/2010/04/conferencia-de-prensa-que-ofrecio-el-secretario-de-gobernacion-fernando-gomez-mont/. Accessed 15 Jan 2016.

Guerrero, Manuel Alejandro. 2010. Los medios de comunicación y el régimen político. In *Instituciones y procesos políticos*, ed. S. Loaeza and J.F. Prud'homme. Mexico City: Colegio de México.

Hernández Norzagaray, Ernesto. ed. 2010. *Elecciones en tiempos de guerra: Baja California, Chihuahua, Durango, Nuevo León, Sinaloa, Tamaulipas, Veracruz*. Culiacán: Universidad Autonóma de Sinaloa.

Heyns, Christof. 2014. Report of the Special Rapporteur on extrajudicial, summary or arbitrary executions, Christof Heyns, on his mission to Mexico (22 April to 2 May 2013). Available online: http://www.ohchr.org/EN/HRBodies/HRC/RegularSessions/Session26/Documents/A_HRC_26_36_Add.1_ENG.DOC. Accessed 3 Feb 2016.

Instituto Federal de Telecomunicaciones (IFT). 2015. Infraestructura de Radio y Televisión. Estaciones autostradas al 14 de Agosto de 2015. Available online: http://www.ift.org.mx/sites/default/files/contenidogeneral/industria/cuadroestadisticodedistribuciondeestacionesagosto2015.xlsx. Accessed 10 Feb 2016.

Instituto Federal Electoral (IFE). 2009. Acuerdo del Consejo General del Instituto Federal Electoral por el que se establecen medidas y compromisos de partidos y el propio instituto, para propiciar condiciones de seguridad, legalidad y transparencia, durante el resto del proceso electoral federal 2008–2009. *Diario Oficial de la Federación*. Jan. 20.

Instituto Federal Electoral (IFE). 2012. Acuerdo del Consejo General del Instituto Federal Electoral para colaborar al fortalecimiento de las condiciones de legalidad, transparencia, rendición de cuentas y control interno de los partidos políticos para el Proceso Electoral Federal 2011–2012. *Diario Oficial de la Federación*. Mar. 6.

Lizárraga, Daniel. 2012. Oculta el gobierno cifra de muertos en la guerra contra el narco. *Animal Político*. Jan. 4. Available online: http://www.animalpolitico.com/2012/01/oculta-el-gobierno-cifra-de-muertos-en-la-guerra-contra-el-narco/. Accessed 23 Jan 2016.

Loret de Mola, Carlos. 2015. Y que se me deje venir el gobernador. *El Universal*. Feb. 10.

Mendoza Hernández, Enrique and Rosario Mosso Castro. 2014. "Los muertos de EPN: 41 mil en 23 meses." *Zeta*. Dec. 9. Available online: http://zetatijuana.com/2014/12/09/los-muertos-de-epn-41-mil-en-23-meses/. Accessed 25 Feb 2016.

Mexican Presidency. 2011. Base de datos de homicidios presuntamente relacionados con La delincuencia organizada. Available online: http://presidencia.gob.mx/voceria_seguridad/. Accessed 30 Jan 2011.

Mexican Presidency. 2013. *Plan Nacional de Desarrollo 2013–2018*. Mexico City: Gobierno de la República.

National Drug Intelligence Center (NDIC). 2009. *Drug Market Analysis 2008. South Texas High-Intensity Drug Trafficking Area*. Washington D.C.: US Department of Justice.

Observatorio Nacional Ciudadano (ONC). 2014. *Reporte sobre delitos de alto impacto. Dec. 2014*. Mexico City: ONC.

O'Neil, Shannon K. 2009. The real war in Mexico: How Democracy can defeat the drug cartels. *Foreign Affairs* 88, n. 4 (July-August): 63–77.

Osorio Chong, Miguel Angel. 2013. Comparencencia ante las Comisiones Unidas de Gobernación y de Seguridad Pública de la Cámra de Senadores. Nov. 8. Available online: http://www.senado.gob.mx/comisiones/gobernacion/reu/docs/version_081113.pdf. Accessed 21 Feb 2016.

Padgett, Tim. 2008. In Mexico's Drug War, Bad Cops Are a Mounting Problem. *Time*. Nov. 22.

Procuraduría General de Justicia del Estado de Tamaulipas (PGJ). 2011. Comunicado de la Procuraduria General de Justicia del Estado. Sept. 26. Avaiable online: http://procuraduria.tamaulipas.gob.mx/09/comunicado-de-la-procuraduria-general-de-justicia-del-estado-4/. Accessed 15 Jan 2016.

Procuraduría General de la República (PGR). 2006. Acuerdo A/031/06 del Procurador General de la República, por el que se crea la Fiscalía Especial para la Atención de Delitos cometidos contra Periodistas. *Diario Oficial de la Federación*. Feb. 15.

Procuraduría General de la República (PGR). 2010. Acuerdo del Procurador General de la República, por el que se crea la Fiscalía Especial para la Atención de Delitos cometidos contra la Libertad de Expresión, la cual se adscribe a la Oficina del Procurador General de la República, y se establecen sus funciones. *Diario Oficial de la Federación*. July 5.

Reporters Without Borders. 2013. *Predators of freedom of information in 2013*. Paris: Reporters Without Borders.

Reporters Without Borders. 2015. World Press Freedom Index. Available online: http://index.rsf.org/#!/index-details/MEX. Accessed 20 Feb 2016.

Sabet, Daniel. M. 2012. *Police reform in Mexico: Informal politics and the challenge of institutional change*. Stanford, CA: Stanford University Press.

Seco, Raquel. 2013. Noches de violencia y silencio en varias ciudades de México. *El País*. Aug. 4.

Secretaría de Gobernación (Segob). 1977. "DECRETO que reforma y adiciona los artículos 6o., 41, 51, 52, 53, 54, 55, 60, 61, 65, 70, 73, 74, 76, 93, 97 y 115 de la Constitución Política de los Estados Unidos Mexicanos." *Diario Oficial de la Federación*. Dec. 6.

Secretaría de Gobernación (Segob). 1998. "Convocatoria y bases de licitación para la venta de la participación accionaria del Gobierno Federal en las entidades denominadas Productora e Importadora de Papel, S.A. de C.V. (PIPSA), Fábricas de Papel Tuxtepec, S.A. de C.V. (FAPATUX), Mexicana de Papel Periódico, S.A. de C.V. (MEXPAPE) y Productora Nacional de Papel Destintado, S.A. de C.V. (PRONAPADE)." *Diario Oficial de la Federación*. Nov. 17.

Secretaría de la Defensa Nacional (SEDENA). 2012. *Informe de Rendición de Cuentas*. SEDENA: Memoria Documental. Operaciones contra el Narcotráfico. Mexico City.

Stratfor 2012a. Polarization and Sustained Violence in Mexico's Cartel War. Available online: https://www.stratfor.com/sample/analysis/polarization-and-sustained-violence-mexicos-cartel-war. Accessed 12 Feb 2016.

Stratfor 2012b. Mexico's Presidential Election and the Cartel War. Available online: https://www.stratfor.com/weekly/mexicos-presidential-election-and-cartel-war. Accessed 5 Feb 2016.

U.S. Tijuana Consulate. 2009. Police murders show the difficulty of bringing down the drug cartels in Tijuana. Available online: https://wikileaks.org/plusd/cables/09TIJUANA732_a.html. Accessed 18 Jan 2016.

United States Department of State (USDS). 2009. *International Narcotics Control Strategy Report*. Vol. I *Drug and Chemical Control*. Available online: http://www.state.gov/documents/organization/120054.pdf. Accessed 15 Feb 2016.

US-Mexico City Embassy. 2009. The battle joined: narco violence trends in 2008. Available online: https://wikileaks.org/plusd/cables/09MEXICO193_a.html. Accessed 22 Dec 2015.

Velasco, José Luis. 2005. *Insurgency, Authoritarianism, and Drug Trafficking in Mexico's "Democratization"*. New York, NY: Routledge.

Washington Office for Latin America (WOLA). 2015a. El Mecanismo de Protección para Personas Defensoras de Derechos Humanos y Periodistas en México: desafíos y oportunidades. Available online: http://www.wola.org/sites/default/files/MX/Enero%202015_El%20Mecanismo%20de%20Protecci%C3%B3n%20para%20Personas%20Defensoras%20de%20Derechos%20Humanos%20y%20Periodistas.pdf. Accessed 29 Jan 2016.

Washington Office on Latin America (WOLA). 2015b. The Mechanism to Protect Human Rights Defenders and Journalists in Mexico: Challenges and

Opportunities. Available online: http://www.wola.org/sites/default/files/MX/Jan%202015-The%20Mechanism%20to%20Protect%20Human%20Rights%20Defenders%20and%20Journalists%20in%20Mexico.pdf. Accessed 29 Jan 2016.

Wilkinson, Tracy. 2009. Mexico crime reporters face deadly perils. *Los Angeles Times*. Dec. 29.

Zacarías, Armando. 1996. El papel del papel de PIPSA en los medios de comunicación mexicanos. *Comunicación y Sociedad* núm. 25–26 (Sept. 1995–Apr. 1996): 73–88.

CHAPTER 11

Land Tenure, Community Space, and Media Engagement as Determinants of Good Governance in a Central American State: The Case of Guyana

Emmanuel K. Ngwainmbi

Overview of the History of Amerindian Land Tenure

The third smallest country (after Surinam and Uruguay) in South America, with Venezuela to its west, Brazil to its west and south, and Suriname to its east, and a landmass and water spanning approximately 215,000 km^2, Guyana has quickly become an attraction to emerging markets because of its minerals, malleable tropical climate, and relative political stability. Forest covers 75% of the land area. The average

Emmanuel K. Ngwainmbi, an expert researcher, lecturer, and writer on the problems in emerging nations, in this chapter focuses on the importance of protecting indigenous land rights and creating opportunities for communities that depend on forest resources for their livelihood.

E.K. Ngwainmbi (✉)
Matthews, NC, USA

E.K. Ngwainmbi (ed.), *Citizenship, Democracies, and Media Engagement among Emerging Economies and Marginalized Communities*,
DOI 10.1007/978-3-319-56215-5_11

temperatures range from 24 to 31 °C, a warm climate moderated by trade winds, rainy seasons (May through mid-August), and mineral deposits, including bauxite, gold, and diamonds (Official Guide to Guyana 2012, p. 82). Bauxite, diamonds, fish, forestry, gold, and manganese are among the products that are exported. The strategic location of the country and its resources have made it an international business beehive, with foreign companies flocking there and exploiting its resources. According to Guyana's Office for Investment:

> Guyana offers potential investors—foreign and domestic alike—a broad spectrum of investment choices, ranging from more traditional industries (such as mining, sugar, rice and timber), to non-traditional export sectors such as aquaculture, agro-processing, fresh fruits and vegetables, light manufacturing, value-added forest products.[1]

The exploitation of local space for economic benefits by domestic and foreign entities raises questions about ancestral notions of land ownership and state-owned land managed by the government. According to the ministry in charge of the affairs of indigenous people, the Government of Guyana set the policy objectives to be accomplished by 2015. One major objective was addressing all land titling issues for Amerindian villages by the end of 2015, including applying for land certificates. The process of applying for land titles had to be based on the principle of free, prior, and informed consent (FPIC), as defined by the United Nations Permanent Forum on Indigenous Issues (UNPFII). The terms of this principle are that a community or indigenous group has the right to give or withhold its consent to proposed projects that may affect the lands it customarily owns, occupies, or otherwise uses.[2] However, the implementation of that concept can have unintended consequences and consultation can sometimes embed existing social, cultural, and economic tensions, especially regarding the tensions between inclusive participation and exclusive rights (Fontana and Grugel 2016). Moreover, there are challenges in building cultures of involvement and inclusion in complex and ethnic diverse democracies in relation to further reflection on participatory governance and collective rights of the people and FPIC implementation, as Fontana and Grugel (2016) found in their case study of Bolivia.

As one of the 193 members of the United Nations (UN), Guyana is required to adhere to UN laws, including demonstrating respect for the rights of indigenous people. Accordingly, the government introduced the Amerindian Act of 2006, which led to Amerindians collectively owning 13.9% of Guyana's land mass. The Act recognized the spiritual and cultural attachment that Amerindians have to their land, which makes Amerindian land inalienable.

However, various media sources in Guyana, as well as leaders of Amerindian tribes and other non-profit groups, have been complaining that the indigenous people are not aware of their rights to own land, while other residents have publicly verbalized their concerns over deprivation of their space. *Stabroek News*, the largest newspaper in circulation in the country, has consistently published reports of those concerns, including failed negotiations between the government and negotiators representing the people to reach a consensus on land tenure. There have been reports from local action groups about miners having challenged the issuing of land extensions (additional space) to Amerindians.[3] What started the conflict between the residents and companies? To have some clarity, we need first to understand the history of land titling in the country.

Brief History of Land Titling in Guyana

The entire Amerindian land titling (ALT) program began with a decision by the Government of British Guyana in 1965 that Amerindians should be granted rights to occupy areas and reservations in tribes or communities where they were residing. Having failed to deal with Amerindian land rights 150 years prior, the British colonialists demanded that the new state of Guyana should begin with granting legal ownership of land to Amerindians. However, some groups argued that the land already belonged to Amerindians and that the government had no right to demarcate it.

After the British colonial administration handed authority to the Guyanese people, successive governments of Guyana have invested considerable amounts of financial and technical resources in the protection of the indigenous land rights of Amerindian communities. To show its intent to respect the freedoms and rights of its indigenous people, the Government of Guyana created a unit called the Ministry of Amerindian Affairs (MoAA), now known as the Ministry of Indigenous People's Affairs (MoIPA), which works with development partners and local communities for the wellbeing of the indigenous people in Guyana. To increase public access to information about Amerindian affairs and promote transparency in its dealings, the ministry manages a website, www.indigenouspeoples.gov.gy, to inform the public on matters affecting the Guyanese, especially indigenous peoples, and to provide another useful communication route and links to online resources, allowing the world to gauge the country.[4]

For some years, the Government of Guyana has received technical and financial support from international development agencies, such as the United Nations Development Programme (UNDP), the United Nations Programme on Reducing Emissions from Deforestation and Forest Degradation (UN-REDD), the United States Agency for International Development (USAID), and the Government of Norway, for the land titling and demarcation project. General meetings and consultations with indigenous communities and with bodies that represent their interests and facilitate knowledge sharing, such as the Amerindian Village Council, have caused greater understanding on both sides. Projects implemented were meant to provide more resources and increasing opportunities for Amerindians. The government attempted to utilize various mechanisms to enable information flow and communication on land titling by engaging communities in dialogue, and setting up and implementing policies based on the United Nations Declaration on the Rights of Indigenous Peoples (UNDRIP). UNDRIP Includes the provision of minimum standards for the survival, dignity, and wellbeing of indigenous peoples. These measures were taken by the colonial administration, and subsequent governments of Guyana only made provision for three categories of Amerindian land and security of tenure to their Amerindian inhabitants.

Government Engagement on Land Titling

A brief review of government engagement in land titling and the rights of the Amerindian people has not been produced. Dialogue with the Amerindian communities has already been initiated for their active involvement, and this process is being tracked and recorded as part of an ongoing stakeholder engagement plan. Also, various consultations with different indigenous groups suggest that people can gain more knowledge about the Amerindian land titling mechanism through a good communication program. For example, during an ALT meeting with Executives of the National Toshaos Council (NTC) held on December 18, 2015, executives cited limited communication to communities regarding ALT and strengthening community relationships, and the involvement of other community associations in the ALT process. Those concerns were raised mainly because the NTC and other associations representing Amerindian interests claimed that they had not been well informed on how the ALT process works.

A policy document produced by Guyana Lands and Surveys of the Land Administration Division lists procedures for issuing a land certificate of title to Amerindian communities, which are the following[5]:

(1) the Community or Village makes a formal Application in writing, signed, approved by two-thirds of the village, and accompanied by a sketch or plan of the area and
(2) submits the application presented to the Minister of Amerindian Affairs that
(3) acknowledges receipt in writing and orders investigation within 6 months of receipt of the application.
(4) The Ministry requests GLSC to prepare a scaled plan of the area requested;
(5) sends a scaled plan to GFC, GLSC, and GMC for their indication of whether there are any overlaps with existing concessions, which
(6) conducts an Investigation to ascertain information from the Amerindian village or community. The Minister then
(7) considers the investigation along with other information before he/she
(8) approves or disapproves the application made by the village.

Examination of Community Space

Land Titling and Human Rights

In examining the ALT project and related documents, we find that Amerindian inhabitants have never had the security of tenure of their land, even after the colonial administration and the Government of Guyana implemented some ordinances and measures to define Amerindian land. Ordinances delivered in 1902 and 1910, as well as the Amerindian Act of 1951 that made provision for three categories of Amerindian land, were not respected. Logan Hennessy's scathing report submitted to the Human Rights Center at the University of California, Berkeley some time in 2002 showed that after three decades of environmental, indigenous, and civil rights movements for ecojustice, local communities were still being marginalized in development, resource management, and conservation agendas (Hennessy 2002). In the study, Hennessy stated that spiritual and material losses of land and resources had forced indigenous peoples to wage national and international protests. Facing more barriers to justice in their countries, environmental and indigenous social movements appealed to international bodies for help in recognizing the shortcomings of their own governments' laws.

Politics of Land Ownership

Land ownership is always a sensitive issue, because it involves having access to natural resources and utilizing space for the advancement of cultural and economic purposes. It also involves handing land ownership over to subsequent generations of family members, or preferred individuals, and selling or utilizing it at will. It is, therefore, necessary for all parties involved in land tenure, including the government, intermediaries (the media, village council), and beneficiaries (people), to continue to share knowledge and information before, during, and after land has been allocated. The overall purpose of sharing knowledge is to promote dialogue and mutual understanding in order to have in place a peaceful environment in which people live and work together for the overall advancement of the nation.

To ensure that all stakeholders were better informed about the land titling mechanism, the Government of Guyana requested technical assistance from the intergovernmental development agency, the UNDP, in 2013 to prepare a communication strategy for the Amerindian Land Titling project. In a gesture of transparency and to obtain a proper roadmap to measure its success, the parties published a bid for proposals on the internet.[6] The expected outcome of the ALT project was that well-informed persons would apply for land titles, and unrestricted grants and certificates of title would be issued to eligible Amerindian communities and village extensions for villages that submit requests.[7] However, when requesting a means of sensitizing the people to obtaining land, the government did not foresee that it was being perceived as playing a dubious role—referee and player—in the land titling process.

Government Interference and Land Ownership

Amerindians who constitute 9.1% of the entire population of Guyana (CIA World Factbook 2014) have not been satisfied with the government's past and present actions in connection with the land they occupy. That could also be one of the reasons why preliminary alliances between Amerindians and international NGOs augmented the fission of internal groupings and increased growing tensions for all Amerindian claims vis-à-vis the state (Klautky 2000; Ishmael 1995). In less than 5 years, the Wai Wai tribe with only 200 people became the largest landowners in Guyana. Although it is a Community Owned Conservation Area without a legal status, the Wai Wai tribespeople designed the area they occupied to preserve biodiversity, their traditions, and their way of life, and to provide community and family development.

Published media reports have made it known that as of August 2016, the Wai Wai people had applied for protected area status under the Protected Areas Act, but state authorities had not decided by the end of that year. With no explanation of how or why what was numerically a small tribe ended up with the majority of the land, we should not be surprised that the remaining eight Amerindian tribes could challenge the government to provide a justification or simply give them their fair share. Meanwhile, we can make the following deductions based on the government outlook on land allocation: rules were not followed, and the indigenous people were not given the means (resources) to help them have land.

Empowerment of Indigenous People to Utilize the Environment

The fact that Guyana, a lower- to middle-income country per World Bank standards, relies on the exploitation of its natural resources (such as agriculture, mining, forestry, and trade in wildlife), which have a damaging effect on biodiversity, explains concerns that the national government and indigenous people may have about repartitioning the land.

Empowering Indigenous people to exploit natural resources is a mandate given by the UN to member states. According to Article 8 (2) of UNDRIP, the state is required to provide effective mechanisms for the prevention of and redress for any action which has the aim or effect of depriving indigenous people of their integrity as distinct peoples, or of their cultural values or ethnic identities; and dispossessing them of their lands, territories or resources. In Articles 20 (25) and 32 (1) of UNDRIP, "indigenous people do not only have the right to own traditionally, occupy or otherwise use lands, waters, and territories, but also to determine and develop those priorities and strategies for their own territory use."

Aligned with those principles is the state's responsibility to properly lead efforts in sharing knowledge on issues about indigenous people's socioeconomic future, and their right to knowledge. Having limited access to information about their rights, limited interactions with the government, or for the group not to be given adequate access to information could also mean deprivation. To that end, the Guyana Forest Act of 2009 has provisions for Amerindians and non-Amerindians to assist in meeting local needs. However, the Guyana Forestry Commission, a branch of the Ministry of Indigenous Affairs, may not be implementing the Act. Further, the ALT project was produced with input from the Ministry of Indigenous Peoples' Affairs and senior members of UNDP's project board, who might not have considered the informed consent and dispute resolution factors. According to an assessment of existing capacities and entry points for free and knowledgeable consent and settlement of differences on the ALT project produced in January 2014 with input from the Ministry of Indigenous Peoples' Affairs of the Government of Guyana, and senior members of UNDP's project board, "in all communities, information about the ALT Project was communicated solely through verbal communication by the Implementers of the Project and the Village Council (VC) ."[8] The report further revealed that over three-fourths (82%, $n = 363$) of respondents recommended that they have other forms of communication for more efficient learning about the project, especially as announcements for meetings were seldom presented early enough for community members to prepare.

In the next section, we analyze the general communication on land titling issues.

Communication and Information Sharing of Land Issues

Best Practices in Communicating the ALT Program Consultation

Communication about land tenure in Guyana has historically taken four main forms: (1) top-down via one-way message delivery; (2) information sharing from the government reminding the people of their rights to freely express their views on public policy; (3) face-to-face meetings between government representatives and the villages aimed at engaging them in discussions; and (4) media coverage, including publications in the *Gazette,* that disseminates information and perspectives and political factors that influence the allocation and demarcation of land.

According to documents and reports produced by the ALT project, two types of dissemination techniques have been used to inform the villages about ALT: the Amerindian Rights Act 2006 and consultations. The Act, for example, states that Amerindian villages are consulted to give their consent to a company, corporation, or any foreign entity to exploit Amerindian land only if that entity agrees to the conditions of the village. Moreover, the village council, elected by the villagers to represent the village's interests, makes decisions about occupation and use of the land. In that context, consultation is the right method, because it empowers indigenous people to generate their own ideas, take responsibility for handling internal matters, and control their actions and decisions. Moreover, as part of the nation, the villagers are accountable for their decisions and actions. At the national level, the government took unusual steps to ensure that people were informed of future actions involving land and their health.

There have been 15 subnational consultations across the country at which 222 communities were present and which 3285 persons attended. Also from October to December 2015, consultations with various indigenous populations' associations that work on behalf of the Amerindian communities, such as the Amerindian People's Association and the National Toshaos Council, revealed that there is a major knowledge gap between the ALT implementing agency (MoIPA) and the Amerindian peoples. Many Amerindians do not know about the ALT project.

Advocacy and Information Sharing

Regarding advocacy efforts, national newspapers, radio news bulletins, advertisements, and TV broadcasts have been used to create general awareness about mining, logging, low carbon development, and other forms of environmental exploitation. In terms of information dissemination quality, the Government of Guyana can be credited for having utilized the internet to share knowledge on issues related to the Amerindian livelihood, as evidenced on www.amerindian.gov.gy, a website of the

Ministry of Amerindian Affairs where users can easily upload files on ALT-related projects such as the GRIF Amerindian Development Fund, Amerindian Heritage, and the ALT itself. Documents on the Amerindian Act 2006, as well as departments within the ministry and contact information, are available with a simple click.

Preliminary Consultations

Verbal communication has a short-term impact on the receiver, especially in legal matters such as land ownership. Unless it is recorded, it is impossible to validate what has been spoken. The verbal communication used by the implementers of the ALT project and the village council also raises important questions that should be investigated, and answers found, to ensure that the communication activities to be carried out can properly inform key stakeholders about the ALT mechanism. The questions are the following:

- Why did the implementers and village council use only oral communication in dealing with such a sensitive, important matter as land tenure, without utilizing a recording mechanism for future referencing of their message?
- Was the audience they spoke to uneducated and unable to read/understand the legalese, including issues associated with the land they occupied or were to occupy?

It is also not clear whether the implementers got any feedback, given that we normally garner more positive results through transparent action in the form of a dialogue between the government, its constituents, and the people it seeks to serve. In the same way that participation is a necessary condition for the promotion of dialogue, dialogue on a national scale can be a step toward achieving greater transparency in the land ownership process. This is especially so when we consider the increase of knowledge, understanding among the villagers, and advising potential land owners within the context of having land certificates. The approach is necessary because it allows groups to share what they know, feel, or want with others and creates a context for their involvement in the setting up and implementation of policies. In fact, through dialogue, key messages can be identified and can accompany communication tools developed based on feedback from communities as well as face-to-face consultations with ALT implementing partners, village council, and the media. This is consistent with the notion that people's empowerment and their ability to hold others to account is strongly influenced by their individual assets, such as land, a sense of identity, and the capacity to aspire to a better future (Blomkvist 2003). It also suggests that government responsiveness to citizens' demands is affected by different types of political participation. Hence, social and economic empowerment is tempered by the quantity and quality of communication actions as well as interactions between lawmakers (power keepers) and law-abiding citizens.

Theoretical Framework

The main purpose of this chapter is to know whether existing knowledge of land ownership, community space, and communication practice can determine the quality of the services that a governing body provides for its subjects or clients. It argues that in shared governance there is better communication and parties become more responsible for their actions than in situations where a party is governed without the benefit of feedback. For there to be shared governance, the governed party (community Ngwainmbi (1994, 1999, 2005) has to be empowered with information and other relevant resources. "Empowerment" is both a value orientation for a community and a theoretical model for understanding the process and consequences of efforts to exert control over decisions that affect one's life, the functioning of the community, and the quality of life (Rappaport 1987; Perkins and Zimmerman 1995). The definition of the empowerment theory that is relevant to this study considers person–space interaction. The Cornell Empowerment Group has seen "empowerment" as an ongoing process centered in the local community. It involves mutual respect, critical reflection, caring, and group participation, through which people who lack an equal share of valued resources gain greater access to and control over those resources (e.g., Lord and Hutchison 1993).

The Conceptual Framework of "Good Governance"

Regarding people living within defined national boundaries, "good governance" is when officials selected by citizens based on certain values and beliefs continually serve the needs of citizens to those citizens' satisfaction. In the same way, governance is said to be good when there is a free flow of information and communication between the selected group (government) and the selectee (citizens). The government proposes policies, actions, and programs and allows citizens to contribute their knowledge, conditions, and expectations. *Social empowerment* is a paradigm of governance. It is best understood as the process of developing a sense of autonomy and self-confidence, and acting individually and collectively to change social relationships and the institutions and discourses that exclude poor people and keep them in poverty (http://www.gsdrc.org). Hence, in the case of Guyana, the citizens, including Amerindians, are expected to have direct access to information about their land rights and to make their decisions about owning and utilizing the land. Similarly, NGOs, local and state authorities (Toshaos), and village councils are expected to work with the indigenous people (Amerindian communities and towns) in shaping policies related to the ALT project and land titling, and determining the actions to be implemented for the common good of the people. Thus, actions led by the government can either strengthen the people's sense of autonomy and responsibility or stifle it.

Within the framework of social/community empowerment, participation by all stakeholders is needed to set up rules and actions for the group for which they are intended, as this allows and empowers the team to be responsible for the actions it takes. It involves sharing perceptions, meanings, and knowledge (2007), and it involves people in decision making (Mody 1991; Servaes 2008; Maurizio 2010). Participation in decision making means that people can initiate, discuss, conceptualize, and plan the activities they will all undertake as a community. Regarding implementation, people are actively encouraged and mobilized to take part in the actualization of projects. Participatory communication comes to life when facilitated by the right people (Yoon 2004) and when they are given certain responsibilities and tasks and required to contribute specified resources (Uphoff 1985). National interests should take precedence over individual interests, and people must be educated before they make the right decisions.

The process of getting stakeholders adequately informed about the land titling process and demarcation should include drawing together knowledge about their thoughts and beliefs and packaging it accordingly. That requires interfacing communication with the various stakeholders. This concept is tied to behavioral change management and better knowledge sharing, in that when people are involved in creating something, they can easily understand how it works and can control, improve, or learn from their experience. Hence, the sharing of knowledge about the ALT project and land titling among the Amerindian communities and villages and other ALT project stakeholders has to follow a two-step approach to be successful. There are two key steps needed: first, communication at the political level, which involves advocacy work: consultation meetings with governments, potential product manufacturers, and development partners; and secondly, communication at the community level, which involves the media and affected population. We posit that no project being set up on behalf of the community can be successful among residents and their representatives without their involvement.

Assumptions

This study was based on the following understandings:

- Effective exchange of information comes through strong partnerships among state, local, and tribal authorities, private-sector organizations, and international development partners.
- Information acquired for one purpose, or under one set of sources, might provide unique insights when combined (ISE 2007) with applicable national principles of prior, free, and informed consent.
- Unrelated information from other sources may foster a culture of awareness in which people at all levels of government and the indigenous communities remain cognizant of the functions and needs of others and use knowledge and information from all sources (ISE 2007) to facilitate the ALT process.
- Information sharing must be a part of all ALT activity, including prevention of situations and an environment that propagate disputes about land, conflicts over demarcation, retention of land certificates, and recovery of demarcated land. The procedures, processes, and systems that support information sharing must draw on and integrate existing knowledge of the ALT process, and must respect established authorities and responsibilities.
- State and local persons are a resource, and they should be included in the national information sharing framework, which will require that executives of indigenous associations and government agencies jointly achieve a baseline level of capability to gather, process, share, and utilize information and operate in a manner that respects individuals' privacy rights and other legally protected rights protected (ISE 2007).

The study considered both mass media and interpersonal communication techniques as effective components of information sharing with indigenous communities and other stakeholders on the ALT project.

Research Method and Procedures

The triangulation approach was used in collecting and analyzing the data. The content of the analysis can be best understood through a compendium of information from all sources related to the ALT project in Guyana; that is, the existing land titling documents and institutional knowledge of Amerindian spaces and livelihood in Guyana. We may recall that triangulation is a way of assuring the validity of research through the use of a variety of methods to collect data on the same topic, which involves different types of samples as well as methods of data collection. Triangulation serves as the glue that cements the interpretation of multimethod results by understanding the world in which one lives and interpreting it from the participant's frame of reference.[9] However, the purpose of triangulation is not necessarily to cross-validate data, but rather to capture different dimensions of the same phenomenon. Moreover, findings are not projectable in a statistical sense. As Holtzhausen (2001) has rightly stated, qualitative research has the unique ability to overcome this by providing insight into the underlying issues most pertinent to the population under study. Furthermore, other constraints (e.g., time, costs) may also prevent efficient use (Holtzhausen 2001). Triangulation helps to explain the complexity of human behavior by studying it from one or more angles. The method was utilized in this study with the aim of enlightening researchers, policymakers, students of communication, political science, international relations, and communication think tanks on the underlying information management issues (message creation, message sharing, access to information, and information dissemination) facing the indigenous people of Guyana and the government with regard to land tenure and land ownership.

A cross-analysis of existing literature on land tenure and the opinions of the key stakeholders was carried out to advise on the creation of a communication program for the target groups: the government and the indigenous people. The analysis included cross-referencing of sources of information to underpin the subsequent analyses and a trail of evidence.

General Approach

The main methods used in collecting data to determine the extent of communication and information sharing on land tenure were desk reviews, consultations with stakeholders in Georgetown (the capital of Guyana), questionnaire administration, surveys, and face-to-face meetings with the Ministry of Indigenous Peoples' Affairs, UNDP, indigenous peoples' organizations, and key partners.

Data was collected by using broad-based random sampling. Persons with shared attributes from the community, such as family heads, young adult men and women, and local leaders, were consulted in the context of town hall meetings. Representatives of local action groups were contacted by phone to attend an information-sharing meeting on land ownership and issues faced by the indigenous peoples. At the level of communities, the local liaisons with working knowledge of the local language and customs also invited a representative from each of the tribes to the town hall meeting.

Consultation meetings were held with senior Ministry of Indigenous People's Affairs staff, Amerindian Development Fund (ADF) and ALT, UNDP, senior editors of radio and television stations and newspapers, and other stakeholders involved with land tenure.

The researcher discussed travel and consultation plans for data collection with two liaisons based in Guyana. The planning meetings took place via Skype before actual consultations with the government/inter-governmental agency representatives, and Amerindian community and local media representatives. The local liaisons organized meetings with the target groups. Their activities were those of (1) providing inputs on the development of the questionnaires; (2) administering the questionnaires; (3) organizing consultations, and facilitating and participating in stakeholder meetings; (4) assisting in collecting data during the consultations; (5) assisting in the organizing of workshops, when necessary; and (6) providing feedback to the researcher on matters related to the ALT project and collecting information.

Survey and Consultations

The results of the study are based on consultations held on December 11, 2015 and April 11, 2016, with the principal stakeholders of the ALT project, and feedback collected from various stakeholders interviewed during that period. The researcher, along with two local liaisons with extensive knowledge of the local culture, conducted face-to-face consultations in Georgetown and Amerindian villages and communities, and organized 13 town hall meetings on December 14, 2015 and January 31, 2016.

The main purpose was to get feedback to assess knowledge with the indigenous people's groups and government ministries involved with land titling and utilize their feedback to assess their level of knowledge of the ALT project being implemented from October 2013 to October 2016, to compare their answers with the actions from previous on the project. The results of the comparison would provide advice for recommendations. The researcher then crosschecked the notes recorded from the consultations held with the local liaisons that had taken place from December 15, 2015, to January 31, 2016 with the views of the communities at the stakeholder town hall held in April, 2016. The content of all the meetings had background information about the ALT project, steps for applying for the LT, and how information about the ALT project should be shared among stakeholders.

Study Participants

The primary targets for this study were the Amerindian communities and villages, also beneficiaries of the ALT project. However, all stakeholders were also targeted to promote information and knowledge sharing, and there was a specific approach for groups that have resisted the implementation of the ALT project. Other stakeholders are (1) government sectors involved with Amerindian land tenure and indigenous peoples' affairs in general (MoIPA, Guyana Lands and Survey Commission, Guyana Mines and Power and Forestry Commissions); (2) the National Toshaos Council (NTC); (3) village councils; (4) Amerindian villages and communities; (5) the media; and (6) investors, loggers, miners, and other users of the land resource. These groups are defined based on consultations, observations, and reviews of the documents on the ALT project. They have a stake in either the ownership of land or policymaking regarding land titling.

Procedures

This study analyzed existing information on the land titling project from printed materials and local online news sources, to point out the best practices and challenges that the Guyanese government and its partners may have faced in communicating messages on land tenure. Other methods used were surveys, in-person interviews, and consultations with MoIPA staff and leaders of Amerindian communities.

The researcher first analyzed data on land ownership and information disseminated through existing electronic and physical documents produced on land tenure in Guyana. The document types used were the following: reports commissioned by the government and intergovernmental agencies in Guyana (UNDP, MoAA, UN-REDD, Forestry, Lands and Survey, Mines). Other sources analyzed included articles posted online and printed newspaper reports and stories. Next, questions were developed from the published reports and press articles on land tenure as well as preliminary consultation feedback and used to conduct the survey.

This researcher, along with two local informants, held meetings with the principal stakeholders in April 2016 after analyzing the preliminary results of the study. The researcher understands that the comments were made in the spirit of fairness and the desire to share useful knowledge with the authorities in charge of demarcating land and ensuring the peaceful coexistence of the indigenous people of Guyana.

Questionnaire Administration

Separate questionnaires were administered to the respective participants: UNDP program staff involved with land tenure. Sets of questionnaires were developed and administered to the three principal subjects: the program staff, media personnel (television, radio, and newspaper managers), and community group representatives, which included indigenous peoples' organizations. The main objective was to get an overview of their knowledge of land tenure challenges in order to design appropriate messages and plans aimed at better informing them.

To facilitate administration of the questionnaires, the questions were developed with inputs from the local liaisons. This approach seeks to make the creation of data as transparent as possible, by not involving administrators and financial providers in the generation of some questions. Bias could negatively affect the types of questions to be asked if those entities participate in the design of questions. Besides, since they are also the subjects, it would be unwise to involve them on issues or matters relating to their past work in informing the villagers.

Where respondents did not understand English, the liaison and questions were asked to the respondents in the native language, and the appropriate response marked.

Interviewing

The purposes of interviewing various groups of people were:

- To understand what they thought and felt about land titling and obtaining land certificates.
- To understand the history of the land titling mechanism in their terms.
- To assess their level of understanding of what it meant to have a title and their expectations from the government.
- To evaluate their willingness to share information and knowledge on land titling and their readiness to collaborate with other groups to ensure that the process would be transparent and less complicated for everyone. They were selected based on analysis of the study and consultation visits to the regions.

This researcher and two local liaisons, two representatives of the MoIPA and one member of UNDP ALT project staff, traveled to the 13 villages and communities from April 4 to April 30, 2015 and met with the villagers. All town hall meetings involving men, women, and young people and their leader (Toshao) lasted an average of three hours. Meetings were conducted mainly in English, and interpretations and transliterations in the local languages allowed everyone the opportunity to share their views.

Following the opening of each session with prayers led by a Toshao, the representative of the government explained the purpose of the visit. The researcher then asked participants to say what they knew about the ALT and land titling, how many times they had heard about it. Participants were also asked to propose methods for receiving and sharing knowledge and information about land titling and the ALT project. Other questions were the following:

- Do you have any concerns or questions you would like to share about the ALT?
- What does demarcation mean to you?
- Are you prepared to apply for a land title or an extension of your land?

It should be noted that the researcher recorded the sessions with electronic devices and through note-taking, and participants in each of the villages were asked the same questions, with limited probing. The main objective of discussing these issues was to gauge the participants' knowledge of the impending project to determine the number of communities applying for land titles. It also sought to determine their readiness to participate in sharing information about the ALT project among their people and with neighbors, and to utilize the handbook and other types of sharing products if accessed.

Those consulted and interviewed were ALT project staff at the UNDP, and representatives of MoIPA, Guyana Lands and Survey Commission, the High Court, GEPAN,[10] executives of groups representing the communities: NTC, National Amerindian Development Foundation (NADF), American People's Association (APA), and The Amerindian Action Movement of Guyana (TAAMOG). Potential respondents such as the NADF, Guyana Organization of Indigenous Peoples, and others could not be reached due to transportation issues. Amerindian communities and villages in five regions representing local customs, geographical relevance, and varying levels of sensitivity over the issue of land titling were selected and reached.

Interview Techniques

The interviews took place in the form of face-to-face meetings, phone calls (to reach key land stakeholders who could not attend meetings), SMS texting, and reading and marking of corresponding answers to questions. The town hall meetings were recorded with express permission, to ensure that discussions were comprehensive.

Questionnaire Design and Administration

As mentioned earlier, a set of questions about the level of awareness of the ALT project was developed with inputs from the UNDP, MoIPA, and the ALT project staff, who had had more consultations with Amerindian communities and villages over the previous 3 years than any other group before this study started in January 2015. The expectation was that the frequently asked questions and similar answers would later be shared with all stakeholders as a repository for knowledge sharing. The questions were also designed to determine the amount of knowledge of the ALT project and land titling mechanisms to which the indigenous people had access. The local liaisons used e-mail, telephone calls, and texts to contact participants, invite participants to the meetings, organize meetings, and share questionnaires.

The types of questions asked appear below:

Q1. Amerindian People's Association (APA) and Guyana Organization of Indigenous Peoples

Why did you stay away from meetings regarding Amerindian Land Titling?

What would it take for you to attend such meetings and negotiations?

Describe how you feel the land titling process should be handled. For example, how should the government organize the demarcation of territory and issue land titles?

What roles should the village heads and villagers play to make the demarcation process easy for everyone?

If you want to share knowledge among the villages about the land titling process, how would you communicate the messages to them?

Q2. Amerindian Action Movement of Guyana. TAAMOG respondents only

Why do you support the Land Titling and demarcation process?

Which reasons have your supporters given for their support of the ALT project?

If you feel people do not have enough information about the certificate program, what should be done to make sure more people are well informed (so they can take a decision)?

Describe how you feel the land titling process should be handled.

For example, how should the government organize the demarcation of territory and issue land titles?

What roles should the village heads and villagers play to make the demarcation process easy for everyone?

Q3. Guyana Organization of Indigenous Peoples (use recording device)

What is not clear about the land titling process which the government has been proposing?

Describe how you feel the land titling process should be handled.

For example, how should the government organize the demarcation of territory and issue land titles?
What roles should the village heads and villagers play to make the demarcation process easy for everyone?
If you feel people do not have enough information about the certificate program, what should be done to ensure more people are well informed (so they can take a decision)?
Is there any other issue you want to tell us about the land titling and getting certificates of land title?

Town Hall Meetings

To find out residents' degree of access to information on land tenure and their knowledge of the history of land tenure and ownership in Guyana, as well as the challenges at the psychological, cultural, and economic levels, the legalities involved in the demarcation and allocation of land, as well as the issuance of certificates of ownership, this researcher and the two local liaisons asked participants whether they had heard about the ALT project or been told about it.

General Findings

Face-to-Face Meetings

By taking part in meetings persons are expected to initiate ideas, discuss, conceptualize, and plan activities as a community. With that in mind, the researcher and the local liaisons held separate meetings with the government, intergovernmental officials, and representatives of the Amerindian communities. The meetings were used to share feedback from the town hall meetings and to determine whether the government officials had intentionally withheld information from the people about land ownership or whether they did not have the appropriate methods and mechanisms to reach the people (see Table 11.1, Part b).

Overall, the expected results of the consultations (town hall meetings and in-person meetings) were to validate the desk review of the ALT project and the press articles; that is, to confirm or refute the conclusions of the electronic documents and physical reports.

Table 11.1 Questions asked at town hall meetings

Q1 Stakeholders
Toshaos, Village Council and residents
Toshaos Council and Village Council
What do you know about the land titling project?
It has been said that announcements for meetings are seldom presented early enough for community members to prepare for meetings
a. What other forms of communication have you been using in your communities to learn about the ALT project?
Are they efficient? If so, how do you know?
Are you satisfied with what you now know about the land titling project?
If you answered no, give your reason(s)
How would you like to be informed about land titling?
If you answered no to question 1 (that you have never heard about land titling), is it something you would like to hear about?
After instituting the Amerindian Act of 2006, are you aware of the ways that the Ministry of Indigenous Peoples' Affairs is addressing disputes and issues around the allocation of land to residents?
Do you interact with the Ministry of Indigenous Peoples' Affairs at all?
If you said yes, what issues about land titling do you deal with? For example, disputes that could not be resolved in your community?
Do you get any feedback from the government through the Ministry of Indigenous Peoples' Affairs about disputes? If so, how often?
If you said yes, are you satisfied with the information they give you? If not, explain why
How would you like to get information about land titling? From the government? Media (type)?
Tell us any other way you would like to get information about land titling
How do you share information about the land with the tribes?
b. Ministry of Indigenous Peoples' Affairs and UNDP
According to a report, the Wai Wai tribe with a population of 200 acquired 2300 square miles of land, the largest in Guyana, in less than 5 years. Describe the mechanisms or reasons for this
The Amerindian Act of 2006 and the Justice Institute Guyana state that the Amerindian Village Council was given the responsibility to resolve disputes around the allocation of land to residents. Was there a mechanism for follow-up by the government to ensure that the residents understood that the government had given the Council the responsibility? If not, state the reasons for not following up
The Amerindian Act of 1976 has been described as the principal source of reference in the description of village borders and that, as stated in Amerindian Act Cap 29:01 Schedule, Part A, "such inclusion has been helpful in providing written confirmation in understandable terms through which Amerindian communities may affirm their demarcation"

(continued)

Table 11.1 (continued)

Q1 Stakeholders
To what extent has the Ministry of Indigenous Peoples' Affairs or any other government sector ensured that through written confirmation Amerindian communities have been able to affirm their demarcation?
Which communication approaches and information tools have been used to interact with the communities?
After instituting the Amerindian Act of 2006, is the Ministry of Indigenous Peoples' Affairs aware of any approach being utilized by the National Toshaos Council and Amerindian Village Councils in addressing disputes around the allocation of land to residents?
Which mechanisms are implementers of the ALT project using to interact with the Village Council other than verbal communication?
Does the Ministry of Indigenous Peoples' Affairs receive reports from the Village Council about land titling? If so, how often?
Does the Ministry of Indigenous Peoples' Affairs entertain concerns from the Village Council about the allocation issues? If so, how often and what types of concerns?
Does the Ministry of Indigenous Peoples' Affairs provide feedback on those concerns? If so, how often and through which means?
Describe the role to be played by the following partners in facilitating knowledge sharing on Amerindian land titling: Ministry of Indigenous Peoples' Affairs, Guyana Lands & Surveys Commission, Guyana Geology and Mines Commission, Guyana Forestry Commission
How would you like to be informed about land titling?
How do you share information about the land with the Wai Wai tribespeople?

The consultations with the representatives of the Amerindian communities following the town hall meetings sought to compare knowledge of the ALT process and to advise on future research or communication programming (action plan) on information sharing, public advocacy for land ownership, and promotion of shared governance between government authorities, intergovernmental agencies in the country, and the citizens.

Quality Assurance

During analysis of the data collected from the questionnaires and consultations, the researcher held regular review meetings with the local liaisons via Skype to discuss and address methodological issues with information gathering among all land tenure stakeholders. The researcher examined data collected from the questionnaires at random, to identify inconsistencies and provide clarifications.

Content Analysis of Electronic and Physical Documents

After reviewing the ALT project and related documents, it was determined that, despite the ordinances and measures that the administration, the Government of Guyana, and the colonial government had undertaken to define Amerindian land, including those of 1902, 1910, and the Amerindian Act of 1951,[11] security of tenure to their Amerindian inhabitants has not been established. Facing barriers to justice in their own countries, environmental and indigenous social movements, some of which demonstrated more than 500 years of struggle with human rights abuses, and Amerindians appealed to international bodies for help in recognizing the shortcomings of their own governments' laws.

The preliminary alliances between Amerindians and international NGOs have augmented the fission of internal groupings and increased tensions for all Amerindian claims vis-à-vis the state (Klautky 2000; Ishmael 1995). There are also legitimate fears that for Amerindians, reconciling the large-scale invasions of foreign companies and conservation agencies for land concessions, fueled by a government anxious to collect or retain revenues from its liberalized economy, is only half of the problem.

The efforts of successive governments of Guyana in addressing the plight of the indigenous people, particularly that of issuing land title to over 90% of land claims, have not been enough. For example, in 1995, an agreement with the Amerindian Toshaos (legally elected village leaders) and village councilors for demarcation of the existing 77 villages, and to address the request for titles by communities, probably did not involve proper prior communication with the people. Further, the government had to amend the constitution in 2003 by including a major rights section. The Amendment states that "Indigenous peoples shall have the right to the protection, preservation, and promulgation of their languages, cultural heritage and way of life." That text suggests that the government has not taken enough action after interacting with the indigenous people. For these people to exercise the right to their way of life that includes owning and utilizing the land, the top-down approach wherein lawmakers (government officials) decide what is best for the citizens cannot be sufficient, because lawmakers need adequate feedback to ensure that the people's way of life is properly preserved.

Advancing the mounting discrepancy is the locus of local organizations such as the Amerindian People's Association (APA), which withdrew from land titling negotiations and the compromising role of the UNDP in Guyana in complicating the process of land ownership for

Amerindians. That shows a lack of trust in the government, a lack of transparency, lack of national dialogue on ethnic issues, and tensions between the action group and the government.

Preliminary Observation

Villagers in all communities reached were reluctant to speak and only applauded after listening to their Toshao. Advised of the historical fact that Amerindians are a hierarchical society where people do not open up to strangers in the presence of their leader, the researcher probed and utilized other persuasive techniques such as laughter and local idioms. So the researcher prompted the Toshao to encourage participants to express themselves and not fear or expect repercussions.

Results of Consultations

Based on consultations with various stakeholders, most communities did not participate in the design of the ALT. People are not clear how many villages will apply for land titles. Therefore, the notion that communities and towns would take the opportunity to apply for land titling if they were well informed was not supported. Instead, communities led by their leaders favored the idea of allowing Amerindians to maintain complete ownership of their land.

Summary of Consultations in the Nine Communities, December 2015

- The APA is of the view that since the Amerindian Act is flawed, the ALT project is inherently flawed.
- There are underlying political problems in the ALT project.
- The APA would like *all* of its concerns regarding both the Amerindian Act and the ALT to be addressed before it states a position on the ALT.
- The APA recommends that other independent persons, that is, non-Government of Guyana and non-UNDP persons, be included on the investigative teams for land issues.
- There has been inadequate and inaccurate demarcation of lands.
- There has been little or no communication to communities regarding the ALT.
- There has been an absence of FPIC.
- There has been a lack of community involvement in the process.

- There has been variation in Government of Guyana–community relationships.
- There is a need for a participatory role by the NTC.
- There is limited or no knowledge of the Amerindian Act and its efficacy in addressing land title disputes.

Summary of Consultations on the ALT Project

- There has been inadequate and inaccurate demarcation of land.
- There has been little or no communication to communities regarding the ALT.
- The issue of land titling divides people. Thus demarcation is not a good idea, but more than 50% of the people reached during the consultations want to learn about the ALT project just to get better informed.
- There has been a lack of community involvement in the design of the ALT project.
- There has been variation in Government of Guyana–community relationships.
- There is a need for a participatory role by the NTC.
- The majority of Amerindians (approximately 70%) do not know anything about the ALT; 25% of Amerindians are not comfortable with land titling and they want the traditional definition of land to continue. For this group, boundaries separate people and land is ancestral property, not something the government should control.
- There are pending land disputes.
- Knowledge of the Amerindian Act and its efficacy in addressing land title disputes is very limited.

Based on the results of the consultations, the government has to share more information with the Amerindian communities and villages and the media, including clarification of the operational meaning of land demarcation, and secondly, the communities and MoIPA need to interact more.

Mechanisms for sharing knowledge and information should be the following:

- Use of information and communication technology such as television, radio, and newspapers.

- Use of social media such as Facebook, LinkedIn, and MySpace.
- Use of spokespersons from all stakeholder groups such as village councils, Amerindian associations, and village chiefs.
- Use of traditional forms of communication including drama and road shows.
- Use of events such as visits of ministers, concerts, and town halls and village council meetings.

The study found that only 20% of Amerindians had heard about the Amerindian Act 2006 and the ALT project document, although the information packages had been available for many years through word of mouth. Many Amerindian communities and villages seem unaware of the Amerindian land titling mechanism and the nature, purpose, and expected outcomes of the ALT project. The village council, charged with managing the land issues, and uneducated Amerindians, especially the villagers, do not seem to understand the Act and the importance of the ALT project in relation to their lives and the lives of future generations of Amerindians.

Despite the extensive consultations with Amerindian communities over the past 3 years and the production of other mechanisms such as land tenure regularization (LTR), which was designed to formalize and standardize procedures, to facilitate effective implementation of LTR and promote a just, speedy, and inexpensive adjudication of claims, villagers have observed that there was no redress or complaints mechanism, and the Amerindian Act, which is said to be "flawed," has been utilized continually. As a communication tool, the Act has not been updated since 2006, although physical and social conditions associated with land titling have changed. The success of the Land Tenure Regularization Manual, which was developed through extensive consultation, discussion, and debate with stakeholders involved with or interested in LTR and stresses the general, guiding principles to be involved in the various processes involved, has yet to be determined. Villagers have stated that they are not familiar with the regularization process, while others say they need more information on the Surveyors Act, which is associated with LTR.

Further, a mechanism is not available to give communities greater access to new technology that would enable them to be better informed about the ALT project. Additionally, there is no clear or systematic explanation of the systems and application processes. Several villages state that MoIPA does not acknowledge written correspondence from the villages, nor does it share reports of investigations conducted during the land titling process. A mechanism for eliciting feedback from the communities and towns targeted is absent from the ALT project design. In other words, the document does not include a section for stakeholder feedback, a critical element in facilitating the land titling process. Arguably, without feedback, there would be no communication.

Crucially, the disclosure of the ALT and land titling did not have clear visual properties such as maps posted in public places indicating demarcations for the villages or communities with land titles. Further, the fact that many villages reported that they had little knowledge of the ALT and the land titling process and were unclear about who owns waterways suggests that they had not understood the results of the consultations, discussions, and engagements led by the government and other teams involved with the ALT project.

The Guyanese Government's Role in Managing Indigenous Peoples' Wellbeing

We argue that the efforts of successive Governments of Guyana in addressing the plight of the indigenous people, particularly regarding issuing land titles to over 90% of land claims, has not been enough. In 1995, an agreement reached with the legally elected village leaders and representative village councilors to demarcate 77 villages and to address the request for titles by communities, probably did not involve proper prior communication with the local people. The government had to amend the constitution 7 years later (in 2003) by including a fundamental rights section to the Human Rights Act. The amendment states that "Indigenous peoples shall have the right to the protection, preservation, and promulgation of their languages, cultural heritage and way of life." This amendment suggests that the government had not taken enough action after interacting with the indigenous people. For the people to exercise the right to their way of life that includes owning and utilizing the land, the top-down approach wherein lawmakers (government officials) decide what is best for citizens is not enough, because lawmakers need adequate feedback to ensure that the people's way of life is properly preserved.

Furthering that argument is the position of local organizations such as the APA, which reportedly withdrew from consultations about land titling and has indicated its position as regards the process to the UNDP and other relevant agencies.[12] The position of the Guyana Organization of Indigenous Peoples regarding the ALT is not clear. According to a local informant, the APA was still in favor of the retention of traditional land by indigenous people. Although other organizations of indigenous populations, including TAAMOG and NADF, are supportive of the ALT project, it is important to determine the rationale and level of support in order to understand how well informed they are and plan a separate information campaign that targets those groups. Further, TAAMOG has a reputation for taking drastic action against some government decisions that it perceives to be unjust. This may suggest a lack of trust in the government, a lack of transparency, lack of national dialogue on ethnic issues, or existing tensions between the action group and the government. In this case, TAAMOG is expected to resist efforts toward facilitation of land titling, meaning that a particular initiative should be developed and implemented to engage its members in continuous dialogue on the topic of land titling.

Surveys and in-Person Interviews

For all stakeholders to be better informed about the land titling mechanism, they have to be engaged in dialogue, to understand the history of land tenure and ownership in Guyana, the challenges at the psychological, cultural, and economic level, and the legalities involved with the demarcation and allocation of land, as well as issuance of certificates of ownership.

The study found huge gaps in the communication of knowledge about land tenure. In the human rights and communication for social change practitioner communities, it is understood that positive results can be garnered through transparent action in the form of a dialogue between the government, its constituents, and the people it seeks to serve. Collaboration is a necessary condition for the promotion of dialogue. Dialogue on a national scale is considered a step toward achieving greater transparency in the land ownership process, particularly in increasing knowledge and understanding among the villages and advising potential landowners on the context of having land certificates. However, verbal communication between the ALT project and village councils raises important questions that should be investigated.

Based on information gathered from consultations with organizations representing Amerindian villages and communities (NTC, TAAMOG, APA), Guyana Lands and Survey Commission, and MoIPA), recent press reports on land disputes and ongoing confusion over demarcation, letters written to the government, and consultations with various Amerindian associations between December 2015 and January 31, 2016, it can be asserted that those stakeholders in the ALT project, particularly the Amerindian communities, are almost clueless about the Amerindian land titling mechanism.

The verbal and written concerns of the representative groups of Amerindian communities such as the NTC over the infringements of Amerindians' rights show in part that most people do not well understand the Amerindian Act 2006 or the ALT project document.

Conclusions

It can be concluded that the rights of the indigenous population to own land as specified in the UNDRIP document were not met. As a reminder, the agency advocates that "indigenous peoples should not be denied the exercise of their rights, [and] should be free from discrimination of any kind." In that sense, there was a lack of good governance in the management of land tenure in Guyana and the government failed to cater to the people's socioeconomic needs and implementation of FPIC.

Other lessons learned were that information on land ownership was not shared effectively. Despite myriad consultations on the ALT project initiated by the government, the majority of Amerindian communities and villages, even the village councils, still had not understood the nature, purpose, and expected outcomes of the ALT project. The village councils and Amerindians did not seem to understand the Act and the importance of ALT in their lives and the lives of future generations of Amerindians.

General Study Limitations

Aware that communication actions do not necessarily culminate in the results expected, this study no doubt had a few glitches in the data collection phase. For example, only a handful of the participants answered or asked questions during the town hall meetings. Only leaders of tribal groups answered or asked most of the questions. To a small degree, participants who identified themselves as students expressed their concerns about the logic of requesting certificates of title, and throughout the meeting also spoke mainly to clarify or help translate their statements. Through those respondents, the researcher learned that the indigenous population does not have much respect for the government, but they consider ancestral land as their "bread of life." So they remained resilient to any idea or action that seeks to challenge their position, including giving answers to the questions asked. It is not clear whether questions posed in English were properly transliterated into the local language, so reactions and some participant responses were probably not accurate or reliable. Moreover, audiovisual materials were not analyzed due to a lack of the resources needed to validate their authenticity.

Participants reported that some people did not attend the meetings due to distance, no transportation, or inaccessible means of travel.

The media was not reached to answer questions as planned, but its response would not have had a significant effect on the results.

General Recommendations

The recommendations provided in this section are justifiably based on consultations with the key stakeholders in Amerindian land in Guyana and analysis of the politics and econometrics of land ownership within the context of good governance and national development. The study finds that the indigenous people, not the government or companies, have the right to own land within national boundaries, and the government needs to properly negotiate with the indigenous people in all matters pertaining to land exploitation. This position is in keeping with the United Nations Declaration on the Rights of Indigenous Peoples (UNDRIP). As a reminder, this declaration is based on international human rights law and it "protects collective rights that may not be addressed in other human rights charters that emphasize individual rights, and it also safeguards the individual rights of Indigenous people."[13]

Further, Article 3 of UNDRIP recognizes indigenous peoples' right to self-determination, which includes the right "to freely determine their political status and freely pursue their economic, social and cultural development." Article 4 affirms Indigenous peoples' right "to autonomy or self-government in matters relating to their internal and local affairs," and Article 5 protects their right "to maintain and strengthen their distinct political, legal, economic, social and cultural institutions." Article 26 states that "Indigenous peoples have the right to the lands, territories, and resources which they have traditionally owned, occupied or otherwise used or acquired." (p2)

Moreover, because the UN also calls for respect for indigenous knowledge, cultures, and traditional practices that contribute to the sustainable and equitable development and proper management of the environment,[14] the requests made by the nine Amerindian villages and their representatives should take precedence over any other recommendation.

Community Action Groups' Recommendations

- A communication strategy should be prepared.
- Mechanisms needed to be put in place to satisfy all aspects of the ALT, and all the parties are required to be involved.
- According to the APA, during one of the ALT consultations earlier in the year, it was noted that Toshaos who were friendly to the then government were allowed to speak, while others who shared a different view were silenced and could not or did not speak.
- If communities were dissatisfied and had grievances the format for investigations was flawed. Citing a case involving demarcation between Chenapau and Karisparu, there was a rush to come out with a decision. The APA noted that there needed to be sensitivity to community's feelings in resolving issues. Although a field visit was held, there needed to be more time given to examining the information, analyze, and then come to a decision.
- The most effective means of communication to the residents of the villages is face-to-face meetings. The leaders stated that they prefer to have the team visit their communities and hold consultation meetings with them, so that they can make their contributions to the document at these sessions. Communication has to be for a day or two (not brief visits and brief interaction with the community). (In many hinterland communities, radio communication, the internet, and phone services are at best minimal.)
- The NTC recommended that information is shared with the NTC, which would facilitate communication team visits with the community for a period, meeting with people in the communities. The villages needed two weeks' notice to mobilize the community.
- There was the view that the NTC should have a participatory role in any review of the ALT. The NTC would go back to the communities and offer feedback, thereby providing a two-way flow of communication to address all concerns.
- The villagers further recommend several village meetings, thus asking for more than one meeting per village, as a series of consultations is needed before views can be solicited.

- The village residents should be more involved in the process and should be allowed to guide the surveyors, so as to reduce the occurrence of boundary disputes. Often the surveyors do not take advice from the village councils.
- The village requesting the land and its neighbor(s) need to be involved shortly after receipt of the application to avoid conflicts and save time. Instead of just submitting an acknowledgment letter, the ministry should meet with the village that submitted the application as well as the neighboring village(s) to ensure that all parties are informed at an early stage. Conflicts with demarcations and other needs that include the spiritual value of the space being requested can be resolved at that stage.

Criteria for Disseminating Knowledge and Information to Relevant Stakeholders

In order to support the implementation of the ALT project and ensure that the stakeholders are better informed about the land titling mechanism in Guyana, two main communication approaches should be exploited (1) implementation of a two-step information and knowledge dissemination flow among all groups directly and indirectly involved with the ALT project; and (2) implementation of a communication and messaging action plan targeting specific groups that have demonstrated resistance to the implementation of the ALT project and limited to no knowledge of the project.

Two-Step Information and Knowledge Dissemination Process

Messages and communication techniques should be developed that enable all stakeholders of the ALT project to share information and knowledge over time, until there is irrefutable evidence that groups and individuals have indeed acquired more knowledge on the ALT mechanism.

The two-step approach will include preparation of spokespersons from all groups to serve as advocates and information sources for implementation of the ALT project. The spokespersons will be trained and prepared on the details of the ALT before they can share information and knowledge with other groups, including the media. It is expected that the tracking measures, if well carried out, would reflect the level and type of information and knowledge shared among the stakeholders over a period of 2 years (2016–2018); and that the future of the communication of ALT and enlightenment of interested parties on the implementation of ALT would depend on the level of success or results from the implementation of the action of this study.

To increase the chances of success, all selected stakeholders (spokespersons) must demonstrate their commitment to reach out to others and share the messages developed. They should be prepared to utilize the available information and communication channels and be ready to take risks in reaching out to persons outside their group and their comfort zone. To incentivize the traveling knowledge-sharing team, the ministry should provide funding for transportation and lodging.

This study offers background information for the Amerindian land titling stakeholders, aimed at kick-starting the process of communication and knowledge sharing about the ALT mechanism.

Topics for Discussion

1. How can communication effectively change the mentality of indigenous people?
2. Do governments truly have the best interests of the rural population in view when it comes to allocating resources to improve economic life?
3. Do you support actions to transform the indigenous communities to urban life? Give your reasons.
4. Should the United Nations be more proactive in settling land disputes in a country and region?

Notes

1. http://goinvest.gov.gy/investment/investment-guide/ Accessed January 18, 2017.
2. Free, prior and informed consent (FPIC) | Forest Peoples, http://www.forestpeoples.org/guiding-principles/free-prior-and-informed-consent (Accessed January 13, 2017).
3. https://www.facebook.com/Amerindian-Peoples-Association-APA-194002507377517/?fref=nf Accessed January 14, 2017.
4. http://indigenouspeoples.gov.gy/ The Ministry of Indigenous People's Affairs (MoIPA) was formerly called the Ministry of Amerindian Affairs (MOAA). The name was changed in a bid to be politically correct, as

there are at least nine other indigenous peoples that make up 9.1% of the population of Guyana.

5. The document is entitled "Procedures for Issuance of Certificate of Title to Amerindian Communities." Bearing the Land Administration Division logo, it was produced on September 4, 2009, when M. S. Huston was Senior Land Administrative Officer.
6. The publication has been accessible to all researchers, media, knowledge management technicians, and so on since 2015. https://jobs.undp.org/cj_view_job.cfm?cur_job_id=55891 Accessed January 14, 2017.
7. The Government of Guyana and the UNDP jointly published information about the low-carbon development strategy aimed at establishing secured land tenure for Amerindian villages and communities. http://www.gy.undp.org/content/guyana/en/home/operations/projects/environment_and_energy/amerindian-land-titling.html Accessed January 14, 2017.
8. Baseline Assessment of Existing Capacities, Capacity Needs and Entry Points for Free, Prior & Informed Consent and Dispute Resolution, p. 14.
9. In a case study, Somarie Holtzhausen (2001) successfully identified triangulation as a powerful tool to strengthen qualitative research design (Holtzhausen 2001).
10. Empowered Peoples' Action Network (GEPAN), a non-profit dedicated to the empowerment of local communities and indigenous peoples in Guyana.
11. The Amerindian Act of 1951, particularly Section 5 (1), states that "no person other than an Amerindian shall enter or remain within any district, area or village or in any Amerindian settlement without lawful excuse or permission in writing."
12. Personal communication from Laura George, Program Assistant of the APA, in 2015.
13. http://indigenousfoundations.arts.ubc.ca/home/global-indigenous-issues/un-declaration-on-the-rights-of-indigenous-peoples.html Accessed January 16, 2017.
14. Ibid., p. 2.

References

Ali, Maurizio. Medios de comunicación, asuntos étnicos e intercultura en Colombia. En Revista Razón y Palabra, 74 (nov.2010/ene.2011). México DF: ITESM Campus Estado de México.

Blomkvist, H. Social capital, political participation, and the quality of democracy in India. In *Paper presented at the annual meeting of the American Political*

Science Association, Philadelphia Marriott Hotel, Philadelphia, PA, 28–31 Aug 2003.

Douglas, Perkins, and Marc Zimmerman. 1995. Empowerment theory, research, and application Perkins. *American Journal of Community Psychology* 23 (5): 569–579.

Fontana, Lorenza B., and Jean Grugel. 2016. The politics of indigenous participation through "free prior informed consent": Reflections from the bolivian case. *World Development* 77: 249–261.

Hennessy, Logan A. 2002. Amerindian environmental politics and resource justice in Guyana. Summer Fellowship Final Report submitted to the Human Rights Center, U.C. Berkeley.

Holtzhausen, Somarie. 2001. *Triangulation as a powerful tool to strengthen the qualitative research design: The Resource-based Learning Career Preparation Programme (RBLCPP) as a case study*. In Paper Presented at Presented at the Higher Education Close Up Conference 2, Lancaster University, 16–18 July 2001.

Information Sharing Environment (ISE). (2007) National Strategy for Information Sharing, Washington, DC: ISE. https://www.ise.gov/sites/default/files/nsis_book_0.pdf. Accessed 14 Jan 2017.

Ishmael, O. 1995. Investing in Guyana. Guyana Ambassador to the United States. Washington, D.C.: Embassy of Guyana, April 10.

Klautky, Colin. Personal Communication, 5 Dec 2000. (Mr. Klautky is the President of The Guyana Organization of Indigenous Peoples).

Lord, John, and Peggy Hutchison. 1993. The process of empowerment: Implications for theory and practice. *Canadian Journal of Community Mental Health* 12 (1): 5–22.

Mody, Bella. 1991. Designing messages for development communication: An audience participation-based approach. Sage, CA.

Ngwainmbi, K.E. 1994. *Communication efficiency and rural development in Africa*. New York, NY: University Press America.

Ngwainmbi, K.E. 1999. *Exporting communication technology to developing countries*. Lanham, MD: Univ. Press of America.

Ngwainmbi, K.E. 2005. NEPAD's development perspective: Bridging the digital divide with good governance. *Journal of Black Studies* 35 (3): 284–309.

Rappaport, Julian. 1987. Terms of empowerment/exemplars of prevention: Toward a theory of community psychology. *American Journal of Community Psychology* 15 (2): 121–148.

Robinson, Lee. 2009. A summary of diffusion of innovations. www.enablingchange.com. Retrieved 30 Jan 2016.

Servaes, Jan (ed.) 2008. *Communication for development and social change*. Sage, CA

The Official Tourist Guide of Guyana-2012. http://www.exploreguyanamag.com/. Retrieved 13 Jan 2017.

The United Nations Declarations on the Rights of Indigenous Peoples (UNDRIP). March 2008. http://www.un.org/esa/socdev/unpfii/documents/DRIPS_en.pdf. Accessed 16 Jan 2017.

UN-REDD Program. The guidelines on free, prior and informed consent. Jan 2013. http://www.uncclearn.org/sites/default/files/inventory/un-redd05.pdf.

Uphoff, Norman. 1985. Fitting projects to people. In *Putting people first: Sociological variables in rural development*, ed. Michael M. Cernea, 369–378. Oxford, UK: Oxford University Press.

Yoon, C.S. 2004. Participatory Communication for Development. In Guy Bassett and C.V. Rajasunderam. *Participatory Development Communication: A West African Agenda*. IDRC & Southbound.

Suggestions for Further Reading

Innovations in Land Information Recording, Management, and Utilization in Sri Lanka. Prepared by Piumi Nisansala Attygallle.

International Encyclopedia of the Social Sciences © 1988.

Securing Africa's Lands for Shared Prosperity.

PART V

Strengthening African Democratic Institutions through Policy and Communication

CHAPTER 12

Moving Beyond "Illiberal Democracy" in Sub-Saharan Africa: Recalling the Significance of Local Governance

Christopher LaMonica

FAREED ZAKARIA'S CHALLENGE TO AFRICANISTS

In a provocative article entitled "The Rise of Illiberal Democracy," published at the end of the twentieth century, Fareed Zakaria convincingly argued that despite holding regular elections, liberal democratic practice in most of the world's newly declared democracies remained elusive (Zakaria 1997). Zakaria warned that the holding of regular elections

This article was first published in the *African Journal of Political Science and International Relations* in July 2015, Vol.9, 7. It has been modified for this book.

Christopher LaMonica's major research interests are comparative politics, African politics, and international relations. In this chapter he argues that a renewed emphasis on the role of local government institutions must take place in the newly declared democracies of Sub-Saharan Africa. He uses the recent experience of Zambia to illustrate and support his position.

C. LaMonica (✉)
US Coast Guard Academy, New London, USA

E.K. Ngwainmbi (ed.), *Citizenship, Democracies, and Media Engagement among Emerging Economies and Marginalized Communities*,
DOI 10.1007/978-3-319-56215-5_12

would now confer the official title of "democracy" on some states, but that many of them should not be thought of as classically liberal or *free* democracies in the sense of guaranteeing Lockean liberties and permitting the unhindered alteration of power. Citing Freedom House's 1996–1997 survey, *Freedom in the World*, Zakaria argued:

> Illiberal democracy is a growth industry. Seven years ago only 22 percent of the democratizing countries could have been so characterized; five years ago that figure had risen to 35 percent. Moreover, to date few illiberal democracies have matured into liberal democracies; if anything, they are moving toward heightened illiberalism. (p. 24)

Zakaria was asking us all to think critically about the sudden rise of democratic elections taking place in the post–Cold War context; something which could undoubtedly have profound implications for interpreting political realities in Sub-Saharan Africa. Over the past two decades, however, Africanists have been slow to respond to this new political situation. It is in response to Zakaria's challenge, then, that this chapter is written, but with a new caveat: for liberal democracy to be realized in Sub-Saharan Africa, policymakers at all levels must place a renewed emphasis on local governance.

Post–Cold War Optimism: Warranted?

The end of Cold War patronage has had dramatic policy implications for Sub-Saharan Africa. The kinds of support on which corrupt African state leaders had come to rely were now gone, leaving them decidedly less at ease. At the beginning of the twenty-first century, all of Africa's leaders remain well aware of a new political reality: Cold War ideology can no longer be used as a basis for US or other state support. In retrospect, many within Africa consider the era of Cold War patronage a politically corrupting force, delaying the democratic hopes of the 1950s–1960s. Yet that is largely an academic view, the kind of argument that might be found in an African university classroom. In practical terms, for a generation of entrenched political leaders all over the African continent, the *end* of Cold War patronage marked the end of their hold on political power and privilege. And for the people of Africa it provided yet *another* reason for democratic hope. Unfortunately, in their analysis of African politics, a good number of Africanists (academic and think-tank specialists of African affairs) have continued their long-established pattern of remaining focused on politics at the central government level. Moreover, many are repeating the error that occurred during the era of Africa's "first independence": interpreting democratic elections in an overly optimistic and, in the end, quite superficial manner.

Africanists of all political perspectives have long maintained that the first real democratic hope for Sub-Saharan Africa came with decolonization—with the "Year of Africa," 1960—when many African states gained their independence from France (Benin, Burkina Faso, Cameroon, Central African Republic, Chad, Côte D'Ivoire, Gabon, Madagascar, Mali, Mauritania, Niger, Senegal, Togo, and the Republic of the Congo); from the UK (Nigeria and Somalia); and from Belgium (Democratic Republic of the Congo); others were soon to follow suit. Many scholars, such as the young Immanuel Wallerstein, were thrilled to partake in these significant historical events and wrote of them with great optimism (Wallerstein 1961, 1967).

In the decades that followed, however, the subject of African politics became decidedly less popular among political science scholars. Even that previous generation who had expressed so much optimism in the 1950s and 1960s now deemed African studies somehow less appealing or even irrelevant. In the words of former Africanist Gavin Kitching, for example, African studies was "too depressing," as he carefully explained the matter in a 2000 issue of the *African Studies Review & Newsletter* (Kitching 2000). Moreover, Wallerstein, who has similarly moved on to other areas of academic inquiry, now considers his optimistic language of the time to be unwarranted (Wallerstein 1995).

The same can be said of the optimistic observations made by many observers of African politics in the immediate aftermath of the Cold War—what Colin Legum referred to as Africa's "Second Independence" (Legum 1990). Writing for the *Journal of Democracy*, for example, Richard Joseph declared: "It is conceivable that by 1992 the continent will be overwhelmingly Democratic in composition" (Joseph 1991, p. 32). Carol Lancaster was similarly upbeat in an article written for *Foreign Policy*, noting that "three-fourths of the 47 countries south of the Sahara are in various stages of political liberalization" (Lancaster 1991, p. 148). The primary reason for these Africanists' optimism was that democratic elections were suddenly taking place across the African continent after decades of single-party and autocratic rule. Just a few years later, doubts were being expressed about the "wave of democratization" that was taking place, not only in Africa but across the globe. It was in 1997 that Zakaria famously remarked: "We see the rise of a disturbing phenomenon—illiberal democracy." He explained: "It has been difficult to recognize the problem because for almost a century in the West, democracy has meant *liberal* democracy—a political system marked not only by free and fair elections, but also by the rule of law, a separation of powers, and the protection of basic liberties of speech, assembly, religion, and property" (Zakaria 1997, p, 22). Zakaria's crucial insight, which has clear implications for today's new democratic states, is that *liberalism* is "theoretically different and historically distinct from *democracy*" (Ibid: 22–23).

It could be argued that today the vague term "democratization," arguably still in vogue in some circles, is gradually being replaced by the notion of democracy *alongside* political liberalization—something that, for many commentators, is more meaningful and more easily subjected to scrutiny and measurement. This is because, as Zakaria points out, the *sine qua non* of democracy is indeed elections; and now that most of the Sub-Saharan African states are holding elections, they can be called formal "democracies." However, there can be little doubt that observers of African politics have always had more in mind when speaking of democratization than the official process of democratic elections. What many of the observers of African politics mentioned above were thinking of was not only "democracy," but also the prospects for political liberalization. This post–Cold War concern is not only more "refined" from what was typically argued during the Cold War, it has also made many observers more sensitive to the need for local institutional support for liberal and other policy aims, such as improved healthcare and education. In short, the post–Cold War era has already taught us that using the term "democracy" is just not enough.

The Blame Game: Is It a Problem of African Leadership?

In the post-independence era it was quickly apparent that neocolonial norms, which prioritized the whims of those in central government, continued to dominate the political cultures of Africa. That is, colonial administrators cared more about themselves than about any form of democratic leadership and, after independence, most of Africa's leaders simply followed suit. Rather than assign part of the responsibility for this non-democratic form of governing to external patronage, which helped to create the conditions for political monsters like Desiré Mobutu, Africanists were freely writing about a "unique" form of African political leadership that was patrimonial, patriarchal, and so on. Harvard's Martin Kilson and Robert I. Rotberg are prime examples of Africanist scholars who based their entire careers on critiquing African leadership. As early as 1963, Kilson et al. were pessimistically describing the "authoritarian and single-party tendencies in African politics" (Kilson 1963), as if there was no connection to the governing norms of the colonial era that had just ended; and Similarly, within the hallowed lecture halls of Harvard University, Rotberg (now pessimistically questioning China's "real motives" in Africa) has been a consistent contributor to the "irresponsible" and "corrupt" African leader angle (Rotberg 2002, 2004). In a 2004 *Foreign Affairs* article he writes, what remains the authoritative way of writing about African politics: "Africa has long been saddled with poor, even malevolent, leadership: predatory kleptocrats, military-installed autocrats, economic illiterates, and puffed-up posturers" (Rotberg 2004, p. 14). Most of today's post–Cold War Africa scholars have followed this career-safe, pessimistic way of interpreting African political realities, whereby the problems within the continent are portrayed as being entirely due to the *internal* shortcomings of Africa and/or Africans.

To continue along the path of one-sided pessimism, I submit, is not only inaccurate, it is irresponsible scholarship: good for careers in political science, but hardly an accurate description of Africa's political realities, past or present. Post-structuralist and postcolonial scholarship—similarly pessimistic in tone—is certainly closer to the mark, in that it emphasizes *external* influences on virtually every aspect of African life, but it can over-emphasize the external and neglect internal dynamics and, most importantly, solutions to African political woes. Table 12.1 demonstrates the general perspectives and developmental agendas of powerful states (e.g., the West) and those of weak states (e.g., within Sub-Saharan Africa). What we can see is that observers from powerful states (political left and right) will tend to focus on the *internal* changes—that is, within Sub-Saharan African countries—that must take place for positive developmental change to occur; conversely, *external* influences tend to be the focus of weak state observers (political left and right).

The majority of Africanists fall into the first three columns: the first two columns represent the broad differences of those involved in the

Table 12.1 Internal vs. external focus on reasons for developmental woes

	Powerful state views		*Weak state views*	
FOCUS	INTERNAL LENS Pushed for by many Western/external participants, to wit: Africa/ns must change *internally*		EXTERNAL LENS Emphasis of many local/internal participants, to wit: the *external* is the source of our woes (left) or the source of our riches (right)	
Political Orientation	*Left* (liberal by Western standards)	*Right* (conservative by Western standards)	*Left* (Marxist-Leninist; local and otherwise)	*Right* (conservative by African standards; local beneficiaries; often colluding with external powers)
Developmental agenda	*Civil Society* *Community* *Education*	*Leadership* *Governance* *Policy*	*Colonialism* *Capitalist exploitation* *Cold War*	*Power, Wealth* *Joint ventures* *"Order"/Non-Democratic Government*
	Empowerment	*Corruption*	*Neocolonialism*	*FDI, MNCs*

Note: *FDI* foreign direct investment; *MNC* multinational corporation
Source LaMonica (2013), p. 274

development industry who tend to focus on the *internal* changes required within African states to achieve "modern" developmental goals. These represent the views on the western majority: Column 1, the "well-intentioned bleeding heart" liberals; Column 2, the cynical "realist" conservatives of whom I spoke of earlies, who are consistently rewarded in powerful state establishment environments. The third column includes many leftist academics who adhere to ... - other Marxist-Leninist views, both within Africa and elsewhere, and though there might be much truth to these arguments, there are few jobs where one can be an advocate for them other than in teaching and/or scholarship within Western power structures; in fact, the dearth of powerful state incentives for emphasizing the significance of *external* influences on African political realities may explain much. In weaker (Sub-Saharan African) country contexts, by contrast, this kind of logic has been the basis of much political support. That is, locally conservative political leaders have tended to take full advantage of their ongoing relations with external political powers. In practice, viewing their precarious circumstances as necessarily liked to the resource extractive norms of the colonial state, local politicians may at once "complain" about one or another external influence for local political support, while simultaneously taking full advantage of corrupt financial and other support from external powers. Because external powers maintain supportive relationships within the mechanisms of the African state, cynical conservative Africans that seek powerful latch onto the state and never let go— ... options, to deep is just too far to contemplate. Outside observers (columns 1 and 2) will often attribute the existence of "corruption" to *internal* dynamics (lack of civil society, poor leadership), without acknowledging the role of *external* actors (columns 3 and 4). In fact, change in the external power structure is where there is the greatest political resistance and, in fact, there are inevitably local beneficiaries of relationships with external actors (column 4). Local beneficiaries are the local powerful who tend to be on the most conservative side of the political spectrum, locally defined.

In short, twenty-first-century Africanists of all ideological stripes must remove themselves from the temptation to over-simplify Africa's many ongoing political dysfunctions—blaming either the *internal* or *external* factors—as had been prevalent during the Cold War period. In other words, to help matters, Africanists must strive to be more balanced, more realistic, and less ideological in their analyses. For too long, the stance of scholarship has been to blame one or another (*internal* or *external*) factor—which changes nothing—and go back to their sheltered offices.

To be clear: the non-democratic phenomena which Kilson, Rotberg, and other African area experts describe do exist and have existed in Africa, but the continent's political dysfunctions cannot be attributed *only* to local politics and politicians; moreover, those ... patterns of governance are not unique to Africa, a basic truth that somehow evades the political science subfield of comparative important politics. As I have argued elsewhere, yes, there is differences among us, ... but there are also commonalities of human experiences and patterns of governance; that is there is a limit to our differences (Lamonica and Omotola 2013). In all African contexts, gauging the "responsibility" of political actors needs to be thought of in a broader historical context, with a clear view of the strong external influences that now exist again, a matter which is not entirely unique to African. Those external influences are empowered by two phenomena that did not exist in the developmental history of today's powerful states: (1) global media; and (2) the speed of capital transfers. With previously unheard-of swiftness, the global media has helped to expose much, but it has also become a permanent tool of politicking, for good and for ill. Moreover, as a growing number of financial observers have argued, capital flight now happens, routinely, with the "click of a mouse," which can have devastating consequences for the state that is being targeted for rapid divestment (Soros 1999; Stiglitz 2003).

External influences on local political dysfunctions need to be included in any discussion of African politics. And this needs to be said, as much of the "development industry"—now seemingly a permanent feature of much of the African landscape—continues to point fingers at Africa's many *internal failings* that include, notably, failings of African leadership. However, as is often to ease for post. Colonial governing structures the norms of African leadership are a construct that is arguably the creation of external powers. As historians have consistently emphasized, the colonial era wreaked havoc on pre-existing African political norms. Peter Schraeder, for example, has stressed that the lack of "checks and balances" in modern African contexts cannot be portrayed as a uniquely African creation: the colonial policies of *assimilation* and *indirect rule* have, perhaps forever, distorted pre-existing checks on the abuse of political power (Schraeder 2004, p. 66). Whereas, in history, a local African political leader's power would be "checked" by, say, a council of elders, extended clan chiefs, or other lines of social interaction (a matter of notable scholarly interest to anthropologists), the colonial powers restructured the dynamics of political power whereby the local African leader was obligated to respond to the colonial administrator, usually residing in the capital. "Democratic" leadership, in other words, was never the aim; in fact, the colonial support of one or another local African leader would often be a betrayal of the desires of local populations. What mattered was allegiance to the power of the colonial state, and that is the norm that remains in place, throughout the African continent. Moreover, Africanists' tendencies to make generalizations about African political realities based solely on corrupt leaders or, at best, central government observations have only further aggravated the distortions that lead to misunderstanding. The role of the local administration matters greatly, but the focus, inside and outside Africa, remains almost exclusively on *central government* matters. As part of an effort to correct these distortions, the next generation of Africanists needs to have a more balanced perspective on the significance of both internal and external capabilities and influences and to refocus its energies on matters of local government.

Worth repeating is that the need for "order" in African and other developing country contexts, before political liberalization can take place, was similarly emphasized by political theorists of the post-independence era of the 1950s and 1960s. In the 1968 book *Political Order in Changing Societies*, Samuel Huntington famously argued that "political decay" was to be temporarily expected in developing state contexts as they liberalize; that is, disorder, Huntington argued, was part of the process of change. In retrospect, of course, such arguments can be seen as providing excuses for delaying progress toward political liberalization; since that initial period of optimism for African political change, standards of living throughout the Sub-Saharan African region have been decreasing. Moreover, in retrospect, while the impediments were many, the years that followed the hopeful wave of African independence movements provided scant evidence of political liberalization on the continent. A process that began with a large degree of optimism for the peoples of Africa led many observers, within just a few years, to great disappointment. The mistake was to conflate promises on "democracy" with prospects for "liberalism," an error that was repeated by liberal optimists twice: first, in the aftermath of Africa's First Independence (the end of the colonial era) and then of Africa's Second Independence (the end of the Cold War). In both eras, the early 1960s and 1990s, political liberalization has remained elusive. Many political scientists, of the left and right, who had been so optimistic in the 1960s, now deem African development a kind of lost cause; so discouraged are they by events of recent decades that some Africanists have chosen simply to walk away from the study of Africa (Kitching 2000). Among those who have remained, there seems to be a focus on either the development of an African "civil society" (bottom-up) or a change in African "leadership" (top-down; columns 1 and 2 in Table 12.1). Yet neither of these groups, roughly representing the Western political left and right, respectively, dares to make direct historical comparisons based on the practical underpinnings of liberal practice. Instead, the ideological assumptions that they might have about political development anywhere are simply transferred to their observations about politics in Africa. The one group of theorists that does emphasize historical circumstances, the historical structuralists (Marxist-Leninists), have deemed Africa's developmental circumstances a kind of lost cause due to the nature of the global capitalist system (column 3 in Table 12.1). In fact, the very idea that comparisons of political development north to South, or developed state versus less developed country, can and should be made has been largely discredited due to the earlier works of modernization theorists, such as Daniel Lerner (1958) or Walter Rostow (1960). Debates on the matter of political development are, in a sense, blocked. Many Africanists simply dismiss direct comparisons of political behavior and experience as "modernization theory" and/or dismiss the prospects for African development because of the global capitalist system, but African citizens themselves are losing any faith in "democracy" that they might have had just a few years ago with Africa's Second Independence, often conflating the meanings of democracy, democratization, and liberalism.

Today, we must address the shortcomings of formal "democracy" and turn our attention to the role of governing institutions in supporting liberalism. This will require true historical comparisons that have thus far eluded the field of African area studies and mainstream comparative politics. Nevertheless, there are a few examples of this kind of effort. For instance, it is undoubtedly with *African* political development in mind that Africanist Robert Bates discusses the structure and purpose of Europe's pre-liberal governing institutions in his 2001 book *Prosperity and Violence*. For him, as with Hobbes, the original purpose of governing institutions is to control violence and, in history, this was most visible at the local level. "Political development," Bates argues, "occurs when people domesticate violence … Coercion becomes productive when it is employed not to seize or to destroy wealth, but rather to safeguard and promote its creation" (Bates 2001, pp. 101–102). For him, Europe's pre-liberal governing institutions, by helping to deter violence, in turn aided European development. Again, with African development clearly in mind, he argues rather provocatively that "Societies that are now urban, industrial and wealthy were themselves once rural, agrarian and poor" (2001, p. 21). To his credit, Bates does emphasize the centrality of local government to political development in history. Yet, like others, he ignores the link between local government development and the new, and historically significant, external influences on development. That is, local governance in Sub-Saharan Africa has been dramatically affected by the dictates of outside (colonial, Cold War, multinational oil, etc.) actors; the same could not be said of the medieval European village. Historical structuralists are right to emphasize the role of history, but, like all schools of thought, the emphasis tends to be on "state"—writ large—development.

Like the neo-institutionalists, Bates importantly brings the focus back to the local level (with the understanding of its centrality to the African context), but his focus is on *economic* over political development (Bates 2001). Looking at data from medieval and early modern Europe, he argues that, over time, while violence was certainly not eradicated, functioning government structures were developed and "prosperity" resulted. That is, along with a growing sense of security and order among the masses, average incomes rose. As stated, similar arguments were made in the 1960s, notably by Huntington (1968); that is, that order is a necessary precursor to democratic development. However, Bates' work focuses less on the provision of government services and more on the requirements of members of society. The eminent Swedish economist Gunnar Myrdal similarly argued: "Even an authoritarian regime cannot record major achievements unless it can somehow mobilize acceptance, participation, and cooperation among the people" (Myrdal 1971, p. 35). Democratic states did ultimately flourish in the European context, but it may well have been citizens' demand for liberalism that made this possible; that is, the internal policy environment. Again, importantly, in contrast to today's internal policy environments in Sub-Saharan Africa, medieval local government development faced fewer challenges from external actors.

In spite of Zakaria's (1997) warning of the rise of "illiberal democratic" conditions, the distinction between democracy and liberalism remains elusive among many theorists in external policy environments. For example, in a 2004 article entitled "Why Democracies Excel," Joseph T. Siegle et al. provide a variety of statistics to make the point that democratic states outperform authoritarian states in virtually every category of developmental change: economic growth, quality of life indices, and avoidance of humanitarian crises. In other words, they conflate the two: liberalism and democracy. However, their argument still represents a significant step away from Huntington's 1968 argument that "political decay" is only part of the process of change and that authoritarian regimes may be a kind of necessary evil as they promote "order" amid chaos. That is, the policy of "order over democracy" may not be as valid as previously thought; democratic states do consistently outperform "orderly" autocratic or aggressive forms of governance. Siegle et al. conclude that we must reject all "development first, democracy later" approaches, especially where it comes to foreign aid (Siegle et al. 2004, p. 71). In this they are probably right, yet nowhere do they mention local governance, nor do they ever distinguish between democracy and liberalism—as Zakaria warns, the two are simply conflated. Moreover, one can only assume that their revised plan still involves central over local government leadership.

Thus the internal demand side of the debates on democratization has been portrayed regarding "civil society." The prevailing logic of civil society proponents is that improved livelihoods, at the individual and local levels, will lead to a variety of developmental improvements, including political demands that will eventually take place within the political system. In African contexts, the hope is that civil society will act, collectively, as a safeguard over otherwise authoritarian forms of government. This makes good theoretical sense, but the efforts to improve livelihoods at the local level have little to do with Lockean ideas related to the protection of "the things we work for." Instead, discussions of civil society are overwhelmingly oriented toward the policy debates within "developmental circles" that relate, specifically, to the provision of public services, such as water and electricity. While the delivery of these public services is undoubtedly a meritorious venture, it is unclear that today's successful democracies developed in such a fashion. Policy debates on democratization framed either as an ideological quest or as a desperate call for water or electricity are, importantly, neglecting the historical underpinnings of liberalism.

The hard fact is that democratic elections are limited in their impact. Further, in today's African context, a fundamental truth is that "democracy," as with previous forms of government, has been handed down from above without any political struggle by a large section of the people. The historical struggle of Africans against the colonial state is one of coercion and violence, of an oppressive power against its colonial subjects. That history has left the vast majority of post-independence citizens wary of both the (non-democratic) political process and the mechanisms of the state. While the media might portray urban protests as a positive sign of political struggle, it is clear that the majority of Sub-Saharan African citizens reside in the countryside, where the kind of coordination required for effective political protest is generally lacking. This, in fact, may be very analogous to what happened in early democracies, where urban protest (later documented by historians) was where the debates of political theory took place, while the masses in the rural countryside were largely removed from the process. "Democracy," in other words, can be thought of as an arrangement of the elites to keep the masses contented; all the while, liberalism is what the masses cared most about. "Democracy," thought another way, was how then reigning elites maintained order, while simultaneously disposing of monarchy—obviously a direct interest of elites who were to take over political power. Faced with an opportunity for establishing liberal state practice, elites were keen to do so, as it protected their own property (thereby avoiding disorder), but it also appealed to the masses in ways that Bates refers to (avoidance of violence) and, gradually, in a sense of new possibilities for the future. In early democratic states, then, as in newly democratic states today, the vast majority of rural and urban residents continue to focus on day-to-day struggle and, if anything, generally have remained politically apathetic and disunited. This reality is not unique to Africa. Democracy is a major step toward political legitimacy, but it is not what heightens the interests of the elites or the masses in their respective futures; liberalism is.

The very fact that individual citizens have no real avenue to pursue effective protest is undoubtedly disappointing to many, but the disappointment, it must be acknowledged, stems from broader theoretical preconceptions of the historical development of *democracy*. Both Western and Marxist models of political development see promise in protest, in the "rising" of peoples to hold their political and industrial leaders more accountable. However, democracy, it must be acknowledged, is not a panacea, as can be seen in the case of the Ancient Greeks, where the masses were kept outside of any democratic experiment.

It would not be an exaggeration to say that this model was carried over into the democratic developments that took place in Europe and America. In fact, scholars such as Charles A. Beard and Richard Hofstadter provocatively argue that the framers of the US Constitution at the Philadelphia Convention of 1787 were highly critical, even fearful, of democracy. According to Beard, the notes of James Madison, which have proven crucial to scholars' understanding of what was discussed at the convention, show conclusively that

> the members of that assembly were not seeking to rationalize any fine notions about democracy and equality, but were striving with all the resources of political wisdom at their command to set up a system of government that would be stable and efficient, safeguarded on the one hand against the possibilities of despotism and on the other against the onslaught of majorities. (Beard 1957, p. 140)

Gouverneur Morris, who was present at the Convention, confirms Beard's conclusion: "An aristocratic body [which he defined as "men of great established property"—aristocracy] will keep down the turbulence of democracy." According to Madison's notes, Elbridge Gerry and others warned of the evils that could be experienced "from the excess of democracy" (Beard 1957, p. 141). Writing on the prevailing logic of America's Founding Fathers, Richard Hofstadter similarly explains:

> To protect property is only to protect men in the exercise of their natural faculties. Among the many liberties, therefore, freedom to hold and dispose of property is paramount. Democracy, the unchecked rule of the masses, is sure to bring about arbitrary redistribution of assets, destroying the very essence of liberty. (Hofstadter 1948, p. 12)

Beard was attempting to demonstrate the *economic* logic behind the US Constitution and his work, therefore, was deemed by many within Western states (and particularly within the US) to be Marxist. To many people, Hofstadter similarly appears to be overly critical of the US democratic experiment. During much of the twentieth century, because they both downplayed idealistic understandings of the development of "democracy," both of these scholars appeared unpatriotic. In particular, linking economic considerations with politics was thought of as leftist at best, Marxist at worst. The works of Howard Zinn on US history have also been deemed unpatriotic or Marxist because of his emphasis on the political concerns of the "masses" (Zinn 2010). With the ideological fervor that characterized much of the Cold War now over, a reconsideration of these views may be in order. Admittedly, some commentators have simply opted to label the works of Hofstadter, Zinn, and others as unpatriotic, Marxist, communist, and the like, but today it is hardly controversial to say that economic considerations are an important part of politics and policy analysis. Conservatives in the US context regularly intertwine the economic with the political, as Marx might have done, yet no one would dare label their ideas "Marxist." For example, CNN quotes Condoleezza Rice as saying "Economics and security are inextricably linked," and countless others—notably Henry Kissinger—have made similar comments throughout their careers (CNN 2003). Indeed, with the passing of this ideological block may come a clearer understanding of the underpinnings of Western political liberalism. The underpinnings are in fact linked to matters of *security*, as argued by Bates (2001), and *economics*, as argued by Owusu (1992)—which may help provide important clues for the development of today's new African democracies.

Upon reflection, it is clear that the average democratic citizen in history has been less interested in theoretical democracy than in the day-to-day struggle for survival. This does not detract from the overwhelming virtue of democracy over other forms of government; the point is to emphasize the practical concerns of citizens at the local level. At this level of analysis, the individual's struggle for political liberalism, viewed regarding citizen demand, can be revealing. To the average citizen of pre-democratic and democratic states alike, the state did help deter random acts of violence, but it also helped legitimize claims to private property ownership, a cornerstone of Western understandings of political liberalism. Because of their geographical proximity, at a time when traveling great distances was especially uncommon, local governments also fostered ties with the central government, for instance through a collection of state tax or tribute and, ultimately, in matters of security. As Bates (2001) has argued, contact with the state was considered worthy insofar as the state authorities provided a sense of protection from violence. Another crucial "spill-over" effect, of course, was to affirm, through civil records of births, marriages, and deaths, a sense of national identity.

Importantly, these local government tasks were largely administrative and not, one might suspect, especially cumbersome, but they had revolutionary results regarding their "liberal" outcome. In the pre-democratic late seventeenth century, British philosopher John Locke described the inextricable link between these very basic local government functions and—what later became—the Western interpretation of "political liberalism." A reconsideration of Locke's work reminds us that, while the role of democratic state leadership is undoubtedly a crucial consideration in democratic states, it is not only central government leaders who underlie liberal state practice. Citizens of liberal democratic states have historically been more closely linked with local administrative procedure, largely out of self-interest, and motivated by the security and protection of what Locke referred to as "the fruits of our labor." Specifically, Locke argued that the input of labor into what nature has provided to all is what legitimately creates a property (Locke 1952, pp. 16–18).

Accordingly, within today's liberal democracies there exists a possible connection between government institutions and the citizenry; what Louis Hartz once termed a "Submerged Lockean Consensus" (Hartz 1955). By this, Hartz meant that there was a popular consensus within liberal states as to what political liberalism entails and what the role of government institutions should be; an interpretation that was first argued by the then radical Locke *contra* the political philosophy of governance, then promoted by apologists of illiberal state practice, such as Sir Robert Filmer. Locke's argument that government institutions should protect our "lives, liberties, and estates," later interpreted as the protection of "life, liberty, and the pursuit of happiness" by Thomas Jefferson in the US Declaration of Independence, is fundamental to liberal practice. The US Declaration of Independence has often been interpreted as an important stepping-stone toward "democracy," but it might better be thought of as a crucial step toward today's predominant view as to what political liberalism entails.

The bounds of political liberalism remain a key matter of policy and debate among liberal states, but the fact remains that there is nearly universal agreement on this essential role of governing institutions in liberal democratic states. Few would counter, for example, the protection of our private property—again, viewed historically as the things for which we work, what Locke termed "the fruits of our labor"—as a fundamental right within liberal states. This interpretation of what political freedom entails remains an underlying principle in liberal practice, and it can be argued that much of the Western "miracle" has relied on this as the basis of liberalism. Indeed, it can be argued that the realization of prosperity (Bates' term) or liberalism (the policy concern of Zakaria and other proponents of freedom in today's new democracies) is a kind of "chicken and egg" phenomenon, where development via private enterprise—that is, economic liberalism—can only occur once property (as Locke terms it, "the things we work for") is secure; that is, once political liberalism is realized. Approaches to liberalism, however, remain mired in such vague notions as the "end of history" rather than what it will require: a more efficient connection between governing institutions and the citizenry that emphasizes specific Lockean or other, locally defined, aims (Fukuyama 1989). The only arrangement that can be considered appropriate and just—part of any democratic hope—must include the collective expression of the hopes, dreams, and desires of the local citizenry. At the beginning of the twenty-first century, many external actors remain tied to vague, often ideological aims that are only shared with central government leaders. Moreover, within the new democracies of Sub-Saharan Africa, Lockean and local notions of political freedom remain largely misunderstood and scarcely expressed, due to the ongoing dysfunction of local governments; again, a problem that is largely a result of the priorities of external powers.

For political liberalism to be realized in Sub-Saharan Africa's new democracies, local government institutions must assume, at a minimum, the administrative roles that they have had within today's liberal-democratic states, for example maintaining civil records (births, marriages, deaths), titles to property, and a locally accountable security force; thus far, they have not. Instead, when local governance is mentioned in Sub-Saharan African contexts, and for understandable reasons, the focus is on the soaring demand for other, more visible public services. As witnessed during the campaign before the 2006 local government elections in South Africa, candidates were quick to make *unrealistic promises* regarding the provision of improved public healthcare, education, and the like, while burgeoning issues that underlie improved local government administration were entirely neglected. In the party manifesto of the African National Congress (ANC), it was declared, for example, that its action plan would make local government "speed up the delivery of services." Other parties, including the African Christian Democratic Party (ACDP), similarly focused on improving "service delivery." While political organizers know all too well that this would appeal to the voting public, there is little visible support for the view that it would happen. Citizens of other early democracies never had these kinds of public service expectations, and one can reasonably assume that the citizens of Sub-Saharan Africa will only develop cynical attitudes toward "democracy" in this sort of atmosphere.

To date, administrative challenges such as keeping track of titles to property, which generally falls under the heading of "land tenure" in the development literature, have been consistently marginalized in discussions of Sub-Saharan state policy. To the extent that land tenure is maintained by government records, there is a tendency to rely on the records of central government authorities, which often date back to the colonial era. These notoriously incomplete records require careful consideration if political liberalism of any kind is to be realized in Sub-Saharan Africa. And, certainly, in the short term there is no guarantee that the process of improved administrative austerity at the local government level will be without controversy. As countless observers have noted in the wake of the harsh property redistribution policies of the Mugabe regime in Zimbabwe, land records are indicative of a history of colonial rule and influence (what the Mugabe regime described as "white" over "black" property ownership). Certainly, there is no intention here to condone Mugabe's approach to the problem; it is an exceptional case on the African continent. Yet the historical result of having state power linked to property ownership has been to alienate many locals from the administrative processes that underlie land tenure. Historically, such procedures have been viewed as linked to agents of the central government, which, since well before the independence era, has been something that local citizens would rather avoid. Improved records of titles to property, and other forms of civil administration, would improve the relationship of people to their local governments, as has been the case in all liberal contexts.

Today, contrary to the very basic expectations of local governments in early and pre-democratic states, what is most often heard from the citizenry in Sub-Saharan Africa is that the state ought to provide better services. It should come as no surprise, then, that the internal politics of local governance is characterized by general avoidance of the issue; because central government authorities view the needs of the local administration as an inept, bottomless pit, local governance is rarely listed on the national policy agenda. Indeed, one is not surprised to see external actors, such as internationally recognized non-governmental organizations (INGOs), in rural areas of Sub-Saharan Africa aiding local communities in a variety of ways. Whether these external actors are motivated by humanitarian concerns, the provision of "basic needs," or an expectation of what a modern welfare state might provide, there is virtually no support for what might be termed Lockean ideas at the local government level. Land tenure remains a concern largely of under-funded anthropologists, while internal and external policymakers frantically address more "pressing" policy matters. As the successes of the Grameen Bank have demonstrated throughout the world, central governments are not especially adept at responding to household-level needs. In the interest of contemplating the prospects for strengthening local government institutions along locally defined lines—that is, of promoting political liberalism—the discussion in the next section addresses the recent history of *internal* policies and debates regarding strengthening the local governments of one Sub-Saharan African state, Zambia. This is followed by a consideration of changes in *external* policies, and how they might hinder or improve the prospects for strengthening local governments. Finally, some of the lessons learned from the decentralization efforts in the Zambian case are considered.

The Case of Zambia

With the collapse of the Soviet Union, it was evident to all that the patterns of Cold War patronage with African states were about to change forever. During that period, Kenneth Kaunda, Zambia's leader after independence, had argued that Zambian citizens should adopt a policy of humanism (what was also called Kaundism). His argument for humanism, which he first expounded in his 1962 book *Zambia Shall Be Free*, was that with independence there would be a significant number of changes, perhaps even turmoil and chaos. Because the traditional village ways of life and culture would now be under the constant threat of change, citizens should make every attempt to be kind to one another during this tumultuous time. Certainly, the logic had appeal for many people, and it must be admitted that Zambia was relatively peaceful in the post-independence years, compared to its neighbors (Angola, former Zaire, and Mozambique). Like other Sub-Saharan African central government powers, the Kaunda regime relied largely on the export of natural resources. The nationalized Zambia Consolidated Copper Mines (ZCCM) has been particularly crucial to central government authorities as, for decades, copper exports alone accounted for over 80% of

Zambia's foreign exchange earnings. As was the case during the colonial era, the "state" was therefore viewed as a stable resource for the few who were lucky enough to maintain ties; within this political power vacuum, local government was little more than an inconvenience.

Coupled with central government ties with Cold War patrons, it should come as no surprise that throughout the Cold War period many people looked to the central government as Zambia's primary resource. However, Kaunda's central government "stability" was threatened by dramatic drops in the world price of copper during the 1970s. With the rising price of oil, the Kaunda government had little option but to borrow funds, notably from the International Monetary Fund (IMF). In a pattern that was replicated throughout the developing world, Zambians found themselves with crippling and historic levels of debt. In 1987, Kaunda announced that he would not allow debt financing to exceed 10% of export earnings and attempted to "delink" from the IMF and World Bank. However, by then it was already clear that his leadership would be challenged. In an atmosphere of growing critique against African forms of socialism and increasing support for "democratization," a young union lawyer named Frederick Chiluba (who had previously been socialist) soon entered into a presidential race against Kaunda and his United National Independence Party (UNIP). As a candidate for the Movement for Multiparty Democracy (MMD), Chiluba represented a growing group of African politicians who were now openly supportive of democracy and capitalism. Despite protests by supporters of UNIP, Chiluba's MMD won the election decisively, with 75.8% of the vote.

In 1991, as had been the case after independence, the prospects for democratization seemed high. This time there would be no Cold War rivalry. Now, it was evident to all that the future developmental path of African states would not and could not be that of the Soviets. The newly elected Frederick Chiluba (1995) remarked, for example:

> The significance of the collapse of communist states should not be underestimated. These events were critical, first because the Eastern European regimes and their constitutions had provided the model upon which the entire structure of government in Zambia's Second Republic came to be the base. Second, the Soviet Union had provided aid to the one-party state in Zambia. A Soviet military attaché was accredited to the embassy in Lusaka [and] East German military instructors could be found in Zambia as recently as 1988. (p. 49)

Following a pattern that had begun during the colonial era, the Chiluba government maintained central government authority and control. However, outside observers, notably donor states and INGOs, began to lobby for policies that would promote "democratization." Importantly, the Lockean ideals of establishing local governments with the primary aims of protecting our "lives, liberties, and estates" were not the focus; rather, decentralization was viewed as an important step toward democratization. During the Chiluba era, the term "democracy" was simply used as a kind of trump card for legitimacy, and local governing issues continued to be framed regarding public services. Many of those involved in public health and education, in particular, argued that these essential services could be more efficiently provided at the local level through a gradual process of decentralization.

In short order, the new regime's Public Service Reform Programme (PSRP) promised the "decentralization and strengthening of local government," with task-based timetables, which were all presented to donor states in a comprehensive text, circulated in 1993. Passage of the PSRP was considered by many commentators to be a remarkable event in Zambia's political history, as it was a policy direction that had been long fought for by proponents of decentralization. In the many discussions that led up to the 1993 PSRP, the 1980 Local Administration Acts that had aimed (on paper) at the devolution of power from central government to councils were openly criticized and considered a failure, if not an outright sham. This new policy, coupled with the significant break with the past—one that had been dominated by former president Kenneth Kaunda—offered Zambians reasons for democratic hope in the first few years of the Chiluba presidency. As supporters of Chiluba reminded eligible voters in 1991, "the hour had come" (extended thumb and index finger to represent the hands of a clock reaching the hour) and, with the 1993 passage of the PSRP, the change was in the air.

However, in the years that followed, specific tasks that had been listed in the PSRP's Proposed Implementation Schedule, notably that the Ministry of Local Government and Housing (MLGH) would complete a Plan for Decentralization by mid-1993, were clearly being delayed. Seeing that strong central government resistance to the PSRP remained, one of the primary proponents of decentralization in Zambia, the British-funded Local Government Support Project (LOGOSP) that had been formally initiated in March 1995, closed its doors in 1997. From 1995 to 1997, brand new white trucks with LOGOSP decals on the doors were a common sight on the roads of Zambia, particularly in Lusaka. However, seeing no real signs of political will to decentralize government authority and control, LOGOSP was to last just over two years. Since then there have been no indications of any plans to have LOGOSP return. In response, Bennie Mwiinga, MP for the MLGH, made every attempt to revamp LOGOSP through the support of other donor states. However, his eleventh-hour efforts proved unsuccessful (LOGOSP Newsletter: 1995). Mwiinga's appeal for what he termed "bridging finance" was only considered as an attempt to keep the MLGH bureaucracy afloat and not as linked, in any meaningful way, to the implementation of the PSRP. Even the draft decentralization plan that was finally circulated in 1996 did not convince donors that central government leaders were taking the issue seriously; indeed, formal consideration of the scheme by parliament was to take another eight years.

Internal Politics: Zambia's Ministry of Local Government and Housing's Desperate 1997 Appeal to Donors

In all fairness, Mwiinga's 1997 appeal to donor states never really stood a chance. The only donor country that could have provided any substantive support to the MLGH was the USA (or, more specifically, the US Agency for International Development or USAID) and, for a variety of reasons, USAID was not prepared to do so. As a leading donor state in Zambia, the consistent position of USAID/Zambia on decentralization is worth noting.

Local Governance: A Non-starter?

First, beyond keeping "democracy and governance" low on this mission's priority list, the task of strengthening local governments through decentralization was consistently portrayed as a non-starter. Throughout the 1990s USAID officials were notably less optimistic than those from other donor states. Observing that there was little central government support for the task, the former democracy and governance advisor of USAID/Zambia commented: "We simply see no political will to allow any localization to take place," adding, "the enabling environment is downright hostile" (Toder Interview: 1999). Nor is there any indication that there will be any change in USAID's position on local governance. For example, in the summaries of its Democracy and Governance Program for Zambia, USAID has consistently made no mention of local governance issues, or of decentralization efforts.

Aid as Obstacle

Second, USAID/Zambia is entirely dependent on the support of a home government that has been, relatively speaking, anti-"aid." The open critique of assistance was especially marked during the 1980s and 1990s and is now commonplace in development circles; one could say, without exaggeration, that the USA has led the global campaign against development aid, to great effect. "Aid as obstacle" has since become the established "common wisdom" among donors; that is, it is accepted that assistance only distorts the proper development of developing states. Donations of free food and clothing have proven to be powerful examples of how even "well-intentioned" aid can devastate the local entrepreneur. Specifically, such cases ask: how can local entrepreneurs possibly compete with an influx of free goods that are sent in the form of "aid"?

Central Government Focus

Third, the democracy and governance (D/G) activities of USAID have historically centered on the observation of, and contact with, central government leaders. The incentive for altering this largely entrenched way of conducting D/G activities remains minimal; rewards for having central government contacts are still higher than what they might be for establishing contacts out in the countryside. Indeed, during the Cold War, donor state missions in Sub-Saharan Africa were expected to *work with* central government leaders—especially since they were often pro-socialist and/or avowedly Marxist. In the ideological climate of the Cold War it should come as no surprise, then, that USAID missions in the Sub-Saharan African region had little difficulty in obtaining home support when submitting requests for funds. During those years, while Kaunda promoted Zambian humanism, other state leaders developed what were considered unique forms of African socialism, including most famously Tanzania's Julius Nyerere (president of Tanzania from 1962 to 1985). Donor state missions from the West, in particular, were therefore cautious of openly criticizing such leaders, lest entire states were lost in a global chess-like battle among states that were considered either pro-Soviet or pro-West. As we progress into the twenty-first century, it is becoming abundantly clear that the post–Cold War world is dramatically different, in that donor state critique of African national leaders occurs with much more ease and, as demonstrated, the use of aid to these same leaders is now openly put into question.

Policy Without Implementation? the 2004 Decentralization Plan

Finally, with the overall stance of donor states being hostile toward "aid," USAID's policy stance will likely have dramatic consequences for the future implementation of Zambia's 2004 National Decentralization Policy; that is, without external funding of some kind, implementation of the policy itself will prove to be a non-starter. While there are other potential sources of financial support for this policy, a consideration of USAID/Zambia's development policies, as viewed through budget allocations, is crucial, as USAID remains the largest single bilateral donor to Zambia, followed by the UK, Germany, Norway, and Japan. In fact, a look at USAID/Zambia's post–Cold War budget figures demonstrates the lack of will, on the part of USAID, to put resources into what is termed "democracy and governance." For example, in order of importance to USAID/Zambia one typically finds that the top two "strategic objectives" are increased competitiveness and improved health; D/G has tended to receive around 5% of the overall annual budget (USAID.gov).

External Politics: The Rapidly Changing Dynamics of Aid

Following the 1980s, a period that has been considered by many commentators a "lost decade" for Africa, US policymakers made it abundantly clear that their policy priority for Africa was *economic growth*; improvements in other areas, including democratization, could only occur after successful rates of annual growth were achieved. Many theorists now refer to this as a "development first, democracy later" approach to African development. Certainly, this was the logic behind what was dubbed the "End of Dependency Act of 1996" for Africa (H.R. 4198), which made specific reference to "sub-Saharan Africa's lack of competitiveness in the global market." Sponsored by Phil Crane (R-IN), Charles

Rangel (D-NY), and Jim McDermott (D-WA), the bill aimed at building "a market-oriented transition path for sub-Saharan Africa from dependency on foreign assistance to economic self-sufficiency." Leading development economist Jeffrey Sachs, former director of Harvard's Center for International Development (formerly the Harvard Institute for International Development) and now director of Columbia University's Earth Institute, strongly supported the initiative. In February 1997, Sachs submitted a paper to the former Speaker of the House, Newt Gingrich, which was then forwarded to members of the US Congress, entitled "A New Partnership for Growth in Africa," which wholly supported the idea of having a new growth strategy for Sub-Saharan Africa. In that paper, Sachs called for an "initiative from the United States to work with the other largest donors to end aid to Africa as we know it" (Sachs 1997). Turning his focus away from his consultations on structural reform in other parts of the world, Sachs, now especially interested in African development, was regularly quoted as a supporter of the objectives in H.R. 4198, calling it a "new way forward for Africa" in the *Financial Times* and arguing in an interview with *The Economist* that "growth in Africa can be done" (*The Economist* 1996). Hearing that this was a viable plan to help Africa grow, African American leaders, following in the footsteps of Charles Rangel, similarly supported the bill. As a senior member of the Congressional Black Caucus, and chief sponsor of the bill, Rangel argued that "at last, like other ethnic groups in America, African-Americans will be able to point to a special partnership that connects the United States to our ancestral homes" (Fox Market Wire: 2000).

Despite the glaring fact that plans for this "special partnership" included continued reductions in aid, opposition to the bill was minimal. By this time the consensus was that dependency on aid diminished the prospects of competition and, hence, economic growth. The lack of any real critique from lobbyists in Washington was mainly due to the renaming of the initiative, from the "End of Dependency Act" (which was understood to be a partisan, that is Republican, initiative) to the more appealing "African Growth and Opportunity Act" (AGOA), which received full bipartisan support. Ralph Nader's group Public Citizen dutifully called on its members to "oppose the misnamed African Growth and Opportunity Act," but to no avail (Public Citizen: 1998). In 1999, with the full support of the Black Caucus, the House passed the renamed bill with a vote of 309–110, followed by a 2000 Senate vote of 77–19. Since then, AGOA has remained the dominant policy stance toward Sub-Saharan Africa, with direct consequences for USAID budgets. Indeed, in the years immediately following the passage of AGOA-I (2000), aid budgets (in thousands of US$) immediately decreased: FY 2004 ($49,487), FY 2005 ($28,297), and FY 2006 ($24,927; USAID.gov). In line with the newer (post–Cold War) mantra "trade, not aid," statistics are regularly posted to http://www.agoa.gov to demonstrate that exchanges between the USA and Africa are rising. Moreover, as US leaders lobbied for this new policy stance, AGOA membership immediately expanded. In December 2005, US President George Bush expressed his hope that 37 African states would be made "eligible" for "AGOA (AGOA.gov). Citing specific sections of AGOA, as well as the US Trade Act of 1974, the president's press release suggested that certain African states were "making continual progress" and considered the prospect of new AGOA designations for African countries; that is, "lesser developed beneficiary sub-Saharan African countries" (AGOA.gov).

Ironically, of course, while this fundamental restructuring of aid to Africa was occurring within US policy circles, others involved in aid were simultaneously pushing for the United Nations' Millennium Development Goals that specify the need for *increased* aid from donor states, to reach a minimum of 0.7% of gross domestic product (GDP). Proponents of increased aid to Africa within Organisation for Economic Co-operation and Development (OECD) states have already run into significant resistance, particularly in US contexts, as the prevailing wisdom remains critical of aid in general. What is particularly ironic, given Sachs' involvement in pushing for AGOA, is that he was actively involved in the promotion of the UN's Millennium Development Goals (UNMDGs), working as special advisor to UN Secretary General Ban Ki-Moon (earthinstitute.columbia.edu). Furthermore, in 2005 Sachs published a bestselling book entitled *The End of Poverty*, which addressed his revised views on aid. Over the past few years, he has given many public lectures and interviews discussing his ideas (Sachs 2005). To him there is no inconsistency: economic growth must be the priority, and (different from the AGOA approach) aid can help to make that happen. For this later, pro-aid policy stance, Sachs has received tremendous support. In fact, all 192 member states have agreed to the highly publicized eight UNMDGs.

The overarching goal, argued Sachs, was to end "extreme poverty" by 2015, although that was delayed due to the 2008 financial crisis (www.undp.org/poverty). And again, much of his work focused on

Sub-Saharan Africa specifically. The (delayed) goal could not be achieved, he argued, by simply cutting aid across the board, but through a careful consideration of the unique circumstances in which a number of developing states now find themselves. While still arguing that developing state policy needs to welcome market liberalization, Sachs now focuses on other factors that have impacts on economic growth, such as *geography*; that is, while some countries have been blessed with access to international markets, others, particularly landlocked countries, have had a difficult time accessing world markets and this has translated into increased operating costs. Further, the *initial income level* of a country may be low and that lack of capital will adversely affect the prospects for growth. Such circumstances, Sachs argues, may warrant a write-off, or easing of, debt burdens and so on. In other words, many of the circumstances that adversely influence the immediate prospects for the economic growth of most Sub-Saharan African states need to be addressed through a variety of development strategies, not by simply cutting aid budgets across the board. Aid can be used in effective ways that aim at promoting economic growth, Sachs seems to argue, contrary to prevailing wisdom; what need to be fostered are the fundamentals of any economy: the support and training of labor, the development of capital, management know-how, and the like. With the view that labor is an abundant and under-utilized resource in many developing countries, Sachs has made a concerted effort to point to public health concerns, notably AIDS, as an impediment to growth. While it might seem difficult to refute his more comprehensive approach to promoting economic growth, his views remain marginalized among many aid policymakers. The popularity of Thomas L. Friedman's book *The World Is Flat* is testament to the ongoing support for the view that, in this era of globalization, opportunities are available to us all and that accordingly, aid can only be considered a handout (Friedman 2006). In fact, during his book tour for *The End of Poverty* (2005), Sachs made a point of criticizing Friedman's perspective. The question remains as to what direction the Washington Consensus will take on the matter.

It is partly as a result of Sachs' new perspective on the subject of aid, and global support for the UNMDGs, that the debate as to whether aid must necessarily hinder developmental patterns, including the development of free markets, has returned. For now, the notion that the assistance can be put to good use, for instance in supporting business initiatives, assisting the workforce in training and education, and helping to alleviate glaring public health concerns, remains controversial. Moreover, the links between these issues and political development, not to mention any improved prospects for liberal political practice, are still difficult to ascertain at best. The question remains as to how all of these political debates on aid that are largely outside of Sub-Saharan Africa will affect the prospects for improved political development *within* Sub-Saharan African states.

There can be little doubt that the external policy debates have profound implications for the strategic direction within Sub-Saharan African countries. For instance, decentralization in Zambia, like other strategic initiatives, has been largely a donor-driven enterprise. While the leading donor to Zambia, USAID, has had other priorities, Britain and other donors have consistently pushed for decentralization plans, including, notably, the increased "capacity" of local governing authorities. The push for political change, from donor states (*external actors*), must be taken into account when attempting to understand recent trends in Sub-Saharan African state policy. While African national leaders may voice contempt for such ideas, Africanists such as Jennifer Widener have consistently argued that in Sub-Saharan Africa "political openings usually take place only in conjunction with international pressure" (Widener 1994; Ottoway 1997). This was certainly the case, for example, with the long-delayed approval of Zambia's National Decentralization Policy in 2004. While USAID took little interest, other donor states lobbied hard for passage of the draft policy (LaMonica 2010). Advocating a new strategic direction, of course, is a delicate issue, but Zambia's central government leaders have long been accustomed to the idea that donor state funding is linked to certain policy initiatives. Indeed, any contempt that some Zambian leaders and citizens might have for such external pressures is mainly due to what is now widely perceived as the donor state's "self-serving" interests during the Cold War. "Why else," goes the refrain of many Zambians today, "would donor states be cutting their foreign aid budgets?"

Conclusion: Recalling the Significance of Local Government Institutions

In the geographically vast region of Sub-Saharan Africa, the proximity of government authorities can play a crucial role. Largely due to the history of capital-centered politics and the "national" formulation of policy, local governments have been thus far considered by many commentators to be a burden or even a luxury. To the extent that colonial administrators have reviewed local authorities, it was to emphasize the maintenance of "order" (through indirect rule, assimilation, or other means) and not to establish local government institutions that had, as their principal aim, the maintenance and security of local property. Moreover, due to the colonial history of Sub-Saharan African states, local citizens have historically viewed local authorities as agents of "the state." In these circumstances, "the state" was something to be avoided and at all costs; this legacy remains. To this day, it certainly is not assumed that a local government authority acts in the interest of the local citizen. Much of this can be explained in relation to colonial history, and the often corrupt practices that continued during the era of "neocolonialism." This chapter has argued that a careful consideration of the limited roles of local government authorities in liberal democratic contexts could be revealing. Within that context, local governance played a largely unsung but crucial role in expanding liberal practice. At least initially, citizens had limited demands. One of the most fundamental functions of local governments in liberal states, then and now, has been the protection of the "fruits of our labor"; that is, our property.

As local—historically agrarian—productivity improved, administrative ties with central government also improved, with the understanding that there could be *positive-sum* gains to be had by those involved. In the Sub-Saharan African context, central government leaders were direct beneficiaries of colonial and Cold War ties, to the detriment of local government development. The relationship then has been viewed as "top-down," *zero-sum* (competing for limited resources), and antagonistic. By contrast, in liberal-democratic states, there have been political debates over the appropriate balance of local–central state authorities, but the largely cooperative connection has always existed. In the sub-Saharan African context, colonial history and its aftermath led to the development of governing institutions that consistently favored centralized over local forms of governance.

Democracy then, in all historical contexts, is a process, not an event. In the post–Cold War environment, it must be openly acknowledged that this has been the case in all democratic states of the world; political freedoms that have become synonymous with democratic practice certainly did not apply to all residents of the early USA, for example, which included a sizable slave population and systematically excluded women. The inclusion of these groups—certain improvements in democratic practice—took place over time. Such views are now being expressed in policy circles as part of the challenge that new democracies must face (Krasner and Pascual 2005). The argument that it takes time may offer little solace to those anxious to implement liberal-democratic practice in new democracies. However, these kinds of historical comparisons that focus on the practical underpinnings of liberalism demonstrate the crucial role of local governance.

There are several important lessons to be learned from the internal and external politics that surround the decentralization efforts in Zambia in the 1990s and 2000s. First, the pressures from international or external actors for decentralization are not uniform. Evidence of this can be found by comparing the *types* of donor state support for the decentralization policies pursued by the Chiluba, Mwanawasa, and Banda governments, including those behind the 1993 Public Service Reform Programme and the 2004 National Decentralization Policy. Indeed, a more careful consideration of donor support for political change in Zambia demonstrates clear differences among donors as to what the policy priorities should be, based largely on prevailing political beliefs among donor states themselves. Broadly speaking, USAID tends to prioritize privatization, increased competition, and business development, while the Scandinavian states tend to support more coordination of aid efforts and civil society development projects. Britain and Germany, as well as international organizations such as the United Nations Development Programme (UNDP) and the World Bank, tend to emphasize the importance of institutional "capacity building." This can also be said of CARE International in Zambia and other INGOs that work extensively on the development of rural agriculture and community-based organizations (CBOs). Over time, donor states develop reputations among Zambians (and within the local development community) for supporting various types of development initiatives (PSRP 1993).

Second, the policies of individual donor states are a reflection of the policy debates that take place within their respective home governments. The parallels between the 1960s expansion of foreign aid and welfare programs, on the one hand, and the 1980s contractions of both, on the other hand, are worthy of note. In the 1960s, while Western states vowed to end poverty at home through a host of new welfare programs, lending institutions such as the World Bank provided unprecedented levels of lending to developing states throughout the world. In retrospect, the parallel is clear: the principal policy aim was to eradicate poverty through the promotion of certain domestic state and international development policies. These loans continued to expand until the 1982 least developed countries debt crisis, prompted by Mexico's refusal to pay debts, and similar refusals only continued throughout the now indebted world. A good way to identify a donor state's position on aid, therefore, is a careful consideration of each respective country's domestic politics. In 1992, US President Clinton announced "the end of welfare as we know it"; the AGOA initiative applied the same logic of "ending dependency" to foreign aid. As Steven Radelet argues, "the African Growth and Opportunity Act ... should hardly be trumpeted as the United States' 'giving' something to developing countries, since the legislation only slightly reduces existing barriers and leaves significant obstacles untouched" (Radelet 2003).

Third, the method of pursuing decentralization points to the extreme imbalances of wealth and power among the various players involved in the process. Discussions with consultants, development practitioners, and Zambia's central government staff led this observer to the conclusion that Zambia's decentralization policies are pursued largely to appease the concerns of international actors (particularly donor states and the dominant lending institutions of the UN, the IMF, and the World Bank). As central government ministries struggle to maintain control, they are constantly under pressure to mention "decentralization" as one of their new policy goals. Unrealistic target dates for decentralization and "strengthening of local government," with little follow-up in policy implementation, have thus far been the result.

Finally, decentralization is but one of the many goals among international actors that have constant, and growing, budget constraints. As the international funds made available during the Cold War gradually disappear, and despite the political will for continued centralized control, decentralization nevertheless occurs; this demonstrates the mere fact that a continued flow of resources is required to maintain central government control. While there are likely a variety of reasons for the passing of the 2004 National Decentralization Policy in Zambia, the combined pressures of privatizing ZCCM and decreasing donor aid left central government authorities with few remaining options but to relinquish some control. However, the immediate results of decentralization are likely to be grim. As those involved in decentralization will readily admit, local government institutions throughout Zambia have little hope of coping with the many new challenges that they face in the shorter term.

Hopefully, we will soon get beyond the point of being told that strengthening local government institutions does not matter—or, in the case of Zambia, that it cannot yet be implemented. A more careful consideration in policy circles of local government function is crucial. In fact, the realization of liberal democracy may well require it.

Topics for Discussion

1. What is "illiberal democracy"? What must happen for the development of liberal democracy to occur in Sub-Saharan Africa?
2. What are Lockean liberties? What is the origin of this term? Do any countries practice Lockean liberties today? Explain your answer.
3. Why are democratic elections limited in their impact in Sub-Saharan Africa?
4. LaMonica argues that "if political liberalism is to be realized within the newly declared democracies of sub-Saharan Africa, a renewed emphasis on the role of local government institutions must take place." Is his argument clear, logical, and well supported? Does the author convince you with his argument? Explain your answer.

Works Cited

Bates, R.H. 2001. *Prosperity & Violence*. New York, NY: W.W. Norton & Co.

Beard, C. 1957. *The Economic Basis of Politics*. New York, NY: Vintage Books.

Chiluba, F. 1995. *Democracy: The Challenge of Change*. Lusaka: Multimedia Publications.

Friedman, Thomas L. 2006. *The World Is Flat: A Brief History of the Twentieth-Century*. New York, NY: Picador.

Fukuyama, F. 1989. "The End of History." *National Interest*. https://ps321.community.uaf.edu/files/2012/10/Fukuyama-End-of-history-article.pdf.

Hartz, L. 1955. *The Liberal Tradition in America*. New York, NY: HBJ.

Hofstadter, R. 1948. *The American Political Tradition*. New York, NY: Vintage Books.

Huntington, S. 1968. *The Political Order of Changing Societies*. New Haven, CT: Yale University Press.

Joseph, R. 1991. Africa: The Rebirth of Political Freedom. *Journal of Democracy* 2: 11–24.

Kilson, M. 1963. "Authoritarianism and Single-Party Tendencies in Africa." *World Politics* 15(2).

Kitching, G. 2000. "Why I gave up African studies." *African Studies Review & Newsletter* XXII(1): 21–26.

Krasner, S.D., and C. Pascual. 2005. "Addressing State Failure." *Foreign Affairs* 84(4): 153–163.

LaMonica, C. 2010. *Local Government Matters: The Case of Zambia.* Saarbrucken: VDM-Lambert.

LaMonica, C. 2013. *Human Security in World Affairs: Problems and Opportunities.* ed. Alexander Lautensach, and Sabina Lautensach, 274.

LaMonica, C., and S. Omotola. 2013. *Horror in Paradise: Frameworks for Understanding the Crises of the Niger Delta of Nigeria.* Durham, NC: Carolina Academic Press.

Lancaster, C. 1991/1992. "Democracy in Africa." *Foreign Policy* 85: 154. 14.

Legum, C. 1990. "The Coming of Africa's Second Independence." *Washington Quarterly* 13(1): 129–140.

Locke, J. 1952. "Of Property" in *Two Treatises on Government.* New York, NY: Liberal Arts Press. (originally published 1690).

Myrdal, Gunnar. 1971. *Asian Drama: An Inquiry into the Poverty of Nations.* London: Penguin.

Omotola, J. Shola. 2009. "Attractions and Limitations of Liberal Democracy in Africa." *Africana* 3(1): 5–30.

Ottoway, M. ed. 1997. *Democracy in Africa: The Hard Road Ahead.* Boulder, CO: Lynne Reiner.

Owusu, Maxwell. 1992. "Democracy and Africa—A View from the Village." *Journal of Modern African Studies* 30(3): 369–396.

Radelet, Stephen. 2003. "Bush and Foreign Aid." *Foreign Policy.* http://citeseerx.ist.psu.edu/viewdoc/summary?doi=10.1.1.483.3680. Accessed 13 Jan 2017.

Rotberg, R. 2002. *When States Fail: Causes and Consequences.* Princeton: Princeton University Press.

Rotberg, Robert I. 2004. "Strengthening African Leadership." Harvard Kennedy School Belfer Center. http://belfercenter.org/publication/strengthening-african-leadership. Accessed 13 Jan 2017.

Sachs, J. 1997. *A New Partnership for Growth in Africa.* Cambridge, MA: Harvard Institute for International Development.

Sachs, Jeffrey. 2005. *The End of Poverty: Economic Possibilities for Our Time.* New York: Penguin Press.

Schaefer, Peter J. 2004. *African Politics, and Society,* 2nd Ed. New York: Thomson Wadsworth.

Siegel, J. et al. 2004. "Why Democracies Excel." *Foreign Affairs* 83.

Soros, George. 1998–1999. "Capitalism's Last Chance?" *Foreign Policy,* No. 113: 55–56.

Stiglitz, Joseph E. 2003. *Globalization and Its Discontents.* New York: W.W. Norton.

The Economist. 1996. "Growth in Africa: It Can Be Done."

Wallerstein, I. 1961. *Africa: The Politics of Independence.* New York: Vintage Books.

Wallerstein, I. 1967. *Africa: The Politics of Unity.* New York: Random House.

Wallerstein, Immanuel. 1995. "What Hope Africa? What Hope World?" in *After Liberalism.* New York: The New Presss.

Widener, Jennifer. 1994. *Economic Change and Political Liberalization in Sub-Saharan Africa.* Washington, DC: Johns Hopkins Press.

Zakaria, Fareed. 1997. The Rise of Illiberal Democracy. *Foreign Affairs* 76 (6): 22–43.

Zinn, H. 2010. *A People's History of the United States.* New York: Harpers.

CHAPTER 13

Use and Misuse of Data in Advocacy, Media, and Opinion Polls in Africa: Realities, Challenges, and Opportunities

Adebayo Fayoyin and Emmanuel K. Ngwainmbi

Data is an important resource in achieving development and equal outcomes, yet various entities often misuse it. The phenomenon called "big data" and advances in digital technology and information processing have resulted in a data revolution. Leading experts, such as Mayer-Schonberger and Cukier (2013, p. 19) and Groves et al. (2014, p. 2),

---

Adebayo Fayoyin and Emmanuel K. Ngwainmbi are both interested in the impact of information and communication technology on emerging nations. In this chapter they advocate stricter regulation of election opinion polls to avoid misinformation and manipulation of the electorate.

This article was published in *Journal of Development and Communication Studies*, 6, 3. 2014. With permission from the editor, it has been modified for this book.

A. Fayoyin (✉)
United Nations Population Fund, Johannesburg, South Africa

E.K. Ngwainmbi
Matthews, NC, USA

E.K. Ngwainmbi (ed.), *Citizenship, Democracies, and Media Engagement among Emerging Economies and Marginalized Communities*,
DOI 10.1007/978-3-319-56215-5_13

now state that big data is poised to shake up everything in life, from business to the science of healthcare, government, education, economics, and the humanities, among other aspects of society. However, there are also constraints on effective data use, especially in a digital world, where information or misinformation goes viral with a click, with limited opportunities for adequate retraction or "corrigendum." Data and social statistics have been misinterpreted and misrepresented, causing major misinformation within interpersonal and mass communication. Within the framework of development, these intricacies in data management may be having adverse effects on countries with fragile democracies.

In light of this challenge, this chapter explores some of the uses and misuses of data and statistics in different areas of public affairs, drawing references from a range of countries. Our goal is to advance scholarly debate on the problems and prospects of data use in a digital age and how data can be a tool of development, good governance, and democracy in Africa. The chapter starts with some conceptual observations on the trend toward big data and the role of data in development. It then examines some of the critical issues in the use of statistics by advocates, journalists, and pollsters. Following the analysis, we propose specific recommendations to enhance data use and mitigate the impact of erroneous data in public affairs.

Era of Big Data

Big data is the lifeblood of contemporary science and business, and modern society is awash with a vast amount of processed and unprocessed data from various domains and platforms, including call logs, online user-generated content, and satellite images. Big data, widely supported by web-based applications and digital devices, continues to revolutionize our society. So do words and phrases, the fundamental building blocks of language and culture, much as genes and cells are to the biology of life, continue to serve as a window into society's intellectual evolution. In fact, big data has always been part of all academic research, scientific activity, and business dealings. In the twenty-first century when communities are focusing on economic development, companies and research institutions are putting enormous amounts of resources into gathering, processing, and utilizing data to create new markets for their products and services or to expand existing markets.

In calculating the volume of data available today, we have moved from binary bytes to kilobytes, megabytes, gigabytes, terabytes, petabytes, exabytes, zetabytes, and yottabytes, and this still continues. Big data has its origin in the integration of digital technology, the science of informativity and high-level analytics. Technological innovations have created a horizontal integration of society and new patterns of social interaction and information flows which are multi-polar, multi-dimensional, and multi-directional (Ayish 2005, p. 25). New sources of information include data exhaust, online data, physical sensors, and crowdsourcing (United Nations Global Pulse 2013, p. 1). Large collections of evidence are now being compiled in centralized data warehouses, allowing analysts to make use of powerful methods to examine data more comprehensively (Weiss and Indurkhya 1998). A new field of data science which is expected to influence various dimensions of life has also emerged.

The digital age, with sophisticated computer automation of the analysis of different data sources and tools, is capable of terminating decision making based on experience, intuition, and other non-data-driven approaches (Provost and Fawcett 2013, p. 51). According to Mayer-Schonberger and Cukier (2013, p. 17), data is no longer regarded as a static or stale resource but as a major raw material in business, a vital part of economic input, and a critical tool for creating new economic value. Neither is it any longer a question of hard-headed statistical packages or dead information available in the archives or remote databases. In the digital age, data is expected to be mined and efficiently utilized for social change and effective decision making (Provost and Fawcett 2013, p. 55). However, with near universal access to big data comes major risks and challenges relating to its correct utilization to avoid misinformation and disinformation. Thus, we argue that the current data environment requires a new level of responsibility and a critical approach by data generators, users, and recipients.

Big Data in Africa

Data has also become a critical input to democracy and good governance. At the advent of globalization, many businesses and observers considered African countries (and other developing countries) to be on the "periphery" in the global information flow. There were concerns that Africa was "losing out" and being "neglected in the global information highway" because of limited access to information and telecommunications technology. The perceived imbalanced and asymmetrical global data flow led to the call (and sometimes acrimonious debate) for "a new world information and communication order" (UNESCO 1980). While we do not suggest that information asymmetry has been totally eliminated on the continent, it is noteworthy that advances in digital technology have created a data revolution in Africa. The continent has one of the highest levels of digital penetration in the world, and young people are able to connect via social media more than ever before. In many African countries, initiatives are revolutionizing the pattern and flow of information and enhancing a vibrant culture of data utilization. For example, through the support of various organizations, data on Constituency Development Funds in Kenya have been made available for public accessibility, helping to track the utilization of funds. Examples of innovative crowdsourcing platforms in Africa include Ushahidi, a crowdsourcing mapping tool capable of obtaining, verifying, and disseminating large volumes of data. Different groups Ushahidi for real-time transmission of information during the 2013 elections in Kenya. The U-Report in Uganda provides real-time coverage of children's rights in the country. However, in light of the differentiated access to digital media, it is essential to observe that some populations and constituencies are still left behind.

Data for Development

Health and international development enjoy some optimism around the use of big data. Data for development is now a major intervention undertaken by different development agencies. The United Nations (UN) has established the Global Pulse, an initiative aimed at bringing expertise from the public, private, development, and academic sectors to harness the power of big data for development policy and action (United Nations Global Pulse 2013, p. 3). Furthermore, the World Economic Forum report *Big Data Big Impact: New Possibilities for International Development* (2012, p. 1) underscores the high potential of the use of new data in development. With concrete examples of financial services, education, health, and agriculture where data has an impact, the report argues that responsible parties should channel the flood of information in the world to actionable information to improve the public good. Several development organizations have also initiated processes to make more program data widely accessible for public access and invariably utilization. Data sites that enable users to map, chart, and compare various forms of indicators and statistics are now in existence. Despite the promise of data use in a democracy, and in development and communication, it is subject to various misuses and abuses, which is a major concern in our digital society. The democratization of information and diversity of content generation present significant challenges for effective data use.

Data for Foreign Assistance: the Case of African Countries

Foreign governments, particularly those in the West and North America, as well as the World Bank, International Monetary Fund (IMF), and other intergovernmental institutions, rely heavily on census data to provide aid to African countries. The World Bank and IMF introduced structural adjustment policies in the 1950s, to give loans to policies that included a drastic reduction of government controls. Those institutions set up adjustment policies to enhance aid effectiveness, implement anti-corruption measures, and advance market competition as part of the neoliberal agenda, but some African countries resorted to falsifying data to meet the banks' terms. The IMF and World Bank saw limited government control and empowerment of the people to control their futures as the right approach to expediting social change and economic growth in Africa. Here again, the need for appropriate and accurate data on government employees would inform the decisions of those organizations.

Non-governmental organizations (NGOs) and other external assistance groups also rely on published data to take action on countries that need immediate interventions. The African Development Bank, a regional finance institution headquartered in Abidjan, Côte d'Ivoire, assists countries in gathering data on various development issues and publishes data on development. Although most governments have statistics divisions set up to collect and process data on different sectors, such as health and population, climate change, or water management, they rarely update the databank. In some cases, it is impossible for the public (e.g., researchers, aid groups, companies) to obtain access to existing data due to bureaucratic red tape, lack of appropriate legislation or policy, and incompetence. The external groups eventually turn to online publications and other secondary sources that are unreliable.

Common Problems with Generation and Use of Data

Statisticians have been attempting to document the challenges associated with the generation and use of numerical data in social sciences and public affairs. One of the pioneering works on the improper use of data is *How to Lie with Statistics*, which has been in existence for around 60 years. Huff (1954) examines various dimensions of the wrong use of statistics, such as sample bias, data manipulation, dredging, and misreporting, and recommends different approaches for data seekers to avoid falling into a web of bad statistics. Other publications have built on Huff's ideas. Two famous works by Best (2001b, 2004) with the interesting titles *Damn Lies and Statistics* and a revised version entitled *More Damned Lies and Statistics* catalogue some of the major uses of bad statistics by politicians, journalists, and activists. According to Best (2004), social statistics describe the society and are tools used for a specific purpose. Thus, entities can retrieve data or statistics (including bad ones) for predetermined agendas, which then affect how others use such information. Other challenges that he identifies are data fabrication, use of wrong statistical basis, and data mutation.

In a digital age, the potential for data misrepresentation is quite high. First, we are living in an age of citizenship journalism, in which everyone is a global communicator without official gatekeepers. The democratization of information technology implies that everyone can decide what to communicate and how they communicate without any major vetting function. This technique has great merit for information devolution, but it also embodies significant challenges as regards information accuracy. While citizenship journalism or "networked journalism" enhances participatory communication, it has great potential for misinformation. In the next section, we examine some of the challenges associated with the use and misuse of processed data such as social statistics in advocacy, health reporting, and election opinion polls.

Data Use and Misuse in Advocacy

Advocacy is an important strategy for achieving health and development outcomes (Johnson 2009; Samuel 2010; Waisbord 2009). Its overall goal is to elicit changes in a vast spectrum of areas such as policies, programs, positions, strategies, practices, and other instruments of governance. Development agencies, NGOs, non-profit institutions, donors, activists, and public health practitioners associate advocacy with actions and efforts intended to influence decisions, behavior, cooperative attitudes, and positions of critical decision makers and influencers on different issues in any society. Those factors are the premise for the design and implementation of a fleet of advocacy campaigns and mobilization programs to influence key individuals or institutions for the public good.

The use of quantifiable evidence is critical for advocacy because of its capacity to present issues and causes in a compelling way. Most advocates agree that measurements, numbers, and statistical evidence are helpful to prove or disprove a belief, assertion, or proposition. For example, Fayoyin (2013, p. 186) found that the strategic use of evidence is a major tactic of argumentation and positioning in advocacy. More than two-thirds of the participants in the study indicated that evidence is the first essential element of effective advocacy communication. They agreed that evidence must come from "accurate, unvarnished, and verifiable research." They also noted that such evidence must not be "massaged or manipulated" for specific ends. According to the interviewees, advocacy without robust and credible evidence is just "shouting or noise making." Experience has shown that inaccurate measurement can be used to promote a good cause (Best 2006, p. 3).

Scholars in the field of advocacy have expressed divergent views on the role of data in designing policies. For Shifman (2007, 2009), institutional arrangements also have an effect on the policy interface and the technical capacity to undertake complex social research. Although there are ambiguities over the impact of research in policymaking, there is a strong consensus that knowledge and policy research are critical to advocacy practice.

There has been an increase in the use of survey data in various advocacy interventions. Development agencies have learned a major lesson that demonstrating evidence is better than a publicity stunt and issue spinning. We examine some of the data utilization and packaging techniques in advocacy in the next section.

Impact of Performance Scorecards

According to Hood (2007), performance management may involve simple, multiple, composite, or complex measures, and focuses on inputs, outputs, outcomes, and throughputs. It also uses ranking and intelligence systems. Focusing on performance evidence helps to move advocacy from mere "noise making" to "evidence-based advocacy." An example is the recent use of performance scorecards on specific issues and indicators by UNICEF in northern Nigeria. The goal was to establish an accountability framework for assessing the effectiveness of collective actions on child health and development indicators. The scorecards or stocktaking reports also take the form of a league table to classify and compare the performance of various states in northern Nigeria. The performance-ranking tool persuaded decision makers to take action on specific issues, because they could see how their states were performing in relation to others. Based on our working experience with political organizations like the African Union (AU) and the South African Development Community (SADC), there is much sensitivity to performance ranking and league tables. Governments, especially those of countries not performing well on indicators being measured, do not like to see their countries compared to others.

Thematic Analysis

Advocates also undertake various thematic analyses to generate a variety of data. These include budgetary allocation analysis, expenditure information, and comparative data across countries, country status reports, facility utilization/data, bottleneck analysis, investment cases, return on investment analysis, cost–benefit analysis, policy or program impact analysis, or strategic modeling approaches. Anyone can present findings from these activities in creative ways, such as interactive maps, infographics, factographs, dashboards, and stories of change, which can target specific decision makers and influencers. The idea is to ensure that decision and actions are based on compelling evidence and not ideology or personal impression.

Situation Assessment

Most development organizations carry out situation analysis of their development support to countries. Usually, this provides the quantitative and qualitative context for development interventions. Such analysis may be developed for specific thematic issues as the backdrop for policy and programmatic change. For example, these authors recall that in its campaign for adolescent girls in Africa aimed at building the health, social, and economic assets of teenage girls, especially those at risk of child marriage, the United Nations Population Fund (UNFPA) developed infographics to inform and influence decision makers to invest in young people. The documents were used to engage different policy makers, the donor community, and media professionals. The package presented complex information on adolescence issues in easy-to-use formats, including for online campaigns and advocacy regarding adolescent girls (UNFPA, 2014).

Challenges of Data Use in Advocacy

The use of data in advocacy is not without its challenges. The first concern is with the "voluntary" nature of advocacy, which is inherently replete with influence and persuasion. To Chapman (2001), advocacy is "unashamedly purposive," while to most development agencies, advocacy is a deliberate process of influence. The following are snapshots of perspectives on advocacy:

- UNAIDS: advocacy is "a strategic process designed to influence."
- UNICEF: advocacy is a "deliberate process of influencing decision makers."
- Pathfinder International: advocacy is a broad "range of activities conducted to influence decision makers at various levels."
- Johns Hopkins University: policy advocacy is "effort to influence law and order through diverse forms of persuasive communication."
- Care International: advocacy is "a deliberate process of influencing those who make policy decisions" (Fayoyin 2015).

Based on those notes, one can characterize messaging aimed at influencing people by a deliberate choice of what to say and how to say it. In reality, therefore, advocates frame issues for specific reasons and use data with the aim of achieving their stated objective. Thus, advocates do not use statistics with neutrality in mind, but in a deliberate and planned intention. As noted by Best (2001a), advocates may skew the use of evidence and data.

One sector of health and development that has seen a robust and targeted use of data to make a case is HIV. To convince the world to take action on HIV, the Joint United Nations Programme on HIV/AIDS (UNAIDS) made the data relevant when it created a compelling picture for the global community. UNAIDS' global reports resulted in "cooking up an epidemic" that finally "hit the headlines (Pisanni 2008)." Over-estimation of the AIDS situation has been a subject of recurring controversy and in 2007, UNAIDS agreed that the extent of AIDS in Africa was over-stated (GAVI Report 2007, p. 4; McNeil Jr 2007, p. 1; Timberg 2006, p. 2). While we may see the faulty methodology as the cause, it does not rule out politics and pure advocacy.

Another example of the careful use of data to "inspire and inform" action is a campaign against rape by the advocacy organization Blow the Whistle in South Africa. According to the organization and a clock on its website, one person is raped every 36 s in the country, resulting in the estimation that 74,400 women were expected to become victims of rape in South Africa in August 2014. The *Times Live* newspaper published those statistics on August 20, 2014, and other local media organizations picked up the story. However, an investigation by a fact-checking organization, Africa Check, confirmed that the NGO's claim was wrong. The investigation concluded that the organization "overstated the number of rapes reported to the police and also seem to have thumb-sucked under-reporting rates" (Africa Check 2014).

Advocacy Data Generation and Research

Some problems with data use in advocacy could be related to how we generate data and how users communicate it. Advocates have used sources of data with various levels of comparability in development. From unstructured interviews conducted with professionals in many African countries, we have identified the following causes of poor data: unreliable sources and an incomplete data set, limited accessibility of data, the collection of inaccurate data, the collection of incomplete data, delays in reporting, inconsistent data for the same type of indicator, under/over-reporting from data collectors, and conflicting data sources. When we include these challenges alongside the use of different reporting and monitoring systems, tools, and modalities by various development agencies and national partners, and the practice of measure fixation and gaming, they create conflicts in the use and dissemination of data.

Data and evidence generation are among the core principles of research, but barriers affect the process and findings. Specifically, in health policymaking research, some of the problems encountered are poor methodological quality, weak internal validity, and haphazard evidence diffusion. In most areas of policy, there are problems with timeliness of research, dearth of primary research, and weak capacity of decision makers to access and apply scientific knowledge in decision making. Without a doubt, these challenges seriously affect data dissemination and utilization.

One additional problem with data use in advocacy is the "politics" of data in development. Data is not just a technical issue; it is a political product, which evokes significant political sensitivities, as mentioned above. There have been instances where agencies do not agree on certain indicators and cases where government data did not match the data from development agencies, which led to action that negatively affected the population. Further, this creates inherent wariness about data acceptability on the part of decision makers.

Another critical issue that determines how aid agencies use data is the need to demonstrate results. Critics of development aid, such as Easterly (2002), have accused development agencies of performing poorly on some variables. For example, Easterly and Pfutze (2008) argue that many development agencies are performing below expectations regarding the effectiveness of the assistance they provide.

In the preceding discussion, we have established that despite the positive uses of statistics in advocacy, there are technical and communication problems, which result in data misrepresentation. Some of the constraints are inherent in the purposive and intentional nature of advocacy communication, and there are errors in the data-generation process. Thus, we argue for greater control and responsibility in data generation and dissemination in general and in journalism in particular.

Data Use and Misuse in Journalism

Data is one of the sources of news in journalism and the reliability of information and accuracy of data form one of the normative principles of contemporary journalism. In particular, media reports are expected to abide by the mantra "facts are sacred, but comments are free." Data are a primary source of information in journalism, but data misrepresentation is also common in the field. Data use in journalism can be neutral and purposive. When utilized by a journalist to present a story, it may be neutral, but when used as part of opinion writing, there is the possibility of intentional use.

In a digital age characterized by decentralization and democratization of information resources, erosion of traditional gatekeeping and agenda-setting functions, enhanced dialogues, and near-instant feedback (Lasica

2003), the potential for data misrepresentation in journalism seems to have increased. The experience of the authors in training media professionals and having effective interaction with development, science, and health journalists is that the latter face many challenges associated with data gathering and dissemination. These include restricted access to health data and statistics, lack of ability to critically analyze and interpret information, and the weak interface between media and scientists. Another major barrier to the effective use of data in journalism is the relatively complex nature of the health and development sector, characterized by social statistics that are sometimes difficult to understand. Such data may include population censuses, demographic and health surveys, sentinel surveys, surveillance systems trend analysis, forecasting, estimates, and the use of projections from different development agencies. Such constraints result in the dissemination of distorted social data, mangled interpretation of statistical findings, laundering of statistics, and transmission of "rogue" statistical information from one channel to another. Therefore, we argue that health and development reporting requires enhanced skills in data processing, interpretation, and presentation. In the following sections, we illustrate some of the challenges associated with data presentation in the media.

Data Use and Misuse in Politics

There are many aspects to the use of data in politics. However, we shall focus on political polling. Polling is a primary source of data and information in a democratic dispensation. It has become an essential part of the contemporary political process, especially during multi-party political elections. While in some cases polls have educated the electorate on political trends, in others they have been embroiled in public controversies because of their misuse. Conceptually, surveys are part of survey research, which helps to describe, understand, explain, analyze, and predict the behavior of a population or its sample. Polling seeks to explore or explain voter preferences on specific political issues and may be useful in guiding voter action. The electorate tends to believe the findings of such polls. However, in many countries political opinion polls have been fraught with several weaknesses. As illustrated below, polls have been found to be misleading and in some cases fraudulent. Although the science of polling has inbuilt techniques to ensure acceptable levels of validity of the process and reliability of its results, in the authors' view many opinion polls during elections have been used to prove whatever the pollsters wanted to prove.

Public Opinion Polls in Africa: Questionable Pollsters, Questionable Statistics?

Since the emergence of multi-party politics in African countries, various bodies have introduced election polling into the democratic polity. We describe the level and scope of election polls in Africa as "poll frenzy." Polling organizations usually conduct professional polling, but others are carried out by media institutions, NGOs, and shadowy institutions with no track records. Findings from many polls have also been the subject of contention among the press, academics, politicians, and opinion leaders. Here are a few examples.

There were numerous opinion polls during the 2013 election in Kenya, especially from leading pollsters such as Infotrac, Synovate, and Strategic Research. Findings from such polls received extensive coverage, many times making headline news. However, commentators used descriptions such as "poll pollution," "corrupt pollsters," or "poll controversies." In an insightful analysis of the role of political polling in the election, Makulilo (2013) identified seven weaknesses of the polls conducted by one of the leading pollsters, which potentially affected the quality and accuracy of the findings. They were sampling bias, the problem with the design of the polls, the contexts of the study, the level of honesty of the responses, the poll design, the timing of polls, the technical competence of the pollsters, and the response rate. From the detailed analysis, Makulilo (2013) concluded that the polls were problematic on all the seven variables of analysis, which caused "overestimation or underestimation in projecting the electoral outcome" (Makulilo 2013, p. 26). Makulilo (2013, p. 1) described the behavior of one of the polling organizations as that of a "weather forecaster," conducting four polls in just a week and projecting for the entire elections. In simple terms, the findings and data presented from the polls were inaccurate.

Various assessments berated the quality of the polls. According to *The Business Day* (2014), pollsters created "misplaced expectations" which could trigger tension and chaos. Other commentators (Ngaji 2013; Gathigah 2013) criticized the accuracy of the polls due to vested political and business interests. According to Chessman (2014, p. 1), some of the polls lacked methodological precision and were flawed in their presentation of data, concluding that "polling methods were frequently misunderstood, overlooked or studiously ignored by politicians and media outlets." The media published unreliable data from the polls, which advocates picked up and used in private and public conversations. It also featured in social media discussions. Such data may have contributed to the political tension in the country during the election.

Election polls from other African countries face the same problems. For example, in an examination of the polls in Tanzania during the 2010 elections, Makulilo (2011) revealed that the pollsters lacked a good understanding of the political structure in the country and eventually produced incorrect results. Cheeseman (2008) described the polls in Zambia in 2006 as "missing the point," thereby producing questionable findings.

Political election polls in Ghana also follow a similar pattern of contention because of poor design and the questionable results they have published. Some of the polls conducted in 2012, reflecting propaganda for specific politicians, resulted in acrimony and controversy. In the 2014 Malawi election, opinion polls created confusion in the electoral process, apathy, and electoral manipulation. Based on corrupt practices with data perpetuated by the media and pollsters, the Malawi Electoral Commission warned the electorate to beware of pollsters with "questionable credentials" who produce "questionable statistics" (*Malawi Voice* 13 May 2013).

Findings from election polls in less contentious political contexts like Uganda have also been subject to controversy. Opposition and media commentators queried the findings and methodology of the election polls in 2011, which showed that President Museveni would win the election. Undoubtedly, some observers questioned the integrity of the agency that conducted the polls, Afrobarometer (Conrol-Krutz and Logan 2011, p. 4). However, Afrobarometer's predictions were proved right in both Malawi and Uganda.

That brief review affirms our submission that election polls and statistics are largely problematic in Africa. At best, observers describe many of the polls as "rogue polls" with deficient data integrity, and they are intended to advance specific political interests. Specifically, Makulilo (2013, p. 5) opines that the polling industry in Africa has remained controversial and progressively incredible. This view is consistent with suggestions in the literature that entities should use opinion polls wisely (Best 2006, 4; Barone 1997: 1).

Effects of Data Management on Development, Democracy, and Public Communication Research

We identify lessons on the impact of data and social statistics for broader development and communication contexts, but we examine three main ones here. Within the political context, reliable data is useful in educating voters on political behavior during elections. However, its inappropriate use can undermine democratic policy, as evidenced by election opinion polls in Africa. They result in voter apathy or manipulation of the electorate. The audience's heavy reliance on print and broadcast media information to form opinions about the conditions of democracy in the country is another problem (Ngwainmbi 1994, 2004, 2005) . During the campaign period, local newspapers, in a mad rush to sell more copies, habitually publish stories without verifying data, hence misinforming and misdirecting voters and politicians alike.

Because of the believability of information from electronic media, the actions and thoughts of the electorate are affected by information disseminated through that source. People have held mass rallies in support of or against elected officials after reading press reports. In their editorials and news coverage, private press reporters in Nigeria, South Africa, Ghana, Kenya, Niger, and Cameroon, where there is relative press freedom, challenge the polls or accuse the ruling party of election fraud. Even though those countries have electoral commissions that should remain impartial and maintain accurate data, journalists have faced difficulties accessing information. Some reasons account for this: (1) lack of capacity and resources to collect the data; (2) incompetence of data collectors; (3) apathy among low-paid employees of the commission; and (4) corrupt officials serving the interests of influential politicians. Hence, it is impossible to educate the electorate adequately about their rights, and the press cannot tell the whole truth to their audience.

We might expect a dramatic change in the sharing of data with growing access to social media products and activities in more African countries. One expects consumers of information technology to twist, i-chat, and Facebook data and statistics from controversial opinion polls within social networks without discernment and critical interrogation. About development and health advocacy, communication practitioners can use data as an effective tool for media advocacy and policy influence.

Conclusion

We have established that data misuse is common among advocates who frame issues based on their own predetermined goals. Data generation and utilization are political tools in advocacy, and it is only matters that attract the attention of activists or those with substantial donor interest that seem to motivate researchers to conduct investigations. Thus, issues that do not achieve "celebrity status" do not get media attention, and various parties do not advocate public and policy discourse. In this case, we foresee the most improper use of data and under-reporting of issues. Within journalism, social statistics are an excellent source of news with the potential for informing and educating the public on various topics. Nevertheless, due to a variety of factors, media misrepresentation of data is a common occurrence. For example, journalists' reporting of data can be a source of public misinformation. We therefore contend the need for a critical mindset in the dissemination of data at all levels to reduce the mass circulation of erroneous data and statistics in the media. All forms of journalism—traditional, digital, or trado-digital—need a critical approach and a skeptical mindset in dealing with data, statistics, evidence, and numbers. That aggressive interrogative attitude will enhance fact checking before publication.

Recommendations

Skills Building in Data Use

Journalists and other media professionals handle information in the process of informing and educating the public. Therefore, improving their skills in data appreciation has become more imperative for the effective dissemination of statistics and data to the public. Here are some recommendations to consider:

(1) Media professionals need sophisticated insight in data interpretation and data communication.
(2) The current revival in data journalism in many countries needs scaling up.
(3) Agencies that produce data for public consumption need to strengthen their interface with media professionals to enhance the fair reporting of data from such fields.

(4) Regular orientation is necessary for journalists to understand emerging trends in health and development to communicate such issues adequately.

Data Alignment in the Public Sector

Inadequate data alignment in the public sector has been one of the factors contributing to data misreporting. To address these issues, data-generating institutions and organizations need to establish a data verification mechanism, conduct regular spot checks, and prepare metadata for all indicators. It is necessary to harmonize the various types and forms of data collected and disseminated by different organizations. Technical and financial investments are also needed to enhance data generation, validation, verification, and contextualization for meaningful dissemination.

Stricter Regulation of Opinion Polls

Because election polls have a great impact on democratic processes in many African countries, strict mechanisms are needed to ensure the effective "policing" of pollsters. The consequences of publishing unreliable data can lead to the election of the wrong candidate and in some cases the death of innocent people. Thus, political structures need have stricter regulations to guide the practice of opinion polling in Africa, to help in the democratization process.

Need for a More Active Role for Fact-Checking Organizations

The role of fact checking is critical in correcting data misuse. In recent times, few organizations have been established in African countries focusing on promoting data accuracy in the media and public debate. It is necessary that many organizations institutionalize this role at the national and regional levels. Academic institutions that deal with data need to invest more resources in ensuring fact checking for various thematic areas, and we cannot guarantee data validity only after correcting errors.

Topics for Discussion

1. Regarding the population, should numbers matter when it comes to measuring the pace of development of a country?
2. Potential aid donors may be relying on data published by the press as data from the respective institutions (research or development agency) might not be easily accessed. Such data is often inaccurate. What should be done to make correct data readily available to all persons? Moreover, what can be done to make citizens aware of the inaccuracies?
3. Some development analysts have been arguing that emerging economies are struggling to leap forward because they do not have adequate resources to sustain their growing population, which is why they continue to rely on foreign aid for technical assistance. Other analysts say that a country with a huge population has the right workforce to invest in its future. Which of these assertions makes sense? Give reasons for your answer with strong data.

References

Africa Check. 2014. Will 74,400 women be raped this August in South Africa? http://africacheck.org/reports/will-74400-women-be-raped-this-august-in-south-africa/

Ayish, M. 2005. From "Many Voices, One World" to "Many Worlds Once Voice": Reflections on International Communication Realities in the Age of Globalisation. *The Public* 12 (3): 13–30, 2 March.

Barone, M. 1997. Polls are Part of the Air Politicians Breathe. *The Public Perspective*, 1–2, April/May.

Best, J. 2001a. Telling the Truth about Damned Lies and Statistics, *The Chronicle Review*, May 4. http://chronicle.com/free/v47/i34b00701.htm. Date Accessed May 13 2015.

Best, J. 2001b. *Damn Lies and Statistics*. Berkeley: University of California Press.

Best, J. 2004. *More Damned Lies and Statistics*. Berkeley: University of California Press.

Business Day. 10 Lessons for Kenya from the 2013 General Election. 2014. http://businessdailyafrica.com/opinion-and-analysis/53948/1737838/-view/. Accessed 04/11/2014.

Casimir, A., E. Omeh, and C. Ike. 2013. Electoral Fraud in Nigeria: A Philosophical Evaluation of the Framework of Electoral Violence. *Open Journal of Political Science* 3 (4): 167–174.

Chapman, S. 2001. Advocacy in Public Health: Roles and Challenges. *International Journal of Epidemiology* 30: 1226–1232.

Cheeseman, N. 2008. The Kenya Election of 2007: An Introduction. *Journal of Eastern Africa Studies* 2 (2):166–184.

Conrol-Krutz, J., and C. Logan. 2011. *Museveni and the 2011 Uganda Election: Did Money Matter?* Afrobarometer Working Papers, No 135. Africa Barometer, September.

Easterly, W. 2002. The Cartel of Good Intentions. F*oreign Policy* 40–49, July/August.

________. 2015. *Advocacy Nuts and Bolts*, Nairobi, Kenya, Nairobi Academic Press. (In Press).

Fayoyin, A. 2013. Advocacy as a Strategy for Social Change: A Qualitative Analysis of the Perceptions of UN and Non-UN Development Workers, Journal of Social Studies 35 (2): 181–193.

Gathigah, M. 2013. Kenya's Electoral Opinion Polling Marred by Suspicion. *Inter Press Service,* Nairobi, Kenya. February 27.

GAVI Report, 2007. HIV Prevalence Estimates: Fact or Fiction 11 (4) July–August.

Grooves, P., S. Kayyali, D. Krust, and S. van Kullen. 2013. *The Big Data Revolution in HealthCare.* New York: McKinsey & Company.

Hood, C. 2007. Public Service Management by Numbers: Why does it vary? Where does it come from? What are the gaps and puzzles? *Public Money and Management* 27 (2): 95–102.

Huff, D. 1954. *How to Lie with Statistics.* New York: W.W. Norton & Company.

Johnson, S.A. 2009. *Public Health Advocacy.* Edmonton, Alberta: Healthy Public Policy—Alberta Health Services.

Lasica, J., D. (Ed.). *We Media: How Audiences are Shaping the Future of News and Information.* (2003) The Media Centre: The American Press Institute.

________. Pfutze, T. 2008. Where does the money go? Best and Worst Practices in Foreign Aid, Brooking Global Economy, and Development, Working Paper 21.

Makulilo, A. 2013. (Poll "Pollution"? The Politics of the Numbers in the 2013 elections in Kenya. *Africa Review* 40 (2): 1–32.

Malawi Voice. 2013. MEC cautions media on opinion polls. Some pollsters have questionable credentials, produce questionable statistics. May 13. http://www.malawi.voice.com/2013/05/13/mec.-cautions-media-on-opinion-polls-some. Accessed 05/11/2014.

________. (2011). *The Dark Side of Opinion Polls in Tanzania. 1992–2010.* Lambert Academy Publishing. Saarbrucken.

Mayer-Schonberger, Viktor, and Kenneth Cukier. 2013. *Big Data.* Boston: Mariner Books.

McNeil, D. G. Jr. 2007. UN to say it overstated HIV cases by Millions. New York Times, http://www.nytimes.com/2007/11/20/world/20aids.html. Accessed 04/11/2014.

MOPAN 2010. *Multilateral Organization Performance Assessment Network Common Approach.* Finland http://www.mopanonline.org/assessments/. Accessed January 13, 2017.

Ngaji, D. 2013. What if Kenya's election violence points to corrupt pollsters? http://www.theafrica.report.com/News-Analysis/what-if-kenyas-election-violence-point. Accessed 2014/11/04.

Ngwainmbi, K.E. 1994. *Communication Efficiency and Rural Development in Africa.* New York: University Press of America.

________. (2004) Glocalization, Local Urban Culture and Change in West Africa: Toward Negotiating Socioeconomic Understanding with Foreign Companies and International Organizations, March. *Columbia University International Affairs Online Journal-*.

________. 2005. NEPAD's Development Perspective: Bridging the Digital Divide with Good Governance. *Journal of Black Studies,* 35 (3):284–309.

Pissani, E. 2008. *Wisdom from Whores.* London: Granta Publications.

Provost, F., and T. Fawcett. 2013. Data Science and its Relationship to Big Data and Data-Driven Decision Making. *Big Data* 1 (1), BD 51–59. March. http://wenku.baidu.com/view/72d8c8c76f1aff00bed51ee3.html. Accessed 7/12/2014.

Samuel, J. 2010. Public Advocacy and People Centred Advocacy: Mobilising for Social Change. In *Deconstructing Development Discourse—Buzzwords and Fuzzwords*, ed. A. Cornwall, and D. Eade. Oxford: Oxfam.

Shiffman, J. 2007. Generating Political Priority for Maternal Health Reduction in 5 Developing Countries. *American Journal of Public Health* 97 (5): 796–803.

Shiffman, J. 2009. A Social explanation for the Rise and Fall of Global Health Issues. *Bulletin World Health Organization* 87: 608–613.

Timberg, C. 2006. How AIDS in Africa Was Overstated. The Washington Post. April 6. http://www.washingtonpost.com/wp-dyn/content/article/2006/04/05/AR20060405025. Accessed 03/11/2014.

UNESCO. 1980. Many Voices, One World: Report of the International Commission on the State of Communication Problems, Paris: UNESCO.

UNFPA: Johannesburg. 2013. United Nations Global Pulse. *Big data for Development. A Primer.* New York: United Nations. http://www.unglobalpulse.org/sites/default/files/Primer%202013_FINAL%20FOR%20PRINT.pdf. Accessed January 13, 2017.

UNFPA 2014. *Investing in adolescent Girls for Africa's Development: Challenges, Realities and Opportunities.* UNFPA: Johannesburg.

Waisbord, S. 2009. Advocacy Journalism in a Global Context. In *The Handbook of Journalism Studies*, ed. K. Wahl-Jorgensen, and T. Hanitzsh, 371–385. New York: Routledge.

Weiss, Sholom M., Nitin Indurkhya 1998. *Predictive Data Mining: A Practical Guide*. Morgan Kaufmann Publishers, Inc.

World Economic Forum. 2012. *Big Data Big Impact: New Possibilities for International Development*. Geneva: The World Economic Forum.

CHAPTER 14

Media Advocacy and Strategic Networking in Transforming Norms and Policies

Adebayo Fayoyin

This chapter explores the powerful role of media advocacy and strategic partnerships in transforming norms and policies in Africa. It is underpinned by the fact that public policies and social practices in emerging economies affect all aspects of the life of the population. Moreover, unquestionably, without effective media engagement and coalition with-different actors, it is difficult to influence policies, programs, and social practices. The chapter presents three case studies from Egypt, Kenya, and Nigeria to demonstrate how engaging with media professionals and political and cultural leaders is central to shifting norms and changing policies. Among the issues examined in the case studies, media advocacy and strategic networking were pivotal to the changes. Thus, the chapter

Adebayo Fayoyin current research interests include advocacy and social development, strategic communication, and the impact of new media on oral media. In this chapter he focuses on how norms and policies in Africa are being transformed by media and supports his stance with case studies.

A. Fayoyin (✉)
Johannesburg, South Africa

E.K. Ngwainmbi (ed.), *Citizenship, Democracies, and Media Engagement among Emerging Economies and Marginalized Communities*,
DOI 10.1007/978-3-319-56215-5_14

argues for the creative deployment of media advocacy and coalition building of influential networks, coalitions, and institutions in changing public policies, programs, and social practices.

Media Advocacy

Media advocacy is an element of a development communication program intended to shape the media coverage of specific issues and ultimately affect the public agenda. It is premised on the pivotal role of the mass media in shaping public debates and keeping issues on the public agenda (McCombs and Shaw 1972). It is thus related to the agenda-setting function of the mass media (Kim et al. 2002; McCombs 2004; Scheufele and Tewksbury 2007). In practice, it is recognized as an invaluable strategy of influencing public debate and amplifying the attention to specific issues through partnerships with media professionals and institutions. Chapman (2004) situates media advocacy within the framework of public health advocacy as the "strategic use of news media to advance a policy initiative, in the face of opposition" (p. 1). Wallack (1993) describe it as a strategy to use the mass media "appropriately, aggressively and efficiently to support the development of healthy public policies" (p. 5).

Advocacy with media professionals helps them to focus on identified social issues (what to cover) and shapes their portrayal in the media (how they are presented). It also enhances the attention of specific actors (those who have power and positions in society) to take appropriate actions (such as laws, legislation, policies, political decisions, or solutions) advanced by advocates. This approach sometimes involves editorializing, catalyzing of public dissent, and mobilization of the court of public opinion, which challenges some of the standard ethos of journalism, such as neutrality and objectivity. By nature, therefore, media advocacy is a pre-planned and deliberate approach to ensure that media practitioners and gatekeepers support the issues being advocated and draw salience to them.

The Imperatives for Media Advocacy

Some imperatives influence media advocacy in different contexts. First, most development agencies are dealing with long-standing and complicated social problems that are susceptible to public apathy, misrepresentation, and controversy. Some of the challenges the media has been facing in reporting of reproductive health issues necessitate effective media advocacy. The challenges include the politics of newsworthiness, weak capacity of media professionals, poor understanding of the reproductive issue, and the negative disposition of editors to soft news because of a desire to sell papers or increase audience ratings of broadcast stations (UNFPA 2012, p. 15). Other challenges identified include sensationalism by journalists, gatekeeping gaffes in treating health issues, and the poor interface between programs and media professionals (Deane and Scalway 2003). On the other hand, there are genuine concerns from media professionals relating to the non-attractiveness of development issues, the preference of the media audience for more interesting and topical issues rather than boring statistics on health, and lack of access to human stories to animate development issues. All these challenges make media advocacy a major element of the operations of development organizations.

Second, development agencies are under constant scrutiny to justify their existence, prove their relevance, and demonstrate their results (da Costa 2008; Da Costa and Network 2009; OECD 2008; Vollmer 2012). Critics of development aid such as Easterly (2002) have accused development agencies of performing poorly on some variables. The fallout of such criticisms is the aggressive use of media advocacy tactics to highlight the activities of various development organizations and enhance their positioning in the development marketplace.

Linked to the previous argument is the competitive nature of the development industry for its mandate and resources. The development industry functions like a quasi-market with intense competition for resources and attention (Harford and Klein 2005). Furthermore, the development landscape is crowded with different agencies who want to draw attention to the issues they advocate. Steinwand (2015) and Aldasoro et al. (2010) have characterized the industry as fragmentary, because of the existence of a multitude of bilateral and multilateral agencies, funds and programs, different non-government organizations (NGOs) and international non-government organizations (INGOs), and foundations and initiatives. Many development organizations have therefore integrated media relations to help them promote their image and the agenda they sell.

Besides the programmatic imperatives outlined, there is substantial empirical justification for media advocacy in achieving social change. Baleta et al. (2012) examine the role of advocacy, social mobilization, and communication in introducing three child vaccines in South Africa. The study noted that engaging with local, regional, and national media and specialized health media assisted in addressing misinformation and negative reactions, and influenced positive public reception to the vaccines. It also found that the integration of advocacy, social mobilization, and efficient communication contributed to the awareness raising of appropriate audiences on pro-immunization messages, which finally facilitated the successful introduction of the vaccines.

In another study, Taroni and Grilli (2008, p. 1) underscore the power of the mass media in promoting public health campaigns. While arguing that public health practitioners need to learn how to harness the power of different media and to compete in a "contested environment successfully," Taroni and Grilli concluded that the quality of news reporting in medicine is widely determined by medical journals, research, healthcare institutions, and individual scientists competing for visibility, funding, and profits. Similarly, Castells (2013) argues that the mass media have become a "battleground for social campaigns" and that, without effective media engagement, it is impossible for social campaigners to be able to influence the public agenda, government decisions, and social practices. This highlights the centrality of the mass media in social transformation processes.

The emergence of digital media has added an interesting dimension to the use of media in achieving social change in contemporary societies. Bastian (2008) found that the internet is now a primary source of information diffusion on health messages, but it is also a source of misinformation. In a study on the impact of information and communication technology (ICT) on public mobilization, Olorunnisola and Martin (2013) wanted to establish the extent to which digital media platforms facilitate or constrain activism in social movements in Africa. Their assessments underscore the critical role of citizens' empowerment and the multiplier capabilities of new media in the formation of social movements. They also found that digital platforms have doubled the capacity of people as creators and disseminators of news and information. This affirms that social media have become an indispensable tool of media advocacy and public communication in emerging economies. However, digital media and online communications do not replace the engagement of traditional media in advocacy and social change.

Strategic Networking

The "network" is a major concept in contemporary social science, development programming, and policy discourse. According to Hudson and Lowe (2009), variations of the network theme can be found in organizational studies, economics, sociology, policy science, and political science (pp. 127–128). The authors also identify different networks in various settings, including policy or national community, professional network, intergovernmental network, producer network, and issue network. While there are many perspectives on network analysis, its relevance is the ability to link macro- and micro-level environments to agenda setting and change in society. Strategic network analysis is rooted in the interdependence of actors in achieving specific goals, and is variously described as coalition building, stakeholder mobilization, strategic alliances, or small group alliances.

About policy change, Adam and Kriesi (2007) argue that government institutions (executive, legislature, judiciary), political parties, supranational governmental and non-governmental institutions, the mass media, policy communities including policy consultants and policy entrepreneurs, and research and professional networks have a contemporary influence on the policymaking process (p. 130). Other actors are private-sector institutions, public-sector organizations, and non-state actors, which sometimes have different motives and goals. The existence of networks in policy and social change implies that governmental actors are only part of the policymaking machinery.

Sabatier and Jenkins-Smith (1988) opine that the policy process manifests inherent complexities and is therefore influenced by different interests and actors. They propose the advocacy coalition framework (ACF), which underscores and highlights the roles of networks and coalitions (p. 196). The model offers a powerful lens for advocates in looking at the complexity of policy change and how to navigate its paradox. Although ACF presents little or no causal link between input and output, it presents valuable lessons on the collective nature of policy outcomes.

In transforming norms and changing policies, a robust network analysis will involve a series of mapping exercises which help to understand the nature of the networks, and their motivations for engaging in a particular issue or problem. In this respect, the author has identified a range of mapping exercises for effective strategic networking in achieving development outcomes. These are:

- Mapping of the main policymakers, officials, and technocrats who are critical for making and implementing social policies, programs, and legislation.
- Mapping of strategic individuals, coalitions, and networks that can influence primary opinion leaders and decision makers.

- Mapping of relevant institutions, public and private sector, civil society, relevant agencies' stakeholders, and interest groups that are critical to the identified social problems.
- Mapping of complementary or competing issues in the public space to determine the position and level of attention being devoted to the social problem being promoted.
- Mapping of social and political power structures and their impact on critical public issues.
- Mapping of the level of interest and power base of influential individuals and institutions.
- Mapping of opposition or resistance groups, including their origin, philosophy, rationale of opposition, source of influence, level of power, and tactics.

Case Studies

This section examines three case studies that demonstrate the role of media advocacy and strategic networking in shifting norms and social practices in selected emerging economies. These highlight how media advocacy assisted in setting the agenda and how coalition building enhanced the creation of a favorable environment in swaying social practices. The chapter subsequently discusses critical lessons from the case studies.

Egypt: Changing Policies and Norms on Female Genital Mutilation

Female genital mutilation (FGM) involves procedures which include the "partial or total removal of the external female genitalia, or injury to female organs for non-medical reasons" (WHO 2010). These may be incising or removing the clitoral hood, removing the complete clitoris, removing the labia minor or/and labia major, or infibulations which narrow the vaginal orifice (p. 1). According to the United Nations Population Fund (UNFPA 2012, p. 9), more than 200 million girls and women have been cut in almost 30 countries in Africa, the Middle East, and Asia, while an estimated 86 million young girls worldwide are likely to experience some form of the practice by 2030 if current trends continue (Koutaniemi n.d.).

In Egypt, the practice dates back thousands of years before the advent of Islam, Judaism, and Christianity, and cuts across religious and tribal divides. It is thus deeply entrenched in the social and traditional fabric of the nation. Most parts of the country have a prevalence rate of FGM of 90–97% (UNICEF 2013). Young girls ranging from 5 to 13 years of age are subjected to the practice by traditional midwives and local practitioners with blunt instruments, "pricking, piercing, incising, scraping or cauterizing the female genital area" (UNICEF, p. 3).

The practice has been justified on social, religious, and traditional grounds. The rationale includes social pressure to do what others are doing, a way of raising girls for adulthood, a belief that it makes girls less sexually active and pure, or a belief that it enhances femininity and erotic modesty. Some adherents believe that it is a religious requirement or a cultural tradition (Wakabi 2007).

Nevertheless, it is a practice with severe consequences to the physical and mental state of victims. There are also immediate impacts after the procedure, such as severe pain, shock, bleeding, tetanus, or even death. Campaigns against FGM started in the early 1920s and mainly involved lectures and meetings with community people on the adverse effects of the practice. In recent times, more concerted and organized mobilization approaches have been instituted, as described below.

International Momentum

The International Conference on Population and Development (ICPD) of 1994, which took place in Cairo, was the turning point for the campaign toward FGM abandonment globally as well as in Egypt. Part of the conference recommendation states as follows:

> Governments are urged to prohibit female genital mutilation wherever it exists and gives vigorous support to efforts among non-governmental and community organizations and religious institutions to eliminate the practice. (McCauley et al. 1995, p. 486)

The conference and its outcome provided a solid platform for sustained media advocacy and partnerships for the elimination of FGM in Egypt. Since then, various international commitments and instruments have been used to pressure key influencers for political and social decisions against the practice.

Strategic Partnerships with Religious Influencers

Engaging with the faith community is one of the major avenues for changing FGM practice in Egypt. Anti-FGM groups developed a strategic approach of mobilizing religious groups. Various Islamic scholars were consulted to clarify the doctrinal position on FGM. The clerics confirmed that FGM was not mandated by Islam. On this basis, advocates of abolition began using this doctrinal clarification to campaign for the practice's eradication. Islamic opinion leaders were exposed to the physical and psychological consequences of FGM, while the long-term implications were discussed with many of the religious gatekeepers. National consultations and workshops were held with high-profile Islamic teachers, which influenced their position and some of them became advocates for FGM abandonment. Through concerted advocacy and outreach, the highest religious authorities in the country were convinced to make statements in support of FGM elimination. They included Sheikh Mohammed Sayed, Tantawy, Grand Sheikh of Al Azah, the representative of the Pope Shenouda 111, Patriarch of Alexandra, who debunked the religious underpinnings of FGM.

Engagement of Positive Deviants

"Positive deviants" (PDs) are "ordinary individuals" in communities who are against a practice in their own right. Between 1998 and 2004, one of the international agencies (Center for Development and Population Activities, CEDPA) initiated a project with local NGOs to identify positive deviants in Egyptian communities. They became motivators and influential community advocates for FGM abandonment. This initiative has been carried out in many communities in different provinces, resulting in the engagement of local authorities against the practice of FGM prctice. Researchers from the Population Council affiliated with UNICEF report that data from the field show that the focus on the physical consequences of FGM leads to increasing the medicalization of the process to avoid such harms (e.g., Refaat and Hadi 2007). Program activities succeeded in empowering volunteers and PDs to be advocates for eradicating the practice and broke the silence on the issue. Refaat and Hadi's study (2007) shows that the number of targeted families constitutes a small minority of village populations.[1]

Mobilization of Civil Society Organizations

Intensive social mobilization has played a critical role in the social activism against FGM. At least 60 community-based organizations, including human rights organizations, academia, feminist groups, doctors' networks, youth groups, volunteer corps, and traditional social organizations, have been involved in integrated social advocacy and community mobilization. Their activities brought an issue which was considered taboo into the open for discussion with local decision makers. This also allowed for public discussion of the health and social impactsof the practice. Advocacy with and by medical professionals has also played a pivotal role in the process of abandoning FGM in Egypt. A group called Doctors against FGM was formed in mid-2000 comprising young medical professionals and university professors, who voiced their opposition to FGM and carried out advocacy with other groups (UNICEF 2013).

Partnership with National and International Agencies

Myriad national and international stakeholders have been engaged in lobbying and conducting outreach toward changing the practice. The partners include UNFPA, UNICEF, UNDP, World Bank, European Union, CEDPA, USAID, UN Women, International Planned Parenthood Federation, Family Planning International, Conrad, Cairo Family Planning Association, Population Crisis Committee, Women in Development, Ministry of Health, and other government institutions. The agencies have been critical in providing technical and financial support for the anti-FGM initiatives in Egypt (CEDPA 2005).

Engagement with Government Institutions

The Egyptian government has also played a major role in the anti-FGM campaign. Evidence shows that since 2002, the national government has been implementing campaigns to influence critical decision makers from the religious and traditional sectors on the issue. State leadership also entailed consultation and engagement with intellectuals and scholars on how best to approach FGM abandonment programs and initiatives. All levels of government machinery, including the executive and the legislature, have played a critical role in the series of decisions that resulted from multistakeholder engagement processes.

Use of Evidence

Advocacy organizations provided a raft of qualitative and quantitative evidence to influence the position of various stakeholders. This included evidence on the health impacts of the practice, qualitative studies on the relationship between Islam and FGM, and several knowledge, attitude, and practice surveys of opinion leaders (Abdel-Tawab and Youssef 2003, p. 4). Country-specific assessments were carried out with the support of organizations such as the World Health Organization (WHO), Human Rights Watch, Population Council, UNFPA, and UNICEF, to assist in framing the issues and recommending appropriate actions at both national and regional levels (UNFPA 2012; UNICEF 2013).

Partnership with the Office of the First Lady

Through the strategic partnership, the former Egyptian First Lady (Susanne Mubarak) became a champion of the campaign for FGM abandonment. Under the auspices of the National Council for Childhood and Motherhood (NCCM), she advocated on several occasions against the practice and used her position to influence policy directions (Koutaneimi n.d.). The NCCM carried out several lobbying activities to influence government decisions on FGM. The council has also used national and international opportunities to step up the anti-FGM campaign (Abdelhadi 2007).

Media Partnerships

The mass media have been critical channels for public sensitization and influencing public opinion against the practice of FGM. Based on the newsworthiness and human interest nature of the issue, it has always attracted significant media coverage. However, the media also assisted in shaping government, public, and private opinion on diverse aspects of the problem through targeted advocacy on its impact. Tools used with the media include regular updates, press releases, studies, and reports on the implications of FGM.

These actions had the following results:

- *Increased public discussion* around an issue which was initially taboo in Egyptian culture. FGM was transformed from a matter strictly of private discourse to an issue of public debate.
- *Enactment of laws against FGM.* In 1997, a law was put in place which banned FGM, but allowed medical personnel to carry it out in exceptional cases. However, in 2007, another law was enacted which completely banned the practice.
- Many *religious leaders* became advocates for FGM abolition. Senior Islamic clerics issued a religious injunction (Fatwa) that supported the prohibition.
- A *grand coalition* of different stakeholders and advocates evolved which developed into a movement against FGM.

Kenya: Changing Child Protection Policies and Norms

Kenya is one of the countries affected by the devastating impact of HIV and AIDS in Africa. As a result, the country experienced a major orphan crisis from the early 2000s. In recognition of the strategic role of the parliament in shaping policies and influencing social change, UNICEF undertook a strategic advocacy program to influence members of parliament (MPs) between 2002 and 2007, to make the orphan crisis a political issue and elicit changes in policies and social practices (UNICEF 2008, p. 3). The activities implemented include those described below.

Multimedia Engagement

- *Partnership with media gatekeepers.* UNICEF engaged with editors and senior media professions in Kenya through thematic forums, capacity building, and targeted presentations. These activities resulted in a new approach to reporting HIV stories in the media. It also assisted in focusing the attention of the national media on the orphan crisis.

- *Capacity building of media professionals.* Orientation and training sessions were undertaken for middle-level media professions to enhance their understanding of HIV issues in Kenya. This also provided in-depth knowledge of the orphan crisis, its impact on society, and the programs implemented by partners. Through the training and media outreach, significant attention was devoted to orphans in the media.
- *Field project visits.* Project visits were organized to offer first-hand information on the orphan crisis. They supplemented the information received in capacity-building sessions and thematic consultations. Such exposure helped to improve the human interest dimension of reporting and media coverage.
- *Development of information packages.* To promote a better understanding of the HIV situation, targeted publications were produced for various media professionals. These involved situation assessment and analysis, research findings, epidemiological information, and technical briefs. The use of fact sheets, press kits, and photo stories enhanced public information on the subject.
- *Multimedia campaign in print and electronic media.* To leverage public opinion and empower voters to demand supportive action from government, an aggressive marketing approach was undertaken, involving billboards, targeted adverts, and use of different collaterals or brochures. Adverts were published to raise awareness and generate interest in the orphan crisis.

Strategic Partnerships

- UNICEF mobilized politicians and the electoral commission to focus on the challenges of orphans and vulnerable children. Signatures from parliamentary candidates who pledged to serve as advocates for children during the elections were collected. The signatures were published in national newspapers as a form of public commitment. In 2007, 562 candidates pledged to support policies that promote the welfare of orphan children in the country.
- A forum for all parliamentarians to discuss the follow-up to the campaign was instituted An *Annual Leadership for Children Report* was published which demonstrated how MPs performed in protecting orphans and vulnerable children. The report assisted in tracking

key indicators of policy change, including overall budget allocations to social services ministries, allocation of resources and expenditure within social-sector departments, and key parliamentary votes on matters that affect children.

- Children's groups were formed to advocate with relevant government agencies. Children were encouraged to "speak up" on the impact of HIV on their health and development through artistic performances, songs, and poetry. Their main message focused on their "missing childhood" as a result of the crisis. Stories and messages of how children were missing their childhood from homes, schools, and the community were shared on various media. Children's parades were organized in the capital city, which showed children demonstrating alongside the statements and signatures of potential politicians.

The implementation of the various advocacy activities resulted in the following outcomes:

- The campaign raised the visibility of the HIV/AIDS epidemic and the orphan crisis in Kenya among politicians, the donor community, and government. Members of the public were also sensitized to the role of UNICEF in the care and protection of children.
- MPs spoke out about the orphan crisis during the campaign and signed a "pledge for children" to advance orphans' issues at national and local levels.
- A parliamentary standing committee was established to lead the development of a situation assessment and plan of action for an emergency response to orphans in Kenya.
- A stronger partnership with development organizations evolved, resulting in the elaboration of joint action toward addressing the crisis.

Nigeria: Influencing Children's Rights Laws and Programs

Nigeria is a signatory to the Convention on the Rights of the Child and the African Charter on Rights and Welfare of Children, which embody the minimum standards of children's rights. Before the advent of these instruments, Nigeria did not have a consolidated legal framework on children. Various elements of children's rights were scattered in different legal instruments such as the criminal code, unwritten laws, and social policies. However, with the children's rights treaties, the country had to align the various legal elements in one legal instrument—the Child Rights Act. This section describes the role of strategic partnerships, social mobilization, and media engagement in that process.

Generation of Evidence

From 1994 to 2008, development agencies produced and disseminated research and evidence to influence the legislative process. This included thematic briefs, situation assessments, scorecards, a performance dashboard, policy briefs, and flagship publications. The documents contain useful data, statistics, and information for public, media, and policy engagement. Many bilateral and multilateral development agencies, NGOs, and foundations also invested in printing collateral materials targeted at the general public on specific issues. In addition to the generation of evidence, several experts were deployed to make a presentation in different forums at national and subnational levels. One of the platforms for wider information dissemination about children and young people is the establishment of the child rights information bureauwithin the Federal Ministry of Information. The bureau enhanced public information on the survival, development, protection, and participation of children in Nigeria among various audience groups.

Media Engagement

The media played a critical role in mobilizing public opinion to promote children's rights and toward the approval of the Child Rights Act (Oyero 2010, p. 26). From the initiation of the process, UNICEF and other partners invested in media advocacy, primarily for agenda setting and coalition building in support for the issue. The collaboration covered the spectrum of media institutions, including the Nigerian Union of Journalists,the Nigerian Guild of Editors, and the Women Journalists Association of Nigeria. Thematic engagement was also undertaken with other subgroups in the media industry, such as correspondents on business, health, and education. Development organizations supported the various journalists' groups to enhance the broader discourse on children's rights in Nigeria. In some cases, field trips and media fellowships were organized for journalists to gain a better understanding of children's rights in the country. This enhanced the level of media attention to children's issues. Also to influence the media's gatekeeping and agenda-setting functions, consultations and briefing sessions were organized by the Nigerian Guild of Editors and the editorial board members of high-profile newspapers and magazines. This was aimed at raising the profile of children's issues in the media and keeping them on the public agenda through focused media attention. Direct engagement with media gatekeepers culminated in more media coverage through news reports, editorials, entertainment pages, specific pages, or on broadcast media.

A media alliance group specifically focused on promoting children's rights was formed in 1997 (UNICEF 2011). This encouraged more investigative reporting on children's rights violations in Nigeria. Media awards were also used to incentivize sustained media interest in less attractive social issues like infant mortality and morbidity. Development agencies established institutional collaborations with communication training institutions as a way of influencing the training of media professionals. Overall, the various media advocacy efforts helped in improving the reportage of children's and youth issues.

National Partnerships

Legal reform requires engagement with different levels of government and intergovernmental institutions. At the commencement of the process of law reform, the Ministry of Youth Development had authority over children's issues in the country. The task was given to the former National Women's Commission, which eventually metamorphosed into the Ministry of Women Affairs and Child Development. These institutions organized a series of government-to-government advocacy efforts, especially during the preparation of the Initial Report for the Convention on the Rights of the Child Committee. The Ministry of Women Affairs and Child Development then undertook a raft of activities including cabinet briefs, interpersonal contact with other directors for buy-in, lobbying of cabinet and the national assembly, and many other techniques. Targeted engagement was implemented with the Ministry of Justice, the National Law Reform Commission, and other relevant government agencies. Specific individuals in these organizations were consulted and briefed and were mobilized in drafting the original bill. The ministry then undertook consultations with policymakers at federal, state, and local government levels for the endorsement of the bill (Fayoyin 2015, p. 3).

Through the activities of the ministry, the government established the National Council for the Review and Implementation of the Convention on the Rights of the Child. This group was also established at the state level and became a platform for multilevel influence at the subnational level. The committee developed and coordinated the implementation of national and subnational advocacy strategies for the popularization of children's rights and also for the enactment of the Child Rights Act. Activities carried out comprise cabinet briefs, interpersonal contact with directors of other government departments, lobbying of cabinet and parliamentary members, orientation sessions, compatibility reviews, internal dialogues, and targeted presentations at national and state assemblies.

NGO coalitions also assisted in promoting the children's rights agenda in Nigeria. They supported the process of preparing state reports to the various international children's rights institutions and promoted campaigns that created a positive environment for the reform of laws relating to children. Through non-violent methods of achieving influence, such as the voices of youth, creative use of evidence, grassroots activism, iconic messaging, and mass mobilization, the NGO community attracted attention to the incidence of children's rights violations in the country as well enhancing the capacity building of various community networks in influencing decision makers.

Several consultations were held with different stakeholders to influence public opinion in support of legislative reform for children. These included NGO dialogues and expert consultation with government institutions involved in various stages. Policy outreach was also conducted by UNICEF, World Vision, Save the Children, and national agencies, such as the Institute of Advanced Legal Studies, Human Development Initiative, Child Welfare League, and many other organizations (Fayoyin 2015, p. 5).

Results

- Decision makers such as presidents/heads of state, MPs, governors, and local government councilors were mobilized to support legal reform.

- Stakeholders in the media, religious institutions, development organizations, political parties, academia, and the legal community were actively engaged in advocacy for children.
- Nigeria enacted the Child Rights Act in 2003 and also developed appropriate implementation mechanisms.

Cross-Cutting Lessons

From the case studies, several lessons and recommendations can be generated, a few of which are examined as follows:

- Public attention to social problems is a finite commodity. In general, social problems addressed by development organizations (e.g., FGM or the status of children in society) are complicated and entrenched issues that require significant time and perseverance to resolve. Most are inherent in the social fabric and do not attract the necessary level of attention to elicit the necessary change. This underscores the pivotal role of multiple stakeholder engagement in issue positioning. We argue that to increase the standard of attention to entrenched social and traditional issues, it is important for advocates to understand the complexity of issue attention, the dynamics of issue competition, and how to galvanize coalitions and networks for issue positioning. The case studies show that the creative engagement of different stakeholders enhanced attention to the matters in question. With effective media advocacy and strategic engagement, it is possible to turn opposition to social issues into action for change. However, coalitions need continuously to navigate the complex domains of the public sphere—people, problem, politics, and power—to transform norms and change policies.
- The framing and portrayal of the issues contributed to the level of attention and final selection of issues for action (Weaver 2007). Media advocacy helped in addressing the "information gap" in the process of policy or political influence and assisted in conferring salience on the issues. However, the media is also constrained by some institutional and systemic challenges which affect its capacity to achieve this function. Therefore, getting the best from the press requires creative media advocacy rooted in sophisticated insights into the contemporary media context, structure, and systems.

Media practitioners need to be adequately equipped to hold development agencies accountable for the promised results of development, and invest in investigative journalism around social and health issues rather than regurgitating press releases and reports churned out by development agencies.

- Digital technologies and social media channels have changed the media landscape in emerging economies, resulting in the advent of digital journalism, network journalism, and cyber advocacy. The traditional gatekeeping and agenda-setting functions seem to have collapsed with the emergence of the new media. Advances in digital media and communications technology have generated considerable optimism about the role of social media in achieving developmental and public health outcomes.[2] The unprecedented availability of digital devices and platforms has also prompted different development institutions to design and implement a range of social media and media interventions for social change. Thus, new modes of engagement to maximize the power of digital media for social development need to be explored. This study calls for the innovative and integrated use of both mass media and mass-mediated communication channels for effective social transformation.
- The increasing tendency of development agencies to engage in public relations and corporate promotions tends to dilute their media advocacy efforts. Field experience shows that different agencies churn out press releases, publish different data, and promote their agenda and organizational brands on the same social issue. However, the desire for visibility and image should be secondary to issue positioning in the public communication programs of development agencies. Similarly, media professionals in emerging countries need to be sensitive to the overbearing posture of some organizations or the combined actions of multilateral organizations in their media engagement practices, as this raises significant ethical dilemmas in media work.
- As already noted, the development industry operates like a quasi-market, with various agencies advancing their mandate with the media and other partners. Even with the new aid modality which promotes the harmonization of development interventions and alignment with the national agenda, program delivery and public communication by development agencies are still mandate driven. This calls for greater integration of both strategic coalition building

and media engagement through joint communication, collaborative policy initiatives, and coherent mobilization, rather than competitive positioning. A coherent media framework and strategic engagement process by development agencies will thus achieve greater success than fragmentary and disparate interventions.

- Evidence continues to play a significant role in shifting norms and policies. However, despite the power of proof in society, policy and social practices never change because of numbers alone. Data can also be subject to various misuses and abuses in public persuasion. Our recommendation is that the use of evidence in advocacy and strategic networking should emphasize internal and external capacity building, the enhancement of knowledge capital, and social accountability.
- Organizations today function within a multidimensional, rights-oriented, and contested corporate environment with possibilities for counter-framings, counter-movements, and significant opposition to social issues. Advocacy is a double-edged sword, which can be used for or against any specific issue or cause. Media advocacy can support political and policy change, yet organizations can use it to achieve changes in policy instruments or even provide different sources of knowledge to influence the same policy instrument. Also, partnerships can be built in support of social issues; conversely, opposition coalitions can be developed against such matters. Thus, in our modern world, a more sophisticated approach is needed to deploy both media advocacy and strategic engagements effectively in promoting social issues and understanding how to counter their use by opposition groups.

Conclusion

This chapter has sought to examine the role of media advocacy and strategic networking in shifting norms and policies in emerging economies. We have established that social transformation involves a continuous process of educating, informing, networking, mobilizing, dialogue, consultations, negotiating, and alliance building, and not coercion or compliance. The case studies have shown that harnessing the powerful combination of media advocacy and strategic networking goes a long way in influencing social practices and public policies in emerging economies. While advocacy helps to mobilize the media to shape public opinion and ultimately affect the agenda, strategic networking assists in mobilizing important allies, coalitions, and groupings for change, converts supporters into champions, and leverages transnational solidarity for policy and social change.

Next Steps

In a rapidly changing African continent, development organizations need to adapt their media and engagement strategy for greater effectiveness and efficiency. They need to assess and reshape their strategy for coalition building, embrace the new drivers of social change, and continuously reframe their narratives in line with emerging public conversations. Furthermore, they need to expand their mobilization strategy beyond the traditional partners, as well as deepen their corporate engagement with a diverse network of institutions which are relevant to national and regional development contexts. Greater alignment of the advocacy efforts of development agencies with the national agenda, bodies, and structures will also be critical in the process of change.

Development agencies need to find new angles to tell stories about the issues they want to change. This would require coordinated social and public communications approaches for the most efficient portrayal. Media professionals need to undertake more investigative journalism to tell the "untold stories" of social practices in society. This will move the narratives beyond the slogans and soundbites of development agencies.

In an age of dwindling public and media attention to social problems, new creativity is imperative. More creative multimedia communication based on dynamic storytelling and compelling images is required. Targeted consultations need to be put in place to generate appropriate frames for different messages for different publics and audiences. New arguments to reposition the issues may also be necessary.

The emergence of digital media has transformed the entire public and media landscape. This development has resulted in increased digital journalism and cyber advocacy. The social media world entails interactivity and user content generation, not a linear model of communication dominated by professional communicators. Advocates need to enhance the symbiotic relationship between the mass media and mass-mediated communication for their advocacy. The era of citizenship journalism heralds new opportunities for more attention to development news and information.

Topics for Discussion

1. Should national governments in emerging economies rely more on strategic networking or the media for rapid, positive change?
2. Are intergovernmental agencies needed in developing countries? Give your reasons.
3. It has been argued that the slow pace of social change is due to various paradigms of development being implemented simultaneously in one country. Explain your perspective.
4. Most developing countries have not managed to transfer or master different kinds of technology. In your views, what are some of the reasons for this failure?
5. Who are media professionals? Would you consider journalists as media practitioners? Why or why not?
6. Describe the obstacles that media professionals could face when implementing advocacy strategies. Consider institutional factors and the role of private enterprise.

Notes

1. *Refeat and Hadi's report is part of an evaluation that was piloted by UNICEF in partnership with the Center for Development and Population Activities (CEDPA) from 2003 to 2006.* More at https://www.unicef.org/evaldatabase/index_45240.html accessed January 10, 2017.
2. Adebayo Fayoyin|Papers—Academia.edu, http://independent.academia.edu/AdebayoFayoyin/Papers (accessed January 10, 2017).

Works Cited

Abdel-Tawab, N., and H Youssef. 2003. Attitudes and Values of Egyptian Opinion Leaders Towards FGM/C: A Qualitative Investigation. https://www.unicef.org/evaldatabase/files/Egypt_2003_804_Opinion_Leaders.pdf.

Abdelhadi, M. 2007. Egypt Forbids Female Circumcision *BBC NEWS*. http://news.bbc.co.uk/2/hi/middle_east/6251426.stm. Accessed 10 Jan 2017.

Adam, S., and H. Kriesi. 2007. The Network Approach. *Theories of the Policy Process* 2: 189–220.

Aldasoro, I., P. Nunnenkamp, and R. Thiele. 2010. Less Aid Proliferation and More Donor Coordination? The Wide Gap Between Words and Deeds. *Journal of International Development* 22 (7): 920–940.

Baleta, A.F., J. van den Heever, and R.J. Burnett. 2012. Meeting the Need for Advocacy, Social Mobilization and Communication in the Introduction of Three New Vaccines in South Africa-Successes and Challenges. *Vaccine* 30: C66–C71.

Bastian, H. 2008. Health Information on the Internet. *International Encyclopedia of Public Health* 3: 678–682.

Castells, M. 2013. *Communication Power*. Oxford: Oxford University Press.

CEDPA. 2005. *New Horizons and New Visions: Mobilizing Communities for Girls' Education in Egypt*. http://www.eldis.org/go/home&id=63596&type=Document#.WUuxIOt97IW.

Chapman, S. 2004. Advocacy for Public Health: A Primer. *Journal of Epidemiology and Community Health* 58 (5): 361.

Da Costa, P. 2008. Managing for and Communicating Development Results. *Background Paper for the OECD Informal Network of DAC Development Communicators (DevCom Network)*.

Da Costa, P., and D. Network. 2009. Study on Communicating Development Results. https://www.oecd.org/dev/development-philanthropy/44836250.pdf. Accessed 10 Jan 2017.

Deane, J., and T. Scalway. 2003. Missing the Message–20 years of learning from HIV/AIDS: Panos, London.

Easterly, W. 2002. The Cartel of Good Intentions: The Problem of Bureaucracy in Foreign Aid. *The Journal of Policy Reform* 5 (4): 223–250.

Fayoyin, A. 2015. Positioning Youth Development Agenda in Public Discourse in Nigeria: An Advocacy Imperative. Open Access Library Journal, 2: e1875. http://dx.doi.org/10.4236/oalib.1101875. Accessed 17 Dec 2016.

Harford, T., and M. Klein. 2005. Aid and the Resource Curse. *Public Policy Journal* 291: 1–4.

Hudson, J., and S. Lowe. 2009. *Understanding the Policy Process: Analyzing Welfare Policy and Practice*. Bristol: Policy Press.

Kim, S.-H., D.A. Scheufele, and J. Shanahan. 2002. Think About it this Way: Attribute Agenda-Setting Function of the Press and the Public's Evaluation of a Local Issue. *Journalism & Mass Communication Quarterly* 79 (1): 7–25.

McCauley, A.P., C. Salter, K. Kiragu, and J. Senderowitz. 1995. Meeting the Needs of Young Adults. *Population Reports. Series J, Family Planning Programs* 41(1).

McCombs, M. 2004. *Setting the Agenda: The Mass Public and the Opinion*. Cambridge: Polity.

McCombs, M.E., and D.L. Shaw. 1972. The Agenda-Setting Function of Mass Media. *Public Opinion Quarterly* 36 (2): 176–187.

Meeri Koutaniemi? The Alternative—Oulun kaupunki, http://www.ouka.fi/oulu/oma/50. Accessed 10 Jan 2017.

OECD. 2008. *Informal Experts' Meeting on Managing for and Communicating about Development Results.* Retrieved from GTZ House Berlin.

Olorunnisola, A.A., and B.L. Martin. 2013. Influences of Media on Social Movements: Problematizing Hyperbolic Inferences About Impacts. *Telematics and Informatics* 30 (3): 275–288.

Oyero, O. 2010. Children: As 'Invisible' and Voiceless as Ever in the Nigerian News Media. http://www.ec.ubi.pt/ec/07/vol2/oyero.pdf. Accessed 10 Jan 2017.

Refaat, Nadia and A. Amal Hadi. 2007. EGY: Evaluation of the Female Genital Mutilation Abandonment Programme in Egypt https://www.unicef.org/evaldatabase/index_45240.html. Accessed 10 Jan 2017.

Sabatier, P.A., and H.C. Jenkins-Smith. 1988. Symposium Editors' Introduction. *Policy Sciences* 21 (2): 123–127.

Scheufele, D.A., and D. Tewksbury. 2007. Framing, Agenda Setting, and Priming: The Evolution of Three Media Effects Models. *Journal of Communication* 57 (1): 9–20.

Steinwand, M.C. 2015. Compete or Coordinate? Aid Fragmentation and lead donorship. *International Organization* 69 (2): 443.

Taroni, F., and R. Grilli. 2008. Mass Media Interventions. *Int Encyclopedia Public Health* 4: 202–210.

UNFPA. 2012. *Report on Media Advocacy for the Campaign on Accelerated Reduction of Maternal Mortality in Africa.*

UNICEF. 2008. *Looking Out for Leaders Who Look Out for Leaders: Partnering with Members of Parliament as Leading Advocates for Children.* https://www.unicef.org/policyanalysis/index_25193.html. Accessed 10 Jan 2017.

UNICEF. 2011. Situation Analysis of Children and Women in Nigeria: 2011. http://www.unicef.org/nigeria/resources_8467.html. Accessed 10 Jan 2017.

UNICEF. 2013. *United Nations Children's Fund, Female Genital Mutilation/Cutting: A Statistical Overview and Exploration of the Dynamics of Change* https://www.unicef.org/publications/index_69875.html (10 Jan 2017).

Vollmer, F. 2012. Increasing the Visibility and Effectiveness of Development Cooperation: How to Reconcile Two Competing Objectives? https://www.die-gdi.de/uploads/media/Studies_67.pdf. Accessed 10 Jan 2017.

Wakabi, W. 2007. Africa Battles to Make Female Genital Mutilation History. *The Lancet* 369 (9567): 1069–1070.

Wallack, L. 1993. *Media Advocacy, and Public Health: Power for Prevention.* California: Sage.

Weaver, D.H. 2007. Thoughts on Agenda Setting, Framing and Priming. *Journal of Communication* 57 (1): 142–147.

WHO. 2010. Global Strategy to Stop Health-Care Providers from Performing Female Genital Mutilation. UNAIDS, UNDP: UNFPA, UNHCR, UNICEF, UNIFEM, WHO, FIGO, ICN, IOM, MWIA, WCPT, WMA. http://whqlibdoc.who.int/hq/2010/WHO_RHR_10.9_eng.pdf?ua=1. Accessed 10 Jan 2017.

Index

E.K. Ngwainmbi (ed.), *Citizenship, Democracies, and Media Engagement among Emerging Economies and Marginalized Communities*,
DOI 10.1007/978-3-319-56215-5

CPSIA information can be obtained
at www.ICGtesting.com
Printed in the USA
LVOW05*1739210917
549571LV00016B/327/P

9 783319 562148